Is Anyone in Charge Here?

Is Anyone in Charge Here?

A Christological Evaluation of the Idea
of Human Dominion over Creation

SELWYN YEOMAN

Foreword by Murray A. Rae

☙PICKWICK *Publications* · Eugene, Oregon

IS ANYONE IN CHARGE HERE?
A Christological Evaluation of the Idea of Human Dominion over Creation

Copyright © 2019 Selwyn Yeoman. All rights reserved. Except for brief quotations in critical publications or reviews, no part of this book may be reproduced in any manner without prior written permission from the publisher. Write: Permissions, Wipf and Stock Publishers, 199 W. 8th Ave., Suite 3, Eugene, OR 97401.

Pickwick Publications
An Imprint of Wipf and Stock Publishers
199 W. 8th Ave., Suite 3
Eugene, OR 97401

www.wipfandstock.com

PAPERBACK ISBN: 978-1-5326-7489-1
HARDCOVER ISBN: 978-1-5326-7490-7
EBOOK ISBN: 978-1-5326-7491-4

Cataloguing-in-Publication data:

Names: Yeoman, Selwyn, author. | Rae, Murray A., foreword.

Title: Is anyone in charge here? : a christological evaluation of the idea of human dominion over creation. / Selwyn Yeoman ; foreword by Murray A. Rae

Description: Eugene, OR : Pickwick Publications, 2020. | Includes bibliographical references and index.

Identifiers: ISBN 978-1-5326-7489-1 (paperback) | ISBN 978-1-5326-7490-7 (hardcover) | ISBN 978-1-5326-7491-4 (ebook)

Subjects: LCSH: Creation. | Creation—History of doctrines—Early church, ca. 30–600. | Jesus Christ—Person and offices.

Classification: BT210 .Y46 2020 (paperback) | BT210 .Y46 (ebook)

Manufactured in the U.S.A.   12/21/20

Unless otherwise indicated, all Scripture quotations are from Common Bible: New Revised Standard Version Bible, copyright © 1989 National Council of the Churches of Christ in the United States of America. Used by permission. All rights reserved worldwide.

Contents

Foreword by Murray Rae | vii
Preface | ix
Acknowledgments | xi
Abbreviations | xv

Introduction | 1

1 | At the Beginning: A Clamor of Many Voices | 4
    Those Who Spoke Before: A Century of Voices in Anticipation | 5
    In the Noise of Battle: Voices in the Aftermath of White | 15
    Where the Voices Have Been Silent, or Only Whispering | 25

2 | In the Shadow of Ozymandias: Dominion and Destruction in a World without, and with, the Bible | 28
    Walking among the Gods—Life in a Divinized World | 29
    Walking with God—Life in a Created Universe | 36

3 | On Irenaeus of Lyons | 48
    On the Goodness of Creation | 51
    Of Adam's Dominion | 54
    Of Other Creatures and the Earth | 62
    On Christ and Recapitulation | 64
    Conclusions | 67

4 | On Athanasius | 69
    On Worshipping the Creatures or the Creator | 72
    On Being Human | 76
    On Being Human in Christ | 78
    Conclusions | 88

5 | On Augustine | 90
  Introduction | 90
  On Interpretation in Genesis | 96
  On God the Creator | 97
  On the Creation | 105
  On the "Resting" of God—The Sabbath | 123
  Conclusions | 130

6 | Monasticism—Reclaiming the Garden, Building the City | 132
  Introduction | 132
  Conclusions | 197

7 | At the Turning of the Ages: Reviewing White's Account of the First Millennium, and Previewing the Second | 199
  Introduction | 199
  The "Psychic Revolution" of Christianity | 201
  On Human Power and Sinfulness | 208
  New Developments in the Second Millennium | 210
  Conclusions | 226

8 | With Christ in the Care of Creation—Part One: Human Dominion and the Resurrected Lord | 228
  Christology and Human Dominion | 230
  Conclusions—Part One | 266

9 | With Christ in the Care of Creation—Part Two: Resurrection and the Vindication of Jesus | 267
  Resurrection as Vindication for Jesus' Proclamation of the Kingdom of God | 268
  Resurrection as Vindication of Jesus' Claims over Sanctuary and Sabbath | 277
  Living the Sabbath of the Kingdom | 284
  Conclusions | 297

Bibliography | 303
Author/Name Index | 317
Subject Index | 323
Scripture Index | 331

Foreword

A NEW ZEALAND POLITICIAN, no longer in office, remarked several years ago that he wasn't especially worried about global warming or about the threat of environmental degradation because science would eventually provide solutions. More recently, a facebook meme brought to my attention the words of a scientist who confessed that he does not know how to solve the problem of global warming because it requires, above all, an alteration of our ways of living and a transformation of hearts and minds. The scientist's instincts are in this case more to be trusted, I think.

That responsible habitation of our environment is inseparably bound up with the condition of our hearts and minds and with the beliefs that shape our lives is not a new insight, however. Lynn White, Jr. famously declared in 1966, that the ecological crisis could be attributed to a religious commitment that is profoundly damaging. White claimed, more specifically, that the fundamental cause of the crisis is the Judeo-Christian notion that human beings have dominion over the earth which exists, in turn, solely to serve the needs and desires of humankind. While Selwyn Yeoman contends in this book against the view that the Jewish and Christian traditions, and the Scriptures upon which they rely, are especially to blame here, he accepts and confirms that the problem has its roots in the misdirected commitment of our hearts and minds. That is a problem that the Christian tradition identifies as sin. What then is to be done?

One part of the solution, directed towards the transformation of our hearts and minds, is to explore again the traditions of biblical and Christian thought concerning humanity's relation to and responsibility for the environment. Those traditions, as it turns out, are both rich and extensive. Those who have studied the Bible with any care will know that there is an abundance of material in the Bible that is concerned very directly with the divinely instituted imperative to take care of what has been given in creation, not merely for our own sake, but for the sake of all that God has made, and to pass it on, still as blessing, to those who will come after us. Less well known, perhaps, is the extensive theological reflection upon this imperative that can be found in the patristic and medieval eras of Christian history. The wisdom to be found there may help us to discern and encourage us to adopt practices that more faithfully embody the divine imperative to have dominion over the things of earth. Such faithfulness requires, of course, careful consideration of what dominion means. To help us in that task, Selwyn engages in extensive biblical and theological study from which emerges a thoroughly and appropriately Christocentric account of what human dominion involves.

Given that the ecological crisis has been brought about in no small measure by the misdirected commitment of our hearts and minds, a second, indispensible, part of the solution is repentance. Repentance is not simply a matter of being sorry, of course, but also of transformation. The New Testament term, *metanoia*, which may be translated as repentance but also as conversion, points to the transformation that is required in the face of human sin. It is a transformation of our minds, to be sure, but also of our way of being in the world. Christian tradition offers the further insight that such transformation cannot be achieved without God's help. All of this confirms that the scientist cited above was right: the basic problem we face of living more responsibly and sustainably in God's good creation is not a scientific one; it is, we might say, a spiritual one. That being so, we need the help of the Holy Spirit who is about the business of conforming us to Christ and enabling our participation in the dominion that Christ himself exercises, and in the kingdom of shalom for all creation that Christ has inaugurated among us.

The careful and theologically rich study of human responsibility toward creation that Selwyn offers in this book offers welcome assurance to those who may be in doubt whether Christian faith really has much to say about contemporary environmental concerns. It offers too, for those already willing to submit their hearts and minds to the transformative work of God's Spirit, an admirably clear picture of where faithfulness to Christ must lead.

Murray Rae

Preface

How are we human beings to understand our place and apparently unique power among all other creatures of the Earth? This may seem a naive question, except that the world of the early twenty-first century is increasingly degraded precisely because of inadequate answers to that question—or refusals to answer it at all. Apocalyptic scenarios surrounding human induced climate change, global conflicts over access to the Earth's bounty, resource depletion, unconscionable disparities of wealth and poverty, and dramatic rates of bio-diversity loss seem frequently to be met with the response, "don't worry. Go shopping!" Consumerism is not only an economic strategy but a therapy, and a way of understanding one's place in the world.

Such indifference is not universal however. In 1967 American historian Lynn White Jr. suggested that our present ecological crisis was deeply rooted in the Judeo-Christian heritage and especially the inspirations drawn from the biblical creation stories in Genesis 1 and 2.[1] His argument was that these stories imagined humanity set apart from the rest of creation by being made in the image of the Creator God, to exercise domination of the world, and indeed, "no item in the physical creation had any purpose save to serve man's purposes."[2]

The purpose of this thesis is firstly, to interrogate White's account of the impact of Christian faith by demonstrating the reality of serious environmental degradation in contexts quite untouched by biblical ideas or the Christian tradition. Secondly, I will explore ideas about creation and human dominion as articulated by the patristic theologians. These were critical influences during the period of which White writes but are completely ignored in his critique, as also are the Promethean experiments

1. White, "Historical Roots," 1203–7.
2. White, "Historical Roots," 1205.

with human power and freedom that have impacted the world since the European Enlightenment.

Trinitarian accounts of God are central to patristic theology and it is in the light of such accounts that I address issues to do with the nature of human dominion. It is the heart of Christian faith that Jesus Christ is the true image of God, and as the word of God embodied in the materiality of creation he is also the authentic human being. To properly understand our place within the ecology of creation we must learn from the humanity of Jesus. To exercise our power rightly we must learn his exercise of power. But the Earth's ecological crisis is ample evidence that humanity is not readily disposed to living well here. This disorientation, in Christian theology, is our sinfulness. It is repaired, not by individual decisions to try and do better, but by deep-seated conversion into the life of Christ, and into participation in the community of his new humanity, which he proclaimed as the kingdom of God.

To assess our power, sources of identity, community or autonomy, orientation of desire, and ecological relatedness, all in the light of Jesus Christ is to engage in a christological evaluation of our humanity. Such an evaluation is a central task of this thesis. Jesus exercises his power or dominion as a servant, and we will explore some implications of serving the well-being of all Earth's creatures. As he embodies the word of God, we examine what it means for us to be formed by that word, and how the contemplative life is a necessary counter to the destructiveness of the consumerist life. As he is the true image of God, we will explore aspects of advocacy and representation, participating in Christ's priesthood for the Earth. By such an evaluation we articulate a way of being that is able to recognize a unique power for responsible nurturing, a fellowship in Christ with all creation.

Acknowledgments

ANY PROJECT INVOLVING BOTH the Trinity and ecology cannot be true to itself without acknowledging the rich network of relationships that has brought it into being. Such relationships I celebrate with deep gratitude.

This project had its beginnings in my childhood. I was privileged to live above a bush-clad gully in which I watched birds build nests, lay eggs and fledge their young. A bulldozer cut a track into this bush so that houses could be built—some of them designed by my architect father. So began a questioning as to how we humans are to live within the fellowship of all creation. I was also introduced to the spiritual nurture of Crusaders (now Scripture Union) and Boy Scouts camping, and the skills for being comfortably at home in the New Zealand outdoors. Thus, my first acknowledgement must be to my parents, Desireé and Martin Yeoman, for the environment of faith, piety, and amazing freedom in which I and my siblings were allowed to grow up.

The Presbyterian Church of Aotearoa New Zealand has welcomed me into its ministry. In three parishes I have been encouraged to help people nurture faith in Christ through engagement with creation. Having begun ministry among farmers and foresters in Central Southland, and never being far from those pursuits subsequently, has meant that I have been held close to the land throughout this project. Many colleagues have supported me, but I particularly note the team and congregations of the Coastal Unity Parish. This is a city parish, and standing between two worlds has also proven constantly thought-provoking. Bruce Hamill earns special mention for his practical involvements, searching questions, wide-ranging conversation and many borrowed books, as also does my brother-in-law, Rev. Rob Yule, whose collection of books on these matters is truly enviable. My thanks also for the church's study grants. These have eased my way and symbolized support for the church's vision to bear witness to Jesus Christ through caring for creation. I trust that support will prove fruitful.

The Presbyterian Church has historic links with the University of Otago and has always promoted education. Consequently it has been easy to move back into the university environment, a move made easier still by the encouragement of congenial staff and office-mates in the Department of Theology and Religion. Professor Gerald Pillay first planted the seed that I could pursue post-graduate study. Professor Alan and the late Jane Torrance, from a great distance, facilitated a truly life-changing experience in conservation and community development in Chinghai Province, Western China. Rev. Dr. John Roxborogh, Associate Professors John Stenhouse, and Winsome Parnell, and Professor Paul Trebilco have all been caring, helpful, and constantly encouraging, for which I am grateful.

Pre-eminent among those to be thanked are my supervisors. Professor Murray Rae, by refusing to hold my hand, but offering insightful guidance, eventually brought me to realize he had more confidence in me than I had in myself. Thank you, Murray. Until his departure to the University of St. Andrews, Associate Professor Ivor Davidson acted as my second supervisor. He too was a blessing by his astute observations, and directions to far more resources than I have been able to take advantage of.

The University was also generous with scholarship support. This too helped make life easier, but even more, encouraged my sense that this research was regarded as worthwhile.

For over thirty years of lunchtime and weekend running, and for great tramping, I thank my friend Alastair McCallum, a farmer by upbringing, and a widely-read scholar by inclination. There are few issues in this thesis that have not been talked over with him. He represents a wonderful network of enriching friendships. Tom Duncan is a very recent addition to the running pack whose conversation and ideas have also proven helpful. Thanks to my dear friend and former secretary, Fran Short, without whose cheerful and patient help with proof reading, formatting and document set-up, this thesis might never have made it to the printer. And equally grateful thanks to Sandi Jull, without whose help it would never have been ready for the publisher. Andrew Shepherd also satisfied his boundless curiosity by insisting upon being a proof reader. Thanks also to the staff of Wipf and Stock, and especially my patient and gracious copyeditor, Emily Callihan. To you all, for your careful attention—thanks so much. The errors however remain my own.

Above all, my thanks to my wife, Natalie, and to our children and their partners. You have laughed off my eccentricities, shared my interests and loves, blessed me by your own enthusiasms, and been constantly encouraging during this project. To Natalie I owe more than I can easily tell. She has been a theological stimulus to me since we first met as students—in her truthfulness helping me to seek honesty, by her hospitality, laughter, and creativity enriching the world. Her spiritual tenacity, even in dark times, shines as a light of hope for me, and a living sign of the ultimate goodness of creation.

Abbreviations

ATHANASIUS

AA	*Orations against the Arians*. Edited and introduction by William Bright. Oxford: Clarendon, 1884.
AP	*Against the Pagans/Contra Gentes*. Edited and translated by Robert W. Thomson. Oxford: Clarendon, 1971.
DI	*On the Incarnation of the Word/De Incarnatione*. Edited and translated by Robert W. Thomson. Oxford: Clarendon, 1971.
SWL	*Select Works and Letters*. Edited by Archibald Robertson, in Nicene and Post-Nicene Fathers 4, edited by Philip Schaff. Edinburgh: T. & T. Clark, 1891.
LA	*The Life of Saint Anthony. The Paradise of the Fathers.* Translated and introduction by Ernest A. Wallis Budge. New York: Burt Franklin, 1907/1972.
LHS	*Letters Concerning the Holy Spirit*. Translated and introduction by C. R. B. Shapland. London: Epworth, 1951.

AUGUSTINE

CG	*The City of God against the Pagans*. Edited and translated by R. W. Dyson. Cambridge: Cambridge University Press, 1998.

CON	*Confessions.* Translated and introduction by Henry Chadwick. Oxford: Oxford University Press, 1991.
DC	*On Christian Doctrine.* Edited and translated by R. P. H. Green. Oxford: Clarendon, 1995.
DT	*On the Trinity: Books 8–15.* Edited by Gareth Matthews, translated by Stephen McKenna. Cambridge: Cambridge University Press, 2002.
LM	*The Literal Meaning of Genesis.* Translated and notes by John Hammond Taylor. New York: Newman, 1982.

BASIL THE GREAT

BLR	"The Longer Responses." In Anna M. Silvas, *The Asketikon of Saint Basil the Great.* Oxford: Oxford University Press, 2005.
HEX	*The Hexaemeron.* In *The Patristic Understanding of Creation*, edited by William A. Dembski et al. Riesel, TX: Erasmus, 2008.
THS	*On the Holy Spirit.* Translated and introduction by David Anderson. New York: St. Vladimir's Seminary, 1980.

IRENAEUS OF LYONS

AH	*Against Heresies: On the Detection and Refutation of Knowledge Falsely So Called.* In Ante-Nicene Fathers 1, translated by Alexander Roberts and W. H. Rambaut, edited by Philip Schaff. Edinburgh: T. & T. Clark, 1885.
DAP	*The Demonstration of the Apostolic Preaching.* Translated and introduction by John Behr. Crestwood, NY: St. Vladimir's Seminary, 1997.

Introduction

ADDRESSING THE AMERICAN ASSOCIATION for the Advancement of Science in December 1966, on "The Historical Roots of Our Ecologic Crisis,"[1] the American historian Lynn White Jr. castigated the Judeo-Christian tradition and Christianity particularly for having created the condition of mind that had issued now in the world's current environmental crises. "What people do about their ecology," he asserted, "depends upon what they think about themselves in relation to things around them. Human ecology is deeply conditioned by beliefs about our nature and our destiny—that is, by religion."[2] Thus religion becomes a key element in environmental discourse, and for White the complex of religious ideas that had shaped Western attitudes were those derived from the Bible and Christianity. The paper is wide-ranging, but at the heart of his critique of what he calls "the greatest psychic revolution in the history of our culture,"[3] he identifies three elements: a story of creation *ex-nihilo*, an account of human beings made in the image of God to exercise some kind of exploitative dominance, and the de-sacralization of nature through the destruction of pagan animism.[4] So ubiquitous and destructive have been these ideas that he pronounces, "we shall continue to have a worsening ecologic crisis until we reject the Christian axiom that nature has no reason for existence save to serve man."[5]

But, to what degree is such pugnacity justified? The purpose of this thesis is firstly to examine White's account historically, and secondly to offer a theological evaluation of the key elements about which he

1. White, "Historical Roots," 1203–7.
2. White, "Historical Roots," 1205.
3. White, "Historical Roots," 1205.
4. White, "Historical Roots," 1205.
5. White, "Historical Roots," 1207.

complains. The first chapter will serve to locate White's critique within a wider discussion regarding religion—particularly Christianity, in relation to environmental concerns. In the second, we shall survey some evidence of devastating human environmental impacts in contexts utterly uninformed by the biblical creation stories or biblical ideas concerning human dominion—a dynamic that seriously undermines White's central thesis. Here we shall also examine how religious visions imagining a highly divinized universe offer no automatic protection at all, to either the Earth or its non-human creatures. One such is ancient Mesopotamia, and in relation to that context we shall review some current biblical scholarship concerning the relevant issues in the Genesis creation stories and other associated passages. In them we discover a theological protest against the animistic vision of the world, which is not indifferent to Earth's wellbeing, nor that of its creatures. In the establishment of Sabbath and the Sanctuary we also discover parameters for human existence quite unacknowledged by White.

A significant part of White's case was not the biblical story itself, but an account of how it had subsequently been received and appropriated. Yet, despite his sweeping claims, White singularly neglects to engage with any key primary sources from the formative centuries of the Christian movement. In attempting our own history of interpretation, we shall engage key patristic theologians in their understanding of the image of God and human dominion, as these relate to the human place and role in creation. This will not be an exhaustive study, but a reasonably comprehensive review of material that has, thus far, been largely neglected in responses to White. We will examine the work of Irenaeus in chapter three, Athanasius in chapter four, and Augustine in five. These three were particularly formative influences in the Western tradition and it is of this tradition that White is especially critical.[6] The former two however were also highly esteemed in the East, and this cross-fertilization thus ameliorates White's contention of a deep division between the two streams.[7] Then, in chapter six we shall explore aspects of Christian monasticism. Monasticism is a valuable field as it enables some comparisons to be made between what people wrote, and what they actually did. The Desert Fathers and Mothers, Basil of Caesarea, Benedictine monasticism and its Cistercian offspring, and the new forms of asceticism represented by

---

6. White, "Historical Roots," 1205–6.
7. White, "Historical Roots," 1206.

Francis of Assisi will also be subjected to a comprehensive, although not exhaustive survey.

In light of this history of ideas and practice, in chapter seven we shall review the adequacy of White's account of the Christian impact, and then address the impact of another complex of ideas which rose to new influence during the Renaissance and subsequent Enlightenment, but which White ignores except insofar as to describe some as Christian heresies.[8]

Finally, drawing on both patristic and contemporary trinitarian study, we shall attempt a christological evaluation of the idea of human dominion over creation. It was the first community's convictions concerning the resurrection of Jesus which led to their affirmations that God had been uniquely present in Christ, and thus to the development of a trinitarian account of the life of God and God's engagement with the world. In light of this resurrection faith, chapter eight will explore some implications of the earliest New Testament confessions that Jesus is Lord, is the incarnate Word, and is the image of God. Resurrection was also regarded as the sign of vindication. Therefore, in chapter nine we shall explore the theme of vindication in relation to Jesus' proclamation of the kingdom of God, and in relation to his claims for authority over two primary symbols of Jewish identity—the Sanctuary and the Sabbath. Trinitarian accounts of the life of God presume that what has been done for us in Christ is somehow worked into us—and us into it, by the operations of the Holy Spirit. Therefore, we shall conclude by exploring some implications in Jesus' account of the Sabbath of the kingdom for the contemporary living of our dominion.

---

8. White, "Historical Roots," 1205.

1

At the Beginning: A Clamor of Many Voices

WHITE'S DRAMATIC EVALUATION OF the impact of Christianity breathed into flames a controversy that hitherto had been merely smoldering, regarding the role of Christianity in the Earth's ecological degeneration. Viewing religion as a crucial element in environmental discourse White suggested that, despite the "fashion to say we live in 'the post-Christian age' . . . we continue today to live, as we have for about 1700 years, very largely in a context of Christian axioms."[1] He argued that a peculiarly high evaluation of technology and a religiously motivated science, previously quite different and separate, had both originated in the medieval Christian West and therefore,

> since both . . . got their start, acquired their character, and achieved world dominance in the Middle Ages, it would seem that we cannot understand their nature or their present impact upon ecology without examining fundamental medieval assumptions and developments.[2]

These assumptions, he suggested, were largely derived from the Genesis creation story, with a particular emphasis upon human beings created in God's image, to exercise some kind of dominion over all the

---

1. White, "Historical Roots," 1205.
2. White, "Historical Roots," 1204–5.

rest of creation.³ In the context of developing democratization these two, formerly unrelated impulses, had "married" in the mid-nineteenth century⁴ "to give mankind powers which, to judge by many of the ecologic effects, are out of control . . . Christianity bears a huge burden of guilt."⁵ To speak thus of guilt is to assert deliberate moral (ir)responsibility, and it may be that by such a rhetorical flourish White both caught attention and generated a response that might otherwise have been absent. If he has done no more than place creation back as a central element in theological discourse we owe him some gratitude. Perhaps more gratitude is owed for having identified religion as a critical element in environmental discourse!

THOSE WHO SPOKE BEFORE: A CENTURY OF VOICES IN ANTICIPATION

White was not the first to have implicated Judeo-Christian faith in environmental degradation. In the same year that he went global with *Historical Roots*, Roderick Nash published *Wilderness and the American Mind*, a re-working of his 1964 doctoral thesis. Exemplifying a deprecatory approach he wrote, "comparison of early Western attitude toward wilderness with that of other cultures dramatizes the great influence of the Judeo-Christian tradition in arousing and nourishing antipathy."⁶ Like White's, I believe Nash's account is selective and tendentious, and it is perhaps revealing that he offers special thanks to White for a pre-publication reading of *Historical Roots*.⁷ Both writers represented the spirit of their age. Nash wrote, "I was lucky . . . I just happened to be right there,"⁸ and produced one of Yale's best sellers ever. Edward de Steigeur suggests, "White's blaming of traditional Christianity may have been startling, yet it was very much in step with the iconoclasm of the late 1960's."⁹ But even earlier, in 1949, Aldo Leopold had complained, "conservation is getting nowhere because it is incompatible with our Abrahamic concept of land.

---

3. White, "Historical Roots," 1205–6.
4. White, "Historical Roots," 1204.
5. White, "Historical Roots," 1206.
6. Nash, *Wilderness*, 20.
7. Nash, *Wilderness*, 19, note 29.
8. de Steiguer, *Origins*, 67.
9. de Steiguer, *Origins*, 102.

We abuse land because we regard it as a commodity belonging to us,"[10] and later, "Abraham knew exactly what the land was for: it was to drip milk and honey into Abraham's mouth."[11] We have not space to expose the theological and historical nonsense embodied in such comments,[12] but they are indicative of a mentality that was already abroad. In fairness we should acknowledge that Leopold also observed, in promotion of a land-ethic, "thinkers since the days of Ezekiel and Isaiah have asserted that the despoliation of land is not only inexpedient but wrong. Society, however, has not yet affirmed their belief."[13]

Behind all of these stands the influential and paradoxical figure of John Muir.[14] An inspirational advocate for wilderness in the late nineteenth and early twentieth centuries, Muir had a remarkable influence in the establishment of the first National Parks and the legislative protection, or at least recognition, of wilderness lands. His deeply Calvinistic upbringing seems to have involved contradictory attitudes towards creation. On the one hand his father had allegedly taught that there could be no knowledge of God discerned from creation, but only from the Scriptures—of which Muir appears to have had an encyclopedic knowledge. Thus, he is found constantly quoting them, while also excoriating Christianity for its failure to provide room in heaven for dead bears.[15] On the other hand he attributed love of wilderness to his earliest childhood in the Scottish highlands and he never tires of discerning the finger of God in all things.[16] His is the Transcendentalist's re-working of Christian faith, which had found earlier expression in Ralph Waldo Emerson and Henry David Thoreau.[17]

Whether the Judeo-Christian tradition was as antipathetic to wilderness as all these suggest is an issue we shall explore. What is clear, but

10. Leopold, *Sand County*, xviii.

11. Leopold, *Sand County*, 240.

12. Brueggemann, *Land*, 15–25, provides a more historically and theologically robust account of attitudes to land in the Abrahamic tradition.

13. Leopold, *Sand County*, 239.

14. de Steiguer, *Origins*, 11–13.

15. Nash, *Loving Nature*, 124.

16. Nash, *Wilderness*, 122–28; while Rod Nash finds only a destructive tension in Muir's Calvinistic upbringing, Santmire on the other hand discerns Muir's spiritual roots in Calvin's appreciative assessment of creation; see Santmire, *Brother Earth*, 156–57.

17. de Steiguer, *Origins*, 8, 59–60.

unacknowledged, is that for them all, wilderness is a place to which one may go from a place of safety. It can function as a place of wonder—even challenge, only because it no longer surrounds one as a daily threat to life. Nash's account of pre-Christian attitudes to wilderness allows some recognition of the human struggle for survival,[18] but for the most part one senses a modern sophisticate's disdain for those who should have known better. Ironically, the almost unrelieved fear he describes is in marked contrast to the sylvan idyll espoused by White. Ray Galvin catalogues the late-medieval experience of famine, pestilence and natural disaster that would generate deep ambivalence about nature and a welcome for any initiative that might hold promise of a more secure existence.[19] To the degree Nash's account is correct,[20] it is little wonder that the Christian gospel found some welcome, with its account of victory over the demonic in a de-divinized creation.[21]

About the same time as Muir's first wanderings George Perkins Marsh published *Man and Nature*.[22] Nash describes this as "the first comprehensive description in the English language of the destructive impact of human civilization upon the environment . . . the first in America to discuss nature protection in ethical terms."[23] Marsh imagined balance and harmonies in nature, disturbed only by the advent of human beings. But such disturbance was an unavoidable aspect of human survival and development, and it is incumbent upon humanity to manage its changes in ecologically fruitful ways. There was a utilitarian element to preservation, for forests maintained water resources, and reduced flooding and soil degradation—processes that would much later be called "ecological services."[24] The burden of the book is that human dominion had been environmentally destructive, not as a Christian doctrine but as a manner of action, long before Christianity appeared on the world stage.[25] Comfortable with the idea of human dominion rightly exercised, he wrote,

---

18. Nash, *Wilderness*, 8–9.
19. Galvin, *Christ and the Good Earth*, 30–31, 34–35.
20. Nash, *Wilderness*, 10–13.
21. For unsympathetic accounts of a similar dynamic in the southwest Pacific, see Park, *Ngā Uruora*, 134–38; and Flannery, *The Future Eaters*, 290–91.
22. Marsh, *Man and Nature*.
23. Nash, *Rights of Nature*, 38.
24. Marsh, *Man and Nature*, 35, 228–35.
25. Marsh, *Man and Nature*, 29–40.

man has too long forgotten that the earth was given to him for usufruct alone, not for consumption, still less for profligate waste. Nature has ... been proportioning and balancing, to prepare the earth for his habitation, when, in the fullness of time, his Creator should call him forth to enter into its possession.[26]

De Steigeur suggests, "Marsh believed that although proper care of the Earth's resources would ultimately have to be resolved through political processes, the problem was at its roots a moral issue."[27] In other observations relevant to this study as it will develop, Marsh describes pre-Christian deforestation in the Levant,[28] and notes Spanish sources that regard the Spanish hatred of trees as indicative of a pagan hatred of the biblical garden of God, rather than a Christian hatred of sacred forests.[29] Yankee Puritan prejudices appear when, having described the destructive, oppressive, and rapacious legacy of the Roman Empire, he sees it only exacerbated under Roman Catholicism when "in the Middle Ages, feudalism and a nominal Christianity ... converted the most beneficent of religions into the most baneful of superstitions."[30] A caution to contemporary environmentalists, not to become alienated from those most directly affected by conservationist decisions, may also be taken from his descriptions of the deep resentment felt by French peasants towards forests—arising from their experiences at the hands of the aristocracy, which issued in an orgy of forest clearance after the revolution.[31]

Far from the British and North American centers of influence even nineteenth-century New Zealand had its nascent environmental theologians. James Beattie and John Stenhouse have demonstrated the previously unacknowledged extent to which settlers drew on biblical imagery to express a spiritual engagement with the land.[32] Certainly "dominion" was understood in terms of developing productive farmlands, but often as a means for peace—exchanging swords for plowshares.[33] Yet frequently with it there was a deep sense that this wild new beauty

26. Marsh, *Man and Nature*, 36.
27. de Steiguer, *Origins*, 9.
28. Marsh, *Man and Nature*, 313, note 35.
29. Marsh, *Man and Nature*, 239–40, note 187.
30. Marsh, *Man and Nature*, 11–12.
31. Marsh, *Man and Nature*, 240–44.
32. Beattie and Stenhouse, "Empire, Environment and Religion," 413–46
33. Beattie and Stenhouse, "Empire, Environment and Religion," 420, 430–31.

reflected the beauty of God, represented a remnant of Eden, and was not to be mindlessly destroyed, for to do so was wanton sinfulness.[34] Preeminent among the many deeply Christian, environmentally sensitive, and eminently sensible who they reference would be William Travers[35] and W. H. Guthrie-Smith.[36] They are not unaware of issues in the world at large. William Travers, for example, draws on Marsh—among others, in discussing the impact of introduced species upon the indigenous.[37] Guthrie-Smith is shown to be a devout Calvinist with a deep sense of his common creatureliness with other creatures in a world that belongs to God.[38] His great work, *Tutira: The Story of a New Zealand Sheep Station*, has been hailed as "one of the great English-language classics of environmental history,"[39] and due to its wealth of scriptural quotations and allusions (mostly unrecognized as such by secularized readers),[40] as something of a devotional reflection on creation.[41] In pensive mood he asked near the end of his life, "have I for sixty years desecrated God's earth and dubbed it improvement?"[42] But he also anticipated

> the dawn of a new and "wiser dispensation" which, like "the scriptural grain of mustard seed," would transform environmental attitudes and behavior. The "future of mankind," declared Guthrie-Smith, is to make our "life-home" an "earthly paradise." This required "cleansing its waterways, staunching its wounds and waste, conserving its fertility, renewing its forests, watering its deserts, beautifying it with color and elegance of plant life," and "reanimating its woods with song and movement of birds."[43]

Also published in 1967, but begun in the mid-1950s and the fruit of over thirty years' labor, was Clarence Glacken's magisterial work, *Traces on the Rhodian Shore. Nature and Culture in Western Thought from*

---

34. Beattie and Stenhouse, "Empire, Environment and Religion," 431–32.
35. Beattie and Stenhouse, "Empire, Environment and Religion," 432–34.
36. Beattie and Stenhouse, "Empire, Environment and Religion," 435–36.
37. Beattie and Stenhouse, "Empire, Environment and Religion," 433.
38. Beattie and Stenhouse, "Empire, Environment and Religion," 435–36.
39. Beattie and Stenhouse, "Empire, Environment and Religion," 436.
40. Beattie and Stenhouse, "Empire, Environment and Religion," 436, note 131.
41. John Stenhouse, personal communication, Dunedin 13 October 2011.
42. Pawson and Brooking, *Environmental Histories of New Zealand*, 116.
43. Beattie and Stenhouse, "Empire, Environment and Religion," 436.

Ancient Times to the End of the Eighteenth Century.[44] Glacken attempted a much more comprehensive survey than any of those we have mentioned above, and he located both the biblical texts and Christian theology within cultural and hermeneutical contexts which are unacknowledged by Nash or White. In an observation which White would wisely have taken account of, he recognizes, with the writer of Genesis 1, that human dominion is described as a result of observation, rather than promoted as a plan of action.

> One must not read these passages [i.e., Gen 1 and Psalm 8—on dominion] with modern spectacles, which is easy to do in an age like ours when "man's control over nature" is a phrase that comes as easily as a morning greeting. Is this idea . . . anything more than a distillation of everyday observation?[45]

Secondly, warning against purely cultural determinism, "it is a mistake to think the history of civilization can be written purely as cultural, social, or economic history."[46] And he further observes, again recognizing a biblical interest in placing humanity within the rest of creation,

> it is no accident that ecological theory—which is the basis of so much research . . . and which has become the basic concept for a holistic view of nature—has behind it the long preoccupation in Western civilization with interpreting the nature of earthly environments, trying to see them as wholes, as manifestations of order.[47]

His biblical survey is also more comprehensive, and while recognizing strands of *contemptus mundi*,[48] much more prominent for him are the senses of "love for and delight in nature and of a belief that it is manifestation of God's handiwork."[49] Thus, "the affirmations of the closeness of the relationship between God, man, and nature are . . . I believe, the dominant ones in the Old and the New Testaments."[50] Nevertheless, like the other historians, Glacken also neglects to read his sources either christologically or eschatologically, and as we shall see, theological

---

44. Glacken, *Traces on the Rhodian Shore*, xi–xii.
45. Glacken, *Traces on the Rhodian Shore*, 166.
46. Glacken, *Traces on the Rhodian Shore*, 709–10.
47. Glacken, *Traces on the Rhodian Shore*, 708.
48. Glacken, *Traces on the Rhodian Shore*, 162–63.
49. Glacken, *Traces on the Rhodian Shore*, 158.
50. Glacken, *Traces on the Rhodian Shore*, 162.

interpretation is a critical issue—and had been from earliest times, not only since the challenge of the 1960s.

None of these[51] approach the Bible with the tools of biblical and theological scholarship (although Glacken does better than the others). Thus, although their caricatures or characterizations are questionable as being what "Christianity" or "Christian theology" taught, they presumably do represent the "popular" reading of these authors themselves, and perhaps those who formed them. Nor do they recognize that Genesis stands at the beginning of a vast sprawling narrative and is only known to us in relation to its place within that canonical account, which includes fall, redemption and ultimately the restoration of all things. It is not to be read in isolation and for most of history has not been.

Meanwhile, at least some preachers and theologians were alert to the emerging environmental challenges, long before White took the stand. Nash, in a subsequent work to *Wilderness,* cites the forester and hydrologist Walter Lowdermilk, who appealed to biblical ideas of stewardship in the 1930s, and in proposing an eleventh commandment, "succeeded in making conservation a moral matter. For him responsible land use was not just the key to 'physical' progress but to 'higher spiritual . . . development' as well . . . Lowdermilk took religion to be the foundation of environmental ethics."[52] In 1949 the influential English preacher D. R. Davies published three sermons under the title "*Modern Materialism and Lent,*" and a fourth, "*The Resurrection and Modern Progress,*" and all addressed issues of environmental degradation and world poverty.[53] Lutheran theologian Joseph Sittler, described by R. J. Berry as "an environmental prophet ahead of his time . . . [who] has not received the honor due to him for his cries from the wilderness,"[54] in 1954 had articulated "*A Theology for the Earth.*" His particular concern was

> neo-orthodoxy's almost proud repudiation of the earth and the feeling of some profound biblical promise distorted thereby, (and) another feeling that earth—because given of God, capable in spite of all of becoming the cradle in which Christ is laid—is a transparency for the Holy.[55]

---

51. That is, Muir, Marsh, R. Nash, White, or Glacken.
52. Nash, *Rights of Nature,* 98.
53. Davies, *Thirty Minutes,* 39–61.
54. Berry, *Environmental Stewardship,* 51.
55. Sittler, "Theology for the Earth," 51.

Sittler gives little sense of attempting something radically new. Rather, in exploring a range of Scripture, poetry and art, even Francis of Assisi, he attempts to rehabilitate a view of the inter-relationship of God, humanity, and nature which can be redemptive and regenerative.

> God—man—nature! These three are meant for each other, and restlessness will stalk our hearts and ambiguity our world until their cleavage is redeemed. What a holy depth of meaning lies waiting for our understanding in that moment portrayed on the last evening of Christ's life . . . Here in one huge symbol are God and man and nature together. Bread and wine, the common earthy stuff of our life when we have it, and of death when we've lost it. Both in the hands of the restoring God-man![56]

> We may not be able to go beyond Ephesians, Colossians, and the eighth chapter of Romans; but we dare not stop short of the incomparable boldness of those utterances. For here heaven and earth are held together in the incarnate Christ; here the Scriptures sink both ends of the arc of the Christ-event in ontological footings.[57]

Sittler addressed the New Delhi Assembly of the World Council of Churches in 1961, setting that body upon a developing path of environmental awareness. All his themes will reappear in our study but they are unacknowledged by the critics of the tradition, nor, disappointingly, in many of those who subsequently set out to defend it.[58]

In 1964, C. F. D. Moule published *Man and Nature in the New Testament: Some Reflections on Biblical Ecology*. John Reumann's Introduction surveys early Jewish and Rabbinical understandings of the *imago*, and a range of approaches to theological interpretation—most especially christological interpretation. Of a number of Pauline passages he writes, "Here Christ is being spoken of as the Man, the Adam, of Genesis 1:26–27 while we are like the man of Genesis 2:7 and chapter 3."[59] From before the Christian era it is clear that *imago* and dominion were not being read with dominationist intent, and it is another sign of weakness in the detractor's case that no attention was paid to these traditions. Patristic writers—to

---

56. Sittler, "Theology for the Earth," 54.

57. Sittler, "Theology for the Earth," 55; see also Jenkins, *Ecologies of Grace*, 17.

58. Jenkins, *Ecologies of Grace*, 17; and Whitney, "Lynn White, Ecotheology, and History," 15, 160.

59. Reumann, "Introduction," viii–xviii.

whom we shall be giving extensive attention, are mentioned, as also is the now much canvassed recognition that biblical language has no concept at all of a realm of nature from which human beings are absent or outsiders.[60] Moule himself pays particular attention to New Testament passages—an uncommon move in the early debate, and is especially interested in Romans 8. That humanity is "intended" to exercise control in creation involves he recognizes, a teleological theological commitment which is beyond the scope of biology or ecology as sciences, "nor can it be part of any non-religious view."[61] Nevertheless, he set about exploring the significance of Romans 8 for understanding the nature of such control. The casual abuse of Genesis 1 is recognized,[62] as also are ethical decisions regarding animals,[63] and the groaning of creation resulting from human abuse of power—particularly in the newly developing practices of industrialized agriculture.[64] There are no independent rights recognized for non-human nature,[65] but he does reference Sanday and Headlam's suggestion, from 1896, that Paul "is one of those (like St. Francis of Assisi) to whom it is given to read as it were the thoughts of plants and animals."[66] The calling of humanity is to live a sonship before God that recognizes the ultimate purposes of God for creation—not our own, and apart from such living creation will be frustrated and dislocated.[67] But such sonship is only lived within the actuality of created being; therefore, integral to the process of putting on eternal life is entering fully into the earthly, bodily, biological experience of decay.[68]

> It is our duty and our destiny to use and use up and consume and part with our mortal frame—to spend and to be spent. What saves this process from being a frustrating and merely negative decay is the conviction that obedient use, obedient subjection to the wear and tear of life, is a constructive process . . . it is along these lines that ethical problems presented by man's power over nature must be solved. Man is placed in the world by God to be

60. Reumann, "Introduction," xvii.
61. Moule, *Man and Nature*, 4.
62. Moule, *Man and Nature*, 1.
63. Moule, *Man and Nature*, 4.
64. Moule, *Man and Nature*, 12.
65. Moule, *Man and Nature*, 12.
66. Moule, *Man and Nature*, 9, note 4.
67. Moule, *Man and Nature*, 10.
68. Moule, *Man and Nature*, 11–12.

its lord. He is meant to have dominion over it and to use it and use it up—but only for God's sake, only like Adam in paradise, cultivating it for the Lord. As soon as he begins to use it selfishly, and reaches out to take the fruit which is forbidden by the Lord, instantly the ecological balance is upset and nature begins to groan.[69]

Salvation, as achieved in Jesus Christ, is not some means of escape from nature but God's reassertion of "the creative principle of harmony and life . . . rescue into purposeful living in the total environment of God's purposes."[70] Restoration is further recognized as he quotes G. B. Caird on Luke 8, "the miracles of Jesus were all 'miracles of the kingdom,' evidence that God's sovereignty was breaking in, with a new effectiveness, upon the confusion of a rebellious world."[71] Moule's work involves commitments regarding humanity that would probably leave subsequent readers uneasy. But he highlights central theological themes regarding humanity and creation, along with unavoidable ecological realities regarding both human power and decay. Despite its relative brevity the book traverses a remarkable range of themes that would subsequently become key areas of discussion.

Others whose work predates White's 1967 paper include Paul Santmire and Richard Baer. Baer is especially appreciated by Nash who, in his 1989 history of environmental ethics, devotes three pages to Baer's, "new light on the chronic Judeo-Christian 'dominion' problem."[72] The great irony in this is that the three principles Nash discerns in Baer will all be found in some form in the patristic theologians—which is not to dismiss the importance of a new voice and a new formulation for the new challenges of the late twentieth century. In 1969 Hugh Montefiore published *Can Man Survive?*—a series of addresses which included attention to environmental issues and specific, sympathetic engagement with Genesis 1 and the idea of human dominion over nature. Possibly Montefiore had not encountered White's seminal paper for it is unmentioned, but Joseph Needham alludes to it in his foreword.[73] Clearly in Britain too, environmental concern as a theological issue was in the air.

---

69. Moule, *Man and Nature*, 13–14.
70. Moule, *Man and Nature*, 21.
71. Moule, *Man and Nature*, 16.
72. Nash, *Rights of Nature*, 101.
73. Montefiore, *Can Man Survive?* 16.

IN THE NOISE OF BATTLE: VOICES IN THE AFTERMATH OF WHITE

In the *zeitgeist* of the late 1960s White's critique was eagerly appropriated. Theodore Roszak, in *The Making of a Counter-Culture*, and Charles Reich, in *The Greening of America*, exemplified a mentality of exegetical laziness and historical carelessness in their polemical accounts of Christian impact. So too landscape architect Ian McHarg, who mounts a vituperative attack upon the supposed impact of the Genesis passage. Of Genesis 1:28 he writes,

> if one seeks license for those who would increase radioactivity, create canals and harbors with atomic bombs, employ poisons without constraint, or give consent to the bulldozer mentality, there could be no better injunction than this text. Here can be found the sanction and injunction to conquer nature—the enemy, the threat to Jehovah.[74]

Apart from the illogicality that God would regard as an enemy that which has just been created, blessed, and declared to be good—and shortly thereafter very good; or the textual carelessness that Jehovah is nowhere mentioned; the great irony lies in his complete failure to consider that the Scottish countryside—about which he waxes lyrical, having been subject to some form of "Christian" influence for sixteen hundred years, might be a more authentic example of faithful dominion than the blighted slums of industrialized Glasgow which were the fruit of a very recently conceived modern confidence.

Elspeth Whitney recounts the speed with which White's ideas were adopted in both academic and popular literature:

> The thesis in "Roots" has been repeated, reprised, and criticized in over two hundred books and articles . . . between 1967 and (1993), and its central ideas have become so embedded in the ongoing discussions . . . that they have been described as part of environmental "folklore."[75]

Her paper surveys and critiques both White and a vast range of subsequent responses.[76] She too recognizes the over-simplifications in White's thesis and therefore the dangers of focusing on one formative influence while

---

74. McHarg, *Design with Nature*, 26.
75. Whitney, "Lynn White, Ecotheology, and History," 157–58.
76. Whitney, "Lynn White, Ecotheology, and History," 158, note 30.

neglecting to address others. Indeed, she suggests it "conveys a far more value-laden and problematic message than is generally acknowledged,"[77] and the emphasis on private religious convictions plays into the hands of a modern American preoccupation with privatized religion and individualized economic life.[78] Following Paul Santmire,[79] Whitney also recognizes that White's primary concern was not with what the biblical writers "meant," but rather with "the interaction of biblical ideas about nature with the activist religious ethic of the medieval West . . . how the Bible had been interpreted in the Middle Ages and after."[80] Yet, except for one passing reference to Irenaeus,[81] neither White, nor Nash in either of his books,[82] refer to any patristic writer and barely to the long history of Christian monasticism.[83] What they suppose to be "the Christian attitude" is constantly asserted but never once demonstrated by reference to primary sources. Even twenty-five years later Clive Ponting could still propose a simplistic, deprecatory account, untouched by historical nuance or investigation—except for a "Whitean" appreciation of Francis, which as we shall see was itself a simplification.[84] Still, in the twenty-first century, I have heard or had reported to me university lectures and study guides that continue to promote White's thesis without any critical analysis.

One of the earliest responses—and especially significant given its author's identification with conservative evangelicalism, was Francis Schaeffer's *Pollution and the Death of Man*, in which were also published as appendices, *Historical Roots* and *Why Worry about Nature?*[85]—another early response advocating the adoption of pantheism. Schaeffer accepts White's contention that worldview shapes all behavior and then sets about articulating his particular Christian one. He argues the absolute

---

77. Whitney, "Lynn White, Ecotheology, and History," 154.

78. Whitney, "Lynn White, Ecotheology, and History," 168–69; see also Djupe and Hunt, "Beyond the Lynn White Thesis," 670–86.

79. Santmire, *Travail of Nature*, 7–8.

80. Whitney, "Lynn White, Ecotheology, and History," 162; See also Harrison, "Having Dominion," 18–19.

81. White, "Historical Roots," 1205.

82. Nash, *Wilderness* and *Rights of Nature*.

83. Nash, *Rights of Nature*, 96, notes Dubos's advocacy of Benedict as an example of a stewardship tradition.

84. Ponting, *Green History*, 118–21.

85. Schaeffer, *Pollution and the Death of Man*, 117–25.

centrality of creation *ex nihilo* if we are to have a proper estimate of the value of all things, with a particular critique of Platonic philosophy—including Platonic forms of Christianity,[86] but without recognition that these had already been central issues in the patristic debates: "Creation is not an extension of the essence of God. Created things have an existence in themselves. They are really there . . . it is the biblical view of nature that gives nature a value *in itself* . . . of value in itself because God made it."[87] By virtue of being created we are inextricably one with the rest of nature. By virtue of being created in the image of God we need not fear nor be subsumed by nature.[88] Other themes he elucidates as promoting a renewed Christian care for creation include the incarnation, resurrection and ascension, the covenants with creation,[89] and the possibility of living a substantial healing of creation.[90] He quotes a now problematic comment from Francis Bacon regarding the prospects for such substantial healing,[91] but fails to acknowledge similar visions held in Christian monastic and Anabaptist movements.

A far more comprehensive response, also from 1970, was Paul Santmire's *Brother Earth*. Claiming to be "in full accord with the sentiments" of White, he wrote of the need for "an 'ecological theology,' a theology which takes seriously the life of man in nature and the life of nature itself . . . a religious vision which will teach us to say, in the depths of our being, 'brother earth.'"[92] Nevertheless, with what I consider to be greater perceptiveness than most of those we have reviewed so far, Santmire also recognized the romantic weaknesses in the Wilderness movements. There were he suggested two conflicting impulses in American history (and of other cultures also): the Ethic of Adoration and the Ethic of Exploitation. Ironically, he finds one exemplified in Thoreau and the other in Thoreau's mentor—Emerson![93] But the Ethic of Adoration had nurtured an individualistic indifference to the issues of the city, and to involvement in forms of public life that might have helped ameliorate the worst

---

86. Schaeffer, *Pollution and the Death of Man*, 40–43.
87. Schaeffer, *Pollution and the Death of Man*, 47.
88. Schaeffer, *Pollution and the Death of Man*, 50–54.
89. Schaeffer, *Pollution and the Death of Man*, 55–61.
90. Schaeffer, *Pollution and the Death of Man*, 65–77.
91. Schaeffer, *Pollution and the Death of Man*, 69.
92. Santmire, *Brother Earth*, 6.
93. Santmire, *Brother Earth*, 180.

excesses of the city. Thereby, the very problems berated by advocates of wilderness—or the slightly less adventurous advocates of farming life, were exacerbated.[94] American churches had played into this dichotomy, participating in a "cultural schizophrenia" that involved on the one hand, programs participating in the flight to nature and idealized rusticity, and on the other, an institutional life where "the emphasis is placed entirely on the utilitarian approach to nature . . . seriously sapping the vitality of the Church's own inner life, its faith, its hope, and its love, and apparently its ongoing Biblical interpretation as well."[95] Concern for biblical interpretation occupies the remainder of the book. Central to his exposition is an account of the kingdom of God, which transcends the problematic dichotomies—and finds a place for the spirituality of Francis.

> If we belong to the Kingdom of God and his righteousness, then we can no longer be primarily children of nature or primarily children of civilization. We can attend to both without opposing either one to the other. The Kingdom of God validates the rights of both nature and civilization: as subjects of the Kingdom, we are free to validate the rights of both as well.[96]

Santmire identifies three biblical themes that will reappear in his subsequent writing: humanity as Overlord, as Caretaker, and as Wondering Onlooker,[97] and he finds these also witnessed, and moderating each other, in the historical theological tradition. His "most important theological word . . . is Christ,"[98] and he offers the rudiments of a christological account framed in terms of "The Restoration of the Present Creation and the Foretaste of the New Creation."[99] Christ inaugurates us into the kingdom and enables in us the proper expressions of Overlordship, Caretaking, and Wonder.

In 1972 Ian Barbour published *Earth Might Be Fair,* and Paul Lutz and Paul Santmire, *Ecological Renewal*. Thereafter, a cascade of responses emerged in critique rather than adoption of White's thesis. The literature

---

94. Santmire, *Brother Earth*, 16–35.

95. Santmire, *Brother Earth*, 78–79; see also his examination of nature-piety unsupported by theological or doctrinal foundations, 62–65.

96. Santmire, *Brother Earth*, 132.

97. Santmire, *Brother Earth*, 145–61; compare Santmire, in "Partnership with Nature," 253–72.

98. Santmire, *Brother Earth*, 162.

99. Santmire, *Brother Earth*, 162–78.

now is vast. Nash in his 1989 history offers a survey of theological responses, more thoroughly than Whitney (and more thoroughly than he had engaged the earlier tradition), and identifies emerging themes which recognize: Firstly, humanity as an integral part of all that God has created; secondly, new understandings of stewardship; third, new explorations of the message of the kingdom of God; and fourthly, the beginnings of the extension of ethical consideration to the non-human creation.[100]

Renewed attention was paid to issues in Genesis that seem to have been neglected in preceding years. For example, John Skinner, writing for the prestigious International Critical Commentary in the late nineteenth century, had surveyed pagan accounts of the *imago Dei*, and considered various possibilities for the biblical version, but committed to none. Dominion he recognized as a consequence of the *imago*, but with no exploration of what it may actually involve. The provision for all creatures indicated a state of harmony, and there is for the writer of Genesis 1 no conception of a "fall."[101] He made no case for a domineering humanity, nor explored issues of Earth-care, but rather, seemed uninterested. But by 1963 Gerhad von Rad committed thirty-one pages—in two sections, to the issues,[102] and in 1974 Claus Westermann gave the relevant passages one hundred and thirty-seven pages[103]—with a further forty-seven if the creation-centered Introduction is also included. With concerns similar to Sittler's regarding the influence of neo-orthodoxy, and Santmire's regarding Karl Barth,[104] Ray Galvin contrasts von Rad's approach—with its indifference, even negativity, to issues of creation but unrelenting emphasis on experience of salvation in history,[105] with Westermann's—with its emphasis that the One who has acted in history to save is the One who is already the Creator, and salvation is always part of the Creator's care for and claim upon the world.[106]

From the specialist world of biblical scholarship an early specific response to *Historical Roots* was James Barr's, "Man and Nature: The Ecological Controversy and the Old Testament." Barr noted that points of

---

100. Nash, *Rights of Nature*, 99–112.
101. Skinner, *Commentary on Genesis*, 31–34.
102. von Rad, *Genesis*, 44–65, 71–83.
103. Westermann, *Genesis 1–11*, 74–211.
104. Santmire, *Brother Earth*, 98, and 212, note 1.
105. von Rad, *Genesis*, 43–44.
106. Galvin, *Christ and the Good Earth*, 49–56; Westermann, *Genesis*, 12–13.

view such as White's were likely to become widely influential, and "a significant challenge to Jewish and Christian religion."[107] He also references other writers who "rage in some ignorance,"[108] and contrasts "the generality and vagueness of [White's] article . . . with the precision and carefully evidenced nature of his own expert work on Medieval Technology."[109] Of the Genesis passage itself he evinces themes that will re-appear constantly in subsequent responses. Noting other Old Testament examples he writes, "the emphasis in Genesis does not appear to lie on man's power or on his exploitative activities."[110] He draws attention to the explicit prohibition upon meat as food, the equal provision made for animals, and that only after the flood

> do we hear that human domination might produce any kind of unpleasant consequences for the animal world . . . Human exploitation is something that comes along later, after a deterioration in the human condition, as a kind of second best. This fact makes a very considerable difference to the total impact of the idea of human dominion within the legends of Genesis.[111]

Among a range of benign uses of the now controversial word *rada*, he notes its frequent use in relation to rulers over their realms, particularly "Solomon's expressly peaceful and extensive dominion."[112] Thus,

> we can expect exegetes will in the future tend to reduce their emphasis on the "strength" of the terminology . . . [a process] . . . already visible in Westermann . . . there is no idea of exploitation, and man would lose his "royal" position in the realm of living things if the animals were to him an object of use or of prey.[113]

Finally, he also observes that the dominant Christian theological exegesis had been one that "connected the image of God . . . with man's immortal soul, his reason, spirituality, and was quite unconnected to any practical questions of control, technology or exploitation,"[114] and he queries,

107. Barr, "Man and Nature," 16–17.
108. Barr, "Man and Nature," 16.
109. Barr, "Man and Nature," 18, note 1.
110. Barr, "Man and Nature," 20.
111. Barr, "Man and Nature," 20–21.
112. Barr, "Man and Nature," 22.
113. Barr, "Man and Nature," 23.
114. Barr, "Man and Nature," 23.

if these influences are as strong as White and others suggest, "why did science not arise sooner, even among the Jews?"[115]

A widespread response among both biblical scholars and Christian apologists was to explore the notion of "responsible stewardship," as the real implication of both the dominion of Genesis 1 and the gardening of Genesis 2. We see this in Santmire's faithfulness to accounts of "overlordship" and "caretaking," despite their developing unpopularity and despite his own passionate commitment to the rights of non-human nature. John Black likewise explored ideas of stewardship in *The Dominion of Man*.[116] In 1977 Calvin College established a new Research Centre whose first initiative was a major project on Stewardship, which issued in the publication *Earthkeeping: Christian Stewardship of Natural Resources*. The authors recognize that it is

> impossible to act any longer as though humankind could be considered apart from the rest of nature . . . therefore . . . we can no longer speak of humanity being saved out of nature: we are redeemed *in* nature, not apart from it. In some way the Christian must include the rest of creation in his or her own salvation.[117]

Nevertheless, they identify deep ambiguities both within the modern world and within the Christian theological tradition. Some secular visions of a world given over completely to humans make White's account of Christianity appear positively benign.[118] Yet Christian thought itself has been divided between conflicting biblical accounts—"on the one hand that humanity (deeply sinful) is bound for a destructive crisis, and on the other that it is growing toward an Edenic Utopia."[119] Their sympathies for a way forward lie with

> those who see the institutions and abilities of humans as gifts of God, redeemable along with humankind. In various ways— from Justin Martyr, through Calvin and the eastern orthodox tradition, to many contemporary Reformed or Sacramental thinkers—these have maintained that for Christians to build the city of man, however haltingly, in an awareness of God's

---

115. Barr, "Man and Nature," 27.
116. Black, *Dominion of Man*, 44–72.
117. Wilkinson, *Earthkeeping*, 3–4.
118. Wilkinson, *Earthkeeping*, 4.
119. Wilkinson, *Earthkeeping*, 5.

working in the world is to build Zion and that ultimate kingdom of peace.[120]

With such a vision, the book sets out to develop "the possibility of a careful Christian stewardship of creation."[121] This stewardship appears to involve management for an absentee landlord, but there is recognition of need for a deep awareness of relational and ecological interconnectedness, some degree of de-militarization, more mutually advantageous trade agreements, and a renewed simplicity of life, centered on sustainable energy consumption, urban/domestic agriculture, and careful stewardship of each other.[122] Despite the apparent utopianism of such a vision,

> Christians, of all people, have the power in Christ to redeem the human character from its perversity and lead it into a new life in which stewardship, husbandry, and nurturing vulnerability is "natural" . . . obedience to the gospel of Christ motivates our treatment of the earth and all its creatures. Only then can we hope to become good and just stewards of the creation which God has placed under our care.[123]

Especially noteworthy is the recognition of Eastern Orthodox contributions to the question of humanity within creation.[124] Many of the book's themes will be developed in this thesis. Nevertheless, I feel that there is inadequate attention paid to patristic theology, and there is yet more room to explore how God is present to creation and how the new life in Christ impacts all aspects of the human presence in creation. Thus it is significant that a central role for humanity, but conceived in terms of priesthood rather than stewardship, was articulated by the orthodox theologian Paulos Gregorios in *The Human Presence*, published by the World Council of Churches in 1978.

Paul Santmire continued his vigorous advocacy for creation with the publication in 1985 of *The Travail of Nature*, and by the end of the century was writing about moving "beyond the Theology of Stewardship."[125] Here he promoted the conception of "partnerships," yet the structure of his argument still reflected his earliest accounts. Concentrating on what

---

120. Wilkinson, *Earthkeeping*, 6.
121. Wilkinson, *Earthkeeping*, 7.
122. Wilkinson, *Earthkeeping*, 261–90.
123. Wilkinson, *Earthkeeping*, 290.
124. Wilkinson, *Earthkeeping*, 221–23.
125. Santmire, "Partnership with Nature," 253–72.

he identifies as the Priestly, the Yahwistic, and the Jobean micro-narratives, he identifies partnerships of "creative intervention . . . sensitive care . . . and awestruck contemplation of nature"[126]—with stewardship appropriately reconceived as a limited aspect of only the first of these three. Douglas John Hall published a comprehensive volume, *Imaging God: Dominion as Stewardship,* in 1986. In 2006 R. J. Berry gathered up key themes in the stewardship discussion with his edited collection, *Environmental Stewardship: Critical Perspectives—Past and Present.* This is a treasure-trove to which we shall repeatedly have recourse.

Other responses were much less sanguine. Feminist critique discerned in the biblical text patriarchal domination that required much more robust criticism. In 1992 Rosemary Radford Ruether published *Gaia and God: An Ecofeminist Theology of Earth Healing,* and Sallie McFague followed in 1993 with *The Body of God: An Ecological Theology.* Even such as these however still recognize,

> humans are not given ownership or possession of the earth, which remains "the Lord's." God, finally, is the one who possesses the earth as his creation. Humans are given usufruct of it. Their rule is the secondary one of care for it as a royal steward, not as an owner who can do with it what he wills. This obviously means that humans are to take good care of earth, not to exploit or destroy it, which would make them bad stewards.[127]

Athalya Brenner's *Feminist Companion to Genesis,* also 1993, addresses a range of issues and passages, but Luise Schottroff's study of the creation narrative especially demonstrates how a feminist reading can throw new light upon, and derive new possibilities from, a controverted text.[128] Other feminist critique suggested that reading Genesis 1 as an account of creation *ex nihilo* involved the depiction of domineering power and therefore the dominion inherent in the *imago* is also seen as inherently violent.[129] But most commentators repeatedly draw attention to the measured tranquility of the process, which arises entirely from God's speaking. One distinguishing feature of the biblical account is that the violent struggles of the Babylonian myths are quite absent—"Genesis 1 is extraordinarily peaceful in its representation of creation . . . verse 26

---

126. Santmire, "Partnership with Nature," 254.
127. Ruether, *Gaia and God,* 21.
128. Schottroff, "The Creation Narrative," 24–38.
129. Keller, *Face of the Deep,* xv–xx.

indicates some form of divine sociality but no hint of disagreement."[130] This debate has been well explored by Richard Middleton in *The Liberating Image*.[131]

As new significance was being discovered in the text by reading it through new eyes, so alongside feminist or liberationist readings there developed "an ecojustice hermeneutic to . . . assist us in reading the text from the perspective of Earth."[132] Thus developed the Earth Bible project. In conversation with ecologists six Ecojustice Principles were identified. These were the principles of Intrinsic Worth, Interconnectedness, Earth's Voice, Purpose, Mutual Custodianship, and Resistance.[133] According to Norman Habel,

> reading the Biblical text from an ecological perspective involves (1) acknowledging the probable anthropocentric bias both within the text and within traditional interpretations; (2) identifying with Earth and Earth community as kin who are subjects in the narrative; (3) seeking to retrieve the perspective or voice of Earth and earth community of whom we humans are but one species.[134]

Valuable as this strategy is, questions remain for me whether it too is an (anthropo-generated) imposition upon the biblical narrative and whether it is integrated to that narrative by any theological vision arising from the text itself—or from the God who the text is ultimately about.

Such a variety of approaches to the biblical text serves as a reminder that modern historical criticism involved, as Stephen Fowl puts it, "a fiction that reading the Bible could be pursued without reference to theological and personal considerations."[135] He argues that outside the academy Scripture has always been read primarily with practical ends in mind, namely, "the struggle to live faithfully before the triune God,"[136] and thus the pre-modern interpretive approaches of the patristic theologians

---

130. Brett, *Genesis*, 24–25. See also Schottroff, "The Creation Narrative," 24.
131. Middleton, *Liberating Image*, 236–69.
132. Habel and Wurst, *Earth Story*, 9.
133. Habel and Wurst, *Earth Story*, 20; note the elements of critique by Deane-Drummond, in "Living from the Sabbath," 13.
134. Habel, "Introducing Ecological Hermeneutics," 8.
135. Fowl, *Theological Interpretation*, xiii.
136. Fowl, *Theological Interpretation*, xiii.

are to be valued as "an authentic part of an ongoing struggle."[137] Thomas Oden argues similarly.[138] David Steinmetz discusses the theological or pastoral significance in the identification of different layers of meaning,[139] and Andrew Louth suggests that the whole patristic approach consisted of "making the text of Scripture shine like a beam of light . . . through the prism of faith in Christ."[140] Christological interpretation thus becomes the key to the Scriptures. Certainly it is for patristic theology, and therefore to "cherry-pick" quotes from patristic writers[141] while failing to recognize their strategy is to both misunderstand and misrepresent their central concerns.

WHERE THE VOICES HAVE BEEN SILENT, OR ONLY WHISPERING

Despite this rich history, I believe there remain significant lacunae to be addressed.

Firstly, White contended that "the victory of Christianity over paganism was the greatest psychic revolution in the history of our culture."[142] If this is so, its nature cannot be understood apart from engaging the key influences prior to the eighth century, namely the thinking of patristic theologians and the emerging practices of Christian monasticism. Oden defines the patristic period as "the era from Clement of Rome (fl. c.95) to John of Damascus (c.645–c.749) . . . including the Venerable Bede."[143] It was patristic theology that defined the Christian faith as it emerged from within Judaism and encountered the worlds of Greco-Roman and tribal paganism. Alongside, and inextricable from, its articulation of trinitarian faith was its advocacy for creation as the good work of God.[144] Central to all Patrisitic theological reflection were the opening chapters of Genesis,

---

137. Fowl, *Theological Interpretation*, xvii. See also Hays, "Spirit, Church, Resurrection," 35–37.

138. Oden, "General Introduction," xxv–xxvii.

139. Steinmetz, "Pre-Critical Exegesis," 26–38.

140. Louth, "Introduction to Genesis 1–11," *Ancient Christian Commentary*, xlviii.

141. Despite their legitimate concerns about the tradition, this, I believe, is the failure of Singer, *Animal Liberation*, 186–93; or Steiner, *Anthropocentrism and Its Discontents*, 112–26.

142. White, "Historical Roots," 1205.

143. Oden, "General Introduction," xi.

144. Louth, "Introduction to Genesis 1–11," *Ancient Christian Commentary*, xlviii.

which according to Andrew Louth, "had arguably a greater influence on the development of Christian theology than did any other part of the Old Testament. In these early chapters the Fathers have set out the fundamental patterns of Christian theology."[145] Louth further observes that,

> the pattern (the early chapters of Genesis) provides of creation and fall is not something that the Jews detected in it: for them the fall was not and is not a cataclysmic event in the history of humankind; it is but one of many examples of human failure to live within the covenant.[146]

Yet, despite this significant and possibly innovative approach to Genesis, White and his acolytes ignore both patristic and monastic theological reflection upon creation and the human place within creation, and neither have they received much attention in the responses we have so far surveyed. Peter Harrison has briefly addressed patristic ideas, but I will argue that although he rightly identifies their concerns regarding "the beasts within," there is nevertheless significant engagement also with issues concerning the beasts of the field.[147] Differences such as these are indicative of differing responses to the variety of hermeneutic strategies adopted by patristic readers of Genesis.[148]

Secondly, largely neglected in the discussion subsequent to *Historical Roots* is any exploration of the significance of the Sabbath—the seventh day, in relation to the place of humans in creation and in the construction and interpretation of Genesis 1.[149] Yet we shall see that patristic theologians and historical-critical scholars both recognize the centrality of the Sabbath for a proper account of the passage and its place in the Old Testament as a whole. Indeed in many respects, especially for Augustine, the Sabbath becomes the key for understanding and inter-relating all the themes found in Genesis 1.

Thirdly, although both Santmire and Wilkinson touch upon christological issues in their suggestions about stewardship and the kingdom of God, and Douglas John Hall explores some trinitarian aspects of *imago* and suggests that at heart this involves the powerlessness of

---

145. Louth, *Ancient Christian Commentary*, xxxix.
146. Louth, *Ancient Christian Commentary*, xlvii.
147. Harrison, "Having Dominion," 17–23.
148. See Steinmetz, "Pre-Critical Exegesis," 26–38.
149. See Bratton, "Sea Sabbaths for Sea Stewards," 208–12; and Deane-Drummond, "Living from the Sabbath," 1–13.

servanthood,[150] for the most part the discussion has not involved robust theological reflection about God! This is not insignificant. We will see that the patristic development of trinitarianism was in large part an attempt to articulate how God may be creator and also be intimately involved with creation. Irenaeus's famous aphorism about the Father working in the world by his two hands, the Son/Word and the Spirit, is one of many examples to which we shall pay more attention. Envisaging such divine involvement engages White's complaint regarding the de-sacralization of creation. I will argue that creation is de-divinized in the patristic account but not de-sacralized, for it is entirely God's work, God remains intimately involved, and those who contemplate creation rightly will also be encountering the reality of God. The question how God is involved in creation has obvious bearing upon the involvement of those who are made in God's image, thus the earlier mentioned issues of christological interpretation are crucial for understanding the full import of human dominion. Finally, the question concerning God's involvement in creation addresses issues regarding the hope of creation or, to frame it slightly differently, how does the gospel of Jesus Christ impact upon creation? Is care of the Earth only a hobby for enthusiasts or is it a necessary aspect of witness to the gospel? Is there a partnership with Christ that extends to the healing of the Earth?

These are the questions we shall be alert to as we move in the next chapters to engage three of the most widely influential patristic theologians, the subsequent life-experiments in Christian monasticism, and eventually a trinitarian and christological account of human dominion.

150. Hall, *Imaging God*, 193.

2

In the Shadow of Ozymandias: Dominion and Destruction in a World without, and with, the Bible

ALTHOUGH MAKING A CURSORY nod in the direction of other environmentally destructive cultures,[1] White fails to consider their significance in undermining his central thesis. Jared Diamond, in *Collapse*, has demonstrated a range of cultures that have proved to be environmentally destructive. It can be demonstrated that many of these outcomes arose from or were associated with religious understandings that were utterly untouched by either the biblical story or experience of Christian mission. Furthermore, examples we shall consider were societies operating within what Harold Turner has characterized as Encapsulated Cosmologies;[2] that is, their universe is thoroughly divinized—the gods or spiritual powers are present within all things. Such a sacral universe is the kind that White suggests was the spiritual abode of the European and other peoples, before the advent of supposedly dualistic and destructive Christianity.[3]

In this chapter we shall examine three examples from three vastly different contexts, and conclude with a consideration of the ancient

---

1. White, "Historical Roots," 1203.
2. Turner, *The Roots of Science*, 21–34.
3. White, "Historical Roots," 1205.

Hebrew response to one of these, which we have in the Genesis creation stories.

WALKING AMONG THE GODS—LIFE IN A DIVINIZED WORLD

Easter Island

In *Easter Island, Earth Island*, Paul Bahn and John Flenley explore the impressive cultural developments on Easter Island, and the subsequent equally impressive environmental collapse, impoverishment and dramatic population decline. Their case is that these collapses are not simply subsequent but consequent, the result of a particular set of social values and religious practices. Although this collapse may seem insignificant in contrast to the global impacts addressed by White, it was in some respects more disastrous than anything we presently experience because for the Easter Islanders it involved the ecological collapse of the whole world they knew. For them it may as well have been "global." Its significance for us lies in a people's readiness to destroy their whole world under the impetus of a worldview untouched by biblical ideas.

Sometime about the middle of the first Christian millennium evidence appears of a "deliberate colonization" of Easter Island.[4] Apart from the arrival of human beings themselves there was also introduced, as all across the Pacific, the Polynesian rat and a domestic hen. Brought to enlarge the varieties of protein available, the rat would in time contribute to a significant ecological collapse through its destructive impact on trees and their seed resources and on birdlife.[5] Earliest artifacts suggest a simple nature religion based on the worship of the creator god *make make*. In time however there developed a more complex system involving the veneration of deified tribal ancestors. Artifacts become larger and more complex, indicative of "a developing culture of competitive 'one-upmanship,' seeking or demonstrating prestige or the prestige of one's ancestors or gods."[6] Eventually the most impressive of these *moai* were graced by the addition of red scoria head-dresses, *pukao*—a stylized *hau kurakura* identified with the spiritual power of the gods. These are "associated only

---

4. Bahn and Flenley, *Easter Island, Earth Island*, 75.
5. Bahn and Flenley, *Easter Island, Earth Island*, 172–73.
6. Bahn and Flenley, *Easter Island, Earth Island*, 160.

with statues on the largest and most important platforms of the late phases . . . a sign of continuing rivalry . . . in the splendor of monuments and homage to the ancestors."[7] To raise these adornments required considerable resources of engineering skill, community cooperation and timber. Although the authors recognize in this "an intensely competitive instinct that was characteristic of Polynesia,"[8] they also find that "the communal subsistence projects common through eastern Polynesia were replaced on Easter Island by these more esoteric pursuits: the construction of monumental structures and statues."[9] In addition, there was developed on Easter Island *rongo rongo*—the only written script found in Polynesia; and, despite the culture of intertribal competitiveness, warfare and weapons manufacture was virtually unknown for a thousand years.[10] The point of these last observations is that the system appeared to be working. The cultural achievements were increasingly impressive. The ever more grandiosely venerated ancestors appeared indeed to be smiling on their people and blessing their efforts.

Then, with a bang rather than a whimper, the whole edifice collapsed. Sometime early in the eighteenth century, as Flenley has described it in another context, "somebody looked over Easter Island, denuded of all its original forest cover, and deliberately cut down the last tree."[11] This, despite the fact they had no knowledge of another world with which they could hope to trade and thus import the resources necessary to sustain their particular form of life. The archaeological record witnesses to significant impoverishments. Jacob Roggeveen, the first known European explorer to sight Easter Island, described it in 1722 as "withered . . . scorched . . . burnt . . . its withered appearance could cause no other impression than of a singular poverty and barrenness."[12] The loss of trees—the canoe-building resource, led to a further shrinking of the islanders' world. No longer could they access the few outlying islands still visited for food gathering, and the sea became only a place for shore-based food-gathering rather than ocean-going fishing.[13] Kirch and Hunt report

---

7. Bahn and Flenley, *Easter Island, Earth Island*, 185–86.
8. Bahn and Flenley, *Easter Island, Earth Island*, 208.
9. Bahn and Flenley, *Easter Island, Earth Island*, 185.
10. Bahn and Flenley, *Easter Island, Earth Island*, 185–86.
11. Flenley, in a lecture at Christianity, Crisis and Conservation Conference, Auckland, Feb 2005.
12. Sharp, *Journal of Jacob Roggeveen*, 93.
13. Bahn and Flenley, *Easter Island, Earth Island*, 171.

that "all native landbirds and most seabirds had . . . been wiped out."[14] Signs of malnutrition and even starvation appear much more frequently and this is reflected even in the gaunt, emaciated carved figures dating from the period.[15] The development of weapons is an eighteenth-century phenomenon, and feuding and wars—the next step up from communal competitiveness, become much more common.[16] In less than a century the population declined by about 60 percent.[17]

Aotearoa New Zealand

Meanwhile in the far southwest of the Pacific those who eventually became Maori were beginning to colonize Aotearoa New Zealand. Here too there were deliberate species introductions intended to enhance the lifestyles of the new arrivals: the Polynesian rat again (and again with ecological impacts), the dog and the kumara. In this situation, however the rat initially proved irrelevant as a food source for the newcomers. Instead, they found one of the biggest and most easily taken protein sources imaginable—the moa; and, to be hunted with only a little more difficulty, the Southern fur seal and other marine mammals. Athol Anderson in, *When All the Moa Ovens Grew Cold*, and *A Fragile Plenty: Pre-European Maori and the New Zealand Environment*, has explored the history of early Maori exploitation of these resources.

Contrary to earlier notions of the moa being an open grassland bird, hunted indiscriminately in large numbers by use of fire, Anderson argues it was rather a forest and scrub-clearing bird that was hunted individually and with deliberation.[18] Nevertheless this does not seem to have been governed by any kind of conservation ethic. He suggests that "at least 100,000 and possibly up to half a million were killed during the early period in southern New Zealand."[19] Archaeological evidence suggests that birds were often processed at "factory" sites rather than at the place

---

14. Kirch and Hunt, *Historical Ecology*, 72.

15. Bahn and Flenley, *Easter Island, Earth Island*, 92, 170; also notes to displays in the Canterbury Museum, Christchurch, NZ.

16. Bahn and Flenley, *Easter Island, Earth Island*, 170, 186; see also Kirch and Hunt, *Historical Ecology*, 148.

17. Bahn and Flenley, *Easter Island, Earth Island*, 213.

18. Anderson, *When the Ovens Grew Cold*, 9–10.

19. Anderson, *When the Ovens Grew Cold*, 11.

of kill and that most parts were discarded.[20] The Wairau Bar and Waitaki River Mouth sites show huge numbers trapped, killed, and not used at all. Other sites reveal *hangi* ovens laid for cooking but never opened. Moa hunting also involved deliberate environmental modification by burning; not as earlier believed to chase the birds into confined spaces but rather to encourage the development of the patchwork shrubby forest fringes preferred as habitat by the moa.[21] In this sense the land was under a much more extensive management regime than was recognized by later European/Pakeha arrivals. With an estimated biomass of up to thirty birds per square kilometer, moa densities approximated modern high country stocking rates and their extinction significantly lowered the human-carrying capacity of the land.[22] By the end of the sixteenth century moa were extinct and the seal population was also in decline. The breeding range contracted from Northland about 1300, to Cook Strait about 1600, and to East Otago by 1800, when European hunting began in earnest.[23] "Conservation" of a kind was practiced for this species by the taking of pups only, which meant hunting became a strictly seasonal activity.[24]

Anderson quotes Caughley, "after A.D. 1400 the major New Zealand grazing systems ceased to exist... the Polynesians did not just eliminate the moas, they eliminated an ecological and evolutionary process developed over more than 50 million years."[25] His own assessment is that "pre-European Maori... had been involved in the loss of 50% of both the primeval forest area and the Holocene suite of birds."[26] These losses were not incidental. Cumberland reports that in parts of the country moa were known as *kuranui*, which he translates as, "'great treasure' or in modern terms 'basic resource,'"[27] yet, "at the peak of their cultural and economic development they exterminated what was... their prime resource."[28]

---

20. Anderson, *When the Ovens Grew Cold*, 11–12.

21. Anderson, *When the Ovens Grew Cold*, 26.

22. Anderson, "Fragile Plenty," 29; Black, *Dominion of Man*, 12, suggests a rate of 750–800 birds per acre.

23. Anderson, "Fragile Plenty," 29.

24. Anderson, *When the Ovens Grew Cold*, 13.

25. Anderson, "Fragile Plenty," 32.

26. Anderson, "Fragile Plenty," 20.

27. Cumberland, *Landmarks*, 47.

28. Cumberland, *Landmarks*, 54.

Mesopotamia

The third story was well advanced before the previous two had begun and relates to Mesopotamia. This region developed as one of the earliest and greatest riverine civilizations, involving massive human interventions to claim water in support of grandiose religio/socio/political schemes. Jacobsen has traced the rise and decay of various Mesopotamian civilizations over three millennia and in concert with those fortunes their various myths and religious practices. Three phases are identified: the earliest—which nevertheless remains always present in all that follows, in which the gods indwell natural objects and forces, and phenomena cannot be conceived of apart from the action of the respective gods. Fertility and plenty are here the dominant concerns. The second presents the gods as rulers, above the earth but inhabiting it and exercising hierarchical rule through the king. Power and stability become dominant motifs and human beings are presented as created for servile tasks to ease the lot of the administering gods. Finally, and perhaps in face of instability, war, and oppression, there develop conceptions of the gods as parents with concerns for the wellbeing of individuals.[29] According to the epic *Enuma Elish*, Babylon was built at Marduk's command to be his royal throne and the center of his heavenly administration upon earth. Here it was that humans were brought into being, "to be burdened with the toil of the gods, that the gods may freely breathe."[30]

These religious visions are closely allied with sociopolitical developments. That the gods and their earthly manifestations may be appropriately honored required the development and material support of significant institutions. "Enormous city walls ringed every city, attesting to a staggering investment of labor . . . the earlier network of small open villages disappeared."[31] Nineveh in the sixth century BC was "surrounded by rich irrigated farmlands, covered nine square miles, and had an estimated population of 120,000 . . . an enormous concentration for the time."[32] Itself the successor of earlier civilizations which had disappeared, Nineveh in time would be supplanted by Babylon and also decay into the desert.

---

29. Jacobsen, *Treasures of Darkness*, 20–21.
30. Jacobsen, *Treasures of Darkness*, 181.
31. Jacobsen, *Treasures of Darkness*, 78.
32. Ehrlich and Ehrlich, *One with Nineveh*, 3.

Jacobsen and Adams survey the changing agricultural fortunes of the Mesopotamian civilizations.[33] In 3500 BC wheat and barley each account for 50 percent of the annual crop. By 2500 BC wheat accounts for only 20 percent, by 2100 BC less than 2 percent, and by 1700 BC it has been abandoned throughout the southern Mesopotamian plain.[34] The reason? Irrigation causes salinization of soil, and the less salt-tolerant wheat proved unable to survive in the changing environment. Not only do crops change however. Their yields also steadily decline. In 2400 BC the land was producing 2,537 liters per hectare. By 2100 it was 1,460 liters per hectare and by 1700, 897 liters per hectare. Although the science may not have been understood the fact of salinization is attested in records of ancient temple surveyors and periodic, partially successful, attempts made to overcome the problem.[35]

> The southern part of the alluvial plain appears never to have recovered fully from the disastrous general decline which accompanied the salinization process . . . cultural and political leadership passed permanently out of the region . . . and the great Sumerian cities dwindled to villages or were left in ruins.[36]

Political power shifted north. Irrigation systems became ever larger and more complex, extending eventually to the construction of a three hundred kilometer long canal, "boldly reshaping the physical environment at a cost which could be met only with the full resources of a powerful and highly centralized state."[37] But this unrivalled engineering competence not only failed to halt the processes of salinization it also exacerbated the processes of siltation, which led in time to the collapse and abandonment of the whole system and with it the cultures it had been built to support. Ehrlich blames the *hubris* and "notoriously hierarchical" nature of these social systems for being so disconnected from the land that they utterly failed to notice "the gradual environmental decay that was undermining the foundations of their civilization."[38] Their fates are much more poetically recalled in Kipling's "Recessional" or Shelley's "Ozymandias."

33. Jacobsen and Adams, "Salt and Silt," 1251–8.
34. Jacobsen and Adams, "Salt and Silt," 1252.
35. Jacobsen and Adams, "Salt and Silt," 1251–2.
36. Jacobsen and Adams, "Salt and Silt," 1252.
37. Jacobsen and Adams, "Salt and Silt," 1257.
38. Ehrlich and Ehrlich, *One with Nineveh*, 5.

In both Easter Island and Mesopotamia one element at least in the development of an environmentally destructive impact were "theologies" that required ever more grandiose veneration of gods or deified ancestors. Cultures of competitiveness intensified the impact—either between tribal groups on Easter Island or as assertions of imperial power in Mesopotamia. Ironically in both cases destructive human power was not exercised on the basis of any doctrine of human dominion over the Earth, but rather of human subservience to the gods! Nor were these gods conceived of as absent from the world, but rather as a potentially dangerous presence in a thoroughly divinized universe, who could nevertheless be manipulated by the exercise of appropriate propitiatory rites. Maori culture never developed the massive cultural artifacts or organization found in the other two contexts. Caution is thus called for in identifying any common elements. Nevertheless, *mana* did accrue to those who exercised guardianship/*kaitiakitanga*[39] over larger domains, or who could demonstrate greater ability in provision of food. Such a dynamic fits within the Polynesian culture of competitiveness alluded to by Flenley and Bahn. Hirini Moko Mead shows that aspects of *kaitiakitanga*—particularly those relating to the conservationist concept of *rahui*, "can be linked back to Polynesia and Melanesia and even the Lapita ancestors,"[40] but in the prevailing culture of competitiveness these could be challenged and often, in regard to conservation, were not appreciated.[41] Patterson recognizes the possibility of "manipulating the environment . . . [for human purposes] . . . using correct application of spiritual laws relating to *tapu*,"[42] and also that even a whole forest could conceivably be cut if it was for a sufficiently worthy use, providing the spiritual balance of all the elements was maintained.[43]

Without doubt, in all three contexts, for many people struggling to survive with their kin from one harvest to the next, incremental environmental changes may well have gone unnoticed and even if not unnoticed, in all likelihood not understood and therefore not able to be corrected—except perhaps by the raising of even greater honors to the appropriate divinities. The critical observation is that these all are untouched by any

---

39. Roberts et al., "Kaitiakitanga," 7–20.
40. Mead, *Tikanga Māori*, 198.
41. Mead, *Tikanga Māori*, 202, 205–7.
42. Patterson, *Exploring Maori Values*, 83.
43. Patterson, *Exploring Maori Values*, 43.

Judeo-Christian influences. They conceived of a divinized universe of the kind White celebrated, yet in the face of human need, greed, competitiveness, or arrogance—even exercised on behalf of the honor of one's gods, such a conception provided no guaranteed environmental protection at all.

WALKING WITH GOD—LIFE IN A CREATED UNIVERSE

The Hebrew Response

To Babylon came the Jewish exiles after the national disaster of 587BC and there, according to the documentary hypothesis, brought together the Genesis stories in the form we have them today. Documentary hypotheses propose that the whole Pentateuch, of which Genesis is the first part, is a theologically motivated collection of material drawn from a number of different sources usually identified as J, E, D and P. J material stems from the southern kingdom of Judah and always names God as Jahveh. E, using the name Elohim for God, is believed to originate in the Northern kingdom of Ephraim or Israel. D is material associated with the book of Deuteronomy, and P identifies material from a group of writers with particularly priestly interests.[44] Genesis 1:1—2:3 is identified as P material and along with other P material frequently reflects and debates with a number of the Babylonian creation myths.[45] This particular Babylonian orientation, the fact that key ideas in this material—although appearing at the beginning and setting the scene for all that follows, are virtually unremarked in all other parts of the Hebrew Scriptures,[46] and the role of this Priestly material in structuring the rest of the Pentateuch,[47] all support the idea that it was a priestly group working in Babylon or in the light of the Babylonian exile, who drew together earlier traditions to form the Pentateuch much as we now have it. Study through the later twentieth century has called in question some of the confident assertions

---

44. Lohfink, *Theology*, 136–39, and 136, note 3. See also Knight, *Theology of the Old Testament*, 23, note 1; and Jónsson, *Image of God*, 15–24.

45. Levenson, "Genesis," 9–10.

46. Anderson, *Creation to New Creation*, 15.

47. Lohfink, *Theology*, 16; or 133, on the relations between the creation story of Genesis 1 and the building of the sanctuary in Exodus 35; or 167, between the commissioning of Genesis 1:28 and the fulfillment in Joshua 18:1.

of earlier advocates of the documentary hypothesis, nevertheless there remains "general agreement of P's association with the first creation story and some of the flood story . . . written either as supplement to the rest or separately and later integrated to provide a unified story."[48] In subsequent chapters P is the nomenclature I shall use in referring both to this particular material and to its writers.

As recognized above, the Babylonian context was a hierarchical command society where "typically only kings were thought of as bearing the image of a god . . . [and] massive human intervention was necessary to sustain its economy, above all through irrigation projects."[49] In the face of such idolatrous but apparently proven and overwhelming power, what options are there for disorientated, dispirited exiles? Only assimilation— or are there possibilities for resistance?

In the context of these conditions we will identify five key themes in the Genesis narrative, which we shall eventually revisit in our christological evaluation.

The Creation Narrative as a Formative Liturgy

Luise Schottroff suggests the creation account is "an attempt to provide a people in misery with a new order and comprehensive cult, a structure which makes a home for the homeless and deported in a manifest relationship to God."[50] Claus Westermann, likewise, argues strongly that this first creation account must be read, even experienced, as confessional in character and is shaped by liturgical considerations. "Creation myths are not firstly intellectual reflection on beginnings but liturgical enactments elucidating our place in the world and ensuring its stability."[51] Jon Levenson notes that "in the Jewish liturgy this passage serves as an introduction to the Kiddush, the prayer over the wine to sanctify the Sabbath . . . the type of repetition suggests it might have served as a liturgy already in antiquity."[52] The liturgical cast of the passage is also suggested in the establishment of the great lights, the sun and moon in Gen 1:14, to

---

48. Birch, *Introduction*, 37.

49. Santmire, "Partnership with Nature," 257–58.

50. Schottroff, "The Creation Narrative," 25.

51. Westermann, *Genesis 1–11*, 21–22; See also Anderson, *Creation to New Creation*, 2.

52. Levenson, "Genesis," 14.

rule over night and day and to mark the times for seasons and festivals. Heather McKay argues that New Moon festivals are referenced more frequently than any other in instructions regarding worship.[53] Therefore, New Moon is not an illegitimate pagan imposition but an integral part of the calendar of Jewish worship; not only the historical events of liberating salvation but also the cycles of creation serve to order, inspire and focus worship; at the heart of their life with God these people are not free to subject creation to their every whim but rather are themselves subject to creation and guided by its cycles. Also, human beings are not the only ones with some kind of commission to "rule" in creation, and this example shows that rule may be of a serving, helpful character.[54] It is through liturgical enactment and experience that worshippers learn to identify God, see the world in new ways, and inhabit an alternative world to that which may seem to be in hegemonous ascendancy.[55]

The Relationship between the Creation and the Sanctuary

Alert to the priestly structuring of the pentateuchal material, we note connections between the creation story in Genesis 1 and the establishment of the sanctuary as recorded in the Exodus narrative. In P material "there are more than 200 references to the tabernacle . . . while the tabernacle is mentioned only three times in E and never in J and D."[56] According to Lohfink, "building the sanctuary is paralleled with the divine building of the world, and the encounter with God in the sanctuary is paralleled with the divine rest on the seventh day."[57] Even the pattern of 6 days and 1 is repeated (Exod 24:16). The God who has formed these people is not one of many in constant conflict, as we have previously noted, nor one who is in unending struggle with the forces of chaos, but rather, one who has brought all things into being by a Word and by that same Word repeatedly declared them all to be good. Therefore the temple is not to be regarded as merely a local tribal shrine to one local god who has now been humiliated by another. Rather, the sanctuary is a model of the whole

---

53. McKay, *Sabbath and Synagogue*, 25–42.

54. Westermann, *Genesis*, 127.

55. On liturgy as a formative activity, see Neville and Westerhoff, *Learning through Liturgy*; and Smith, *Desiring the Kingdom*.

56. Miller and Huber, *The Bible: A History*, 34.

57. Lohfink, *Theology*, 131. See also, Westerman, *Genesis*, 170, who explores parallels in his notes on Gen 2:2a.

creation. In *The Eschatological Economy*, Douglas Knight in a section on "Creation and the Temple" notes,

> the temple is a complex sign system and working model of creation that relies on the logic of the microcosm. The temple represents the land and provides a matrix of analogies with which complex theological statements about God's relationship to his people and the world he gives them may be made . . . The building and maintenance of the temple form an analogy for and microcosm of the cultivation and rule of the world . . . the now ordered waters of chaos appear as the spring that waters the world . . . The Sabbath is here, and all things in the completed creation are very good.[58]

The Sabbath as the Integrating Element in the Creation Liturgy

The creation of human beings is not the end of P's creation account and neither is it the end and goal of the creation. Rather, the end and goal is the establishment of the Sabbath. We will find this constantly recognized in our ancient sources but completely ignored in White's critique. Bauckham speaks for many in the observation that the passage is not anthropocentric but theocentric, and the end of it all is the Sabbath.[59]

P is a tightly structured systematic narrative,[60] which moves seamlessly, almost hymnically, from the sixth day in Gen 1:31 to the seventh day at the beginning of chapter 2. It is on the seventh day, not the sixth, that we are told "God finished the work that he had done, and he rested on the seventh day from all the work that he had done" (Gen 2:2). Thus the finishing and the resting are an integral part of the whole creation account. Then follows a blessing of the seventh day (Gen 2:3), which reflects the blessings pronounced earlier upon the creatures of sea and air on the fifth day (Gen 1:22), and upon the humans, and all other land-dwelling creatures with them, on the sixth day (Gen 1:28). We noted earlier that many themes in Genesis 1 are virtually unmentioned in all the rest of the Old Testament.[61] Quite the opposite is true in regard to the Sabbath.

---

58. Knight, *Eschatological Economy*, 149–50.
59. Bauckham, "Modern Domination of Nature," 46.
60. Westermann, *Genesis*, 127.
61. Reference to man being made in God's image is found at Gen 9:6 in P's account of the flood and is thus considered the same age. The closest similarity otherwise is in Ps 8, which is regarded as being older.

Sabbath is a recurring theme in the Hebrew Scriptures, drawn out in many different directions. In our final chapter, as we explore Sabbath in the light of the ministry of Jesus we shall examine its themes in greater depth. Here it will suffice to note the following:

Sabbath as God's Covenantal Communion

God's Sabbath rest and the repose of humanity in God's presence and provision are so central that Moltmann writes,

> Sanctifying the Sabbath means being entirely free from the striving for happiness and from the will for performance and achievement. It means being wholly present in the presence of God. The Sabbath is sanctified through God alone—through grace alone—through trust alone. The peace of the Sabbath can be viewed as the Jewish "doctrine of justification."[62]

Such a vision identifies Sabbath as a sign of God's covenantal commitments including those with Noah, all his descendants and all creation; with Abraham; and with the whole community of Israel. "Sabbath . . . provides both a literary and theological *inclusio* that binds together the whole history with its system of covenants,"[63] leading to God's ultimate covenant and self-disclosure. By this covenantal connection Sabbath becomes a defining feature of Jewish identity.

Sabbath as Eschatological Sign

At the beginning of his section on "The Hospitality of the Estate," Douglas Knight suggests that "Israel's liturgical task is the labor of imagining, modeling, and preparing for the new creation, and so participating in its arrival."[64] Sabbath thus takes on an eschatological and messianic orientation. It is intimately linked with all the legislation regarding rest for the land, release from debts, and jubilee years. In its various forms it becomes the primary image of creation healed, of a world where justice is at home and where all things may rest in the presence of God.

---

62. Moltmann, *God in Creation*, 286.
63. Anderson, *Creation to New Creation*, 137.
64. Knight, *Eschatological Economy*, 96.

> The Sabbath... divides up human time. It brings interruption, interval and rhythm into human temporal experience. But of course all the other "festal" divisions of time do this too. What is special about the Sabbath commandment is, on the one hand, the *remembrance* of God's eternal Sabbath of creation, from which the command to sanctify the Sabbath springs; and on the other, the *promise* of the eternal Sabbath of the messianic era.[65]

Time may be linear but it is broken up by the rhythms of the recurring Sabbath. Time has a purpose and an ending, not inherent in some historical process but in the loving purpose of God, and this future is continually presented to us within time in the Sabbath. Thus Sabbath becomes one of the most prominent images in the eschatological visions of both the Hebrew Scriptures and the subsequent Christian ones.

Sabbath as Context for All of Life

The tendency to think of six days of creation (and work) with a seventh tacked on for rest means that "the meaning of life is identified with work and busy activity; and rest, the feast, and joy in existence are pushed away, relegated to insignificance because they are non-utilitarian."[66] In fact the Sabbath is an integral part of the account and of the action of God in the world, not disconnected from it. Thus the whole seven-day cycle becomes one integrated unit of time. "The days each have their goal in a particular day which is different from the rest—a day which is holy and apart. Days of work are not the only days which God has created. The time which God created is structured; days of work have their goal in a day of rest."[67]

The integration of days of work with days of rest also suggests that the nature of the work must conform to the nature of the day. The complaint of the prophet Amos was not that his people did not rest on the Sabbath, even if resentfully, but that the work they were eager to return to was the antithesis of all that the Sabbath was meant to mean (Amos 8:4-6). Other examples suggesting that Sabbath was understood to impact upon daily life we will explore further in our final chapter.

---

65. Moltmann, *God in Creation*, 286.
66. Moltmann, *God in Creation*, 277.
67. Westermann, *Genesis*, 171.

Creation, Sanctuary, and Sabbath—The Dwelling of Humans in the Image of God

Only in the context of all the foregoing does the biblical writer locate human beings. Rasmussen notes that "the modern capacity to image human beings apart from the rest of nature is largely lost to Jewish exegesis because Rabbinic Hebrew, like biblical Hebrew, has no word for nature as a realm separate from human being."[68] Westermann also observes that there is "no creedal distinction between humans and all other creatures,"[69] and Anderson, "what we distinguish as two realms constituted for Israel a single realm of Yahweh's sovereignty, as one can see from the Exodus story where both 'natural events' . . . and 'historical events' are regarded equally as signs of Yahweh's activity."[70] The identification of human beings with the rest of creation is clear in both creation stories. In Genesis 1 they are made on the same day as all the other animals. In Genesis 2, the man is formed by God from the dust of the earth and there is no reference to any *imago* by which he may be set apart from everything else. Furthermore, in the conclusion to the subsequent flood story, "animals too are *nepes hayya* and every *nephesh* has its direct connection to God and its own value which does not depend on human will or pleasure."[71] These considerations set the parameters within which we consider what it might mean to be made in the image of God.

Historically, accounts of the *imago* attempted to identify some quality or capacity inherent within human beings, with constantly conflicting accounts as to what it was.[72] But when attention is paid to context no such quality can be discovered. Rather we find a "functional" understanding, of which von Rad writes, "the text speaks less of its nature than of its purpose . . . man is placed upon earth in God's image as God's sovereign emblem. He is really only God's representative, someone to maintain and enforce God's claim to dominion over the earth."[73]

The Genesis material differs significantly from other ancient stories in that this "image bearing" does not belong to the king alone, but to the

---

68. Rasmussen, "Symbols to Live By," 175. See also Anderson, *Creation to New Creation*, 143.

69. Westermann, *Genesis*, 25.

70. Anderson, *Creation to New Creation*, 113–14.

71. Anderson, *Creation to New Creation*, 149.

72. Westermann, *Genesis*, 148–55.

73. von Rad, *Genesis*, 58.

whole human race; and it involves an honorable partnership rather than servility. At heart is the notion of being God's counterpart, "one whom God can address as 'You' and an 'I' who is responsible before God . . . To say that a human being has been created as being like God means that a person is capable of entering into a relationship with the creator."[74]

Also, in contrast to the situation in the Babylonian mythologies, "it is directed away from the life of the gods and the cult towards the life of this world."[75] This orientation to the fields does not conflict with Knight's account above concerning the temple, for the whole land is sanctuary, and all that happens there is (or is supposed to be), an expression of their life with God. "People are orientated to the fields and to the world which has been given to them. It is here that everything will take place concerning God's dealing with his people. One can understand then how this history leads ultimately to God becoming human."[76]

Moltmann observes, "God 'implants' his image and glory in his earthly creation, the human being, which means that he is himself drawn into the history of these creatures of his."[77]

These are counter-cultural and subversive elements by which Israel was able to cultivate faith in a different kind of God and nurture its identity with a different view of humanity, learning new things about the world even while enduring exile in a strange land.

Bearing This "Image" Involves a "Dominion" of Companionable Care

The "dominion" that arises from bearing this image in the world is not exploitative but preservative.[78] The words *radah* and *kabash* have however aroused considerable suspicion for allegedly domineering overtones, trampling grapes and even connoting rape. This was noted by von Rad.[79] But context is everything and Simkin represents many in observing that the words are "not necessarily violent . . . the human beings are not given

---

74. Westermann, *Genesis*, 151–52.
75. Westermann, *Genesis*, 159.
76. Westermann, *Genesis*, 67.
77. Moltmann, *God in Creation*, 217.
78. Westermann, *Genesis*, 159.
79. von Rad, *Genesis*, 58.

animals to eat and the animals are not afraid of them."[80] Nahum, a Jewish exegete, recognizes the royal power inherent in the dominion, but

> this power cannot include the license to exploit nature banefully . . . the sovereignty is not inherent but by grace alone, the context is the Israelite model of highly circumscribed and accountable kingship, a "very good" world of entirely harmonious and mutually beneficial relationships[81]

which he compares to the vision of the ideal kingdom envisaged in Isaiah 11:1-9. Moltmann too argues, "not all conceptions of humanity, nor all forms of rule, constitute legitimate dominion but only those that truly reflect the image of God."[82] Elsewhere he has already argued that this is a communal, relational existence rather than an individualistic one.[83] Numerous others also draw attention to the specific provision made by God for all creatures, to the blessing of their fecundity, and to the vegetarian restraints placed upon the human beings. There is no free right of disposition, and this sense of being under some kind of restraint will reappear in varying tones in the subsequent history of interpretation.

Lohfink develops a different line of thought with the argument that "the real root of 'radah' may be 'to lead about,'"[84] and thus rule is not trampling but guiding and leading, and therefore the shepherd appears throughout the Old Testament as the symbol of the ideal ruler. Elsewhere he notes that in Psalm 68:27 Benjamin exercises this leadership in the festal procession,[85] a usage that strengthens the case that this is liturgical material and the commission of the human beings is to accompany the rest of creation in some form of priestly, representative role. Miller and Huber observe that "in the P texts the priest is the ultimate authority; prophets play no part,"[86] which may imply, even if it is not explicitly asserted, that Adam's authority was understood as being priestly in nature. Ancient Jewish commentators certainly understood it as such: "The whole of creation was called into existence by God unto his glory, and

---

80. Simkins, *Creator and Creation*, 201.
81. Sarna, *Genesis*, 13.
82. Moltmann, *God in Creation*, 225.
83. Moltmann, *God in Creation*, 216-25.
84. Lohfink, *Great Themes*, 178.
85. Lohfink, *Theology*, 11.
86. Miller and Huber, *The Bible: A History*, 34.

each creature has its own hymn of praise wherewith to extol the creator."[87] Each day of creation was seen as a type of some part of the tabernacle culminating in the creation of man: "so will Israel set aside a man of the sons of Aaron as high priest for my service."[88]

Knight explores similar ideas with reference to Israel, suggesting that,

> Israel is the servant of its Lord inasmuch as it takes up its work as steward of the economy of God's creation . . . it is Israel's task to host the peoples of the world. It is for Israel to lead the gentiles. Israel must bring them into the house of its Lord. Israel must supply to them the being its Lord intends for them . . . Israel's host gives his people the means to play host and return hospitality. Lordship is not about the simple exercise of domination but about the exercise of bringing up people into the form of life enabled by that economy.[89]

He suggests that the world does not work without Israel's effort and explores an ecological complex of hospitable and interdependent relationships involving Israel, the land and the poor.

Bauckham, uncomfortable with the idea of human priesthood,[90] argues that God's rule is on behalf of all creatures, the dominion is set within the framework of God's creative intention so that human beings use it responsibly, and that the only human rule approved of in the Old Testament is the "king as brother."[91]

In recognition of the Babylonian provenance and themes encountered in the story, Anderson and Simkins both suggest that the dominion given to the divine representative has to do with the control of chaos. Whether this is by the application of technology or liturgy it is for the wellbeing of all the creatures.[92] "Humans are part of the creation and so must conform to the created order . . . dominion is the means by which they maintain this order."[93] This theme too is found in ancient Jewish interpretation: "If Israel accepts the Torah, creation will continue and

---

87. Ginzberg, *Legends of the Jews*, 44.
88. Ginzberg, *Legends of the Jews*, 51–52.
89. Knight, *Eschatological Economy*, 97–98.
90. Bauckham, "Modern Domination," 49.
91. Bauckham, "Modern Domination," 46.
92. Anderson, *Creation to New Creation*, 28.
93. Simkins, *Creator and Creation*, 205.

endure; otherwise I [God] shall turn everything back into chaos again."[94] Thus creation is kept in suspense until Israel's acceptance of the Torah at Sinai.

Bauckham also references Genesis 2:15, regarded in documentary theory as older J material, and notes that the instruction "to till and keep" may equally well be read as "serve and preserve."[95] Von Rad similarly argues, "that man was transferred to the garden to guard it indicates that he was called to a state of service and had to prove himself in a realm that was not his own possession."[96] This story contains the account of naming the animals, seen by White as yet another sign of establishing dominance.[97] A hermeneutic of suspicion may be content with that reading but the goal of the story is to make a statement about the nature of the relationship between men and women, specifically husbands and wives (Gen 2:23–24). The naming is the process by which the man pays attention to the nature of each animal and then decides whether it can be a suitable companion for him.[98] Indeed it could be argued that in being found unsuitable as intimate companions for the man the animals are in fact set free from a certain complex of obligations. Furthermore, Santmire references Isaiah 56:5 being an example of name-giving as recognition and establishment of a relationship.[99] Anderson notes that in the subsequent flood story the animals are once again brought to the man, in order that he may be the agent of their protection (Gen 7:9–16).[100]

Drawing all this together we quote Anderson again:

> In view of the overall pattern of the account it is apparent that the emphasis falls not so much on anthropology, that is, the supremacy of humanity, as on ecology, that is, the earthly habitation that human beings share with all other forms of "living beings."[101]
>
> There is no suggestion of competitive violence until after the flood (Gen 6–9), the picture is that of a paradisical peace in

---

94. Ginzberg, *Legends of the Jews*, 52.
95. Bauckham, "Modern Domination," 46.
96. von Rad, *Genesis*, 78.
97. White, "Historical Roots," 1205.
98. Westermann, *Genesis*, 87–88, 228.
99. Santmire, *Partnership*, 262.
100. Anderson, *Creation to New Creation*, 146.
101. Anderson, *Creation to New Creation*, 139.

which human beings and animals live together in a peaceable kingdom. Those who have supposed that the *imago Dei* entitles human beings to exploit and destroy the animals overlook the fact that the *dominium terrae* is a call to responsibility.[102]

Indeed, after an exhaustive survey and analysis of the literature, Westermann concludes, "Humanity is created as the counterpart of God; the intention is to make possible a happening between creator and creature. And this for P is directed toward the holy event in which history reaches its goal, as indicated in Genesis 2:1–3, that is the Sabbath."[103]

This capacity of human beings to participate in "a happening" with the creator is the essence of being made in the image of God. The essence of the attendant dominion is to bring the rest of creation also into that "happening." Creation does not exist solely for human purposes, and what dominion the humans do have is of a representative, caring and serving kind in order to foster participation in a relationship between creator and creation. How such a vision may be brought to fulfillment is a messianic calling, and in that light we now embark upon an historical review involving christological interpretation.

---

102. Anderson, *Creation to New Creation*, 144.
103. Westermann, *Genesis*, 158.

3

On Irenaeus of Lyons

IT IS IN THE writings of Irenaeus of Lyons that we find the first extensive engagement with the passages that are our concern. His significance for us lies in "his defence of the goodness of the material creation . . . without equal in the history of theology,"[1] his account of God's intimate engagement with creation whereby "both creation and redemption are mediated by the two hands of God,"[2] and his eschatology which imagines the whole creation directed towards its divine destiny.[3] Irenaeus's major work is *Against the Heresies* (*AH*).[4] The oldest known fragment, from Oxyrhynchus in Egypt, is dated before the end of the second century. It soon appears in Clement of Alexandria, Tertullian of Carthage, and Hippolytus of Rome. The whole survives in Latin from the third or early fourth century. Greek fragments appear in Eusebius and Epiphanius, and much later, in the ninth century, in Photius of Baghdad, and parts also in old Armenian.[5] Irenaeus's other major work, *The Demonstration of the Apostolic Preaching* (*DAP*), was known of but not known until the discovery of an Armenian version at Erevan in 1904.[6] That both works

---

1. Gunton, *Triune Creator*, 62.
2. Gunton, *Triune Creator*, 62.
3. Gunton, *Triune Creator*, 56

4. Irenaeus, *AH*. The text in this edition is presented in an extremely dense format. To facilitate access to quotations, I have opted to provide a book/chapter/section reference within the body of the tex (e.g., *AH*, 1.1.1).

5. Grant, *Irenaeus of Lyons*, 6; and Irenaeus, *DAP*, 4, for the reference to Photius.
6. Irenaeus, *DAP*, 4.

found such wide acceptance so quickly, both throughout and beyond the empire, undermines White's contention of a deep divide between Eastern and Western forms of Christian thought.[7] Rather, it exemplifies a remarkable Christian interconnectedness which Michael Thompson has called a "holy internet."[8]

Robert Grant summarizes the five books of *Against the Heresies* thus:

> The first concerns the Valentinian Gnostics and their eccentric predecessors . . . The second provides rational proofs that their doctrines are false . . . The third supplies proofs from the apostles, that is, the gospels taken as a whole. The fourth book emphasizes the sayings of Jesus, especially his mysterious parables, and shows the unity of the Old Testament and the Gospel, while the fifth, relying especially on other words of Jesus and the letters of Paul, culminates in Irenaeus' old-fashioned Asian picture of the future reign of God on earth.[9]

Although consisting of one corpus, it is clear that each book was written and delivered separately. Each begins with a summary of the previous ones and each "recapitulates" various of Irenaeus's key themes. Thus similar material is found in each of the different books.

Irenaeus was not of course attempting to address twenty-first-century environmental concerns, but he was addressing questions about the nature of God and of God's engagement with creation, and the place of humanity in this scheme of things. J. T. Nielsen summarizes the situation,

> The gnostic systems described by Irenaeus posit an unknown divine power that is transcendent and has nothing to do with this visible world. This unknown divine power that is at the beginning of everything, is spoken of in negations.
>
> The creation resulted from a mistake made by a potency which in some way or other (e.g. by emanation) had originated from the primordial deity. Through this primordial fault the Demiurge

---

7. White, "Historical Roots," 1206—at least throughout the patristic and early medieval periods. After the expansion of Islam and the "Great Schism" clear differences begin to appear but they are outside the time frame of White's allegations and of this study.

8. Thompson, "Holy Internet," 24–38.

9. Grant, *Irenaeus of Lyons*, 6. For a similar summary see Neilsen, *Adam and Christ*, 3–4.

> comes into being, who then brings the cosmos into existence. The cosmos and everything in it is regarded as evil.[10]

So Irenaeus claims of the heresies he is refuting,

> they deny that he [Christ] assumed anything material into his nature, since indeed matter is incapable of salvation (*AH*, 1.6.1) . . . They assert that the Maker of heaven and earth, the only God almighty, besides whom there is no God, was produced by means of a defect, which itself sprang from a defect, so that, according to them, He was the product of a third defect. (*AH*, 1.16.3)

He critiques Marcion for "setting aside the teaching in which the Lord is recorded as most clearly confessing that the Maker of this universe is His Father" (*AH*, 1.27.2), and arguing that "salvation is for souls only . . . the body, having been taken from the earth, is incapable of sharing in salvation" (*AH*, 1.27.3). Irenaeus counters such conceptions by developing his scriptural understanding of creation by the Word, and of Christ's recapitulation of Adam.

> The core of Irenaeus' argumentation is, that the Word was made flesh, and dwelt among us (cf. John 1:14). In none of the Gnostic systems was this taught (AH, 3.2.3). For Irenaeus the flesh taken on by the Word was the flesh of Adam (AH, 1.9.3). Thus for Irenaeus also Adam is *tupos* of Christ (cf. Rom 5:14).[11]

> The main concern of Irenaeus is the unity of the Creator God and the God and Father of Jesus Christ (cf. AH, 3:1–15), the unity of Jesus Christ himself (cf. AH, 3:16–25) and the unity between the Old Testament and New Testament (cf. AH, 4:9).[12]

All this has bearing on our discussion for it relates directly to questions about the value to be placed upon the material creation, whether the world was as thoroughly desacralized as White contends, and how free the humans were to do as they pleased with the earth in which they were placed?

I propose to explore firstly what Irenaeus says about the goodness of creation as background to how it should be valued, secondly, what he says about the nature of Adam's dominion and thirdly what he says about

---

10. Neilsen, *Adam and Christ*, 40.
11. Neilsen, *Adam and Christ*, 5–6.
12. Neilsen, *Adam and Christ*, 5–6.

other creatures or the earth itself, or what we might legitimately infer from what he says. Finally, we shall examine how all this is viewed in the light of Irenaeus's doctrine of Christ's recapitulation of Adam.

ON THE GOODNESS OF CREATION

Robert Grant argues that Irenaeus's method for handling his resources and his argument is found in the art of rhetoric.[13] Three terms which appear constantly throughout *Against the Heresies* are *hypothesis*, *oikonomia* (economy=ordering) and *anakephalaiosis* (recapitulation). An hypothesis is "the presentation (sometimes in a summary) of a plot or structure intended by an author."[14] Irenaeus's hypothesis is the same as that of the Scriptures: "It starts with belief in one God, maker of heaven and earth and everything in them."[15] Of course the gnostic heresies did not contest that affirmation at one level but they did deny that this creator god was himself/itself uncreated and was also the Father of Jesus Christ. So Irenaeus extends the argument,

> But we hold fast the rule of truth, [i.e. the hypothesis] that there is one almighty God who founded everything through his Word and arranged it and made everything out of the non-existent, as scripture says: "By the Word of the Lord the heavens were made firm and by the Spirit of his mouth all their power (Ps 32:2)," and further, "All things were made through him and without him nothing was made (John 1:3)." Nothing is excepted from this "all things."

> Through him the Father made everything . . . He did not make them through angels or powers separate from his will, for God has no need of anything at all; but by his Word and his Spirit he makes everything, disposes everything, governs everything, gives existence to everything. He made the world, for the world is part of "all things." He fashioned man. He is the God of Abraham, the God of Isaac, the God of Jacob. There is no other God above him, nor a beginning or a power or a pleroma. He is the Father of our Lord Jesus Christ, as we shall show. Holding fast to this rule, we can easily show that . . . they have deviated from the truth . . . (they) say there is one God, but they change him by

13. Grant, *Irenaeus of Lyons*, 46–51.
14. Grant, *Irenaeus of Lyons*, 47.
15. Grant, *Irenaeus of Lyons*, 49.

> their perverse doctrine, being as ungrateful to him who made them as the pagans are through idolatry. They despise the work fashioned by God, rejecting their own salvation. (*AH*, 1.22.1)

Key themes linking all creation with Christ, the Father, and the Spirit, and using Hebrew Scriptures to demonstrate truths about Christ are traversed in this one passage. Furthermore, to reject creation is both ingratitude and a rejection of salvation—and it is a bold claim to make for creation, that in some way it is necessary for salvation! If there should be any doubt he reiterates similar themes at the beginning of book 2:

> We must begin with the primary and most important point, with God the Demiurge who made heaven and earth and everything in them, whom these blasphemers call "fruit of deficiency," and we shall show that there is nothing either above him or beyond him, and that he freely made everything, not moved by another but on his own initiative, since he is the only God and the only Lord and the only Creator and the only Father, the only one who contains all and provides being to all. (*AH*, 2.1.1)

At its simplest, creation is good because it is the work of God by the Word and the Spirit, thus ensuring no gnostic separation may be drawn between Christ and creation. Christ is creation! The goodness of creation is inseparable from the goodness of God. So important is this connection that Irenaeus quotes a quite remarkable affirmation from Justin, *Against Marcion*,

> "I should not have believed the Lord himself had he proclaimed a God other than the Creator." But since from the one God, who made this world and formed us and contains and administers everything, the only Son came to us, recapitulating in himself what he had formed, my faith is firm in him and my love unshakeable toward the Father, since the Lord provides us with both faith and love. (*AH*, 4.6.2)

This partnership of the Word and the Spirit appears constantly throughout *Against the Heresies*, one example being,

> God needed none of these [i.e., angels, other gods, or distant powers] to make whatever He had foreordained to make, as if He did not have hands of His own. For always with him are his Word and Wisdom, the Son and the Spirit, through whom and in whom he made everything freely and independently, to whom he also speaks when he says, "Let us make man after

our image and likeness" (Gen 1:26), taking the substance of the creatures from himself as well as the pattern of the things he adorned. (*AH*, 4.20.1)

This intimate interplay with creation also appears as one of the foundations for *The Demonstration*,

> As God is verbal (logikos), therefore He made created things by the Word; and God is Spirit, so that He adorned all things by the Spirit ... Thus, since the Word "establishes," that is, works bodily and confers existence, while the Spirit arranges and forms the various "powers," so rightly is the Son called Word and the Spirit the Wisdom of God. Hence, His apostle Paul also well says, "One God, the Father, who is above all, and through all and in us all"—because "above all" is the Father, and "through all" is the Word—since through Him everything was made by the Father—while "in us all" is the Spirit, who cries "Abba, Father" and forms man into the likeness of God. (*DAP,* 5)

This is no Deistic conception of the relation between God and creation. Creation has not been ordered by the Word and then set adrift, independent of the sustaining power and presence of the Word and Spirit, but arbitrarily visited and interfered with occasionally. Both its substance and its pattern are from God himself. The Word and Spirit remain integral to the existence of creation, ordering, sustaining and adorning it yet in some sense hidden, in humility and service allowing creation its own freedom. Nor are these merely impersonal powers, for ultimately this creating Word and sustaining Spirit reveal through Christ that God is Father and awaken in us the faith and love that have the confidence to cry "Abba."

Although Irenaeus is frequently at pains to make the point that God does not need the creation he also appears to make one exception, and it is one that further strengthens the whole case that creation is intimately connected to God and with the economy of salvation, and is indeed necessary for the full revelation of God. In book 3 he writes, "Inasmuch as He had a prior existence as a saving being, it was necessary that what might be saved should also be called into existence, in order that the being who saves should not exist in vain" (*AH*, 3.22.3).

As we shall see below in greater detail, Irenaeus in book 5 develops a eucharistic theology of creation. We are nurtured by the Word and Spirit in the sacramental bread and wine because the Word and Spirit are already present and at work in all creation constantly nurturing us. "As a corollary to remaining open and responsive to the Creator, Irenaeus . . . repeatedly exhorts his readers to enjoy God's bounty and to use his gifts, the world which he has prepared for man's nourishment and growth, with thankfulness."[16]

The goodness of creation and its inseparability from the ultimate purposes of God is finally asserted in the doxological conclusion to *Against the Heresies*,

> The Word should descend to the creature, that is, to what had been molded, and it should be contained by Him; and on the other hand the creature should contain the Word, and ascend to Him, passing beyond the angels, and be made after the image and likeness of God. (*AH*, 5.36.3)

OF ADAM'S DOMINION

The Arts and Sciences

In specific terms frustratingly little is said about the dominion of Adam. Of human capacities generally one implied example is found in *AH*, 2.32.2. Here Irenaeus criticizes the negative gnostic assessment of creation for its neglect of the good arts and sciences—those things which are approved as good by all and which beautify or improve life. Rather than enlarging appreciation of life their experience is shrunken, but not their spiritual arrogance (*AH*, 2.32.2)! Furthermore, the pursuit of these good arts and sciences is provided with a theological undergirding, even perhaps a scientific theoretical base, when he writes,

> the Word of God . . . our Lord, who in the last times was made man . . . is inherent in the entire creation . . . who governs and arranges all things . . . communicating with invisible things after the manner of the intellect, and appointing a law observable to the outward senses, that all things should continue each in its own order. (*AH*, 5.18.3)

Because the Word is inherent in and governing creation, and has become human in Christ, there is a correspondence between human capacity and creation, and thus the exercise of intellectual and observational activity will enable the discernment of law and order in the creation. This will not

---

16. Behr, *Asceticism and Anthropology*, 120-21; see also 72-74.

however be any form of human observation or intellectual activity but only that which is shaped and informed by the Word as it is made known in the incarnation.

In a section on ethics in Irenaeus, Gustaf Wingren further observes, regarding *AH*, 4.24.1–5,

> Irenaeus holds that the "natural laws" are the heart of all morality and that the righteousness which receives expression in this law is primordial and was in existence before Moses . . . Christ has not only resuscitated the natural laws, which are grounded in Creation, He has also extended and enlarged them.[17]

Given what is being discerned by those who observe attentively, and reflect intellectually upon what is observed, we may legitimately infer that "natural laws" of ethical behavior, grounded in creation, may now be seen to extend to embrace ethical behavior towards creation. The Word, inherent in creation and incarnate in Christ, leads us into the field of environmental ethics.

The Number of Human Beings

During a discussion about the nature of the soul Irenaeus addresses an issue relevant to contemporary concerns about human population numbers. He suggests that God intends a limit to the growth of human numbers and on the completion of this number procreation should cease and the harmony formed by the Father be preserved (*AH*, 2.33.5).[18] Is this time arbitrarily imposed by God or is there, presented to us, the possibility that human numbers should be limited as part of our mature exercise of dominion? Given all that Irenaeus believes about the Word present in all creation, it is likely that such a time is not arbitrarily imposed but is to be discerned by us as we observe all those factors that hasten the breakdown of balance and harmony. In *AH*, 3.22.4 he has already suggested that procreation itself should only occur where there is a suitable degree of maturity.[19] Would such a limit upon numbers also require the abandonment of sexual relations between men and women? The passage itself hints at this possibility but Behr argues that Irenaeus

---

17. Wingren, *Man and the Incarnation*, 177.
18. Behr, *Asceticism and Anthropology*, 113.
19. Behr, *Asceticism and Anthropology*, 112.

never restricts human sexuality to the function of procreation. Procreation shall cease once the fore-ordained number has been reached; human existence as male and female will not cease, for it is the condition and framework, as created by God, for the man's never-ending maturation and growth towards God.[20]

According to *AH*, 3.23.5 Adam and Eve engage in a self-imposed sexual continence, which far from being what God required, was another sign of their making a law for themselves. This self-imposed discipline was found to be fretful, impeding their growth toward God who in his mercy released them from it.[21]

This complex of issues around the theological possibility and demographic pressure for a limit to numbers opens new fields of discussion regarding Christian asceticism. We may need to limit our numbers and our resource consumption but we need also to live in dependence, thankfulness, and in love. It is clear that for Irenaeus a positive evaluation of the flesh is vital for a proper understanding of human being, and with this, a sense of the vital connection between being in the flesh and participation in the material creation. This connection, the problems and possibilities associated with attempts at celibacy, and the possibilities for growth found in the companionship of marriage all suggest the need to seek new forms of ascesis. The traditional formulation, "poverty, chastity, and obedience," might well be reconfigured as "simplicity, faithfulness, and community." We shall address this further in a later chapter.

As Representing God

A more comprehensive statement about the nature of dominion comes late in *Against the Heresies*, and then only as an aside, when Irenaeus writes of the devil acting "out of envy for man who had the glory of a king's representative" (*AH*, 5.24.4). This representational understanding is significant as it is in keeping with the overwhelming weight of contemporary critical study and it stands somewhat in contrast with those ideas about image and dominion that have seen it in terms of some innate human capacity such as reason or creativity.

---

20. Behr, *Asceticism and Anthropology*, 113, see further 209–11; also Wingren, *Man and Incarnation*, 179.

21. Behr, *Asceticism and Anthropology*, 119.

Nevertheless, Irenaeus has been criticized for elsewhere suggesting that the image of God is located in human reason—"man, being endowed with reason, and in this respect like God" (*AH*, 4.4.3), and Brunner has blamed his distinction, in *AH*, 5.16.2—between the image which was retained in the fall and the likeness which was lost, as having led to a millennium and a half of theological confusion![22] Behr suggests that it is Clement rather than Irenaeus for whom the intellect is in the image of God and the source of free will.[23] He argues, from *AH*, 4.6.6, 5.6.1, and 5.16.2 and also *DAP*, 32, that what "Adam lost in the apostasy was the strength of the breath of life . . . and his "natural and childlike mind" . . . seeing God through the creation, recognizing the fact that he is created and therefore dependent upon his creator, an attitude of thankfulness and obedience."[24]

All this then is relational, rather than to do with some inherent capacity. At its heart is the loss of willingness to live in humility and dependence. The overwhelming weight of contemporary biblical studies would suggest that no distinction at all should be drawn between "image" and "likeness." We are simply encountering another example of the ubiquitous Hebrew device of parallelism.

Human Freedom

It seems vital for Irenaeus that this representational glory is characterized by freedom. He writes that "without freedom there is neither goodness nor understanding nor pleasure nor responsibility in doing good" (*AH*, 4:37:2). He goes on to celebrate "the independent will of man, and . . . the counsel which God conveys to him . . . without, however, in any way coercing us" (*AH*, 4:37:3). In other passages he writes of God as "also our counselor, giving advice; not compelling as God, even though He is Mighty God" (*DAP*, 55), or of God,

> The Word, very man, redeeming from the apostasy His own property, not by violent means . . . but by means of persuasion,

---

22. Brunner, *Man in Revolt*, 503-6.
23. Behr, *Asceticism and Anthropology*, 212.
24. Behr, *Asceticism and Anthropology*, 115. See also, Wingren, *Man and Incarnation*, 21, and 157-8, which is roundly critical of those who have focused on this separation in Irenaeus—"*similitudo* is quite typically used as being synonymous with *imago* and *similitude*."

> as becomes a God of counsel, who does not use violent means to obtain what he desires; so that neither should justice be infringed upon, nor the ancient handiwork of God go to destruction. (*AH*, 5:1:1)

Since Irenaeus is at some pains to argue that God is neither violent nor coercive, we may conclude that as God's representative the human beings are expected not to be either.

The importance of freedom appears also in *The Apostolic Preaching*, where Adam is described as "free and self-controlled, being made by God for this end, that he might rule all things that were upon the earth. And this great created world, prepared by God before the formation of man, was given to man as his place, containing all things within itself" (*DAP*, 11).

The nature of this "rule" is nowhere detailed but towards the end, as he looks towards the age to come, he hints at what will be involved and might have been earlier had Adam not fallen into sin: "creation, being restored to its primeval condition, should without restraint be under the dominion of the righteous . . . which is deliverance from bondage into the glorious liberty" (*AH*, 5:32:1). Irenaeus is drawing here on Romans 8, in which the whole creation groans in bondage as it awaits the freedom of the glory of the children of God. In this vision the dominion of the righteous will not hold creation in any kind of bondage but will involve deliverance for all. This is not dominion as conceived of by White, where "nature has no reason for existence save to serve man,"[25] nor as it may have appeared at some periods in history. For Irenaeus, however, true dominion is exercised not by claiming rights of free use but rather by seeking to ensure freedom for the subjects, while being inspired by them to grow towards God in dependence, thankfulness and love.

Relationships of Peaceful Existence

The visionary future is alluded to in both books. In *The Demonstration* he writes of "the elders,"[26] who, in reference to Isaiah 11, envisage a time when formerly fierce animals will be at peace with each other. At present, however, he sees the passage as figurative of human beings, who having

---

25. White, "Historical Roots," 1207.

26. Irenaeus, *DAP*, 113, note 164, refers to Papias—whom Irenaeus specifically names, and also Eusebius and Justin.

once been enemies and "most vicious, to the point of passing no work of ungodliness, [have] learned of Christ and believing in Him, been changed.... This has already happened" (*DAP*, 61), and is thus a sign of the fullness to come. Similarly, in *Against the Heresies* he anticipates a future where there will be peace between people and all kinds of animals, "but some other occasion, and not the present, is to be sought for showing that the lion will feed on straw" (*AH*, 5:33.3–4).

Further, although he had written of "this great created world . . . given to man, as his place" (*DAP*, 11), need anything of domination be read into this? Does it not rather serve as a reminder that *this world of created materiality* is where we human beings belong and it is in *this place* that God will have dealings with us? Given the task Irenaeus is about: affirming both the goodness of creation and the engagement of God with us in it, this sense of place is significant—and could be for contemporary purposes too. Much current scholarship views the Genesis 1 creation story as affirming, against the chaos and rootlessness of the exile, a vision and hope of a place in which to take root, belong and find identity. This, rather than uncontrolled world domination, is what is envisaged by Gen 1:28.[27] We shall consider further the significance of "place" in our reflections on the incarnation.

Freedom for Growth

Whatever the nature of human freedom or dominion it would seem that initially not much could have been done with it, for a source of intrigue over the centuries is the suggestion that Adam and Eve were first formed as children (*AH*, 3:22:4). They were to grow from infancy, not being overwhelmed by glory, but only gradually becoming able to receive the things of God (*AH*, 4:38:1), and furthermore, "the sentient faculties of the soul were still feeble and undisciplined" (*AH*, 4:38:2). Throughout *AH*, 4.38 and again in *AH*, 5.28.4, this process of growth into the image and likeness of God is presented as something ongoing through the whole history of the creation. Thus, through the whole history of the economy we are learning how to be human and how to exercise our human commission. In *The Demonstration* also, we find the image of the child formed to grow into maturity, with the observation that "the man was a young child, not

---

27. Brueggemann, *Land*, 135–37. See also Schottroff, "The Creation Narrative," 24–38.

yet having perfect deliberation, and because of this he was easily deceived by the seducer" (*DAP*, 12).

Here we should distinguish between ideas about the goodness of creation and its perfection, and especially the alleged perfection of Adam. For Irenaeus, creation is good because it has both its origin and its destiny in God. But the humans are to grow into the love of God, and that openness to growth necessarily leaves open the possibility of misdirection. That openness alone is the nature of any alleged "imperfection" in creation. "This is what makes the fall, however unsurprising, such a devastating affair. In the fall man is 'turned backwards.' He does not grow up in the love of God as he is intended to. The course of his time, his so-called progress, is set in the wrong direction."[28]

> Redemption or salvation is that divine action which returns the creation to its proper direction, its orientation to its eschatological destiny, which is to be perfected in due course of time by God's enabling it to be that which it was created to be. By virtue of their trinitarian mediation, both creation and its restoration in redemption are acts of the one God in and towards the whole created order. In turn that means that Irenaeus must not be thought to operate with a naively linear conception of time.[29]

Growth in Christ is Not Progress to Power

Such growth does not involve extending domination over anything but does involve growth in love and thankfulness. And thus we have grounds for a critical examination of all modernist notions of progress. Progress for Irenaeus is assessed eschatologically—what is its direction and end? Is it toward and into Christ or away? Given Irenaeus's understanding of the relation between the Word in creation and the Word in Christ, growth in communion with Christ will also involve growth in communion with creation—not separation that was the gnostic goal, nor mastery.

But for modernity the question of ends and goals is excluded for nature is believed to have none. Progress is devoid of moral or personal content and has become simply the power to make changes in the material world. Indeed, as we shall see, it is often conceived in terms of breaking free from the constraints imposed by nature or religion. Lohfink observes

---

28. Farrow, "St. Irenaeus of Lyons," 348, cited in Gunton, *Triune Creator*, 56.
29. Gunton, *Triune Creator*, 56.

"growth" has become a mindset, a myth, so deeply embedded as to make life unimaginable or terrifying were it to be called in question or to fail.[30] Indeed he regards the P creation story as part of a manifesto for stability in life with God, not for dynamic change. Clive Ponting, writing from a perspective much less sympathetic to the biblical narrative than Lohfink, suggests that the idea of progress developed in the eighteenth century as a counter to widespread older mythologies that viewed human history as a story of decay. "By the late 19th century the idea of progress had become . . . so ingrained in the unspoken assumptions of nearly all European thought that almost any change could be automatically equated with progress."[31]

Ultimately, to counter any suggestion that Irenaeus's vision of human growth and progress could be equated with modernist notions of progress, we observe that for him the surest sign of growth into the likeness of Christ is the willingness to experience martyrdom!

> Irenaeus would have us keep our attention fixed on the two quite definite points of Christ's *death* and His *Resurrection*, the two points that have shattered the modern immanent and romantic idea of Jesus, and which transfer man's goal from the development of his personality to the resurrection of the dead. For this reason therefore growth takes place at the time of martyrdom . . . at the point of martyrdom man is formed in the *imago* and *similitudo* of God.[32]

Freedom and Growth in the Presence of Restraints

Also intriguing is the suggestion that, while the humans had been placed as lords there were also "in this domain, in their tasks, servants of that God who fashioned everything, and the steward, who was placed over his fellow servants, kept this domain: the servants were the angels, and the steward was an archangel" (*DAP*, 11).

Unlike the human children, these servants "were in their full development" (*DAP*, 12). Angels and archangels may be fantastical for modern people but they were an integral part of the pre-modern worldview. Their presence in Irenaeus's cosmology strengthens an argument that although the creation was de-divinized it had not at all been depopulated

---

30. Lohfink, *Great Themes*, 167–68, 196–98.

31. Ponting, *A Green History*, 151.

32. Wingren, *Man and Incarnation*, 34–35. See also Behr, *Asceticism and Anthropology*, 76–79.

of spiritual beings who had some kind of responsibility, both to "keep" the domain and to oversee us during our growth to maturity.

Finally, again in contrast to assertions that man was free to do as he pleased, "in order that man should not entertain thoughts of grandeur nor be exalted, as if he had no Lord . . . a law was given to him from God, that he might know that he had as lord the Lord of all" (*DAP*, 15). Humans are to live here as those who are both dependent and obedient.

OF OTHER CREATURES AND THE EARTH

In book 5 we find reflection on creation, which is here given a eucharistic cast.

> We are nourished by the creation . . . sun . . . rain . . . the cup—which is part of the creation, as His own blood from which He bedews our blood; and the bread—also part of creation—He has established as His own body, from which He gives increase to our bodies. (*AH*, 5.2.2)

> Vines or corn increase, by the Spirit of God, who contains all things, and then, through the wisdom of God, serves for the use of men, and having received the Word of God, becomes the Eucharist. (*AH*, 5.2.3)

In these passages although the creation serves humankind in the provision of food, this is not in response to any domineering human action but rather by the work of the Word and the Spirit. Further, this food becomes eucharistic for us not by being set apart from creation but because it is part of a creation where Word and Spirit are already present and active. In such a view Christ is present to us in all creation, and the eucharistic meal of the gathered faithful is itself a type of that presence in creation. Every meal may be holy and function for our increase. In a similar vein he suggests that the garden of paradise is a type of the church, in which we are placed again for our pleasure and growth, and in which we are to live in humility and harmony (*AH*, 5.20.2). One cannot hold such a eucharistic view and also hold that creation is simply raw material available for human beings to do with whatever they like.

Of animals Irenaeus says almost nothing and some may read this as a sign of indifference. But he does speak of our "animal bodies, which shall by the Spirit's instrumentality rise to eternal life" (*AH*, 5.5.7). While not speaking of animals as such, does the choice of this term allow that this restoration may involve the rest of creation also, since this sentience is something that we share with other animals, and we cannot be what we are apart from our connections with the rest of the natural order? Animals are specifically mentioned at *AH*, 5.8.4, where the figurative meanings of various kinds are suggested. This figurative understanding of animals was touched on by White,[33] and explored by Harrison at depth as evidence that before the modern period the interest in animals was to learn moral lessons from them but in no other way to take control of them.[34]

A partnership with the Earth itself is described in speaking of

> Adam working the substance from which he was taken (Gen 3:19) . . . and the Lord using this substance for His purposes from the beginning even to the end, forms us and prepares us for life, and is present with His handiwork, and perfects it after the image and likeness of God. (*AH*, 5.16.1)

The substance that Adam worked with is the same as that which the Lord continues to work with. That the substance of the earth is taken by the Lord, formed and ultimately perfected, invites the suggestion that we do not exist as humans apart from our "earthiness," and that the Earth itself will be included in the blessing God is working towards.

Certainly this partnership is of such mutuality that Irenaeus writes of creation sustaining the Word and thereby showing itself to be God's own and not the result of some ignorance or defect (*AH*, 5.18.1). That creation sustains the Word, alongside the much more common confession that the Word sustains creation, is an idea sufficiently unusual and of sufficient significance that it bears further reflection. For the Word to be sustained by creation implies that the Word needs creation! This runs counter to all that Irenaeus wants to say about the freedom of God. But it does suggest that there is an intimacy of partnership—that the purposes of the Word cannot be pursued without creation.

The section begins with a reflection on the cross and continues to one on the whole life of the incarnate Word in the world. Creation recognizes even the cross as part of the purpose of the Word and supports the Word in that work. Further, the Word is sustained in the sense of being supported or shown for what it is by creation, and thus without

---

33. White, "Historical Roots," 1206.
34. Harrison, "Having Dominion," 19–20.

creation we would not come to know these things about the Word. It is certainly true that in the incarnation of the Word in Jesus Christ creation did sustain the Word, and without creation the Word could not have been made known.

All of which further undermines the suggestion that the Christian vision was of a universe not only de-divinized but also thoroughly de-sacralized. Rather, John Zizioulas suggests that by these connections it is possible to respect the sacrality of nature while not reverting to paganism.[35]

ON CHRIST AND RECAPITULATION

All the foregoing might stand as disconnected fragments, even misconstrued, apart from Irenaeus's integrating conception of "recapitulation." Stated most simply, this is that Christ has recreated the human race by becoming Adam again and living well in every part the life that Adam spoiled. We quote him at length:

> The Lord took dust from the earth and formed man; so did He who is the Word, recapitulating Adam in Himself, rightly receive a birth, enabling Him to gather up Adam into Himself, from Mary, who was yet a virgin . . . since the first Adam was taken from the dust, and God was his maker, it was incumbent that the latter also, making a recapitulation in Himself, should be formed as man by God, to have an analogy with the former as respects His origin . . . (it is of Mary not the dust) so that there not be another being which should require to be saved, but that the very same formation should be summed up in Christ as had existed in Adam, the analogy having been preserved. (*AH*, 3.21.10)

> We are a body taken from the earth, and a soul receiving spirit from God. This, therefore the Word of God was made, recapitulating in Himself His own handiwork; and on this account does confess Himself the Son of man, and blesses "the meek, because they shall inherit the earth (Matt 5:5)." (*AH*, 3.22.1)

The bodily needs also are signs of a life derived from Mary and "these are all tokens of the flesh which had been derived from the earth, which He

---

35. Zizioulas, "Priest of Creation," 289.

had recapitulated in Himself, bearing salvation to His own handiwork" (*AH*, 3.22.2).

By this process of recapitulation the very dust of the earth is taken up into the salvation of God. So Irenaeus could write, "the final result of the work of the Spirit is the salvation of the flesh" (*AH*, 5.12.3). Works of healing also stand for Irenaeus as a promise of the resurrection (*AH*, 5.12.6). The remainder of book 5—chapters 12 and 13, is an extensive reflection on 1 Corinthians 15, Colossians 1 and other passages expounding the possibility of the salvation of the flesh on the basis of both the incarnation and the resurrection. Nielsen suggests that at this point Irenaeus lacks the Pauline sense of a deep tension running through creation as the result of human sin, and finds a conflict between Irenaeus and Paul over whether or not flesh and blood can inherit the kingdom of God (1 Cor 15:50). Irenaeus argues that flesh and blood do inherit the kingdom of God, not by virtue of their own will or power but by being made new in Christ by the Holy Spirit. He makes his case by reference to Paul's own image of the olive branch in Romans 11:17 (*AH*, 5.10.1–2), and by an extended reflection on the incarnation which he explicitly relates to the Corinthian passage about flesh and blood (*AH*, 5.14.1). Nielsen claims that Irenaeus has "let go Paul in order to maintain the Adam-Christ typology . . . (AH, 5.14.2), in face of gnostic rejection of 'flesh and blood.'"[36] But we might ask whether Nielsen has overspiritualized Paul's conception of resurrection and, if not making himself something of a Docetist, is certainly disparaging the flesh in the economy of God![37]

I have explored this issue at some length because it is in the Corinthian passage (1 Cor 15:24–28) that Paul writes of Christ "gathering up all things," and he envisages not only human beings. Irenaeus appears to recognize this in writing,

> the Creator of the world is truly the Word of God: and this is our Lord, who in the last times was made man, existing in this world, and who in an invisible manner contains all things created, and is inherent in the entire creation, since the Word of God governs and arranges all things; and therefore He came to His

---

36. Neilsen, *Adam and Christ*, 82—but in a footnote he does reference Joppich, "who deems the divergence between Paul and Irenaeus a mere matter of terminology." Grant, *Irenaeus of Lyons*, 195, note 25 suggests that Neilsen is alone in this criticism of Irenaeus.

37. Behr, *Asceticism and Anthropology*, 80, and note 144, outlines the company—both ancient and modern, in which Neilsen finds himself on this issue.

own in a visible manner, and was made flesh, and hung upon the tree, that He might sum up all things in Himself . . . He has the power from the Father over all things, since He is the Word of God, and very man, communicating with invisible things after the manner of the intellect, and appointing a law observable to the outward senses, that all things should continue each in its own order. (*AH*, 5:18:3)

What is present but invisible in all creation becomes visible through the incarnation; "The Word which dwelt in man was made Son of man" (*AH*, 3.20.2). Similarly in the *Demonstration*, Irenaeus shows the Lord "appearing to the world as man, the Word of God gathering up into Himself all things that are in heaven and that are on earth" (*DAP*, 30), and shortly afterward arguing that if he was not incarnate in the flesh then his death is of no significance and neither could there be any resurrection (*DAP*, 38–39; see also *AH*, 3.22.1).

For Irenaeus the incarnation is not a divine visitation to alien territory, as by a space invader or a deep-sea diver, but rather the Word which is already inherent in the entire creation comes to his own in a visible manner to recapitulate in Christ the life of Adam—that part of the creation which had fallen from its divinely intended purpose (*AH*, 5.16.2). Thus it may be that the reason for the relative paucity of detail about Adam's exercise of his dominion is firstly because Adam failed to maintain that place, and secondly because Adam was himself an image, "created in His [i.e., the Son's] own image and likeness" (*AH*, 3.23.1): "The Word (is that) after whose likeness man was created" (*AH*, 5.16.2). Or in the *Demonstration*, "the image of God is the Son, according to whose image was man made; and for this reason, He appeared at the last times, to render the image like himself" (*DAP*, 22).

Irenaeus's primary interest is in exploring the nature of Christ's dominion, for it is only in and through Christ that we learn what it means to be human and what human dominion means. Every example above of aspects of human dominion is linked by Irenaeus to a statement about Christ. These are not in the first instance universal human capacities but powers belonging to Christ. To exercise them properly requires being in Christ and discerning the nature of Christ's exercise of power and Christ's connectedness to creation. The first task is always a theological one. Thus Behr sums up Irenaeus's case, "Jesus Christ, not Adam, is the first manifestation in history of the true, fully human being."[38] It is by meekness

---

38. Behr, *Asceticism and Anthropology*, 61.

that he inherits the earth (*AH*, 3.22.1). In the *Demonstration*, writing of Isaiah 9:6, "the government upon his shoulder, refers, allegorically, to the cross, upon which His shoulders were nailed: for that which was and is a reproach for Him, and through Him for us, the cross, that, he says, is His government, which is a sign of His reign" (*DAP*, 56).

We have already seen that this dominion is exercised in patience, by reason, and not by violence or coercion. If so for Christ, so too for those made in his image. Thus, Behr concludes, "for Irenaeus, both protology and eschatology are Christocentric: man, from his initial formation and throughout the pedagogy of the economy, can be understood only in the light of Christ."[39]

CONCLUSIONS

Although "de-divinized" the creation remains for Irenaeus a place of God's presence and action—not occasionally but constantly. It is never outside of the Father's two hands—the Son and the Spirit. It does not exist for human beings to use as they please but in order to reveal something of the nature and purpose of God. Thus creation provides us with a means of encounter and communion with God. To abuse or disparage creation is to abuse God since God is always present in all things and it is by means of creation that God has drawn near and been made known to us.

Humanity for Irenaeus is not in any way separable from the rest of creation—neither now nor in the salvation to come. It is true that we are not fully human apart from our participation in the life of the Spirit, but it is equally true and necessary that we are not fully human if we repudiate the flesh. This flesh is from the dust and we share it with the animals, and this is what the Lord has taken upon himself. By both the incarnation in the body and the resurrection of the body we have the clearest demonstration that materiality is vital to God's purpose, and in Christ has—in a way beyond our understanding—been taken up into the life of God.

Humanity has no independent right of dominion but is entirely dependent upon Christ. That it is Christ, who in his humanity gathers up all things, suggests a place of primacy for humanity, but it is only Christ's humanity. One cannot avoid some sense of human primacy in Irenaeus. Writing of *AH*, 4.14.1 Behr states, "Irenaeus concludes this section . . . by emphasizing man's participation in the glory of God as the inspiration

---

39. Behr, *Asceticism and Anthropology*, 85.

for creation,"[40] or, of *AH*, 5.29.1, "Man belongs to the world of changeable things, yet differs from the rest of the world, in that the world was created to enable the growth of man into the immortality of God."[41]

This is not a primacy that replaces or supplants the rest of creation but rather one that is integral to its well-being. Such a conception may be rejected as speciesism—privileging human beings above all others, but it is better understood as recognizing that humanity in Christ has a responsibility for the well being of creation. It is the ministry of Christ to gather up all things to God. Humanity in Christ shares in that priestly service and if neglectful of that service neglects its essential identity. It is difficult to see how an argument can be made for the exercise of human responsibility towards the rest of creation unless there is recognition of some kind of human primacy. If humanity is to be regarded as no more than one evolved creature alongside all others, it is not at all clear, from nature alone, that we carry any more ethical responsibilities than any other creature. But we exercise powers and consciousness that are not exercised by others, we have an overwhelming capacity to make impacts for blessing or destruction, and, for Irenaeus, all this humanity must be incorporated into Christ. Otherwise, there is nothing in Irenaeus of humans extending any kind of power over creation. Creation exists to serve the glory of God. It supports human life and there is not one voice of warning in the whole environmental debate that is saying otherwise!

Thus we see that during the formative period ideas about human dominion were overwhelmingly focused on Christ as the one with dominion, and furthermore that the Earth remains a focus of God's loving presence and action and is not humanity's to do with as we please.

---

40. Behr, *Asceticism and Anthropology*, 37.
41. Behr, *Asceticism and Anthropology*, 42.

4

On Athanasius

ATHANASIUS OF ALEXANDRIA (C.295–373) came to prominence about a hundred and twenty-five years after Irenaeus. His importance for us lies in his theological contribution to critical debates concerning Christ, which produced affirmations about the relationship between God and creation that remain central to the whole church's confessional identity. He also critiques conceptions of a divinized world in which gods or spirits are present within places or processes, and demonstrates that such conceptions encourage conflict and acquisitiveness, to the abuse rather than the well-being of creation. Like Irenaeus, Athanasius also exerted profound influence across the whole church. Two of his five exiles were spent in Western regions (Treves and Rome). Johannes Quasten observes, "The Greek Church called him later 'the Father of Orthodoxy,' whereas the Roman Church counts him among the four great Fathers of the East . . . His contact with the West was to exercise vast and lasting influence."[1] Thus again, White's contention of a deep divide between East and West must at least be modified or located at a much later period.

Quasten reviews an extensive literary output covering a period of about fifty years. Our main sources will be the two major works, from early in Athanasius's career, *Against the Pagans* (henceforward *AP*), and *On the Incarnation of the Word* (*De Incarnatione*—henceforward *DI*). In addition we use the *Orations against the Arians* (*AA*), the *Life of Saint Anthony* (*LA*), the *Select Works and Letters* (*SWL*), the *Letters Concerning*

---

1. Quasten, *Patrology*, 20–21.

the Holy Spirit (*LHS*), and various other letters. His career is associated with his theological opposition to Arianism and his exposition of the doctrine of the incarnation. Not only his major treatises but also the more pastorally orientated "Festal Letters" and *Life of Saint Anthony*, are shot through with the issues of this controversy, although Quasten dates *Against the Pagans* and *The Incarnation* from "about 318 before Arius' doctrine became widely known."[2]

At the heart of the controversy was the question concerning Christ. Arius rejected trinitarian accounts of the being of God, believing that Christ was not divine but the first of God's creations, and therefore "there was a time when he was not." Athanasius's Orthodox counter-argument was that if Christ is created then he is not God come among us, and if God has not come to us we remain unreconciled. Furthermore, neither is creation obviously engaged by God and therefore its goodness is also called into question. Arius's position is summarized in his own letter to Eusebius of Nicomedia.

> We say that the Son had a beginning, but that God was without beginning. This is really the cause of our persecution; and likewise, because we say that He is from nothing. And we say this because He is neither part of God, nor of any subjacent matter.[3]

Athanasius himself, admittedly not a sympathizer like Eusebius, quotes at length from Arius's *Thalia*, part of which reads,

> The Unbegun made the Son a beginning of all things originated; and advanced Him as Son to Himself by adoption. He has nothing proper to God in proper subsistence. For He is not equal, nor one in essence with Him . . . Not intermingling with each other are their subsistencies. Foreign from the Son in essence is the Father, for He is without beginning.[4]

Athanasius, however, was committed to asserting, on the one hand, Christ's essential oneness with the Father and, on the other, his essential humanity in the incarnation. His case is well expressed in the famous aphorism, "He became man that we might become divine; and he revealed himself through a body that we might receive an idea of the

---

2. Quasten, *Patrology*, 25.
3. Arius, "Letter to Eusebius," in Quasten, *Patrology*, 10.
4. Quasten, *Patrology*, 12.

invisible Father; and he endured insults from men that we might inherit incorruption" (*DI*, 54).

Similarly, in the *Life of Anthony*, he has Anthony teaching,

> the Son of God is not a creature nor has He come into being "from non-existence" but He is the eternal Word and Wisdom of the substance of the Father. Hence too it is impious to say, "there was a time when He was not," for the Word was always coexistent with the Father . . . they, by saying that the Son and Word of God the Father is a creature, are in no respect different from the pagans, who worship the created in place of God the Creator. And you may be sure that all creation is incensed against them because they count among created things the Creator and Lord of all, to whom all things owe their existence. (*LA*, 58)

Furthermore, in maintaining that "'once the Son was not,' they rob God of his Word . . . make the fountain of life dry . . . imputing to God an absence of reason" (*AA*, 5.14). C. R. Shapland observes, "by denying the eternity of the Word it imputes to God *alogia*, and thus makes Him less than personal."[5]

The debate about Christ, although at first glance unrelated to this study, is of critical significance because ultimately it is about the nature of the incarnation and whether God was truly engaged with the world or keeping at an untouched distance. If God is indeed keeping distant from material creation then, of course, serious doubt arises as to the value to be placed upon creation, its place (if any) in the purposes of God, whether there may be any knowledge of, or encounter with, God through creation, and whether human responsibility extends to creation. It is not only the nature and honor of God at stake. The extract quoted above (*LA*, 58), shows that creation itself recognizes an interest in the issue—its own value and sustainability are at stake.

Two central concerns are interwoven throughout *Against the Pagans*, and their resolution is unfolded in the subsequent related volume, *The Incarnation*. We identify the dynamic of idolatry and the meaning of being human. *Against the Pagans* begins within an uncompromising statement that the most important knowledge we may have of God is that which is given us through the cross of Christ. It is precisely this, however, that is the butt of pagan mockery and opposition (*AP*, 1). Thus,

---

5. Shapland, "Introduction," in Athanasius, *LHS*, 60, note 9, also 152, letter 2/3.2 and note 2.

Athanasius proceeds to explore how it is that we have degenerated to such ignorance of God and corruption of our own humanity.

ON WORSHIPPING THE CREATURES OR THE CREATOR

The significance of this theme lies in Athanasius's demonstration that the divinization of the universe is in fact a process of projecting onto the world our own human desires and drives, and that this does not issue in greater respect for or tenderness towards the non-human order but rather the opposite, as all things become the objects of our lusts and manipulations. If the earth is to be properly respected, its status as creation sustained by the divine Word must be rediscovered. Thus, closely allied to his exploration of idolatry is an associated argument concerning the essential goodness of creation as the work of God. A central element in the *Orations against the Arians* (*AA*) is that creation is good and valued by God and thus it is neither impossible nor inappropriate that the Word of God should be present in creation—both unseen in its whole ordering and also visibly in the incarnation of Jesus Christ.

On De-divinizing Nature

Throughout *Against the Pagans* Athanasius outlines a process by which humanity turns from the contemplation of the Word and the Father of the Word to the worship of phenomena as gods, then the deification of human lusts, evil, and desires, and finally the irrational deification of material things, or those who have died, or those who in life we have loved, feared, or manipulated and whom we know to be less than ourselves. All forms of idolatry are projections of ourselves. In chapters 10 to 26 he outlines how these many gods issue in the abuse of human persons and in increasingly degenerate behavior, in 18 how human skill and the beauty of nature are both erroneously attributed to these idols—and nature also is devalued when such attributions are made. In 22 and 23 this multiplicity of local, racial, and national gods are shown to breed fear, violence, and conflicts among peoples.

Of course, there are those of higher mind among the pagans who also recognize the folly of popular idolatry (*AP*, 27). They turn their worship to the heavens and to the cosmos as a whole. But even these various forces of nature or heavenly bodies are not, for Athanasius, adequate for our worship. These different parts are recognized by him as being all interdependent, "none self-sufficient, but all in need of mutual service and only subsisting through mutual support . . . How then could these be gods when they stand in need of others' care?" (*AP*, 27–28). In fact, these many different and, often mutually, conflicting parts are "far removed from our ideas of God. For God is a whole and not separate parts; he is not constituted of different elements but is himself the creator of the composition of the universe" (*AP*, 28). Furthermore, these things are still subject to decay and to manipulation by human beings (*AP*, 28–29). But all these potentially discordant elements,

> recognizing the Lord who has joined them, are in harmony with each other, and though naturally opposites, yet by the will of the ruler they are reconciled . . . How could man have appeared on earth at all, if the elements were at strife with each other, and one was the strongest yet by itself insufficient for the creation of bodies? (*AP*, 37)

By Athanasius's argument all ideas about the divinity of the cosmos are excluded. But its value is not diminished for it is affirmed as creation, the handiwork of

> the living and acting God, the very Word of the good God of the universe, who is other than created things and all creation . . . who has ordered all this universe and illuminates it by his providence. He is the good Word of the good Father, and it is he who has established the order of all things, reconciling opposites and from them forming a single harmony. (*AP*, 40)

On Re-sacralising Creation—Contemplating the Word in All Things

The demons may be banished from the springs, rivers, woods, and stones (*DI*, 47), but that has not left the creation untouched by God. Rather, "God so ordered creation through his Word that although he is invisible by nature, yet he might be known to men from his works" (*AP*, 35). Athanasius then quotes from both Romans 1:20 and Acts 14:15–17. Robert Thomson notes, "the order of the cosmos indicates that it has a creator. A traditional argument developed by Stoicism . . . and frequently echoed in the apologists."[6] The same theme appears in *Against the Arians*, when Athanasius writes, "If through the Son creation has come to be, and 'in Him all things consist,' it must follow that he who contemplates creation rightly, is contemplating also the Word who framed it, and through Him begins to apprehend the Father" (*AA*, 1.4.12). He continues, writing of Paul who accuses the Greeks of "contemplating the harmony and order of creation without reflecting on the Framing Word within it (for the creatures witness to their own framer) so as through the creation to apprehend the true God, and abandon their worship of it i.e. creation" (*AA*, 1.4.12).

The argument from design, alluded to by Thomson above, need not itself indicate the immanent presence of God, nor any call to particular reverence. But Athanasius seems not to conceive of an absentee mechanistic ordering of the cosmos. Rather, he uses the analogy of a city in which, despite the immense diversity of inhabitants and activities, there is peace because of the presence within it of the king. One can think also of the soul ordering and balancing all the organs and functions of the body, or a musician drawing harmonies from a lyre, or a great choir (*AP*, 38 and again at 42–44). "In the same way, since the order in the whole world is completely harmonious . . . one must consequently think that there is one leader and king of all creation, not many, who moves the universe and illuminates it with his own light" (*AP*, 38). The suggestion of a purely mechanistic ordering is even more directly addressed and rejected when he writes,

> by Word I do not mean the word involved and innate in every creature, which some are accustomed to call seminal: it has no life of its own neither can it reason or think, but it acts merely by an extrinsic art according to the skill of him who set it in the creature . . . I mean the living and acting God, the very Word of the good God of the universe, who is other than created things and all creation; he is rather the sole and individual Word of the good Father, who has ordered all this universe and illuminates it by his providence. He is the good Word of the good Father. (*AP*, 40)

Furthermore, although things could have come into existence from nothing by the Word, their nature is nevertheless one of instability, in

---

6. Thomson in Athanasius, *CA* 97 note 2.

a state of flux and dissolution. But God is kind and wishes all things to exist so,

> He did not abandon creation . . . But being good, he governs and establishes the whole world through his Word who is himself God, in order that creation, illuminated by the leadership, providence, and ordering of the Word, may be able to remain firm, since it shares in the Word who is truly from the Father. (*AP*, 41)

Creation shares in the Word. The Word is not merely an external force but an active, ongoing, immanent presence. Athanasius concludes his case with a quotation from Colossians 1:15-18, "For he is the image of the invisible God, the first-born of all creation, because through him and in him subsist all things, visible and invisible, and he is the head of the church" (*AP*, 41).

The subsequent chapters continue to explore the relational nature of the presence of the Word in creation. We need not live in ignorance of him

> for the road to God is not as far from us or as extraneous to us as God himself is high above all, but it is within us and we ourselves can find its beginning, as Moses taught: "*The word of faith is within your heart.*" This the Savior also indicated and confirmed, saying: "*The Kingdom of heaven is within you.*" So since we have faith and the kingdom of God within us, we can quickly come to contemplate and apprehend the King of all, the saving Word of the Father. (*AP*, 30)

Thus the contemplative life is presented as the way of faith, and faith as the foundation of a contemplative life. The remainder of the book then develops this possibility as it explores ideas about the soul as the rational, reflective capacity of the human person, the relation of the soul and the body, the soul as mirror of the Word, and the presence of the Word available to us in creation and harmonizing all those elements in creation which without the Word would be in destructive conflict.

Although nature has been de-divinized, it has not been delivered to human beings as raw material for them to use however they please. On the contrary it is creation brought into existence and sustained by the presence of the Word of God and existing for the glory of God. Alvyn Pettersen argues, "the material world exists . . . for its own sake, not simply human utility. Its *raison d'etre* is simply the overflowing goodness of

God . . . as sustained it also expresses God's purposes and intentions and is therefore sacramental."[7]

Whilst primarily regarded as a theologian of the incarnation rather than of creation, Athanasius's arguments for the incarnation are inextricably tied up with his understanding of the living presence of the Word in creation. Creation is thus re-sacralised and takes on a truly revelatory function, requiring that it be appropriately honored.

ON BEING HUMAN

Alongside its critique of pagan conceptions of the gods, *Against the Pagans* also explores a second theme—the question of what it means to be human. For Athanasius, the truly human person lives a contemplative life, focused upon and sustained by the Word, and having minimal impact upon the creation of which they are an integral part. But as demonstrated above, we have turned from this contemplative existence to one focused on the desires of the body, and this has issued in selfishness, greed, violence, and the abuse of creation.

In the early sections human beings are portrayed as enjoying fullness of life as they live in the contemplation of God.

> God, the creator of the universe and king of all, who is beyond all being and human thought, since he is good and bountiful, has made mankind in his own image through his own Word, our Savior Jesus Christ; and he also made man perceptive and understanding of reality through his similarity to him, giving him also a conception and knowledge of his own eternity, so that as long as he kept this likeness he might never abandon his concept of God . . . but retaining the grace of him who bestowed it on him, and also the special power given him by the Father's Word, he might rejoice and converse with God . . . he continuously contemplates by his purity the image of the Father, God the Word, in whose image he was made, and is filled with admiration when he grasps his providence towards the universe. (AP, 2)

Creation in the image of the Word, understanding through perception of similarity, keeping the likeness, holding to the special power, and the description shortly thereafter of Adam living in "unembarrassed frankness

---

7. Pettersen, *Human Body*, 86.

... in the contemplation of intelligible reality" (*AP*, 2), are all references to the rationality inherent in the Word.[8]

All of this leads to recognition of the Word of God in the providential care of creation. Therefore, the point must be forcibly made that the contemplative existence is not divorced from creation, nor from reflection upon creation! Indeed, chapter 4 is explicit and extensive in describing how the truly contemplative person will see, listen to, and touch creation and, in so doing, will encounter God.

It is also critical to note that from the very beginning of this treatise the Word is identified as "our savior Jesus Christ," with whom there may be rejoicing and conversation (*AP*, 2). Thus, as demonstrated above, the Word is not to be conceived solely as pure rationality or as mechanistic power. Always there is a personal and relational element involved, and the "similarity" and "likeness" referred to (*AP*, 2) involve relationality as well as reason, encounter as well as observation.

Such contemplation requires that "men's mind has no intercourse with the body, and has nothing of the latter's desires mingled with it from outside but is entirely superior to them" (*AP*, 2). So Athanasius could be regarded as both separating humankind from the rest of creation and adopting a negative attitude towards the body, but chapter 3 reveals the issue he is really addressing: "Men, contemptuous of the better things and shrinking from their apprehension, sought rather what was closer to themselves—and what was closer to them than the body and its sensations" (*AP*, 3). This quest for sensation and pleasure is, for Athanasius, the abandonment of the contemplation of intelligible reality and the beginning of enslavement to unreality because evil has no real existence except in the conceits of corrupted minds. It is the beginning of a descent into irrationality, powerlessness and fear, lustful acquisitiveness, dissatisfaction, and eventually into murder and injustice. The corruption and misdirection of desire issues in the fear of death which itself arises from the fear of loss of these misconceived loves. This process is unfolded through the book. Its significance for our study is in what it reveals about insatiable demands for ever new material goods and sensual experiences—"consumerism," that arise from corrupted desires and corrupted ideas about God.

It is this loss of contemplative capacity, including its relational element, which needs both healing and rescue. How this is achieved is the

---

8. Thompson in Athanasius, *CA* 7, notes 3 and 5.

subject of the second book, *On the Incarnation of the Word and His Manifestation to us through the Body* (*DI*).

ON BEING HUMAN IN CHRIST

The two books are connected not only by frequent repetitions, for which Athanasius seems to have drawn criticism (*DI*, 20), but more importantly by the opening sentences. "The renewal of creation was effected by the Word who created it in the beginning ... the Father worked its salvation through the same one by whom he created it" (*DI*, 1). After having reiterated something of the process of human corruption, Athanasius asks,

> what was God to do? ... except to renew again that which was in his image, in order that through it men might be able once more to know him? But how could this be done, unless the very image of God were to come, our savior Jesus Christ? (*DI*, 13)

Thomson describes this as "an essential theme in Athanasius ... frequently repeated."[9] Christ comes as a recreated humanity in the reality of a human body.

> Since men's reason had descended to sensible things, the Word submitted to being revealed through a body, in order that he might bring men to himself as a man and turn their senses to himself, and that thenceforth, although they saw him as a man, he might persuade them through the works he did that he was not merely a man but God, and the Word and Wisdom of the true God ... For in two ways our Savior had compassion through the incarnation: he both rid us of death and renewed us; and also ... by his works he revealed and made himself known to be the Son of God and the Word of the Father, leader and king of the universe. (*DI*, 16)

It is necessary here to clarify that although the incarnation does have an element of rescue and repair about it, it does not arise from God being taken by surprise, nor does it entail the revelation of something that would otherwise have remained hidden. In his final appeal, at the conclusion of *Against the Pagans*, Athanasius reiterates a theme that people are unsound in their thinking, "who do not recognize God and do not worship his Word, the Savior of all, our Lord Jesus Christ, through whom the Father orders the universe and contains and provides for all

---

9. Thomson in Athanasius, *DI*, 137, note 3.

things" (*AP*, 47). Thus the ordering and sustaining of the universe by Christ the Word is also to be regarded as the work of salvation. He is present and actively involved in the whole history of creation as much as in the particular historical events of redemption. Pettersen suggests that in Athanasius there is little to separate creation and revelation,

> the tendency to drive a wedge between nature and grace, and to present the logos incarnate as the *antithesis* of nature, rather than nature's completion and meaning is ever to be resisted. The orderliness, with which the logos graciously created and sustains the world and which points all to see that the world is God's handiwork is universal and all-pervasive, the logos' assumed humanity being no exception.[10]

Nevertheless, humanity is in need of renewal, and this renewal in Christ is understood as having two aspects for us. Firstly, the true nature of God is revealed and the power of the demons is broken. This has comprehensive significance because the demons in Athanasius are all those powers that draw human beings into the realm of unreality, the deification of bodily desires, and the idolatry, lusts, greed, conflicts, and violence thus generated. But in the humanity of the incarnate Christ we see what God is truly like and what we also might be like. We see reality. Secondly, the power of death and the fear of death are also broken. What Athanasius writes about death has significance for environmental theology in a number of respects.

Death Is Natural

At some point, according to Athanasius, humans were gifted immortality and this set them apart from other animals. This immortality was secured by the imposition of a law and a place, but, if in their freedom, humanity was "to transgress and turn back they would incur that corruption by death that was theirs by nature" (*DI*, 3). The argument continues, "the transgression of the commandment turned them to what was natural ... man is by nature mortal in that he was created from nothing" (*DI*, 4), and, "men are ... corruptible by nature, but by the grace of the participation of the Word they could have escaped from the consequences of their nature if they had remained virtuous" (*DI*, 5). Immortality is not a given, intrinsic, natural part of being human. It is a gift to be enjoyed only so

---

10. Pettersen, *Human Body*, 17.

long as humans remained in a pure contemplative relationship with the Word. When that relationship is lost or abandoned, we are exposed again to our natural condition, which is the natural process of death.

As the Arian controversy dragged on, another somewhat contrary misunderstanding of the incarnation developed. In a long letter to Epictetus, Athanasius addressed the idea that "the Lord's body is of the Essence of the Triad . . . that the body is not newer than the Godhead of the Word, but was coeternal with it always."[11] If this is true, he argues, then the human response of Mary is irrelevant and the church's commemoration of her obedience is unnecessary. Rather,

> it is time to say openly that He was born of earth (4) . . . A great addition has accrued to the human body itself from the fellowship and union of the Word with it. For instead of mortal it has become immortal; and though an animal body, it is become spiritual, and though made from earth it entered the heavenly gates (9) . . . the body itself being of mortal nature, beyond its own nature rose again by reason of the Word which was in it (10).[12]

The human body is naturally mortal. Only by union with the Word may it become immortal. At this point Athanasius is writing explicitly about the resurrection of Jesus. For the rest of us, the gift of immortality and incorruption must await the time of our own deaths and the general resurrection of the dead. "Now no longer as condemned do we die, but as those who will rise again we await the general resurrection of all, which God in his own time will reveal" (*DI*, 9).

Not only is the human body created mortal, but Athanasius seems quite untroubled by death in nature. It is not an outcome of human sin. Rather it appears to be simply the way God has made things; it is natural. It is certainly not a sign of the fallenness of the non-human parts of creation. In arguing why it was necessary for the Lord to come as a human being he writes,

> nothing in all creation was in error in its ideas about God, save man only. So neither the sun nor the moon nor the sky nor the stars nor the sea nor the air changed their course, but knowing their creator and king the Word, they remained as they had been

---

11. Athanasius, *SWL*, "Letter to Epictetus 1," 1392–97.
12. Athanasius, *SWL*, "Letter to Epictetus 1," 1392–97.

made. But men only turned away from the good and henceforth invented nothings instead of the truth. (*DI*, 43)

Continuing this line of thought he clarifies that although the Lord touched all parts of creation and freed and undeceived everything of all error, it was not the things themselves which were in error but the way in which they were being perceived by human beings (*DI*, 45). The capacity of creation to recognize its Lord is also evidenced by its responsiveness to the word of Christ in the gospel miracles (*SWL*, 11.4; 29), and in the events surrounding Easter: "the whole of creation was confessing that . . . Christ who was on the cross was God, and that the whole creation was his handmaid and was witnessing in fear to the coming of her master" (*DI*, 19). Similarly, "the sun itself, seeing its creator suffering in His outraged body, withdrew its rays and darkened the earth."[13]

Thus Athanasius can conceive of a creation that has not become alienated from its creator but in which death is nevertheless a natural process. Recognizing death as necessary in nature is critical to the operation of natural systems, energy cycles and the whole science of ecology. To recognize, as Athanasius appears to do, that death is natural in what God has established may raise some difficult questions about pain in animals, but it will also rehabilitate nature and natural processes. The natural world is not to be disparaged as incorrigibly fallen. As Moule reminded us in chapter 1, nature's processes, including those of the body,[14] are the work of the good God.

Christ Is Life

In *The Incarnation* Athanasius introduces a phrase that in its frequent use becomes almost a title for Christ. Writing of Christ's resurrection, he says, "he rose up whole since the body belonged to no one else but *life itself*" (*DI*, 21) (my italics). It was necessary that "the life of all, our Lord and Savior Christ . . . accepted and endured the cross . . . in order that when it had been destroyed he might be believed to be life" (*DI*, 24). He continues, "would anyone doubt . . . that Christ is alive, or rather that he is life?" (*DI*, 30). Christ's body "was unable not to die . . . but it was also unable to remain dead, because it had become the temple of life" (*DI*, 31).

---

13. Athanasius, *SWL*, "Letter to Epictetus 1," 1397.
14. Athanasius, *SWL*, "Letter to Amun 48," 1358-59.

By Christ's death, "salvation was effected for all and all creation was saved ... He it is who is the life of all" (*DI*, 37).

The phrase occurs repeatedly in chapter 44 as Athanasius outlines why it was necessary for the Word to touch and take a body, rather than effect salvation by simply a word or a nod. The body must "put on life," in order to put off corruption and rise to immortality. This vindicates Christ, otherwise, "how would the Lord be shown to be life, unless he had given life to what was mortal?" (*DI*, 44). This putting on life is the definitive demonstration that death will not have the last word. We are saved from corruption and dissolution into nothingness by the incarnation and resurrection of Christ.

Thomas Torrance explicitly engages Athanasius to address and reject the idea that the resurrection is some kind of interruption of the natural order, or an intrusion into the natural processes of the world.

> The difficulty with a resurrection of that kind is that there is no consistency between it and the nature of the resurrected One, but it is entirely different with the kind of resurrection to which the New Testament bears witness when it speaks of the resurrection of Jesus Christ... The actual resurrection of Jesus from the tomb was recognized to be in entire accordance with his nature and person.[15]

Thus the resurrection of Jesus is a "natural" outcome for one who is

> the Creator-God among men, at work even in the midst of death and corruption and perdition and nothingness ... the whole life of Jesus, together with his resurrection was the manifestation among men and on earth and in time of the ultimate and original and final creative activity of God.[16]

The importance of this argument lies in the reminder that these acts of God are not an imposition upon the universe, nor an invasion contrary to its own inherent nature. Rather, God is intimately involved. Christ is its life. Since he is

> the head in whom all things, visible and invisible are reconciled and gathered up, the resurrection of Christ in *body* becomes the pledge that the whole physical universe will be renewed, for in a fundamental sense it has already been resurrected in Christ.[17]

---

15. Torrance, *Space, Time and Resurrection*, 76.
16. Torrance, *Space, Time and Resurrection*, 76–77.
17. Torrance, *Space, Time and Resurrection*, 155. At this point, in note 19, Torrance

On the Ascetic Life

The Incarnation concludes with some reflections on the role of ascesis. It is to enable those who are believers to clear their eyes or to prepare for a journey, so that they may see more clearly, understand better, and enter more fully into the life of the Word in creation, Scripture, and the theologians (*DI*, 57). Such discipline was for Athanasius the way of faithful discipleship. To provide a pastor's example for others to model, he wrote the *Life of Anthony* (*LA*). This enabled a protest against the perceived dilution of the Christian identity since its adoption by Emperor Constantine, and it articulated a new form of existence liberated from the old Classical constraints and more immediately engaged with God, the self, others, and creation itself.[18] Within the story he also engages with various contemporary theological debates.

Firstly, Athanasius's ascetical theology is not born of a negative assessment of creation nor of the body, but of a recognition that as human beings abandon the contemplative existence they actually develop an increasingly abusive relationship with creation.

Adam and Eve's fleshly desires and nakedness are not conceived as being anything to do with sex, but entirely with "being stripped of the contemplation of divine things" (*CG*, 3). In his letter to Amun, perhaps 30 years after *Against the Pagans*, he addresses an issue that has troubled or intrigued generations of adolescent males. All things made by God are beautiful and pure, for the Word of God has made nothing useless or impure including all the bodily passages and natural secretions. Specific mention is made of "seminative channels." After an appeal to medical science he concludes, "When any bodily excretion takes place independently of will, then we experience this, like other things, by a necessity of nature . . . what sin is there . . . if the Master who made the body willed and made these parts to have such passages?"[19]

Certainly, he observes, the devil may use these things to sow thoughts of uncleanness or defilement but this is not in the nature of creation itself. Such misguided thoughts are rather another fruit of our having fallen from the truly contemplative existence, which is the intelligible

---

refers to *DI*, 29ff and notes the beginning of contrasts between Eastern and Western theological traditions, with the Western seen as "world denying" in character, and the Eastern as "world affirming."

18. Cowan, *Journey to the Inner Mountain*, ix–xi.

19. Athanasius, *SWL*, "Letter to Amun 48," 1358–59.

understanding of the work of the Word in creation. The virgin birth itself is not necessitated by some need to avoid the supposed evils of sex, but solely in order to demonstrate the creative action of God, who is "Lord of the providence of the universe" (*DI*, 17).

Pettersen, rejecting an argument that Athanasius was a Platonist, writes,

> for Athanasius, the experience of being human, whether in the case of his anthropology or his Christology, is not about being trapped in the weakness of the body (for that is the experience of being less than human): it is the experience of having fallen from true humanity, where the body is not a trap, but the medium in and through which each lives in the free service of God.[20]

Later he adds,

> the body is a person's physical prerequisite to a full existence; it is that part of an individual in and through which he or she lives and expresses him—or herself; and it is the base for the operation of irrationality in the sinner and of the Logos in the saint.[21]

The contemplative life rejoices in what may be known of God through the contemplation of the Word in creation including one's own body, and it is lived in thankfulness and generosity. Thankfulness, the rejection of self-indulgence, and care for the poor are recurring themes in the "Festal Letters."[22] These are not simply things to be done but are the essence of the feast. "We demonstrate that we are clothed with Him when: we love virtue . . . engage in temperance . . . aim to live without undue luxury . . . have strength of mind . . . do not forget the poor but open our doors to all . . . assist humility and hate pride" (*SWL*, 4).

Thankfulness and generosity imply the importance of creation and createdness in being human, in no way undermined by any commitment to simplicity of life. "Festal Letters" (6.10) asserts that the whole creation keeps the Easter feast with the whole company of heaven. Letter 11 stresses the centrality of the theological confession of creation, "before all things believe there is one God who created and established all things, and from non-existence called them into being" (*SWL*, 11.4), and continues by drawing a connection between the work of God the Word

---

20. Pettersen, *The Human Body*, 8.
21. Pettersen, *The Human Body*, 30, see, e.g., *AP*, 4.
22. Athanasius, *SWL*, "Festal Letters," e.g., 3, 5, 6:10, 7:2, 10:4, 11:1, 14:5, 19:8.

in creation and the renewal of creation exhibited in the miracles of the gospel. In the same letter the church catholic, when united in praise, is for Athanasius a sign of hope for all creation (*SWL*, 11.11).

Secondly, neither is asceticism antisocial; certainly, there have been examples of individualist and misanthropic asceticism but this is not the Athanasian vision. His pastoral letters affirm people in their social and marital relationships and consistently urge neighborliness and peacemaking. The exemplary life of Anthony includes the admonition to "work so as to enable relief of the poor and needy" (*LA*, 37); Anthony accepts invitations and practices table fellowship in order "to be mindful of the Word . . . and to affirm that ye are members of each other" (*LA*, 38), therefore seek first the kingdom and do not allow the body to dominate the soul. Moses too, despite having fed on the vision of God, and while doing so being released from the need for food, is commended for returning from Sinai to the social community and to common food (*SWL*, 1).

Protestant and post-Enlightenment assessments of Christian asceticism have tended to critique such movements as essentially negative in their view of creation and the human body. Given Athanasius's uncompromising commitment to the goodness of creation, including the human body, there may be real value in exploring instead the idea that ascesis is not an attempt to escape but rather to engage. It is an attempt to encounter the Word, in creation and beyond creation, with as little intervening impediment as possible. Such a view has significant environmental implications, for as noted earlier, the contemporary consumerist economy involves both unsustainable resource consumption and increasing disconnectedness and separation from creation.

The contemplative existence, pursued by an ascetic life, is for Athanasius the antithesis of the idolatrous existence. This vision, so central to theology and praxis in the pre-modern era, is nowhere touched upon by White. Yet it is neither possible to describe this period nor to analyze it if these elements are not recognized as central.

Humanity and the Natural World

For Athanasius, what Christ restores to humanity is not the power to manipulate creation but the power to contemplate. Nevertheless, we have also seen that humanity exists in the body so the question remains how Athanasius may understand the relationship between humanity and the rest of the natural world. In *Against the Pagans* the soul's power of rationality sets humanity apart from animals, not in order to dominate them but in order to contemplate the Word in creation (*AP*, 31). We have also observed the extensive argument derived from the harmonies of creation and living things, of which we are a part (*AP*, 37). To recognize the providential ordering of the Word in all this is to find a manner of existence quite different to that which Athanasius identifies in the pagan conception of a divinized universe. In that world all things are in conflict and people live in constant fear of both demonic petulance and human enemies whose loyalties lie with particular localized powers (*AP*, 47).

The matter of harmonious relationships is taken up again in *The Incarnation* in order to make an analogy about the incarnation. Athanasius observes that Greek philosophy might allow for the recognition of the Word as Creator and providential Lord, but it mocks the idea that the Word could be revealed in a human body. But why, he asks,

> since they rightly say that the world is a great body . . . if the Word of God is in the world, which is a body, and he has passed into every part of it, what is wonderful or unfitting in our saying that he came in a man? . . . For the human race is a part of the whole; and if the part is not suitable to be his instrument wherewith to make known his divinity, it would be most unfitting that he should be known through the whole universe. (*DI*, 41)

He continues similarly in chapters 42 and 43, drawing analogies between the soul and the tongue and the toe and the body. Although used to demonstrate some important aspects of the incarnation, what is significant for us at this point is that the whole argument is based upon the complete oneness of humanity with the rest of creation. Christ also shares in that experience of being made one with the rest of creation, and as the Word he has passed into every part of it. This sense of intimate connectedness is in total contrast to White's assertion that "Christianity not only established a dualism of man and nature but also insisted that it is God's will that man exploit nature for his proper ends."[23]

Chapter 43 goes on to explain that the choosing of man was because the Lord came

> to teach and heal those who were suffering . . . to be of service to those in need, to appear in a way that they can bear, lest by his

---

23. White, "Historical Roots," 1205.

superiority to the need of those who were suffering he trouble the needy and the coming of God be of no help to them. (*DI*, 43)

That the Lord exercised his power in a spirit of service and humility is further recognized as being a model for us in various of the "Festal Letters." Letter 1 tells us that Christ's blood does not cry out for vengeance. Our feet are shod with the gospel and we carry a shepherd's rod for comfort. There is the oft-repeated encouragement to remember the poor and not forget kindness to strangers. Letter 2 reminds readers that learning of Christ means learning the lesson of John 13, the story of the foot washing: "Not only do we bear His image, but He gives us His life as a pattern of heavenly behaviour, so that we can follow him" (*SWL*, 2). None of these references are explicitly about human relations with the natural world, but they do make the case that bearing the image of the Word is not about domination but about humility and service.

Chapters 47–53 of *The Incarnation* reflect on the changes to social relationships that have occurred with the coming of the gospel. The fears, loyalties, and conflicts associated with different places and cults have all withered away at the presence of Christ.

> He has joined in peace those who hated each other. . . . Barbarians who cannot bear to remain a single moment without the sword . . . when they hear the word of Christ turn from war to farming, and instead of arming their hands with swords they stretch them out in prayer. (*DI*, 52)[24]

It is with Anthony in the desert that we come closest to anything specific concerning human engagement with the world around. In *The Life of Anthony*, chapter 27, demons and charlatans pretend to foretell natural events and thus enslave and confuse their pagan hearers. This is a misuse of creation. Rather, urges Anthony, "get understanding concerning the things of this world and you will obtain preservation of your mind from these unsettling demonic storms" (*LA*, 28). He further refers to the knowledge and experience of physicians and seafarers, but concludes with the reminder that the real issues of life are not about foretelling but about doing good (*LA*, 28). Chapters 42 and 43 show Anthony tending his fragile garden and having it damaged by visiting animals. "Quietly and laughingly, he asks them, 'why do you do harm to me seeing that

---

24. Ironically this development can issue in wildlife conservation conflicts, for territories which humans previously avoided for fear of enemies now become available for occupancy!

I do no harm to you? . . . get gone' . . . From that hour this was a command from heaven to them and they never again did harm to the place" (*LA*, 42–43). This may not count as warm friendship but neither does it represent domineering abuse. We are told that "he was not wearied by the desert, and his soul had no fear of the wild beasts . . . but Satan suffered torture for these things" (*LA*, 43). Sometimes the demons visit him in the guise of animals, but their true nature is revealed when they are addressed in the name of Christ and "they are straitway driven off . . . like a sparrow before a hawk" (*LA*, 44). Later in the account domination of a rather different kind occurs when the arrogant and overbearing official Balacius is attacked and killed by his own horse, and this is taken as a warning to all in authority not to be puffed up nor to magnify themselves over the people (*LA*, 70). Finally, and in marked contrast to the advice offered by many contemporary economic or spiritual consultants, we read, "what poor man ever came broken by poverty who did not afterwards, by reason of his words and the sight of him despise all riches?" (*LA*, 70).

CONCLUSIONS

For Athanasius there is nothing in creation that is not sustained by the living presence of the Word of God. Demons may have been banished but God has not been. This Word is not merely a force but personal. That this is a trinitarian work is made clear when Athanasius writes,

> it is clear that the Spirit is not a creature, but takes part in the act of creation. The Father creates all things through the Word in the Spirit; for where the Word is, there is the Spirit also, and the things which are created through the Word have their vital strength out of the Spirit from the Word.[25]

God's intention for humanity is that we fellowship with this Word by the Spirit, through faith pursued by contemplation. Creation does not exist for us to exploit at all, but rather to reflect the glory of God and to help us nurture humility, love, and thankfulness. Liberated from demonic confusion we live not dominating creation but in contemplative openness, alert to the order, harmony, and interconnectedness of the universe with ourselves as an inextricable part of it. This oneness with creation receives its clearest expression in the incarnation of the Word in Jesus Christ. In

---

25. Athanasius, *LHS*, 2/3.5.

his own human body he ties God inextricably to creation. There is nothing in Athanasius of a desacralized universe and nothing to suggest that the world is given to human beings to use as they please.

White had stated that "in the early church, and always in the Greek East, nature was conceived primarily as a symbolic system through which God speaks to men . . . this view of nature was essentially artistic rather than scientific."[26]

In fact, rarely in Athanasius have we found any references to animals as symbols nor to animal characteristics as sermon illustrations or moral examples. The creation is not mined by Athanasius to find peculiar, interesting curios. But he does urge people to get understanding of nature's cycles, harmonies, and processes, not in order to control nature but to banish those demonic influences that corrupt and misuse nature, darken our minds, and sow fear and confusion. White continued, "in the Latin West by the 13th century natural theology was . . . ceasing to be the decoding of the physical symbols of God's communication with man and was becoming the effort to understand God's mind by discovering how his creation operates."[27]

Athanasius was advocating much the same thing almost a millennium earlier. To find it already present in the fourth century and having no destructive impact suggests that we must look for other influences to determine why something for so long benign should eventually become destructive.

With freedom from fear may come the opportunity to misuse the gifts of creation, and we have been alerted to such possibilities in chapter 1. But the gospel is liberation into the life of Christ—not into any kind of libertarian autonomy. Therefore, the person who by the renewing power of the Holy Spirit is truly putting on the likeness of Christ will live their new freedom being formed in Christ's manner of life. On the other hand, it is a critical issue whether the fears generated by a divinized universe are really an adequate basis for understanding even a little of the processes of creation, for feeling at home within it, or for developing robust environmental ethics. What it means to live in the light of the Word who is Life will be explored further in chapter 8.

---

26. White, "Historical Roots," 1206.
27. White, "Historical Roots," 1206.

5

On Augustine

INTRODUCTION

IN ENGAGING THE WESTERN Christian tradition we find everywhere the fingerprints of Augustine of Hippo (354–430). Alister McGrath suggests that in Augustine, "we encounter what is probably the greatest and most influential mind of the Christian church."[1] Similar accolades are extended by such varied voices as Ivor Davidson,[2] Eleonore Stump,[3] Gareth Matthews,[4] Jaroslav Pelikan,[5] R. P. H. Green,[6] and even Bertrand Russell.[7] In his own lifetime he cultivated what Peter Brown has styled "a far-flung intellectual empire,"[8] which extended around the Mediterranean from Mauretania to Palestine, Constantinople, North Italy, and west through the Pyrenees to Gibraltar. In subsequent centuries it reached to Poland in North Eastern Europe and Northumbria and Ireland in the North West. Numerous copies of *The Literal Meaning of Genesis* (*LM*)

1. McGrath, *Christian Theology*, 12.
2. Davidson, *Public Faith*, 193.
3. Stump and Kretzmann, *Cambridge Companion to Augustine*, 1.
4. Matthews, *Augustinian Tradition*, ix.
5. Pelikan, "Foreword," *Augustine through the Ages*, xiii–xiv
6. Green, "Introduction," in Augustine, *DC*, ix–x.
7. Russell, *History of Western Philosophy*, 352–3.
8. Brown, *Augustine*, 465.

have been found in locations as disparate as Italy, Poland, Great Britain and Ireland, and Spain,[9] and by 700 the Venerable Bede was commenting on his sermons.[10]

Brown, in writing about the *Confessions* (*CON*), suggests that much of Augustine's thought is surprisingly contemporary.

> The more we have been enabled to place Augustine against the wider landscape of late antiquity, the more we have come to realize that many of the aspects of his thought which seem closest to modern persons were often those which struck his contemporaries as the most idiosyncratic ... his discovery of the self represents a notable step forward in the history of human thought. His intervention proved decisive for the emergence of a distinctive notion of the individual in Western culture. Augustine has been called "the inventor of our modern notion of will."[11]

First, and foremost, his motivations were those of a teaching bishop. His work is characterized by "unremitting circumstantiality,"[12] intended to "speak in such a way as to instruct, delight, and move" (*CG*, 4.74), and thus make a difference to the way all his flock understood and lived their lives.

The Book of Genesis was a recurring focus of Augustine's interest. In 388, within 18 months of his baptism, he had written *A Commentary on Genesis: Against the Manichees*, followed in about 392 by *The Literal Meaning of Genesis: An Unfinished Book*. Between 397 and 401 he wrote probably his most enduring work, *The Confessions* (*CON*), and books 12–13 of this are a further series of reflections on Genesis. *The Literal Meaning of Genesis: A Commentary in Twelve Books* (*LM*) was written over a longer period from 401 to 415. Near the end of this time, in 413, he began his magnum opus *The City of God* (*CG*) whose books 11 and 12 again revisit crucial themes in Genesis.[13] In recognition of this prodigious output and impact we shall require a chapter much longer than the preceding ones. Yet, despite his pastoral orientation, intense interest in the passage at the center of this study, and his overwhelming influence Augustine goes unmentioned by White.

9. Augustine, *LM*, 12.
10. Brown, *Augustine*, 444.
11. Brown, *Augustine*, 502–3.
12. Brown, *Augustine*, 444.
13. Augustine, *LM*, 2.

The opening chapters of Genesis enabled Augustine to address three of the great controversies which embroiled his life—Manichaeism, Donatism, and Pelagianism.

Manichaeism, a gnostic movement of Persian origin, was the formative religious influence of Augustine's youth and some commentators suggest he was never completely liberated from it.[14] Brown writes of the Manichees,

> they were dualists: so convinced were they that evil could not come from a good God, that they believed that it came from an invasion of the good—the "Kingdom of Light"—by a hostile force of evil, equal in power, eternal, totally separate—the "Kingdom of Darkness." "The first thing a man must do," says the Chinese Manichaean catechism, "is to distinguish the Two Principles (the Good and the Evil). He who would enter our religion must know that the Two Principles have natures absolutely distinct."[15]

In such a universe Augustine's own self was similarly divided—a division that promoted at once both self-satisfaction and despair.

> I still thought that it is not we who sin, but some alien nature which sins in us. It flattered my pride to be free of blame and, when I had done something wrong, not to make myself confess to you that you might heal my soul . . . but the whole was myself and what divided me against myself was my impiety. (*CON*, V.x.18)

Manichaeism remained for almost a millennium a potent force both within and beyond the Empire with its vigorous mission, exotic appearance, and ongoing appeal to others as it had had for Augustine.[16] Through all his years of writing he never ceases to name it and to engage deliberately with its ideas.

Donatism, by contrast, was a uniquely Christian, rigorist movement which had arisen in North Africa among those who believed that they, or their predecessors in the faith, had remained faithful under persecution

---

14. Gunton, *Triune Creator*, who writes of Augustine's "residual Manichaeism," 77, and his "scars of Manichaeism," 79; and Brown, *Augustine*, quoting the attacks on Augustine by Julian of Eclanum, 386, 388, 396–97.

15. Brown, *Augustine*, 37.

16. Brown, *Augustine*, 33, 43; see also 485, note 3.

in a way that many Catholics had not.[17] But Donatist "purity" lay only in distant history, "that is, from a crime committed by total strangers in a conveniently distant past."[18] In the present Augustine could easily demonstrate that Donatists were no more "pure" than anybody else. More importantly, their notions concerning purity were seriously theologically flawed. African Christians had developed a tradition of wearing, after baptism, special sandals lest their "pure" feet touch the earth.[19] The world was for them a place of malevolent demonic powers and only in a pure church, characterized by Old Testament commitment to a code of law, to ritual purity, and to deeply demarcated separatism,[20] could there be found personal purity and spiritual protection.

Both W.H.C. Frend and Carol Harrison suggest that there are connections to be drawn between Donatism and Manichaeism in their shared negative evaluation of the material world and their attempts "to separate the kingdoms of darkness and light into two clear and distinct, readily identifiable groups."[21] The attempt to draw such a demarcation also functioned, for Augustine, to perpetuate the tragic divisions of the human race. Conversely the Catholic Church, by virtue of its universal character, was Christ's means for expressing his universal lordship and reconciling the divided races of humanity.[22]

While issues with Donatism dominated Augustine's early episcopal career, those with Pelagianism consumed his later years. Pelagius was an ascetic teacher, probably a Briton, living among aristocratic Romans who in the early fifth century were spearheading a new ascetic movement. Deeply troubled by the evident moral laxity of Roman society and the many signs that Christian profession appeared to have made little difference to personal and social relationships, Pelagius embarked upon a transformative moral crusade.[23] The sad irony is that many of his concerns were shared by Augustine and the ascetic principles he espoused

---

17. Brown, *Augustine*, 210.
18. Brown, *Augustine*, 215.
19. Brown, *Augustine*, 207.
20. Brown, *Augustine*, 213–14.
21. Harrison, *Augustine*, 200; Frend, *Donatist Church*, 113.
22. Brown, *Augustine*, 220; see also, Hartranft, "Introduction to the Anti-Donatist Writings," 374.
23. Brown, *Augustine*, 347–48.

were already widespread.[24] At the heart of his message was a perfectionism about which Brown writes,

> this message was simple and terrifying: "since perfection is possible for man, it is obligatory." Pelagius never doubted for a moment that perfection was obligatory; his God was, above all, a God who commanded unquestioning obedience . . . he had no patience with the confusion that seemed to reign on the powers of human nature . . . he refused to believe the power of self-improvement as having been irreversibly prejudiced; the idea of an "original sin" . . . struck him as quite absurd.[25]

Augustine on the other hand was not so sanguine. Reflection on his own inner struggles and the frustrations of pastoral ministry led him to a less optimistic assessment of human capacity. Pastoral psychology was not his only recourse in this debate. He also reflected theologically on Romans 5 and what it meant for all humanity to be "in Adam," and more generally on the role of Christ, the necessity of grace, and the work of the Holy Spirit.

> Augustine recognized that the issues at stake in his disputes with the Pelagians lay at the heart of the Christian faith . . . Is sinful behaviour merely the result of a corrupt environment, or is it an inevitable part of our natural state, from the effects of which we cannot extricate ourselves? Is Jesus only an example to which human beings choose to respond, or has God acted decisively in him to bring about a state of affairs that we are incapable of achieving for ourselves?[26]

For the disputants many of the issues revolved around the nature of the soul and Augustine addressed these at length in book 10 of the *Literal Meaning*.[27] Harrison recognizes in this debate a long-standing issue in antiquity.

> Throughout his life Augustine wavered between the creationist answer (that each individual soul is created by God at birth) and the traducianist solution (that the soul of each person is inherited from their parents and ultimately from Adam) (e.g. [*LM*] books 7 and 10) . . . most often, but not without much agonizing,

---

24. Brown, *Augustine*, 465, 469–71.
25. Brown, *Augustine*, 342–43.
26. Davidson, *Public Faith*, 189.
27. Augustine, *LM*, 280–81, note 56.

he opts for the latter as a better way of explaining the inheritance of original sin and the practice of infant baptism.[28]

By this account Augustine's conception makes inescapable the interconnection of the whole human race. Writing to Simplicianus he describes humankind as a, "*massa peccati,*' one lump in which the original guilt (of Adam) remains throughout" (*Simplic.* 2.17, 20).[29] Pelagianism, on the other hand, in dismissing the significance of such connections, would foster theories of energetic individual responsibility.[30]

Despite their many differences, these three movements raise some common questions concerning the nature of God's engagement with creation, the goodness and unity of creation, the role and capabilities of human beings within creation, and, above all, the extent of Christ's writ over and within creation. For Augustine, all of them could be addressed by the opening chapters of Genesis and to that book we now turn. We have four main sections: issues of interpretation, God the Creator, the creation— with five sub-sections, and finally, the significance of the Sabbath.

A key text is *The Literal Meaning of Genesis* (*LM*). Written during the first decade of the fifth century, it reflects both the underlying influence of Manichaeism and the vigorous debates about Donatism, with its constant refrains concerning the goodness and sustaining presence of God within creation and the all-embracing universal purposes of God for creation. *Confessions*, written early in Augustine's episcopal career as something of a personal apologia, is significant in revealing aspects of his personal spirituality and devotion and the development of his thinking by that time about Manichaeism, Platonism, and the book of Genesis (*CON*, xi–xiii). *On the Trinity* (*DT*) begun in 399 but probably completed soon after 420 is a more systematic attempt to present his doctrine of God and is significant both for its engagement with Arian ideas and for the degree to which Augustine constantly relates things about God to things about creation. *The City of God*, the product of his mature years, began as a response to the fall of Rome in 410 but became, in the end, a survey of the history of God with the creation. There is of course a range of other occasional material.

---

28. Harrison, *Augustine*, 109–10.
29. Cited by Harrison, *Augustine*, 28.
30. Brown, *Augustine*, 350–51.

ON INTERPRETATION IN GENESIS

Augustine begins by discussing issues of interpretation and demonstrating the varieties of different meaning which may be taken from the same text. We have previously noted the centrality of this issue in reading the Fathers and the total neglect of it by those critical of the tradition. Regarding the distinction between allegorical or figurative interpretation, and literal or proper interpretation, the question, according to Augustine "is whether everything must be taken according to the figurative sense only, or whether it must be expounded and defended also as a faithful record of what happened. No Christian will dare say that the narrative must not be taken in a figurative sense" (*LM*, 1.1.1).

Indeed, the issue for Augustine, and many of his readers, was whether it could ever be taken in any way *other* than a figurative sense. Figurative interpretations had an honorable history (*LM*, 1.1.1), and in *Confessions* xiii.13, his own allegorizing inclinations find their head with all of Genesis 1 being interpreted in terms of the church. It was literal interpretation that challenged Augustine, and learning that process was part of his journey out of Manichaeism. He recounts in *LM,* book 8 that his early attempts to read Genesis literally were fraught with difficulty and eventually he abandoned the enterprise until a much later date (*LM,* 8.2.5). But now, in *The Literal Meaning of Genesis,* he has returned to the task with renewed confidence. "I have started here to discuss sacred scripture according to the plain meaning of the historical facts, not according to future events which they foreshadow" (*LM*, 1.17.34). In one example among many, he writes concerning the tree of life in the midst of the garden, "we should take care not to be compelled to turn to allegory and end up with these not being trees at all but something signified by the name of a tree. For it is said of wisdom, '*She is a tree of life for all those who lay hold of her*'" (*LM*, 8.4.8). Then follow a number of biblical examples of persons or events which although later seen as having prophetic or figurative significance, "none the less they themselves existed in the world of material reality" (*LM*, 8.4.8). The importance of there being real events and real trees is because "God did not want man to live in paradise without the mysteries of spiritual things made present in material things" (*LM*, 8.4.8).

By insisting more than some of his predecessors on taking seriously the biblical reports of real trees, real people, and real events, Augustine was actually making a case for the value in God's purposes of the material world. By continuing to read this world figuratively he was also imbuing it with spiritual significance and vitality, a point he is at pains to make at the beginning of book 8 (*LM*, 8.1.1–4). Again, there is simply no support for White's view that the material world had been evacuated of spiritual significance.

ON GOD THE CREATOR

Augustine's Manichaean struggle had centered on the imagined dualistic tension between the material world and a holy God. His subsequent Neoplatonic struggle was not so much with God's distant holiness but with his incarnate humility. The dramatic account of his conversion culminates in the encounter with the word of Scripture, "'put on the Lord Jesus Christ and make no provision for the flesh in its lusts (Rom. 13:14)'" (*CON*, VIII.xii.29). From then on for Augustine, God will be known in Jesus Christ and it is in Jesus Christ that he will be reconciled with God. This Jesus Christ is the Lord, the incarnation of the Word who is in the beginning with the Father. From this trinitarian conception, Augustine will not henceforth waver, and whatever he wants to say about creation, it will always be said in the light of what he wants to say about God.

> Where the name of God occurs, I have come to see the Father who made these things; where the "Beginning" is mentioned, I see the Son by whom he made these things. Believing that my God is Trinity, in accordance with my belief I searched in God's holy oracles and found your Spirit to be borne above the waters. There is the Trinity, my God—Father and Son and Holy Spirit, Creator of the entire creation. (*CON*, VIII.v.6)

The key thing that Augustine the trinitarian Christian wants to say is that God is the beginning of everything. We humans cannot, however, see this directly because being created ourselves we are unable to see beyond or outside of creation (*DT*, 8.1.27). Thus we have instead to trust and herein we encounter one of the most basic of Augustine's convictions; that "we must believe before we understand" (*DT*, 8.5.8). This believing is expressed in love and conversely love is expressed in believing (*DT*, 8.5.8). It is in this disposition of believing love that we may discern, underlying all the changeable goods of creation, the goodness that is "God who is to be loved, not as this or that good, but as good itself" (*DT*, 8.34). As God is goodness—rather than having attained it from beyond himself, so also God is wisdom. "God has not obtained the wisdom by which He is wise, but He Himself is wisdom" (*DT*, 17.5.7), and blessedness—"You alone are in absolute simplicity . . . because you are your own blessedness" (*CON*, XIII.iii.4). This is the simplicity of God which relates also to time.

> It is idle to look for time before creation, as if time can be found before time . . . We should, therefore, say that time began with creation rather than that creation began with time. But both are from God. For from Him, through Him and in Him are all things. (*LM*, 5.5.12)

He argues similarly in *The City of God*, "beyond doubt, then, the world was made not in time, but simultaneously with time" (*CG*, xi.6). Time, which is a measure of change, is a property of creation. One simply cannot speak of a "before" the beginning. There is nothing apart from God. From this recognition of the absolute simplicity of God arises the doctrine of creation *ex nihilo*—out of nothing.

Creation *ex nihilo* subverts both the Manichaean dualism of two eternal principles utterly opposed to each other, and the Neoplatonic conception of creation as an emanation from the divine One with the associated conception of eternal formless matter with which the creator struggles in order to bring the form of the universe into being. Apart from what God creates there is nothing. Or perhaps more accurately, apart from what God creates there is only God. Thus creation *ex nihilo* involves no divine imposition upon anything but simply, a divine giving.

In keeping with this character of God the divine giving suffuses the whole creation and the whole Trinity partners in the work of creation,

> for, when the Scripture says, *In the beginning God created heaven and earth*, by the name of "God" we understand the Father, and by the name of "Beginning," the Son who is the Beginning, not for the Father, but first and foremost for spiritual beings He has created and then also for all creatures; and when Scripture says, *And the Spirit of God was stirring above the water*, we recognize a complete enumeration of the Trinity. So in the conversion and in the perfecting of creatures by which their species are separated in due order, the Blessed Trinity is likewise represented. (*LM*, 1.6.12)

Augustine discerns signs of the Trinity throughout the fabric of creation. An analogy he uses in the *Confessions*—"being, knowing, and willing" (*CON*, XIII.xi.12)—becomes the basis for a much more extensive exposition in *On the Trinity*. The lover, the beloved, and the love (*DT*, 8.10.14), mind, knowledge, and the mind's love (*DT*, 9.12.18), memory, understanding, and will (*DT*, 10.11.17–18), object, sense, and perception (*DT*, 11.2.2), are all for Augustine signs of the trinitarian life of God pervasive of the whole created order. These are however analogies not obviously related to the persons of the Trinity. But elsewhere he outlines how the persons of the Trinity are present to creation, and of particular importance is his understanding of the Word.

> For the Word of God, true God in the bosom of God and the only son of God, is co-eternal with the Father; and yet through this utterance of God in the eternal Word, creation has been brought about in time. It is true that the words "when" and "sometime" refer to time, but the when of something that must be created is eternal in the Word of God; and it is created when in the Word there is exigency for its creation. But in the Word Himself there is no when and no eventually, because the Word is in every way eternal. (*LM*, 1.2.6)

This encapsulates much that Augustine will say in many other places about creation being in the Word (*LM*, 1.1.2; 1.4.9; 1.5.9; 1.5.10; 5.12.29; 5.15.33). All things have their exemplars eternally in the Word (*LM*, 1.4.9) and it really is more appropriate to think of things existing in the Word than of the Word being found in things beyond itself. It is this being in the Word which establishes the unity of all creation, binding all things together despite their many differences. In a meditation on John 1 Augustine writes,

> there is but one Word of God, *through which all things were made* (Jn. 1:1–6), which is unchanging truth, in which all things are primordially and unchangingly together . . . and all things there are life and all are one, and indeed there is but one "one" and one life (*DT*, 4.1.3).

The Holy Spirit also is active in Augustine's creation. He writes at length in *Confessions* XIII about the role of the Holy Spirit—borne above the waters, diffusing love and drawing us in love upwards to freedom in God, and similar activity is described in *LM*, 1.5 where he writes of "the Spirit forming . . . so that each would be established . . . in the good will and benevolence of God" (*LM*, 1.5.11). Even the seven-day ordering of the creation story is a sign of the perfection of the Holy Spirit (*LM*, 5.5.15).

Nevertheless, Colin Gunton has some grave misgivings. Although Augustine is deeply committed to the Word of God, the second person of the Trinity, being the creator and sustainer of all that is Gunton's concern is that this is entirely a Christology of the eternal son, quite devoid of any incarnational reference. "What is manifest and critical is Augustine's appeal only to the eternal Son; unlike Irenaeus he shows no interest in the relation between the Son's becoming material and the status of the material world."[31] Gunton sees this neglect as indicative of a persistent Neoplatonic influence, "a distrust of the material world,"[32] which in his view vitiates much of Augustine's work on the relationship between God and creation. The supposed simultaneous creation of all things in the eternity of the Word[33] indicates for Gunton an inability to "interpret the text in the light of the economy, by which I mean generally God's actions taking place in time according to the biblical account . . . divine action becomes abstract and essentially at variance with the spacious movement of the author of Genesis."[34]

He also identifies Augustine's distinctions drawn between formless matter and spiritual beings as further signs of Neoplatonist, even Manichaean, hierarchies of being and distaste for the material, and the alleged absence of incarnational Christology as leading to an arbitrary voluntarism in God's act of creation. Lost he claims, "is the Christological orientation to the love of God in creating, so that it is sometimes difficult to understand why this God should want to create."[35] There is some mitigation of this. Augustine himself had written,

> I read there (in the Platonic books) that the Word, God, is "born not of the flesh, nor of blood, nor of the will of man, nor of the will of the flesh, but of God." But that "the Word was made flesh and dwelt among us" (John 1:13-4), I did not read there . . . That "he took on himself the form of a servant . . . being made obedient unto death, even the death of the Cross so that God exalted him from the dead" . . . that, these books do not have. (*CON*, VII.ix.14)

---

31. Gunton, *Triune Creator*, 75.
32. Gunton, *Triune Creator*, 74.
33. See e.g., Augustine, *CON*, XI.vii.9; and *LM*, 1.2.6.
34. Gunton, *Triune Creator*, 76.
35. Gunton, *Triune Creator*, 76.

The Neoplatonists did not value faith as the beginning of knowledge. Neither to Augustine's mind did they value the humility that he had come to see as necessary in the face of his own struggles, nor the humility that he had found expressed in the incarnation of the Word come seeking us in love (*CON*, VII.xx.26). Nevertheless the point is made that Augustine appears to pay less attention, than, for example, Irenaeus, to the materiality of the incarnation for a more comprehensive understanding of how God actually does encounter and act within creation. Carol Harrison, without reference to Gunton or his conclusions, also observes, "it is significant that Augustine did not write a work specifically on the incarnation or Christology."[36] Her ensuing review of Augustine's writing about the incarnation reveals it to be almost entirely concerned with the redemption of sinful humanity.

But neither the incarnation nor the redemption it achieved are regarded by Augustine as any kind of afterthought or "plan B." They are prefigured in the very fabric of creation. So it is that Christ's one death which provides salvation from our two deaths, and his one resurrection which bestows two resurrections upon us (*DT*, 4.1.6), enables Augustine to embark upon an extended study of relationship between the numbers 1, 2, and 6—the perfect number, and to find these numbers and their proportions everywhere built into creation, history, and the life and ministry of Christ himself (*DT*, 4.2.7–10). Creation thus becomes a "sacrament, and . . . all the sacred and mysterious things that were shown to our fathers . . . were likenesses of him, so that all creation might in some fashion utter the one who was to come and be the savior of all" (*DT*, 4.2.11). In addition, *Literal Meaning* 1.7–8 is a reflection upon the love of God operative through the Spirit in both the making and the sustaining of creation.[37] Taylor quotes another passage making the point that "love is greater than knowledge,"[38] and by implication criticizing the austere rationality of the Neoplatonic conception of the Word. Furthermore, as we will see below in relation to Augustine's response to idolatry, the beauty of Christ incarnate is central for Augustine in that it allows human beings to love and worship something in the created order without engaging in idolatry.[39]

---

36. Harrison, *Augustine*, 30.
37. Augustine, *LM*, 26–27.
38. Augustine, *LM*, 227; see note 31.
39. Harrison, "Taking Creation for the Creator," 179–97.

Rowan Williams rejects any suggestion that Augustine's reflections on matter and form are indicative of residual Manichaean dualism. The process of "formation" is not to be seen as

> some "spiritual" force struggling with the world of concrete stuff ... the action of form on matter is not the imposition of one thing on another, let alone one system on another: it is simply the process of actualization itself, the process by which organization appears.[40]

In exploring this process of formation, Williams engages with Augustine's ideas derived from *Wisdom* 11.21, "Thou has ordered all things in measure and number and weight."[41] He used them first in *A Commentary on Genesis: Against the Manichees*,[42] where he writes of the qualities he has contemplated in the bodies of animals, and in *LM*, 4.3.7 he explores the question whether these processes of creation—"measure, number, and weight" existed before creation and God is thus in some sense subject to them, or are they in some way to be identified with God?

> How can God be identified with measure, number, and weight? ... He is surely not identified with things as we know them in creatures ... but ... God is identified with these three in a fundamental, true, and unique sense. He limits everything, forms everything, and orders everything. Hence ... we must understand that the words mean ... "Thou hast ordered all things in Thyself." (*LM*, 4.3.7)

Taylor summarizes Augustine's thought,

> Augustine sees a profound spiritual and theological meaning in *Wisdom* 11.21 ... All creatures, spiritual and material, have measure, number, and weight (4.4.8–10). Every creature has a limit (*mensura*) to its nature, for as a creature it is distinct from its Creator precisely because it is not all-perfect and necessary being but is rather contingent and finite. Secondly, every creature has a specific form or perfection (*numerus*), imitating the eternal form or perfection in the Word of God, through whom it has been made. Finally, the perfection of each creature is established (by its *pondus*) in a state of stability or rest in God, who draws back to Himself whatever He has made ... These

---

40. Williams, "'Good for Nothing'?" 17.
41. Augustine, *LM*, 248, note 8.
42. Williams, "'Good for Nothing'?" 12.

three things are in God even before He creates, for "He limits everything, forms everything, and orders everything" (*LM*, 4.3.7). These three things in creatures are an image of the perfection of the Trinity.[43]

Measure, number, and weight are the processes by which the Word orders creation and the Spirit draws things to their proper place. This dynamic understanding of the action of God is important for Augustine in two respects.

Firstly, it engages with the notion of "turning" or "conversion" which Augustine draws upon frequently. So,

> The Word recalls His imperfect creature to Himself, so that it may not be formless but may be formed according to the various works of creation which He produces in due order. In this conversion and formation the creature in its own way imitates the Divine Word, the Son of God . . . But it does not imitate this exemplar in the Word if it is turned away from its creator and remains formless and imperfect. (*LM*, 1.4.9)[44]

By this dynamic of "turning" Augustine was able to conceive a non-dualistic conception of the goodness of creation, which incorporated all that was and allowed for both corruption and growth. Evil was no longer the sign of a Manichaean dualism but of "a turning away into separateness . . . a losing contact with something bigger and more vital than itself."[45] Evil is thus an orientation or turning away from the creature's exemplar in the Word and from the recognition of radical dependence upon God, but it cannot be conceived as a "substance," something created.

> I saw . . . that you made all things good, and there are absolutely no substances which you did not make. As you did not make all things equal, all things are good in the sense that taken individually they are good, and all things taken together are very good. For our God has made "all things very good" (Gen. 1:31). (*CON*, VII.xii.18)

Thus the goodness of creation is its capacity to respond, to turn, and be formed in accord with the purposes of God.

Secondly, the idea of 'measure, number, and weight' introduces a dynamic quality into all the operations of the universe. To be a created

43. Taylor in Augustine, *LM*, 248, note 8.
44. See similarly Augustine, *LM*, 1.5.10, 24.
45. Brown, *Augustine*, 91.

being is to be subject to change (*CON*, XI.iv.6), but this is not a sign of failure or imperfection. It is rather a sign that the Word and Spirit of God are present in creation, drawing all things in love toward their appropriate perfection in God.

> Measure and proportion govern the reality of things that are made to change, and "weight" is what pulls them to their proper place . . . the world is so ordered that at any point in time the balance of things or agencies is being adjusted towards equilibrium: as individual things develop and their relation to other things consequently alters, *pondus* continually guarantees an overall balance, so that there is not, in the natural order, a chaos of conflictual agencies.[46]

Rather, there is integration of the whole. The meditation in *Confessions* VII.xii.18 reflects on those things in creation that taken in isolation we might be tempted to think of as evil due to "a conflict of interest." But upon the earth itself they have a congruence that is good, and their functioning together represents a goodness that would be lost if any of them were to be removed for his convenience. "I no longer wished individual things to be better, because I considered the totality . . . that all things taken together are better than superior things by themselves" (*CON*, VII.xiii.19). The observation is remarkably similar to that in which Athanasius finds a unity in the harmonies of creation which is the antithesis of the pagan conception in which each of the divinities is in conflict.[47] Thus Williams argues that *pondus* involves "a purposive totality, rather than just an ensemble of specific orderly processes."[48]

Human beings are as much subject to the possibilities and limits of this process as everything else. Measure, number, and weight also operate in the realm of the soul, mind, and spirit with regard to activities, the quest for wisdom, and the orientation of the will to love. "There is a Weight without weight, to which are drawn those beings whose repose is joy undefiled, and there they find their rest" (*LM*, 4.4.8). In *Confessions*, reflecting upon himself as a human creature drawn by the love of the Holy Spirit he writes, "my weight is my love. Wherever I am carried, my love is carrying me" (*CON*, XIII.ix.10). Weight for Augustine is love, and

46. Williams, "'Good for Nothing'?" 14.

47. See Athanasius, *AP*, 37; also Augustine, *CG*, xix.17, where Augustine describes the multiplicity of pagan gods, each with their own sphere of influence, "who must be induced to take an interest in human affairs" (946).

48. Williams, "'Good for Nothing'?" 15.

this love is the way of the Word in drawing all creatures to their stability, their rest, in God. This love involves a quite different kind of dualism; that is, a real difference between the lover and the beloved—a difference that is lacking in all ideas of emanationism. Augustine's doctrine of creation *ex nihilo* does not conceive of God "domineering" in any sense of forcing the divine will upon some already eternally existing "other." Rather, God brings that "other" to be from nothingness, in order that in loving relationship with God it may flourish.

ON THE CREATION

For Augustine, all creation is inextricably tied up with its creator. The Father creates and continually sustains through the Word—the Son, and the Spirit broods over all things, drawing them in love towards God. In this dependence is creation's goodness, and in this goodness its capacity to be responsive to the divine purpose. This is a dynamic quality of goodness whereby we should expect change rather than regret it.

In light of these affirmations of the creator's vital and continuous engagement, we come now to explore aspects of Augustine's thinking about the creation, particularly those elements most immediately relevant to this study of the place, role, and impact of human beings within the created order.

The Heavens and the Earth

Having established the priority of a literal reading of the text—a reading that asserts the significance of the material creation in the purposes of God, Augustine engages with the passage, "In the beginning God created heaven and earth (Gen. 1:1)" (*LM*, 1.1.2). Although exploring numerous different angles on the subject he suggests we are reading here of spiritual or rational or intellectual beings which are the angels. He is at pains to avoid having the eternal God being subjected to the changes inherent in time, and so proposes that "the heavens" are spiritual beings who can contemplate the eternal forms of things as they exist eternally in the Word and then be God's means for "speaking" these things into existence. Thus God creates the heavens and the earth in the Beginning—which is Christ the Word, and broods over them by the Holy Spirit, but does not speak until saying "Let there be light" (Gen 1:3). Then,

> If He spoke in time, He did not speak by His eternal word but by a creature subject to time; and so light could not be the first creature, because there already existed a creature by which He said in time, *Let there be light.* Thus we must suppose that before the beginning of days, He wrought the work referred to in the words, *In the beginning God created heaven and earth.* And then by the expression "heaven" we must understand a spiritual created work already formed and perfected, which is, as it were, the heaven of this heaven which is the loftiest in this material world. (*LM*, 1.9.15)[49]

These beings appear repeatedly in Augustine's cosmology in the first nine chapters of book 1, then again repeatedly in book 4.

> The holy angels . . . always behold the face of God and rejoice in His Word, the only-begotten Son, equal to the Father; and in them first of all wisdom was created. They, therefore, without doubt know all creation, of which they are the creatures first made, and they have this knowledge of the Word of God Himself, in whom are the eternal reasons of all things made in time, existing in Him through whom all things have been created. And then they have this knowledge in creation itself, as they look down upon it and refer it to the praise of Him in whose immutable truth they behold, as in the source of all creation, the reasons by which creatures have been made. (*LM*, 4.24.41)

Referring creation to praise seems sometimes to mean offering praise for what the angels have contemplated in the Word and in things themselves, and other times to mean providing the rational consciousness and voice for praise that inferior creatures do not have in themselves. Since nothing in all creation has existence apart from the Creator, true existence, fullness of life, always consists in turning or being referred towards the Creator in loving recognition of this gift of existence. This loving recognition is the life of praise. To promote this realization is one role of the angels. Thus there is an intimate relationship between the angels and the creatures which they are said to know and over which they have influence. Of profound significance in the debate whether Christian theology has desacralized the world, we find this description of the role of angels,

---

49. See also Augustine, *CG*, xi.9, but here Augustine vacillates between either the heaven or the ensuing light as being a reference to the creation of the angels, 459–60.

> every corporeal being, every irrational life, every weak or wayward will is subjected to the heavenly angels ... and the angel's purpose is to accomplish in or with these subject creatures what the order of nature demands in all according to the decree of Him to whom all are subject ... moving themselves through time and moving bodies through time and space in accordance with what is proper to their activity. (*LM*, 8.24.45)

The angels are present to, and active upon, every created being—the corporeal and irrational as much as the higher creatures. This activity is neither arbitrary nor irrational, but orderly and integrative because it is all in accordance with the divine decree. A similar conception is found repeatedly in *The Trinity* where the angels are described as exercising a sovereignty in creation until such time as the now hidden Christ hands over the kingdom to God the Father (*DT*, 1.3.16), or where "the power of God's will ... extended to producing through created spiritual agents sensible and perceptible effects in the material creation'" (*DT*, 3.1.6). Augustine is not naive in discussing angels and recognizes that secular science may not discern their work because science, while accurate as far as it goes, only deals in "proximate and secondary causes" (*DT*, 3.1.7). He suggests that God uses angels in creation in the manner of a man using other human helpers, animals and even inanimate objects in pursuit of his will (*DT*, 3.1.9). Furthermore, in *Christian Doctrine* he argues that the command to love our neighbors extends to loving the angels as our neighbors, "who perform so many acts of compassion on our behalf" (*DC*, 1.71). In *City of God*, while arguing forcibly that they are not to be worshipped—indeed faithful angels would abhor our worship but rather will point us to the worship of God (*CG*, x.7)—Augustine nevertheless recognizes angels as "powers whom we venerate and love as our most blessed fellow citizens during this our mortal pilgrimage" (*CG*, xix.23). Augustine's world is everywhere inhabited by angels. They are present to all things, not merely as an intellectual idea but as spiritual beings we may venerate and love for their service in creation and their encouragement of us. They are a living reminder that human beings do not in fact stand at the top of a ladder of power in the order of creation. They are not the divinities of pagan animism but they may perhaps be identified with "guardian spirits." Their presence is yet another sign that Augustine's world has not been at all desacralized but rather they make it living and personal. If anything, it is more spiritually charged than the world of pagan conception but it is also one to which we may draw nearer with love.

Augustine knows the pagan divinization of the world, whose loss White and others bemoan as the beginning of our environmental troubles. Perhaps he knows it better than they do. He recognizes connections to be made with pagan ideas—"certain philosophers have assigned to each element its own living beings . . . those of the air are demons . . . those of the heavens are gods (and of these last we say that some are the lights of heaven and others are angels)" (*LM*, 3.9.13),[50] but corrections also; In book vii, 19–26 of *City of God* he exposes the violence, cruelties, inner contradictions, and immoralities of this divinized world, "in order to secure the growth of seed and to repel enchantment from the fields: a matron was compelled to do in public what even a prostitute would not have been allowed to do in the theatres" (*CG*, vii.21). Later still he compares the honorable biblical stories of angels engaging visibly with human beings to the many stories of the "gods of woodland and fields commonly called *incubi* who have often behaved disgracefully towards women" (*CG*, xv.23). In *Christian Doctrine* book 2, he reflects on the many practices by which people hope to control their lives or mollify the many spirits which they believe surround them, "it amounts to selling uneducated people into a wretched form of slavery. When free people go to see such an astrologer, they pay money for the privilege of coming away as slaves to Mars or Venus, or rather all the stars" (*DC*, 2.78–79).

The divinization of the pagan world was not all sweetness, and as one reads Augustine's account of the poems, myths, stories and practices it is easy to imagine people ready to welcome some good news of liberation.

Nevertheless, despite the ubiquitous presence and active role of the angels in Augustine's world they remain completely unmentioned in White's critique. Rather, White suggests that cults of the saints are a pallid and misguided attempt to reestablish some sense of holiness in the world.[51] In fact the saints were not necessary for this as angels were still present for that task. The role of the saints was to set before Christian people models of holy living—which frequently involved living peaceably with other creatures, or inspiration in the face of the possibility of martyrdom. By ignoring the centrality of angels White has significantly misrepresented the spiritual fullness and integration of this vision of the world.

---

50. See also Augustine, *CG*, 931 (xix.9).
51. White, "Historical Roots," 1203–7.

Human Beings Made in the Image and Likeness of God to Have Dominion

When in *Literal Meaning* book 3.19 Augustine comes to the central and controversial passage concerning humanity made in the image of God, his initial concern is only to clarify how the whole Godhead—Father, Son, and Holy Spirit, is involved. Nothing else is said of the *imago* until he comes to discuss the nature of the associated dominion. "From this we are to understand that man was made to the image of God in that part of his nature wherein he surpasses the brute beasts. This is, of course, his reason or mind or intelligence, or whatever we wish to call it" (*LM*, 3.20.30).

This is virtually all that he has to say about dominion. Throughout *The Literal Meaning* and in *The Trinity*, he shows no interest in developing separate ideas, but appears content to include it within his discussions of the *imago*. Thus he continues with a reference which conflates Ephesians 4:23–24 and Colossians 3:10, about putting on the new man who is being renewed unto the knowledge of God, according to the image of his creator, "by these words he [i.e., Saint Paul] shows wherein man has been created to the image of God, since it is not by any features of the body but by a perfection of the intelligible order, that is, of the mind when illuminated" (*LM*, 3.20.30).

In a complex discussion of masculine and feminine characteristics within one person, he goes on to clarify that "the image of God is found in that part which is devoted to the contemplation of immutable truth" (*LM*, 3.22.23). The critical significance of these sections is that there is nothing at all about control over either animals or the inanimate world. Indeed, in this last section (*LM*, 3.22.34), Augustine separates the capacity for contemplation from that for administration and action, and he identifies the former as being the image of God. This is a dynamic capacity. The *imago* does not consist in some discrete, autonomous, concrete possession. Rather, one is formed to the image of God, as one turns and is illuminated (*LM*, 3.20.30).[52] Similarly, in *City of God* book xi he explains that man is made in the image of God, yet this image consists not in any autonomous possession but in a potentiality to be drawn nearer to God by the hearing of God's Word. This capacity is powerless in itself and "needs to be renewed from day to day, and healed, and made capable . . .

---

52. See also Augustine, *LM*, 1.4.9 and 1.5.10, on "turning" and "conversion" in an intellectual creature.

and so it had first to be imbued with faith" (*CG*, xi.2). This must be mediated by Christ and only as we are in Christ is the image of God formed in us. In 26–27 Augustine observes that we are made to the image of the Trinity, but this is in closeness not in possession of some autonomous, concrete capacity and thus this image "still requires to be reformed and perfected to be a still closer likeness" (*CG*, xi.26). All this reflects aspects of our earlier discussion concerning *pondus*, love and desire. Williams, relating this to *The Trinity*, writes,

> this perspective introduces something quite fresh into theological discussion of the image of God in the human subject, which is no longer to be identified with a single feature or cluster of features, but with the orientation of the subject to God, with the radically *unfinished* character of thinking and wanting.[53]

This identification of orientation and openness as integral to Augustine's understanding of image and dominion raises questions about emphases in the history of interpretation. Ruth Page, for example, asserts that "Augustine fathered a tradition of finding the image of God in human reason. That set the pattern of believing in a divinely ordained gulf between humans and 'unreasoning beasts.'"[54] Certainly Augustine identified "reason" with the image of God, which is given extended treatment at *LM*, 6.12.20–22, but this is always to do with orientation rather than possession. Whether Augustine himself conceived of "a divinely ordained gulf" is, I believe, open to question. He argues that

> if man does not understand this honor and live a good life in accordance with it, he will be on a level with the beasts over which he has been placed. For Scripture says, *Man, for all his dignity has not understood; he has been joined with senseless beasts and become like them* (Ps 48:13). (*LM*, 6.12.21)

In section 22, immediately following, he argues that the beasts too were created by the Word and Wisdom of God from the earth in exactly the same manner as was man, and he uses this fact in rejection of arguments that would separate humanity from animals (*LM*, 6.12.22).[55] Adam had a natural body—from the earth like that of animals—which was able to die. This natural mortality is evidenced in the necessity of the divine

---

53. Williams, "'Good for Nothing'?" 15.
54. Page, "Fellowship of All Creation," 102.
55. See also Van Bavel, "Integrity of Creation," 12.

provision of food and in the provision for procreation, and was Adam's condition even before his sin. There was however potential immortality in that he was able not to die. "This immortality was given to him from the tree of life not from his nature. When he sinned he was separated from this tree, with the result that he was able to die" (*LM*, 6.12.22).

This sense of differences between humans and animals within a larger realm of similarity reappears in *City of God*, following the sections we have already noted on the *imago* as a potential for formation into the likeness of Christ. Book xi, 27 observes that the passion for existence which reflects this image is something which humans share with all other animals. The difference between humans and animals lies in the human consciousness of it, which issues in human beings in a passion "for knowledge, which is found in no mortal creatures apart from man" (*CG*, xi.27), and in an ability to make judgments concerning justice and truth.

In book xii.4 Augustine re-visits the idea of a greater beauty in the interrelatedness of all things, even the dependence for life of some things upon others. But we human beings

> take no delight in the beauty of this order, because, being ourselves only parts of it, woven into it by virtue of our mortal condition, we cannot perceive that those particular aspects which offend us are blended aptly and fittingly enough into the whole. This is why, in those circumstances where we are less able to perceive it for ourselves, we are most rightly instructed to have faith in the Creator's providence. (*CG*, xii.4)

This interdependence is not an unnatural result of the fall, but is rather an expression of the "measure, number, and weight" by which God establishes and upholds creation (*LM*, 3.16.25). It applies even in the case of human remains which have been eaten by animals (*LM*, 3.17.26)! Bodily decay is discussed during a reflection on the nature of peace, and this process too he regards as part of the Creator's peaceful and integrative ordering of the universe.

> Even when the flesh of dead animals is devoured by other animals, it still finds itself subject to the same laws: to the laws which are distributed throughout the universe for the preservation of every kind of mortal creature, and which give peace by bringing suitable things suitably together. This is true no matter where it is taken, no matter with what substances it is joined, and no matter what substances it is converted and changed into. (*CG*, xix.12)

Whatever the nature of their reason, human beings are inextricably bound to the rest of creation in being subject to such natural processes.

Subsequently Augustine describes humanity as "the greatest adornment of things earthly, to whom the Creator has given certain good things appropriate to this life" (*CG*, xix.13). The list of goods then enumerated is entirely about provision and nothing at all about the right to dominate or control. Indeed tyrants, bandits and domestic bullies pursue unjust peace by prideful domination (*CG*, xix.12) and are rejected, for "he who uses temporal goods ill, however, shall lose them, and shall not receive eternal goods either" (*CG*, xix.13).

If there is an element of control, mastery, or domination to be found in Augustine's treatment of humanity in the image of God, it has to do with control of one's self. Peter Harrison critiques White's account of the impact of Genesis 1 on the grounds that in the patristic and mediaeval periods "allegorical and 'moral' readings . . . were commonplace . . . the 'beasts' that were to be mastered were nothing other than fractious human passions that had become wild and uncontrollable as a result of the Fall."[56] He references Origen—at length—John Chrysostom, and Augustine (without identifying the source). Augustine himself, in his highly allegorized *Confessions* xiii, writes,

> restrain yourselves from the savage cruelty of arrogance, from the indolent pleasure of self-indulgence, and from "knowledge falsely so called" (1 Tim. 6:20). Then the wild animals are quiet and the beasts are tamed and the serpents are rendered harmless: in allegory they signify the affections of the soul. (*CON*, , XIII.xxi.30)

Harrison further observes that ascetic disciplines were not "completely internalized, for it was also believed that a sign of self-mastery was the capacity to exercise control over wild beasts."[57] Augustine himself makes such an association when, writing literally now, he refers to Daniel's encounter with the lions and St Paul's encounter with the viper (*LM*, 3.15.24). In both cases it is to be noted that the mastery was in the establishment of peaceable relations. In *CG*, xix.15 he quotes Genesis 1:26 then continues,

> He [i.e., God] did not intend that His rational creature, made in His own image, should have lordship over any but irrational

---

56. Harrison, "Having Dominion," 19.
57. Harrison, "Having Dominion," 20.

> creatures: not man over man, but man over beasts. Hence the first just men were established as shepherds of flocks, rather than as kings of men. This was done so that in this way also God might indicate what the order of nature requires. (*CG*, xix.15)

In contrast to its implications for human sociality this would appear to justify domination over animals. However, in the preceding section 14, he has explained that this order of nature includes peace for animals, "which consists in an harmonious relation of soul and body" (*CG*, xix.14), achieved by the adequate satisfaction of their bodily appetites. To ensure this is the responsibility of those with animals in their power, for rule properly exercised is about love and care and "in the household of the just man . . . even those who command are the servants of those whom they seem to command" (*CG*, xix.14). That rule is about service is reiterated in his *Rule for a Monastery* (7.3).[58] There is nothing here of domineering or destructive rule over either people or animals. Their wellbeing is a necessary element in the harmony of creation. If anything, the human dominion is in order to take responsibility for the wellbeing of the animals.

In summary, Augustine recognizes that humans are made to the image of God which he calls reason. But this reason includes the operations of love and is not an autonomous, concrete possession. It is rather a potentiality that is only formed as by faith we are turned towards the Word (the only true Reason) and are made into the likeness of Christ. None of this has anything to do with either domination over the rest of creation or of separation from it. Human beings are animals with some particular possibilities which may only be properly pursued as we recognize our place in the interconnectedness of all created being—an interconnectedness that is established and upheld in the Word of God. Human reason is given not to set humanity apart from creation but rather to integrate us into creation, with a role of care for the rest of the creation. Human beings should rule as shepherds and as servants but mastery is to be exercised primarily over themselves. Should they turn away from their divine calling humans can become like the animals, although there is a sense in which this is unfair to the animals because such fallen humanity will lack both the innocence and the instincts that are proper to animals. Even if a case could be sustained for a divinely ordained gulf between humans and animals, this in no way diminishes Augustine's conception of an

---

58. Lawless, *Augustine of Hippo*, 101.

integrated creation in which every part is necessary, has its own unique life before God, and participates with the whole in creation's hymn of praise.

Of Adam in the Garden

It was God's breathing upon the man in the garden that made him a living soul (Genesis 2:7). Although called the breath of God, this soul must not be conceived as something of God's own life. It is not the Holy Spirit. Souls can change for good or ill; God cannot (*LM*, 7.2.3). All this is argued at some length, both to ensure that creation *ex nihilo* is maintained and to reject Platonic and Manichaean ideas about the transmigration of souls between humans and animals. Animals have their natures and these cannot be lost to them (*LM*, 7.10.14–15).

In *LM*, book 8 Augustine considers Adam placed in the garden to cultivate and guard it. Cultivation is clearly not a punishment for there is as yet no sin. Indeed, there are those who find such joy in cultivation that it is punishment for them to be deprived of it (*LM*, 8.8.15)! But this is another example of the harmony with which God has established all things.

> Where is human reason better able to speak, as it were, to nature than when man sows the seed, plants a tree, transplants a bush, grafts a mallet-shoot, and thus asks, as it were, each root and seed what it can or cannot do, why it can or cannot do it, what is the extent of the intrinsic and invisible power of numbers within it, and what can be attributed to the extrinsic factors applied by human effort? (*LM*, 8.8.16)

Quoting from 1 Corinthians 3:7, he notes that nature's capacities and those of human beings are both enabled by the work of God, and it is the achievement of this understanding that is the true end of all such engagement with creation. This sense of conversational partnership leads to a discussion of natural and voluntary providence—which includes the human capacity for intelligent work. Van Bavel writes,

> human effort helps God in developing creation, because through our labor God's gifts come forth from the earth in a more abundant and productive way. The human mind lifts up its gaze from agriculture to the whole world like a great tree of many realities (see *LM*, 8.9.17).[59]

---

59. Van Bavel, "Integrity of Creation," 11.

He continues,

> it is on the basis of the cultivation of the earth that Augustine builds his vision of the world: a philosophy of nature (the intrinsic natural movement of things), a gnoseology (the human person knows itself by understanding the world), a political doctrine (the ordering of society), and aesthetics (the practice of art and trade).[60]

Carol Harrison observes that all these activities are envisaged as part of life before the fall. Indeed, Augustine suggests that the work of gardening is as important as nurture of the soul, "what negligence is in cultivating a tree, that unconcern about healing is in respect of the body, and indifference about learning is in relation to the soul" (*LM*, 8.9.18). This is an integrated, holistic vision of the place of humanity in the world. Thus, Harrison argues, Augustine has enlarged upon the classical ideal of *otium*.

> The idea of philosophical *otium*, of withdrawing from the world in order to pursue a life devoted to wisdom, or of a cultured sabbatical in the middle of one's career . . . was a common one . . . Augustine's actual example, however—of gardening, rather than the more well-known and widely accepted one of life devoted to wisdom—might well suggest an implicit criticism of the classical ideal, or at least a desire to broaden it out.[61]

She also appeals to Augustine's ideas about voluntary providence which we have already noted. Augustine himself writes,

> man was placed in paradise with the understanding that he would till the land not in servile labor but with spiritual pleasure befitting his dignity. What is more innocent than this work for those who are at leisure, and what more provocative of profound reflection for those who are wise? (*LM*, 8.9.18)

Thus the life of gardening is understood as a contemplative activity directed towards a deeper appreciation of both the life and presence of God, and the life of nature.

As cultivation was not a punishment for sin, so the guarding could not have been against external enemies. Rather, "he was placed there to guard this same Paradise for himself, so as not to commit any deed

---

60. Van Bavel, "Integrity of Creation," 11–12.
61. Harrison, "Augustine and Gardening," 16.

by which he would deserve to be expelled from it" (*LM*, 8.10.22). This guarding of themselves is of course what the human beings failed to do, and all the disastrous impacts of the fall are the result. Misdirected desire is central to Augustine's conception of fallenness and Harrison and Van Bavel both address this in relation to Augustine's distinction between *frui* and *uti* (enjoyment and use), in our use of the things of the earth.

> The Fathers . . . never considered created realities in a merely functional way, or according to their utility and practical value alone. Augustine's distinction between *frui* and *uti* (God alone is to be enjoyed, created realities are to be used) is not to be interpreted in this sense. *Uti* . . . does not exclude love for created things, and is certainly no denial of their intrinsic importance and value. The Augustinian use of *uti* means that our love should not be attached to created things as the ultimate goal of human life, but that we have to love them in relation to the Creator Himself.[62]

It is this struggle to love the creation in the appropriate way that generates our deep ambivalence about work. Harrison explores a distinction between "free work" and "enforced work."

> Augustine suggests that real work, true work, ideal work, is that in which man freely engages because he loves it, for the delight and . . . the "spiritual pleasure" it affords, and which leads him to engagement with the nature of reality. This is "free work" and is the ideal, natural state of humankind. Work undertaken purely out of necessity, "enforced work," is alien to human existence and a mark of its fallenness.[63]

Augustine still regards "free work" as a possibility (*LM*, 8.8.15; 8.9.18), but it is one constantly vitiated by the impacts of the fall. Even "enforced work" can however take on the character of "free work" as one orientates it towards God, learns to see the ordering of the Word in creation in what one works with, and as it is done in love. Harrison quotes Arbresmann,

> "The labours of those who love are never tiresome, but they are even a source of pleasure . . . It all depends on what one loves, for there is either no weariness in work that is loved, or the weariness itself is loved" . . . this is a reminder that, for Augustine, it

---

62. Van Bavel, "Integrity of Creation," 9–10. See also Harrison, *Augustine*, 63–64, 98–100; and Zumkeller, *Religious Life*, 211.

63. Harrison, "Augustine and Gardening," 15–16.

is in love, above all, that God's redemptive grace makes itself felt and makes possible the free action of man's fallen will, even in contexts which might otherwise be regarded as necessitated by the Fall.[64]

For Augustine, it was within the monastic community that one could most deliberately and with mutual support attempt to practice the life of love. This was the Christian version of the classical *otium*, and here one might find again something of the "rest" that had originally been God's intention for us all. "Only in subjecting themselves to God, and in acknowledging their complete dependence on him, can men and women enjoy 'rest' and therefore the freedom to engage in true work, the freely chosen, pleasurable activity of Adam the gardener."[65]

White suggested that illustrations in early medieval calendars depicted a new attitude of domination over nature.[66] It might just as well be said, in light of the Augustinian vision, that what was envisaged was a partnership, a conversation with nature and a relocation of human beings within nature—neither to abject enslavement (for the peasants) nor indifferent disconnection (for the philosophical elite). The new Christian *otium* involves a contemplative conversation with nature but no domination.

Of Adam among the Animals

In *Literal Meaning* book 9 Augustine discusses the story of the formation of Eve, within which occurs the bringing of the animals to Adam. Despite the significance which White and others attach to "naming" it appears relatively insignificant to Augustine. Chapters 1 to 11 address a range of other issues and only at chapter 12 do the animals appear. In all three sub-sections Augustine asserts that there must be a figurative or prophetic significance in the event, although nowhere does he explain what it might be. But this parade was necessary, "that the man also should recognize his need and thereby receive his wife as a more precious gift because, in all flesh created under heaven ... he found nothing else like her" (*LM*, 9.12.21). He acknowledges that there is in man a power over animals both domestic and wild, by which he is able to shape their behavior

---

64. Harrison, "Augustine and Gardening," 21.
65. Harrison, "Augustine and Gardening," 33.
66. White, "Historical Roots," 1203–7.

to some degree (*LM*, 9.14.25). But this observation is made not to justify human domination but to support an argument that angels, who are also rational beings, have an even greater role in moving creatures in accordance with the will of God.

We have already considered the significance of angels for Augustine, in their oversight and moving of all that God has made and in their role of enabling and offering praise. But this task does not belong to them alone. In *Confessions* book V he writes,

> your entire creation never ceases to praise you and is never silent. Every spirit continually praises you with mouth turned towards you; animals and physical matter find a voice through those who contemplate them. So from weariness our soul rises towards you, first supporting itself on the created order and then passing on to you yourself who wonderfully made it. (*CON*, V.i.1)

Or, again, "your works praise you that we may love you, and we love you that your works may praise you" (*CON*, XIII.xxxiii.48). The conception of an unbridgeable gulf between humanity and animals is fundamentally called in question. The contemplation of animals and physical matter turns the human heart towards God, and it then becomes the task of those with the power of contemplation to give voice to the rest of creation in praise. Creation supports us in our turning to God. Our fulfillment is in speaking with, through and for creation. As the rational creature of Augustine's conception humanity has a unique role in giving rational voice to the praise that is offered irrationally by the rest of creation. By its contemplation of the Word in creation humanity is able to see all things together,[67] and recognize the rationality and the relationality that is in all. The relationship is one of interdependence.

Although this offering of praise with and on behalf of all creation can properly be conceived of as a priestly role, Augustine nowhere uses the language in relation to humanity. In *Christian Doctrine* priesthood is conceived entirely in terms of Christ as an offering to take away human sin,[68] and this is the focus of Zizioulas's critique of Augustine.[69] A priesthood so confined appears to exclude the animals, but they may not be in need of such a priestly ministry. Augustine does not regard animals

---

67. Southgate, "Stewardship and Its Competitors," 192.
68. Augustine, *DC*, 259.
69. Zizioulas, "Priest of Creation," 277.

as guilty of evil or sin because they lack the "rational" capacity to make the choices involved. Even the snake, so central in the first deception and temptation (Gen 3:1–5), bears no responsibility in Augustine's mind. The animal was used by the devil in the same way as a thinker uses a pen, or a speaker their tongue (*LM*, 11.29.36–37). Nevertheless animals may still share in the ultimate consummation. In a christological exposition of Psalm 8 (the passage most similar to Genesis 1), he detours into Psalm 36:6–10, observing that "men in conjunction with beasts are made whole together with these beasts, not by inward illumination, but by the . . . mercy of God, whereby His goodness reaches even to the lowest things."[70]

In *The Trinity* he identifies connections to be drawn between the death of Christ and our salvation to life, and appears to extend their significance to the whole creation.

> This match—or agreement or concord or consonance or whatever the right word is . . . is of enormous importance in every construction or interlock—that is the word I want—of creation. What I mean by this interlock, it has just occurred to me, is what the Greeks call *harmonia*. (*DT*, IV.1.4)

Hill notes that the primary meaning of *harmonia* is "not musical . . . but a joint, fastener, or clamp,"[71] (although Augustine himself goes on to develop the musical image). Thus not humanity only but all of creation are interlocked in receiving the benefits of Christ. Also, on the seventh day which has no end "the whole of creation, whatever its state, in spite of all changes it undergoes, will not cease to be, it will always remain in its Creator, and so after that morning there was no evening" (*LM*, 4.18.35). Thus, despite Zizioulas's concerns, there is here sufficient evidence to suggest that all living creatures not just the human soul, share in the benefits of Christ's priesthood and will ultimately share in the eternal glory.

Of Adam "Fallen"

The tragic and universal impact of human sinfulness is a theme that threads its way through all Augustine's work. At its core lies a human desire for autonomy from God. This quest for self-sufficiency arises from pride, which is

---

70. Augustine, *Expositions on the Psalms*, 30.
71. Hill in Augustine, *Trinity*, 177, note 13.

> an appetite for a perverse kind of elevation . . . to forsake the foundation upon which the mind should rest, and to become and remain, as it were, one's own foundation. This occurs when a man is too well pleased with himself; and he is too well pleased with himself when he falls away from that immutable good with which he ought rather to have been pleased than with himself . . . if the will had remained unshaken in its love of that higher and immutable Good by which is bestowed upon it the light by which it can see and the fire by which it can love, it would not have turned aside from this Good to follow its own pleasure. (*CG*, xiv.13)

Many of the effects of this fall are also its punishments. The will is corrupted and "a wrong action of the will is not, as for Kant, a choice which he can then undo, rather it is something which determines his whole being."[72] Thus, in relation to the focus of this study, the desire to express one's reasonable dominion will be constantly corrupted by the corrupted will. We are no longer able to "rule without pride" (*CON*, X.xxxvi.59). This is true even within our own persons.

> The soul . . . because it had of its own free will forsaken its superior Lord . . . no longer held its own inferior servant in obedience to its will. Nor could it in any way keep the flesh in subjection, as it would always have been able to do if it had itself remained subject to God. (*CG*, xiii.13)

As corrupted will also creates a corrupted reason, that grace which somehow distinguishes humanity from the animals is lost. "To be sure, man did not fall away from his nature so completely as to lose all being. When he turned towards himself, however, his being became less complete" (*CG*, xiv.13). This corruption of reason means we are no longer able to respond to the Word which is God's reason, and neither are we able to properly read the Word in creation. Hence Augustine's critique of the self-sufficient rationalism of the Neoplatonists, his recognition of the need for authority beyond ourselves if we are to begin the pursuit of truth, and his approach to biblical interpretation which, as Brown describes it, presupposes a deep fracture dislocating the whole human consciousness.[73] Furthermore, since reason for Augustine includes the capacity for love, with corrupted reason comes corrupted desire. By "measure, number, and weight," the capacity for desire is built into the

---

72. Harrison, *Augustine*, 92. See also *CON*, 140 (VIII.v.11).
73. Brown, *Augustine*, 257–58.

universe in order to direct and draw it towards a divine end. But if desire has become corrupted the focus and the practice of love are perverted, and it is in the misdirection and misappropriation of desire, frequently for consumerist ends, that William Cavanaugh finds many of the real roots of our ecological crisis.[74] Augustine also connects this corruption of desire with avarice and an elevation of the private self, which despite contemporary adulation of autonomy, he sees as leading to privation and thus being ultimately self-diminishing. "Where pride, then, seeks to excel, there it is cast down into want and destitution, turning from the pursuit of the common good to one's own individual good out of a destructive self-love" (*LM*, 11.15.19).

The pride in independence from God which issues in all these forms of corruption and loss is related by Harrison to Augustine's doctrine of creation *ex nihilo*. Without recognition of its absolute dependence creation itself too easily becomes the object of worship, and this is the truly serious nature of idolatry.

> If we were to summarize Augustine's attitude to idolatry, then, we would probably say that created things reveal God, but only to the one who can see them aright; in other words, to one who, in faith, sees them as wholly dependent on the creator who has drawn them from nothingness. The obverse of not seeing right is idolatry, whereby created things are taken as an end in themselves, instead of their creator, and thereby lead human beings to diminish themselves, by abandoning the source of their existence and moving back to the nothingness from which they were formed.[75]

The beauty of creation should function to point us beyond itself to the source of all beauty—and in that sense is sacramental, but our weakness now is such that frequently the beautiful thing becomes the end of our love. Nevertheless, the very tendency towards nothingness resulting from this idolatry is also the restlessness that Augustine regards as our hunger for the wholeness of God, and is thus a providential means for moving us beyond idolatry. Harrison suggests that the mutability of creation is, for Augustine, one of creation's pointers beyond itself.[76] A second has to do with eschatology—"just as we do not wish a piece of

---

74. Cavanaugh, *Being Consumed*.
75. Harrison, "Taking Creation for the Creator," 184.
76. Harrison, "Taking Creation for the Creator," 191.

music or poem to end in the middle of a bar or phrase, so we should look towards the fulfillment of history for its meaning and not remain stuck in the present."[77] Yet another is the way language functions to direct us beyond the sign to its meaning.[78] Most important however is the incarnation. On the one hand,

> begotten of God, not created, Christ was able to reveal the nature of divine form, or beauty to human beings, and yet by taking flesh, he did so in a manner which fallen humanity could grasp, so that, by inspiring faith, hope and love in himself, he was able to reform fallen humanity to the divine image . . . for if we love the human, temporal Christ, we are not, as would be the case with every other aspect of temporal reality, setting up an idol, but even in his human form we love no more and no less than divine beauty itself.[79]

But this is a different beauty, for the incarnation also involves ugliness and deformity—which are not likely to be idolized, as Christ is revealed as the crucified servant.

> It is precisely in his deformity that . . . [Christ] fully reveals his divine beauty and love, and inspires the faith, hope and love which will eventually work our reformation from the deformity of sin. Christ's deformity reforms our deformity, because whereas our deformity is the result of sin, his, like that of the righteous old person or disfigured martyr, is a revelation of his truth, goodness, beauty and love.[80]

Finally, the incarnation reveals important elements in Augustine's thinking about the relation between body and soul. Unlike either Manichaeism or Neoplatonism he does not locate the source of all this corruption in the material life of the flesh but rather in the soul. Harrison suggests that Augustine "rejects dualistic interpretations and is clear that sin is in reality due to the corruption of the soul, not the body."[81] Brown similarly observes that "Augustine was exceptionally careful to point out, in frequent, patient expositions of the letters of Paul, that *the flesh* was not simply the body: it was all that led the self to prefer its own will to

---

77. Harrison, "Taking Creation for the Creator," 191–92.
78. Harrison, "Taking Creation for the Creator," 192–93.
79. Harrison, "Taking Creation for the Creator," 193.
80. Harrison, "Taking Creation for the Creator," 196.
81. Harrison, *Augustine*, 92.

that of God."[82] Augustine himself states, "rebellion began in the soul . . . but the whole man committed the sin. It was then that the flesh became sinful flesh, whose faults could be healed only by the one who came in the likeness of sinful flesh."[83] Again, if any more reminders are needed, materiality is not for Augustine the source of our ills but an integral element of human being and a critically important means of God's self-revelation and engagement with us.

ON THE "RESTING" OF GOD—THE SABBATH

The creation account (Gen 1:1—2:3) concludes with God's resting and establishment of the Sabbath. The whole of *Literal Meaning* book 4 is devoted to exploring the significance of the seventh day—the day of God's resting. The famous aphorism, "you have made us for yourself, and our heart is restless until it rests in you," announces says Chadwick, "a major theme of Augustine's work,"[84] and four decades later, as Augustine approached the end of both *The City of God* and his own life, the vision remains central of

> the seventh day . . . our Sabbath, whose end will not be an evening . . . the eternal rest not only of the Spirit, but of the body also. There we shall rest and we shall see, see and love, love and praise. Behold what will be, in the end to which there shall be no end! (*CG*, xxii.30)

Chadwick and Taylor both suggest connections may be drawn between this vision of rest and that of Plotinus[85]—and indeed the whole Platonic/Neo-Platonic conception of the soul's emanation and return. Nevertheless there are also some critical differences.

> The fundamental difference between neo-Platonic and Christian mysticism is that in the former, the soul attains union with the One without any assistance from the One. Moreover, as Louth also observes, Plotinus' One cares nothing for the soul; there is no personal character to the contemplative and unitive

---

82. Brown, *Body and Society*, 418. See also Augustine, *LM*, 110–12 (10.12.20-21), and *CG*, 584–86 (xiv.3).

83. Augustine, "Against Julian," 77 (5.4.17).

84. Chadwick in Augustine, *CON*, 3, note 1.

85. Chadwick in Augustine, *CON*, 3, note 1, and Taylor in Augustine, *LM*, 249, note 9.

experience. In Christianity, on the other hand—and here Augustine breaks with his neo-Platonic roots—union with God is not ineluctable but comes about only because of God's gracious transformation of the soul.[86]

Thus Augustine's conception of the journey towards rest is radically different from a Neo-Platonic one in that it incorporates rather than abandons the body; it is enabled by grace and is made in the consciousness of love.

Resting in God is central to Augustine's vision of the relationship between creator and creation and functions at a number of different but interconnected levels.

Firstly, it provides the model for his eschatology. Augustine's creation, in keeping with the Genesis account, is not complete until the Sabbath is established. The whole purpose of creation is that all things might finally find fullness of existence resting in their creator. Then,

> we shall know that He is God: that He is what we ourselves desired to be when we fell away from Him and listened to the words of the tempter, "Ye shall be as gods," and so forsook God, who would have made us as gods, not by forsaking Him, but by participating in Him . . . But when we are restored by Him and perfected by His greater grace, we shall be still for all eternity, and know that He is God, being filled by Him when He shall be all in all. (*CG*, xxii.30)

The end or goal of time is likewise to be found in the timelessness of the creator of time. The significance of the seventh day having no end is that it points to the possibility of eternal rest, "since the whole of creation, whatever its state, in spite of all changes it undergoes, will not cease to be, it will always remain in its creator, and so after that morning there was no evening" (*LM*, 4.18.35). Brian Daley demonstrates the variety in Augustine's treatment of the seventh day. Sometimes he regards the world as grown old and senile but in its old age renewed by Christ; sometimes he adapts a Roman conception of history as a cosmic week concluded with a golden age; sometimes the days of creation are compared to the "ages" of human life, and sometimes to periods in biblical history. In some early works he identified the Sabbath with the millennial kingdom of Revelation 20, but later tended to prefer a realized eschatology in which the

---

86. LaCugna, *God for Us*, 92. See also Davidson, *Public Faith*, 164.

Sabbath is identified with the age of the church.[87] Nevertheless, in none of these does he conceive any notion of progress whereby each age succeeds its predecessor in an idealized journey of human improvement. But the Sabbath in the end will incorporate the whole created order, inclusive of a transformed materiality. "It is entirely credible," writes Augustine,

> that, in the world to come, we shall see the bodily forms of the new heaven and the new earth in such a way as to perceive God with total clarity and distinctness, everywhere present and governing all things, both material and spiritual . . . God will then be known to us . . . in such a way that we shall see Him by the spirit in ourselves, in one another, in Himself, in the new heavens and the new earth, and in every created thing which shall then exist. (*CG*, xxii.29)

This vision of the transformation but preservation of materiality runs counter to Zizioulas's objection that "in St Augustine's vision of the last things there is no place for nature; it consists of the survival of the eternal souls."[88] Daley argues that Augustine anticipates

> nothing less than total . . . transformation of our material reality, and that of our world, which God will work at the moment of resurrection. Without destroying human identity as flesh and spirit, without annihilating the world in which that identity has been realized.[89]

Secondly for Augustine Sabbath speaks of Christ. We have observed how Augustine sees Christ witnessed in creation by the measure and proportion of its numbers. In *The Trinity* he demonstrates the same patterns present in the incarnation and the ensuing redemption worked by the whole life, death and resurrection of Jesus (*DT*, IV.2.9–10). As a day of rest Sabbath prefigures Christ's resting in the tomb.

> On the Sabbath day He rested in the tomb, and he passed this whole day in a kind of holy leisure after he had finished on the sixth day or the day of the Preparation . . . all His works, fulfilling on the cross what was written of Him . . . therefore God, wishing in this way to foreshadow the day on which Christ was to rest in the sepulchre, rested on one day from all His works,

---

87. Daley, *Hope of the Early Church*, 132–33.
88. Zizioulas, "Priest of Creation," 277.
89. Daley, *Hope of the Early Church*, 132.

although after that He would work the unfolding of the progress of the ages. (*LM*, 4.11.21)

By his Sabbath resting in the tomb Christ does the work of our salvation (*LM*, 4.13.24), yet from the very beginning this salvation is declared in the constitution of creation by the seventh day—the day of rest. Nevertheless, while Sabbath speaks of Christ's rest, "my Father is working, even until now, and I also work" (*LM*, 4.11.21), upholding and unfolding creation, and if this was not the case "the universe would pass away in the twinkling of an eye" (*LM*, 4.12.22). Sabbath then is a perpetual reminder that all our existence is one of utter dependence upon God. The death and resurrection of Christ also confirm for Augustine the ultimate salvation of our materiality, for Christ's resurrection overcomes the struggle and separation between body and soul that have marked our human journey.

> The one death of our savior was our salvation from our two deaths [i.e., of both soul and body], and his one resurrection bestowed two resurrections on us, since in either instance, that is both in death and resurrection, his body served as the sacrament of our inner man and as the model of our outer man (*DT*, IV.1.6).

In addition, writing of the restoration that is both daily progress and resurrection hope (*DT*, XIV.5.23), and referencing 1 Cor 13:12, 2 Cor 3:18, and 1 Jn 3:2—"we shall be like him, because we shall see him as he is," he includes the body.

> In this respect too we will be like God, but only like the Son, who alone in the triad took a body in which he died and rose again, carrying it up to the heavenly regions. This too can be called the image of the Son of God in which like him we shall have an immortal body, conformed in this respect not to the image of the Father or the Holy spirit but only of the Son, because of him alone do we read and receive on wholesome faith that *the Word became flesh* (Jn 1:14). (*DT*, XIV.5.24)

That by the incarnation and resurrection the Godhead has taken materiality into itself is the clearest affirmation possible that material existence is never a matter of indifference, nor will it be eventually transcended but is rather a matter of ultimate significance. That significance is expressed in the outworking of daily life.

The third aspect of Sabbath significance for Augustine is that it provides the template for Christian living. We live in eschatological hope of Sabbath rest but we also begin to enter that rest now. Indeed, Sabbath is experienced not on one day only but every day, and all of them in hope of the day of rest that is to come. Baptism, as a resting with Christ in the tomb, enables release from the burden of one's own works into the daily recognition of the works that come as gifts of God's love (*LM*, 4.13.24).[90] Concluding his reflections about rest in *City of God*, Augustine suggests that good works done of ourselves, to justify ourselves before God, are "servile works" not born of our resting in the grace of the Sabbath (*CG*, xxii.30). Grace however elevates our good works—rather than diminishing them, because they are now the warm expression of love (*CON*, XIII.ix.10). "Obedience motivated by fear or hope of reward, such as the Pelagians urged . . . is servile when compared with the obedience which springs from inner delight, desire, and love of God. It is in the love that grace inspires that man's true freedom is found."[91]

Resting in Christ is the foundation not only of work, but also of the contemplative life, which itself reflects something of the life of God.

> Even in Himself, who toils not in His work, repose is more important than activity. This truth as applied to man is taught us in the Gospel, where our Savior says that Mary has the better part because she sat at His feet and rested in His word, rather than Martha, in spite of the fact that out of devotion she served Him, busying herself about many things, and thus performed a good work. (*LM*, 4.14.25)

Mary models both the contemplative life in the present time and the happiness that will be ours when Christ hands over the kingdom to God and the Father. She sits "at the Lord's feet, intent upon his words; at rest from all activity and intent upon the truth, in such measure as this life allows of, and thereby nonetheless foreshadowing that joy that is going to last forever" (*DT*, 1.3.20). Martha's work is not dismissed as being of no account. She is simply reminded that such service, valuable as it is, will not be necessary when need is brought to an end. Remarkably, Hill suggests that Augustine

> is firmly of the opinion that charity, and attention to the needs of ourselves and of our brothers, compel us to devote most of our

---

90. See also Augustine, *CON* (XIII.xxxvi.51), 304.
91. Harrison, *Augustine*, 110–11.

energies in this earthly life to activity. He never, so far as I am aware, speaks of the contemplative life as a mode of life on this earth to which some Christians are called.[92]

Was White correct that "the Greek saint contemplates. The Western saint acts"?[93] In fact all action for Augustine is of a contemplative kind. Love is itself an expression of Sabbath rest for,

> God gave rest in Himself to the rational beings He had created, among whom man is included, that is, that after their creation He gave them this rest by the gift of the Holy Spirit, by whom charity is poured forth in our hearts, that we may be drawn to God by a desire and yearning for Him, and reaching Him may find rest, and want nothing besides. (*LM*, 4.9.16)

We have also seen Augustine's expansion of the contemplative life to include the manual labor involved in gardening. Conversation with nature enables some vision of the glory and love of God, it contributes to God's providential care of the earth, and even in this life it may have the character of "free work," but it eschews lust for material goods and it recognizes that the seventh day of rest is the sign that all that is needed for a good and Godly life has been provided (*LM*, 4.12.22). Zumkeller[94] argues that Augustine is advocating such a mix of action and contemplation when he writes, "we have been looking for a kind of rational couple of contemplation and action in the mind of everyman, with functions distributed into two several channels and yet the mind's unity preserved in each" (*DT*, 12.3.19). A healthy life involved both action and contemplation, and Zumkeller demonstrates that Augustine came to see monastic life not as a private pursuit of perfection, but as a community of love in the service of the church.[95] Subsequently, monastic orders based upon Augustine's *Rule* blended the active and contemplative lives in worship, education, hospitality, and hospital care.[96] But such a holistic life is for all Christians and "no one ought to live a life of leisure in such a way that he takes no thought in that leisure for the welfare of his neighbor; nor ought he to be so active as to feel no need for the contemplation of God" (*CG*, xix.19). This stress on the role of the contemplative life, both within and

---

92. Augustine, *Trinity*, 94, note 56.
93. White, "Historical Roots," 1206.
94. Zumkeller, *Religious Life*, 208, note 224.
95. Zumkeller, *Religious Life*, 197.
96. Smetana, "Augustinian Canons" and "Augustinian Friars," 659–60.

outside the monastic community, is important. It is the contemplation of the Word that provides the proportion in which life may properly be viewed. The disciplines of the contemplative life nurture attentiveness and contentment, which are the spiritual antidote to culturally induced pressures to haste, superficiality and dissatisfied consumerism. Furthermore, the peaceable relations characteristic of the Sabbath may even now be witnessed in the lives of holy persons. Thus the contemplative life does not require disconnection from the earth nor from a certain mode of work nor abandonment of loving relationships, but all these are to be enjoyed as gifts of grace, part of the enjoyment of God himself.

Fourthly, the seventh day is the sanctified day because on it God rested *from* his works not *in* them (as would be the case if the Sabbath was prescribed for the sixth day) (*LM*, 4.14.25–17.29). We are thus reminded that although all things are in God, God is not in any way dependent upon that which he has made. God's rest is rest in himself who

> does not owe His happiness to the fact that He has made creatures, but rather to the fact that having no need of what He has made, He has rested in Himself rather than in them. Therefore, it is not the day of His work but the day of His rest that He has made holy; for He has revealed that He is happy not by making creatures but by having no need of those He has made . . . He rests from the finishing of His creatures who needs no finishing of creatures to increase His happiness. (*LM*, 4.17.29–30)

This state of affairs is not indicative of a monumental divine indifference. We have already seen that all things have their existence in God who has created them in love. Rather, it is profoundly liberating. What could be more servile than to find, as in the Babylonian mythologies, that we have been brought to existence in order to attend to dirty work that God is unwilling to touch? What could be more terrifying than to discover that we had been brought to being, like a court jester, for the task of making God happy? But for Augustine, God's whole purpose is that we should find our joy resting in God who has made us; not that we should have somehow to make God happy but that we might enjoy his happiness. To do this there is no call to dominate the earth but simply to enjoy it and enjoy being part of it, in the contemplation of the Word which sustains it.

CONCLUSIONS

We have demonstrated that, despite Manichaean and Neo-Platonic influences, Augustine was converted enough to vigorously promote a doctrine of creation *ex-nihilo*. All creation is sustained by the Word of God, and it is by orientation towards or away from the Word that creatures move towards their fulfillment or dissolution. The mobility of creation is a defining feature of Augustine's doctrine, expressed in his ideas about "weight," restlessness, love and desire—and involving much more than mere rationalism. This potential for movement is pursued by human beings in the contemplative life, and it is this loving relationality that for Augustine constitutes the image of God.

The associated dominion is exercised over oneself by pursuing this life with God, and over other creatures through recognizing their particular needs and natures and exercising good governance accordingly. To do the latter requires an attention to creatures that makes Augustine's Christian vision of the contemplative life radically different from his earlier Neo-Platonic one. Thus, conversation with nature experienced in gardening became a significant element in the contemplative life. This clearly is not a conception of destructive domination over creatures even if it does involve governance. The ultimate sign for Augustine of engagement with materiality is seen in the Word himself taking flesh and coming to us in humility.

Angels are everywhere present in Augustine's creation, providing the spiritual impetus for the movement of non-human creatures and providing support and encouragement to humans. The angels' task is to awaken praise. Thus, although de-divinized, Augustine's universe is still thoroughly spiritually alive—not mere materiality for human projects.

Augustine's vision of mobility—restlessness, finds its fulfillment in his understanding of the Sabbath. Sabbath, not humanity, is the goal of God's creative work whereby the whole creation will be drawn to ultimate rest in its creator. This is the eschatological vision that infuses all Augustine's work. This too is pre-figured for creation in Jesus' death and resurrection and we can begin to experience it now by faith, through the contemplative life.

The contemplative life, engagement with creation as a place of encounter with God, and some experience of the Sabbath future in present life all became key elements in the development of Christian monasticism. Heaven could be anticipated here in the new society of the monastic community. The implications of this vision for the exercise of human dominion over creation will be the subject of the next chapter.

6

Monasticism—Reclaiming the Garden, Building the City

INTRODUCTION

AUGUSTINE'S VISION FOR THE transformation of life was ideally pursued in the context of a monastic community. His own conversion had been facilitated by the story of Anthony,[1] and from the outset his Christian vision was shaped by communal experience; first in the attempt to establish a retreat at Cassiciacum, then briefly at Ostia, thereafter at Thagaste, and finally in the grounds of the episcopal residence at Hippo itself. Although giving the monastic vision his own stamp, in none of this was he doing anything radically new, but was rather, a relative late-comer. Athanasius had used the life of Anthony to promote his vision of transformation by ascesis, and Anthony himself began his ascetic life under the tutelage of others already long experienced.[2] Monasticism is only one expression of a much broader and older ascetic impulse in Christian spirituality. Herbert Workman's great work on *The Evolution of the Monastic Ideal* was subtitled, "a second chapter in the history of Christian renunciation"; the first chapter being his study on martyrdom and persecution.

---

1. Augustine, *CON*, 142–44.
2. Dunn, *Emergence of Monasticism*, 3. See also Davidson, *Public Faith*, 139.

He writes, "the root principle of monasticism lay in the intense desire for self-surrender."[3]

The importance of monasticism for this study is that in monasticism we encounter a movement that is at once intentional—in the sense of being a lifestyle deliberately chosen, and integrated—in that every aspect of life was to be brought subject to the relevant monastic discipline. In such a movement one may hope to see with greater clarity how ideas and convictions are expressed in the practicalities of daily life, thereby presenting a model of Christian existence to the surrounding world. Being about renunciation and transformation it addresses questions of the believer's life with God, as well as relationships with both others and the material creation, with all their implications regarding human habitation of the earth, and the use and/or abuse of the earth and its creatures. Monasticism, especially in its Benedictine form, is widely recognized as having become a pre-eminent influence in the formation and shaping of Western European culture.[4] Therefore we will look to see how ideas and practices that originated within monastic communities may have been appropriated in the wider society. Since as a movement monasticism appears to have originated in the east and then spread westward, we shall follow that geographical trajectory in tracing its influence. We shall begin with the Desert Fathers and Mothers, then review the monastic visions of Basil of Caesarea, and thirdly Benedict of Nursia and the Benedictine movement. Indicative as they are of new social movements, we shall defer until the next chapter examination of the new forms of discipleship associated with Francis of Assisi.

Seeds in the Desert: The Desert Fathers and Mothers

During the second half of the third century, increasing numbers of people, in Egypt initially, abandoned settled lives in towns or on farms and retreated to the desert in an attempt to respond more faithfully to the call of Christ. Workman saw this movement primarily as reaction to the loss of the early church's chiliastic conceptions and millenarian hopes, and to its supposed fateful accommodation to secular power.[5]

Marilyn Dunn surveys a number of other possible factors:

3. Workman, *Monastic Ideal*, 29.
4. Butler, "Preface," in *Benedictine Monachism*. See also White, *Rule of Benedict*, vii.
5. Workman, *Monastic Ideal*, 6–10.

> It was a response to the imperial adoption of Christianity . . . a call to return to the values of Christian martyrdom or a result of a widespread and deep-seated anxiety. It . . . might simply be a continuation of the Jewish ascetic tradition . . . and of the communal traditions of early Christian groups imitating the way of life of the Apostles . . . it might . . . have been located in an economic crisis in third-and fourth-century Egypt.[6]

In addition to all these Davidson also notes the challenge to Christian authenticity which was posed by the ascetic traditions in pagan philosophy,[7] and these were certainly present to Augustine.

Emerging Themes

VALUING CREATION

The definitive model for the monastic life was promoted by Athanasius as being the life of Anthony,[8] whose call came to its culmination in hearing the Gospel passage, "if you would be perfect, go sell what you possess and give to the poor and you will have treasure in heaven."[9]

This renunciation is not necessarily indicative of a rejection of one's creatureliness, nor of creation itself. The golden thread running through all the *Sayings of the Desert Fathers* must be the joy that they find in their oneness with creation. Macarius the Great recounts how he retreated to a lake in the desert. Wild animals gathered to drink, and among them two human forms which he in his city-dweller's fear presumed to be demons. They however assured him that they were monks, men like himself, an Egyptian and a Libyan living together. "It is God who has made this way of life for us. We do not freeze in the winter and the summer does us no harm."[10] In similar vein, "Abba Bessarion's disciples related that his life had been like that of a bird of the air, or a fish, or an animal living on

---

6. Dunn, *Emergence of Monasticism*, 2–3. See also Workman, *Monastic Ideal*, 1, and 59 on pre-monastic asceticism in the West; Gould, *Monastic Community*, 1–3; Davidson, *Public Faith*, 133–34; and Silvas, *Asketikon*, vii.

7. Davidson, *Public Faith*, 134.

8. Dunn, *Emergence of Monasticism*, 2. See also Augustine, *CON*, (VIII.vi.14–15) 142–44.

9. Athanasius, *LA*, 19.

10. Ward, *Sayings*, 106.

earth, passing all the time of his life without trouble or disquiet,"[11] and Isidore the Priest likened a monk's cell to the safety of an animal's lair.[12] The theme of oneness with animals appears in Abba Paul's reflections on handling snakes, "if someone has obtained purity, everything is in submission to him, as it was to Adam, when he was in Paradise before he transgressed the commandment."[13] Poemen suggested, "to become nothing means to place one's self beneath irrational beings and to know that they are without blame,"[14] and Xanthia said, "a dog is better than I am, for he has love and he does not judge."[15] Yet none of this entails negativity about one's humanity. Netras, bishop of Pharan, regarded his asceticism not as a necessary assault upon his body but as contributing to his good health, commenting, "in the desert there was *hesychia* and poverty, and I wished to look after my body in order not to be ill and have to look for something I did not have."[16] Poemen argues, in response to Isaac's surprise at finding him washing his feet, "we have not been taught to kill our bodies, but to kill our passions."[17]

Despite this particular pearl of wisdom, and all the foregoing, Workman preferred to find signs of Gnosticism everywhere infecting the lives and thought of the desert fathers,

> the tales . . . bear witness to the Gnostic ideal . . . that spiritual life can only find its highest perfection in the wildest asceticism . . . the ideal monk of the earlier days stood opposed to a world which no Psalmist can claim as the Lord's, and over whose creation the morning stars should have wept rather than sung aloud.[18]

Certainly some of the bizarre austerities he describes would justify such an assessment.[19] Marilyn Dunn also explores the eastern monastic's

11. Ward, *Sayings*, 35.
12. Ward, *Sayings*, 91.
13. Ward, *Sayings*, 171.
14. Ward, *Sayings*, 145; see also the lives of Sisoes, 180, and Tithoes, 198.
15. Ward, *Sayings*, 134.
16. Netras, in Gould, *Monastic Community*, 174. See also Ward, *Sayings*, 132—that asceticism is good for the body is also witnessed in the great ages mentioned for Anthony, 1, Arsenius, 16; Macarius, 128; and Sisoes, 183.
17. Ward, *Sayings*, 162.
18. Workman, *Monastic Ideal*, 39, 40–41.
19. Workman, *Monastic Ideal*, 41–48. But at least one he records—Sisoes's life-threatening vigil against sleep over the precipice at Petra, is concluded by an angelic

constant dalliance with Manichaean ideas but acknowledges, "Athanasius' emphasis on the distinctive and orthodox nature of Antony's asceticism represents a conscious attempt to minimize any superficial or programmatic resemblances between it and that of the demiurgics and Manichaeans."[20]

Many of the stories are told with considerable awareness of contemporary theological debates about creation, and many sayings clearly promote creation as good and the place of divine engagement. John Chryssavgis recognizes the centrality of this theme not only for animals but for the elements themselves, "Creation is filled with the presence of God on account of the event of the Incarnation: 'Everything is sanctified through his presence,' writes the Great Geron Barsanuphius" (Letter 575).[21] Anthony is said to have urged "understanding of the things of this world [i.e., the processes of Creation], and so obtain preservation of your minds free from unsettling demonic storms" (*LA*, 28). In a saying that is succinct, comprehensive in naming key issues, and pastorally astute, Abba Sopatros said,

> do not allow a woman to come into your cell and do not read apocryphal literature. Do not get involved in discussions about the image. Although this is not heresy, there is too much ignorance and liking for dispute between the two parties in this matter. It is impossible for a creature to understand the truth of it.[22]

Apocryphal literature was the primary inspiration for gnostic speculations that all tended to denigrate the value of creation. On the other hand, a tale recounted by Arsenius promotes a sacramental vision of creation in addressing the issue whether the communion bread is really the body of Christ, or only a symbol.[23] Numerous others recount visions of the divine glory resting upon the eucharistic priest. Elias in a pagan temple hears the demons claim "this place belongs to us," while contesting his claim is that "no place belongs to you." In the ensuing spiritual tussle he encounters the reality of Jesus always and everywhere with

---

rebuke which Workman does not acknowledge. See also Ward, *Sayings*, 184.

20. Dunn, *Emergence of Monasticism*, 12.

21. Chryssavgis, "Sacredness," 350.

22. Ward, *Sayings*, 189. In an editor's footnote Ward writes, "this [i.e., the reference to the image] refers to the doctrine of the image of God in man, the interpretation of which was a burning issue in the desert."

23. Ward, *Sayings*, 44.

him.[24] Theodora (one of the "Mothers"), in discussion with a Manichee, presents a positive vision of both the body and of ascetic discipline, in arguing, "give the body discipline and you will see that the body is for him who made it."[25] In response to a question on the nature of resurrection, surely a defining issue in the debates about creation, the same Theodora replies, "as pledge, example, and as prototype we have him who died for us and is risen, Christ our God."[26] Gnostic suspicion about creation and the Old Testament is addressed by Sisoes, who in response to a request for a word replies, "I read the New Testament, and I turn to the Old."[27] There is nowhere one can go in the desert to get away from the presence of God. The divine fire, it seems, is waiting to break out upon people anywhere. "Who shall separate us from the love of God?" asks Daniel. "God is in the cell, and on the other hand he is outside also."[28] "One contemplated the world," writes John Chryssavgis,

> as a revelation of God's beauty. For to contemplate nature is to become aware of things divine. There can be no renunciation unless there is, first, a true esteem of the world as created by God. Sin is precisely the failure to accept and assume the world as a gift from God. The ascetic struggle betrays the authentic hermit not as hard, but as intensely loving, recognizing in creation the unique "icon" of divinity.[29]

Even Workman, despite his frequently acerbic treatment of the Desert Fathers, nevertheless recognizes in them,

> a new love of nature . . . larger sympathies with beasts and birds . . . they abound with evidences of a new oneness with nature . . . The hermit who began with an almost Gnostic hatred of the created world, as the medium of temptation and the abode of sin, oft-times ended in an identification of himself with nature itself. But this made his Gnosticism an impossible belief.[30]

Monasticism did indeed involve flight from the city, the structures of empire, and the corruptions of the church, but all these renunciations

---

24. Ward, *Sayings*, 61.
25. Ward, *Sayings*, 71.
26. Ward, *Sayings*, 72.
27. Ward, *Sayings*, 184.
28. Ward, *Sayings*, 44.
29. Chryssavgis, "Sacredness," 346–51.
30. Workman, *Monastic Ideal*, 34–37, see also 36, note 1.

were to enable flight towards an immediate encounter with creation—and through that direct encounter with creation to encounter also with the Word which sustained creation. Thus, in light of all the foregoing, the first thing to be said about monasticism for the purpose of this study, is that it does not, or does not necessarily, involve a negative assessment of nature as creation. Creation is the place of meeting and in the emptiness of the desert one realizes the boundlessness of grace.[31]

Living Lightly within Creation

How then did these ascetics inhabit the earth for which they often held such positive regard? Whether in prayer, pastoral care, or physical labor, Theodore of Pherme said, "everything you do as a command of God is the work of the soul."[32] Anthony kept a garden, and when animals dug it up "quietly and laughingly asked them, 'why do you do harm to me, seeing that I do no harm to you?' . . . from that hour they never again did harm to the place . . . He was not wearied of the desert, and his soul had no fear of the wild beasts" (LA, 42–43).[33]

The work of sowing and harvesting, of weaving ropes and baskets, or of baking bread, is a theological as much as a simply physical necessity. John the Dwarf learned the hard way that it was not possible for him, a man, to pursue the life of angels—"You are a man and must once again work in order to eat,"[34] as also did the arrogant brother who berated the monks for their manual labor, preferring to spend the day with a book emulating the better way of Mary.

> When the ninth hour came the visitor watched the door expecting someone would be sent to call him to the meal. When no-one called him he got up, went to find the old man and said to him, "Have the brothers not eaten today?" The old man replied that they had. Then he said, "Why did you not call me?" The old man said to him, "Because you are a spiritual man and do not need to eat that kind of food. We, being carnal, want to eat, and that is why we work. But you have chosen the good portion and read the whole day long and you do not want to eat carnal food." When he heard these words the brother made a

---

31. Chryssavgis, "Sacredness," 349.
32. Ward, *Sayings*, 64–65.
33. Athanasius, *LA*, 42–43.
34. Ward, *Sayings*, 73.

prostration saying, "Forgive me, abba." The old man said to him, "Mary needs Martha. It is really thanks to Martha that Mary is praised."[35]

White claimed that "the Greek saint contemplates; the Western saint acts."[36] But these are heroes among the Eastern saints—and they work! Such work, according to Lucius, contributed to one's life of ceaseless prayer,[37] it enabled almsgiving,[38] and support both for oneself[39] and the poor,[40] participation in community,[41] and helped develop discipline without excess.[42] But there is no suggestion it is done in order to dominate over nature. If anything, the opposite is true. Poemen realistically observed, "there are three things which I am not able to do without: food, clothing and sleep; but I can restrict them to some extent."[43] Such restriction may involve the austerities for which these monks gained both fame and notoriety, but there was considerable variety as to its nature. What was simplicity for Arsenius was improvement of life for a former peasant.[44] Epiphanius urged the study of books,[45] while Serapion charged that those who owned them had stolen from widows and orphans.[46] A saying from Isaac suggests that at least one group engaged, not in casual labor for others, but in working land they themselves owned.[47] Minimal impact, however, remained the goal. When the monks around Silvanus moved the fence to enlarge the garden, he gathered his gear and prepared

---

35. Ward, *Sayings*, 187.
36. White, "Historical Roots," 1206.
37. Ward, *Sayings*, 102.
38. Ward, *Sayings*, Agathon, 20; Poemen, 148; Pambo, 264.
39. Ward, *Sayings*, Agathon, 19; Eucharistos the Secular, 51; Theodore of Pherme, 66.
40. Ward, *Sayings*, Eucharistos the Secular, 51; John the Dwarf, 82; Macarius the Great, 108; Poemen, 143, 146.
41. Ward, *Sayings*, Poemen, 138; Benjamin, 36.
42. Ward, *Sayings*, Anthony, 3; Evagrius, 54; Matoes, 121; Poemen, 144; Pistamon, 168.
43. Ward, *Sayings*, 185.
44. Ward, *Sayings*, Arsenius, 14; An Abba of Rome, 175.
45. Ward, *Sayings*, Epiphanius, 9.
46. Ward, *Sayings*, Serapion, 190.
47. Ward, *Sayings*, Isaac, 85.

to leave,[48] and Anthony, Isidore of Pelusia, and Sisoes, all have explicit and dire warnings about the dangers of desire for possessions.[49]

Despite differing approaches to ascesis, we encounter a strong element of affirmation regarding creation and the fruits of simple work. Joy is to be found in the gifts of creation, the fruits of their work, and in eating and drinking together.[50] Simple gifts of fresh fruit—Arsenius took special and thankful pleasure in savoring one piece of each of the newly harvested fruit,[51] dried fruit cake, loaves of bread, flax for weaving, or a basket of onions are all received with pleasure and thanksgiving, as signs of both the goodness of God and brotherly affection. All of this work is recognized as a gift of God. Serinus said, "I have spent my time in harvesting, sewing and weaving, and in all these employments if the hand of God had not sustained me, I should not have been fed,"[52] and, according to Isaiah, "avarice is not to believe that God cares for you."[53]

Nevertheless, despite the recognized necessity of work, the culture of work, as seen in the *Sayings*, is very definitely voluntary and *laissez faire*—rather reminiscent of the hippie communities of the late 1960s! When the aging Abba Theodore of Pherme was asked why he never gave instructions about work to his disciple Isaac, he replied, "am I a cenobite, that I should give him orders? As far as I am concerned, I do not tell him anything, but if he wishes he can do what he sees me doing."[54] Probably Theodore had in his sights the alternative form of monastic life that was developing under the leadership of Anthony's contemporary Pachomius. A converted former soldier, Pachomius was instrumental in developing a much more deliberately communal form of monasticism.[55] Workman finds it a matter of considerable regret that Athanasius did not write a life of Pachomius—whom he knew, visited, and approved of, rather than the one he did write of Anthony![56] The Pachomian system involved a common Rule of life and a system of discipline to maintain it. The daily

48. Ward, *Sayings*, Silvanus, 188.
49. Ward, *Sayings*, Anthony, 4; Isidore, 84; Sisoes, 182.
50. Ward, *Sayings*, Anthony the Great, 3.
51. Ward, *Sayings*, Arsenius, 10.
52. Ward, *Sayings*, 191.
53. Ward, *Sayings*, 60.
54. Ward, *Sayings*, 85; see similarly Poemen, 158, and 160–61.
55. Davidson, *Public Faith*, 142. See also Dunn, *Emergence of Monasticism*, 26–32; and Decarreaux, *Monks and Civilization*, 77–79.
56. Workman, *Monastic Ideal*, 87.

order included work, teaching, regular meals, and twice-daily common worship. From Pachomius came the idea of the *coenobium* or community (derived from the Greek *koinos bios* meaning "common life"),[57] and with it the commitment to a community of goods after the pattern described in Acts 2:42–47 and Acts 4:32–35.[58] Hospitality was practiced and

> Pachomius is said to have insisted that a generous measure of cooked food was placed on the refectory tables every day so that the brothers might have the possibility of deciding individually to abstain. He does not appear to have imposed his own fasting practices upon the community as a norm, and even abandoned the usual monastic practice of avoiding meat when he ordered a kid to be cooked and served to a sick brother.[59]

Meat, or its avoidance, is a matter of particular theological and ascetic significance, full of implications regarding attitudes to other living creatures. But, as with Pachomius, there are varying degrees of austerity. When Archbishop Theophilus, himself recognized as a monk, invited monks to Alexandria on a mission task, he offered them veal to eat, which they declined.[60] Nevertheless there is recognition that this particular fast has its particular susceptibilities. "If fasting makes you proud," warned Isidore the Priest, "better for a man to eat meat than to be inflated with pride and to glorify himself,"[61] and Hyperechios advised similarly, "it is better to eat meat and drink wine and not to eat the flesh of one's brethren through slander."[62] Poemen recognized instances where, at the same meal, refusal of meat by some would cause offence while, if he were to eat, that would cause confusion.[63]

John Berkman has surveyed attitudes to meat eating in the tradition and identifies three common reasons for abstinence.[64] Firstly there are health reasons, but as he also notes, "when Patristic authors advocate a simple, meatless diet in the interests of health, they have foremost in

---

57. White, *Rule of Benedict*, 110, note 1.
58. Davidson, *Public Faith*, 142. See also Dunn, *Emergence of Monasticism*, 26–32.
59. Dunn, *Emergence of Monasticism*, 31.
60. Ward, *Sayings*, Theophilus the Archbishop, 69.
61. Ward, *Sayings*, 91.
62. Ward, *Sayings*, 200.
63. Ward, *Sayings*, Poemen, 160.
64. Berkman, "Consumption of Animals," 174–90.

mind health as a kind of spiritual purity."⁶⁵ A meatless diet was for both Christians and others "a prerequisite for spiritual or philosophical (rather than athletic) ascetic practice."⁶⁶ Secondly are ascetic reasons. Rather than current concerns about the moral status of animals, "what is central for the early Christians is that all their practices are to be ordered to the love and service of God."⁶⁷ Meatlessness he argues was a key element in the Christian response to the capital vice of gluttony. Dominant medical theory held that animal flesh, being excessively nutritious, produced excessive increases in bodily secretions, including semen. So too did sleep! "Hence . . . abstinence . . . was a means of controlling the two major sins of the flesh—gluttony and lust."⁶⁸ These attempts at control were often dramatic, and even so sensible a monk as Pachomius is reputed to have forced himself for fifteen years to sleep standing up.⁶⁹ Such control however imagines no ideal of domination over nature, except in respect of mastery over one's own mind and body.⁷⁰

A third argument for meatless cuisine was the eschatological, by which one envisioned the world as it was before the Fall, or as it will be at the end of the age. For John Cassian, Jerome, and others, "diet is particularly relevant to the goal of embodying the Edenic state, because they consider the original sin of Adam and Eve to be gluttony."⁷¹ Subsequently, following Genesis 9, flesh eating is allowed as a concession to human hardness of heart, but it is neither necessary nor preferred.⁷² Furthermore, for Basil of Caesarea and Jerome, "fasting from flesh foods is an image of life as it was in the Garden of Eden because in paradise there was no sacrifice of animals or eating of animal flesh (see Gen 1:29–30)."⁷³ The Eucharist of course involves bread and wine. Other ritual meals may include oil, vegetables, salt, milk, cheese, honey, and olives—but not meat, because of a desire to avoid the shedding of blood.⁷⁴

65. Berkman, "Consumption of Animals," 176.
66. Berkman, "Consumption of Animals," 176.
67. Berkman, "Consumption of Animals," 177.
68. Berkman, "Consumption of Animals," 179. See also Dunn, *Emergence of Monasticism*, 16–17.
69. Workman, *Monastic Ideal*, 49.
70. Ward, *Sayings*, Anthony the Great, 7.
71. Berkman, "Consumption of Animals," 179.
72. Berkman, "Consumption of Animals," 179.
73. Berkman, "Consumption of Animals," 179.
74. Berkman, "Consumption of Animals," 181.

Douglas Burton-Christie references stories of intimacy with animals from a range of different sources, all expressing "a conviction which the desert fathers cherished: that they were recovering in their life in the desert a small taste of paradise."[75] Similarly, according to Chryssavgis, "the dream of a restored creation is the ultimate vision of the desert."[76] This eschatological aspect of asceticism is also a key element in the monastic experience of eucharistic prayer.

The Centrality of Prayer

If joy in creation is the golden thread running through the Sayings of the Desert Fathers, thanksgiving is what they weave with it. "Be joyful at all times, pray without ceasing and give thanks in all things," is the advice of Benjamin.[77] All monastic activity can be seen as pursued in this spirit, and the daily round of Psalms (frequently referred to) keeps this consciousness alive. Robert Taft, quoting from the *Canons of Hippolytus* (27), argues that the night prayer was especially important, both for joining the monks' prayers with the praise of the whole creation and for its eschatological orientation as they anticipate the coming of the light with the awaited bridegroom (Matt 25:6), and watch for the coming that may be at midnight or at cock-crow (Mark 13:35).[78] From here develop the seven "hours" of prayer that became the hallmark of all subsequent monasticism.[79] The priority of this prayer in shaping life may be discerned from the primary place it has in the regulations of both Augustine and Benedict.[80] Benedict considered his an easy discipline, referring to "our holy predecessors [who] had the energy to perform in a single day what we, with our lukewarm faith, aspire to carry out in the course of a whole week."[81]

---

75. Burton-Christie, *Word in the Desert*, 232.
76. Chryssavgis, "Sacredness," 347.
77. Ward, *Sayings*, 37.
78. Taft, *Liturgy of the Hours*, 35.
79. Ward, *Sayings*, see Epiphanius, 48–49; and An Abba of Rome, 175.
80. Lawless, *Augustine of Hippo*, 75.
81. White, *Rule of Benedict*, 39 (section 18). White, in a footnote, relates this claim to the story in *The Lives of the Fathers*, in which two monks meet for a meal but before eating take time to pray. One recited the whole Psalter and the other, two of the prophets. They then go their separate ways, having quite forgotten the food!

Alongside the formality of the Psalms is the spontaneity, and often the ecstasy, of the monks' free prayer. Lucius, in a story specifically intended to correct the dualistic and over-spiritualized (and non-working) Euchites, describes how he is able to combine his manual labor with his prayers,[82] while others regard ceaseless prayer as that which is done with regularity. "There is no need to make long discourses," advises Macarius the Great, "it is enough to stretch out one's hands and say, 'Lord, as you will, and as you know, have mercy.' And if the conflict grows fiercer say, 'Lord, help!' He knows very well what we need and he shows us his mercy."[83]

According to Poemen, "Paphnutius was great and had recourse to short prayers."[84] And the same Paphnutius advised a brother who was questioning his calling, "go and stay in your cell; make only one prayer in the morning and one in the evening and one at night. When you are hungry, eat, when you are thirsty, drink; when you are tired, sleep. But stay in your cell and take no notice of this thought."[85]

Whatever the forms of prayer, they all anticipate communal prayer on Saturday and Sunday, the *synaxis* which also incorporated the *agape* or eucharist. As the hart longs for cool water (Ps 42:1), having devoured venomous reptiles, so monks according to Poemen, "long for Saturday and Sunday to come to be able to go to the springs of water, that is to say, the body and blood of the Lord, so as to be purified from the bitterness of the evil one."[86] Of this particular saying Burton-Christie comments,

> a further point of interest in this passage is the explicitly Christological reading of the Psalm. The naturalness of Poemen's interpretation indicates how readily this Christological hermeneutical principle, which was so important in patristic exegesis, was accepted in the desert.[87]

Such fellowship necessitates the breaking of one's fast and many monks appeared to agonize about doing so.[88] Others recognized that to eat and drink with joy was vital, for while fasting was a command of men which

---

82. Ward, *Sayings*, 102.
83. Ward, *Sayings*, 111.
84. Ward, *Sayings*, 163.
85. Ward, *Sayings*, 171.
86. Ward, *Sayings*, 144.
87. Burton-Christie, *Word in the Desert*, 201.
88. Gould, *Monastic Community*, 142–150.

could be taken up or laid aside at any time, hospitality was the command of God.[89] At this meal people experience the life transforming power of the Word in Scripture,[90] they catch visions of the divine glory resting upon one or another,[91] and they encounter a tenderness that is not always associated with these ascetic heroes.[92]

Phocas records a practice whereby the monastic habit, which had been received upon taking one's vow, was worn only to the Eucharist and at, or in preparation for, burial.[93] Thereby, the monk's death to the world and resurrection hope are drawn together at the eucharistic meal. In this and other ways the sacramental meal becomes a sign of the sacramental character of the whole creation, and of the eschatological hope of the restoration of creation. Anna Silvas also links monasticism and eschatological vision, through the particular medium of the liturgy, "the eschatological dynamic of the Divine Liturgy: our being drawn even on earth into the life that is to come . . . is the soul of the life of monks and nuns . . . thus they become a beacon to other Christians of *the mystery which is Christ in you, your hope of glory* (cf. Col 1:27)."[94]

A New Community

To the degree that Workman was correct in seeing the rise of monasticism as an attempt to redress the church's loss of millennarian vision (Workman used the Greek equivalent *chiliastic*), Robert Clouse's observation takes on added significance that,

> although most Christian theologians discuss death, immortality, the end of the world, the last judgement . . . they often limit themselves to the prospects for the individual . . . In contrast,

---

89. Ward, *Sayings*, Cassian, 96–97; Moses, 118–19; Matoes, 121.

90. Ward, *Sayings*, Paul the Simple, 172–74.

91. Ward, *Sayings*, Isaiah, 59; Isaac the Theban, 94; Mark the Egyptian, 127; Sisoes, 180.

92. Ward, *Sayings*, Poemen, 151 and 158. See also Agathon, 19. Numerous other sayings in the section on Agathon portray a person who, despite his personal austerities, is rich with human warmth and compassion, a far cry from the reclusive misanthropy often attributed to the desert monks.

93. Ward, *Sayings*, 201. On the connection of the habit with the eucharistic gathering, see also Theodore of Pherme, 67, and Poemen, 141.

94. Silvas, *Asketikon*, x.

millennialism is concerned with *the future of the human community on earth* [my italics].⁹⁵

In this light, monasticism was at least in part about developing a form of communal life that would bear witness to the vision of the millennial kingdom; an assessment further justified by certain aspects of Pachomian monasticism in which "the *koinonia* seems to have existed in a state of permanent expectation of the Second Coming of Christ . . . a theme later repeated, thanks to St Jerome's translation, in the Rule of St Benedict."⁹⁶ Gould also recognizes, even among the allegedly individualistic Desert Fathers, that

> this renunciation of society . . . was not an individual quest like the self-determination of a small farmer. It did lead to the creation of a new community, a new social ideal . . . and it was in the institution of the *agape* the communities possessed a means of cohering into an identifiable group.⁹⁷

This developing sense of relationship between the eucharistic common life and the eschatological vision ensures that communal monasticism will become increasingly important. Older histories have presented the earliest monasticism as being incorrigibly individualistic, even competitive.⁹⁸ The word "monk" is derived from the Greek *monachos* and traditionally carried connotations of being one, alone, or solitary.⁹⁹ While monastics in the eastern traditions may have conceived of *monachos* as the quest for "singularity" or union with God, within fifty years of Athanasius writing the *Life of Anthony*, Augustine understood the use of "monos/monachos" in a thoroughly communal sense.

> The Greek "monos" means "one," but not "one" in any sense. A man in a crowd is one, but he can be called "one" only in association with many others. He cannot be called "monos," that is "one alone." The Greek "monos" means "one alone." Therefore, "monos," that is, "one alone" is correct usage for those who live together in such a way as to make one person, so that they really possess, as the Scriptures say, "one heart and one soul" (Acts

---

95. Clouse, "Millennium," 715.
96. Dunn, *Emergence of Monasticism*, 28.
97. Gould, *Monastic Community*, 185.
98. Workman, *Monastic Ideal*, 41–50. See also Butler, *Monachism*, 13.
99. Dunn, *Emergence of Monasticism*, 8. See also Davidson, *Public Faith*, 135.

4:32)—many bodies but not many souls, many bodies but not many hearts.[100]

Alongside eremitic and communal forms of monasticism we should also acknowledge those forms of monasticism that purists would subsequently dismiss: married couples, families, or larger households that lived under some form of common, intentional, ascetic discipline, but not under the discipline of an Order or formal Rule. Such renunciates receive favorable mention in (some of) the *Sayings*. Eucharistos the Secular and his wife are sought out for spiritual advice by two monks, in response to a divine instruction. Reluctantly they divulge some aspects of their life, including elements directly related to life on the land. "Here are these sheep; we received them from our parents, and if, by God's help we make a little profit, we divide it into three parts: one for the poor, the second for hospitality, and the third for our personal needs."[101] Poemen invites a secular to teach his monks.[102] Silvanus, in a vision reminiscent of the warning of Jesus (Matt 21:31–32), "was taken up to see the judgement and I saw there many of our sort coming to punishment and many seculars going into the kingdom,"[103] and Syncletia, whose admonitions feel more severe than most in the *Sayings*, can nevertheless acknowledge,

> we are like those who sail on a calm sea, and seculars like those on a rough sea. We always set our course by the sun of justice, but it can often happen that the secular is saved in tempest and darkness, for he keeps watch as he ought, while we go to the bottom through negligence, although we are on a calm sea, because we have let go of the guidance of justice.[104]

These alternative forms of monasticism are practiced by those who for various reasons have not abandoned the challenge of owning and working property and attending to public obligations. Subsequent to these cautious affirmation in the *Sayings*, we find that Basil's *Longer Rules* "are prefaced with an address to a group of Christians who had gathered to escape the outside world for one evening only."[105] Such less formal

---

100. Augustine, "Commentary on Psalm 132.6," cited in Lawless, *Augustine of Hippo*, 158.

101. Ward, *Sayings*, 51.

102. Ward, *Sayings*, Poemen, 153.

103. Ward, *Sayings*, 186.

104. Ward, *Sayings*, 197.

105. Dunn, *Emergence of Monasticism*, 36. See also Silvas, *Asketikon*, 153–60, especially (1) and note 1, 153.

expressions of monastic commitment will reappear in the tradition. No doubt some will deserve Benedict's astringent dismissal of the sarabaites as, "the third and most detestable kind of monks,"[106] but not all. Dunn instances numbers of small and informal communities springing up throughout Gaul and Italy.[107] They do not receive special benefactions and dispensations, nor tax and tithe relief, but wish nevertheless to deliberately give the resources of their lives to the call of Christ. How they then live in the land will be as important as the practice of their vowed and more reclusive monastic brothers and sisters.

Here then are four characteristics central to the monasticism of the desert: A valuing of creation as the place of divine encounter, a desire to live lightly and closely with creation, eucharistic prayer, and some attempt to express together the vision of paradise restored—the new age of the eschaton. These elements reappear, and it is to this monasticism of the desert that later writers refer their readers when wanting to offer inspiration and encouragement.[108] Although there will be debate and changing emphases, these characteristics from the desert provide both foundation and framework for all that will subsequently develop.

Living in the Liturgy: Basil of Caesarea, the Cappadocian Fathers, and Their Big Sister Macrina

Born about 329 into an aristocratic Cappadocian Christian family—"the most remarkable family in Christian history,"[109] according to Anna Silvas—Basil was from childhood exposed to a culture of saintliness, ascetical commitment, theological debate, and public responsibility.[110] Both his parental families had known persecution, dispossession, and exile for their Christian faith, so a vision of demanding discipleship was a commonplace rather than a surprise in Basil's own spiritual history. In the Hellenistic world of Cappadocian Caesarea, Constantinople, and Athens, his first educational and professional forays were into medicine and rhetoric.[111] Both interests would impact on his later exposition of

---

106. White, *Rule of Benedict*, 11 (section 1).
107. Dunn, *Emergence of Monasticism*, 90.
108. White, *Rule of Benedict*, 104.
109. Silvas, *Asketikon*, 51
110. Silvas, *Asketikon*, 51–64.
111. Kaiser, *History of Science*, 41–42.

Christian faith, but before that could occur there were other journeys for him to make.

About 355 Basil took a teaching appointment in Caesarea, but by 356–57 he was on a study tour among the monks of Egypt, probably following Eustathius—a long-time family friend and mentor from childhood. Basil and Eustathius would eventually make a painful parting of their ways—partly over Eustathius's ongoing sympathies for Arianism and partly over hyper-ascetic elements in his conception of the monastic life.[112] Nevertheless his influence remained in the radical social teachings and the commitment to service of the poor embodied in the Basilian/Macrinan monastic vision.[113]

Meanwhile his older sister Macrina, after the death of her fiancé, had adopted her own form of domestic asceticism as a virgin-widow; his brother Naucratius, already a monk, had drowned in hunting accident along with Chrysaphius—his former slave become monastic brother; and his widowed mother Emmelia had followed Macrina's persuasion and herself adopted a monastic life on the family estate at Annisa. By late 357 Basil had received baptism, and as a sign of this conversion returned to the family estate and to a semi-secluded monastic life. In 360 he was ordained as a Reader, in 362 as a Presbyter—an office which allowed a vastly expanded teaching ministry, and in 370 he became Bishop of Caesarea.[114] Eventually two other brothers, Gregory—later bishop of Nyssa, and Peter—later bishop of Sebasteia, would also follow the monastic calling.

In all these developments the seminal role of Macrina cannot be underestimated. Silvas describes her as "the hub of a galaxy of saints . . . a spiritual mother and teacher to her own mother Emmelia and to each of her four brothers"[115] This influence must be regarded more seriously than simply that of an overbearing or especially doting big sister! It was deeply theological. She continued to work on Basil, eventually weaning him from an essentially Hellenistic conception of monasticism to one thoroughly formed by exposure to the Christian Scriptures.[116] Emmelia's monastic reconstruction of the estate entailed the establishment of a

---

112. Silvas, *Asketikon*, 55.
113. Dunn, *Emergence of Monasticism*, 35–36.
114. Fedwick, *Basil of Caesarea*, 7–11.
115. Silvas, *Asketikon*, 52.
116. Silvas, *Asketikon*, 86–89. See also Fedwick, *Basil of Caesarea*, 6.

radically new social order—most clearly exemplified in the dissolution of all signs of hierarchical class distinctions,[117] which Basil would call "the citizenship of heaven."[118] It was Macrina who, with brother Peter, had developed the model of communal life into which Basil would move from a life of seclusion and extreme privation,[119] to one more flexible in its austerities and which always engaged with the church, the local bishop, and ministry to human need.[120] Most importantly from the perspective of this study, she provided significant theological reflection of her own upon nature and the place of humanity within it.[121]

Basil—Aesthetical and Ascetical Theologian

Silvas has traced the development and interrelations of Basil's monastic rules. These are not an ideal conceived in private but are themselves the fruit of lived pastoral and communal experience. Not only are they presented as a complete and theologically integrated statement of the Christian faith (much more so than either Augustine's or Benedict's subsequent Rules would be), they are also framed around a eucharistic narrative, frequently quoting or alluding to various of the Basilian liturgies.[122] Thus the questions that especially concern us, regarding Basil's account of nature and the place of humanity in relation to nature, are addressed in the *Rules* only in the context of a complete theological and pastoral synthesis. George Kustas has explored in much greater depth than we can review here this integrative feature of Basil's work in "Saint Basil and the Rhetorical Tradition."[123]

Nature in the Theology of Basil

The patristic interest in the theology of creation is exemplified in Basil's *Hexaemeron* (*HEX*), a series of Lenten studies on Genesis chapter one. At the outset Basil reminds his hearers that the goodness of the creation

117. Gregory, "Vita Sancta Macrinae," in Silvas, *Asketikon*, 67.
118. Basil, "Letter 207," in Silvas, *Asketikon*, 73.
119. Workman, *Monastic Ideal*, 115.
120. Silvas, *Asketikon*, 72–73, 93. See also Dunn, *Emergence of Monasticism*, 35.
121. Butler Bass, "Michael Vick Versus Gregory of Nyssa."
122. Silvas, *Asketikon*, 169, note 82.
123. Kustas, "Rhetorical Tradition," 221–79.

is inextricably bound up with the purpose for which God has brought it into being.

> You will finally discover that the world was not conceived by chance and without reason, but for a useful end and for the great advantage of all beings, since it is really the school where reasonable souls exercise themselves, the training ground where they learn to know God; since by the sight of visible and sensible things the mind is led, as by a hand, to the contemplation of invisible things. "For," as the Apostle says, "the invisible things of him from the creation of the world are clearly seen, being understood by the things that are made." (*HEX*, 1.6)[124]

Although the creation enables "reasonable souls . . . to learn to know God," we note that it does not exist for them alone but "for the great advantage of all beings." It is this mutuality of advantage for all beings which constitutes for Basil one of the key reasons that reasonable souls should read the signs of God within it. Thus, the beauty of the universe is a reflection of, and a pointer towards, the beauty of God (*BLR*, 2.14–22).[125] "I want creation to penetrate you with so much admiration that . . . the least plant may bring you to the clear remembrance of the Creator" (*HEX*, 5.2). Beauty—which includes goodness,[126] is a key element in both Basil's account of nature and his ascetical discourse. Through sixteen verses near the beginning of *The Longer Responses* (*BLR*), Basil reflects on the longing that beauty may inspire in the soul (*BLR*, 2.9–25).[127] The saints, he writes,

> insatiable in their desire of the vision of the divine beauty, prayed that their vision of the sweetness of the Lord might extend into eternal life (cf. Ps. 15:11, 26:4). So then, human beings are by nature enamored of and love the beautiful. Now what is truly beautiful and lovable is the good. But *it is God who is good* (cf. Luke 18:19). Thus, if all things tend to the good, then all things tend to God. (*BLR*, 2.24–25)[128]

By inspiring such yearning beauty becomes an element in the quest to fulfill the two great commandments to love, the call to which

---

124. See also Basil, *HEX*, 312 (3.10), and *HEX*, 316 (4.6).
125. Basil, *BLR*, 165.
126. Silvas, *Asketikon*, 164, note 54.
127. Basil, *BLR*, 164.
128. Basil, *BLR*, 166.

constitutes both the beginning and the whole structure of *The Longer Responses* (*BLR*, 1.1–2.8).[129] This orientation to love, in thankful recognition of benefits received, is something we can also observe in animals, and indeed we may learn from them (*BLR*, 2.28–38).[130]

Because nature in its beauty has this role in pointing us to God, Basil takes nature seriously as nature.

> I know the laws of allegory, though less by myself than from the works of others. There are those truly, who do not admit the common sense of the Scriptures, for whom water is not water, but some other nature, who see in a plant, in a fish, what their fancy wishes . . . like the interpreters of dreams who explain visions in sleep to make them serve their own ends. For me grass is grass; plant, fish, wild beast, domestic animal, I take all in the literal sense. "For I am not ashamed of the gospel." (*HEX*, 9.1)[131]

Basil knows nature as it is. He recognizes that not all plants have been created "in view of the wants of our bellies . . . but that some plants poisonous to us are food for others" (*HEX*, 5.4). He has witnessed the seasonal migrations of the fish and knows their predatory ways, along with the cunning food gathering of the crab (*HEX*, 7.3–5); he describes in detail the communal life of bees and the remarkable mathematics of their engineering (*HEX*, 8.4); he recognizes emotion and communality in animals and sees this as a sign that they too are possessed of souls, "they express by cries their joy and sadness, recognition of what is familiar . . . need of food, regret at being separated from their companions, and numberless emotions" (*HEX*, 8.1). He identifies the necessity of fecundity in herbivorous animals in comparison to carnivores, and recognizes significance in their different morphologies (*HEX*, 9.5). "Think of all these creatures . . . recognize everywhere the wisdom of God; never cease to wonder, and, through every creature, to glorify the Creator" (*HEX*, 8.7). While he rejects allegorical accounts of nature, which fail to take nature seriously in its own created actuality, he is nevertheless quite happy to use what he sees as sermon illustrations! The predatory fish, for example, do not deserve our reproaches, because they are only keeping their place in the scheme of things.

---

129. Basil, *BLR*, 160–64.
130. Basil, *BLR*, 167–68.
131. See also Basil, *HEX* (3.9), 311.

> A fish does not resist God's law, but we men cannot endure his precepts of salvation. Do not despise fish because they are dumb and quite unreasoning; rather fear, lest, in your resistance to the disposition of the Creator, you have even less reason than they . . . they have not the gift of reason, but they have the law of nature firmly seated within them to show them what they have to do. (*HEX*, 7.3)

Nevertheless, Basil is astute enough not to make his theological account of nature too dependent upon any one scientific account. In Homily 1 he describes a number of different suggestions regarding what it is that the earth rests upon, and without opting for any particular one, concludes, "we must remain faithful to the thought of true religion and recognize that all is sustained by the Creator's power. 'In His hands are the ends of the earth'" (*HEX*, 1.9). Of the Ptolemaic conception he suggests, "if there is anything in this system which might appear probable to you, keep your admiration for the source of such perfect order, for the wisdom of God" (*HEX*, 1.10). He revisits this issue in Homily 9, recognizing many cosmological conjectures that remain unaddressed by Scripture, not because creation is unimportant but because, "Scripture [has] in view the edification and the making perfect of our souls" (*HEX*, 9.1).

In all of this we find a delicately balanced sacralizing and desacralizing—or more accurately a de-divinizing, of nature. The Word of God which spoke creation into being at the beginning continues "pervading creation" (*HEX*, 9.2) and calling forth obedience, while the Holy Spirit "cherished the nature of the waters as one sees a bird cover the eggs with her body and impart to them vital force from her own warmth . . . that is, prepared the nature of water to produce living beings . . . and took an active part in the creation of the world" (*HEX*, 2.6).

Thus, Basil's is a thoroughly trinitarian creation, "the Originator of all things is One: He creates through the Son and perfects through the Spirit," and—in the verse so loved by patristic writers on creation—"'By the Word of the Lord the heavens were made, and all their host by the Spirit of His mouth (Ps 32:6 LXX)'" (*THS*, 16.38).[132]

Furthermore, in both the *Hexaemeron* and *On the Holy Spirit*, Basil writes of "pure intelligences who fill the essence of the invisible world" (*HEX*, 1.5), or of angels "as helpers, fellow-servants, faithful witnesses of the truth . . . set in command over men as teachers and guardians"

---

132. Basil, *THS*, 62.

(*THS*, 13.29–30).¹³³ Every action of life "is accomplished in the presence of the earth and the skies, and they will also be present on that day when every man is judged,"—and the psalms, Moses, Isaiah, Jeremiah, and Paul all call upon the natural world to bear witness—"Joshua . . . even calls a stone to give testimony" (*THS*, 13.30).¹³⁴ The Earth is described as "a universal Mother" (*HEX*, 2.1), who "was in travail in virtue of the power that she had received from the Creator . . . waiting for the appointed time and the divine order to bring forth" (*HEX*, 2.3).

Basil recognizes however that "if matter is uncreated, it has a claim to the same honors as God, since it must be of equal rank with Him" (*HEX*, 2.2),¹³⁵ and he is uncompromising in rejecting any such divinizing of creation. Harold Turner suggests that arising from his reading of Genesis 1,

> basic in Basil's view was the creation of the universe out of nothing, by divine fiat, and its being given a relative autonomy and orderly form we discover and express in the laws of nature. In these ways it is contingent upon and represents the freedom and rationality of its creator. This was quite unintelligible and foreign to the Greek mind, where the universe was of divine nature, eternally co-existing with God.¹³⁶

Georges Florovsky likewise argues that the debates about Arianism were not simply about the incarnation and the doctrine of the Trinity, but equally about the nature of the relationship between God and creation. The Chalcedonian formulation of the "two natures" doctrine served to clarify that

> the real existence of a created human nature, that is, of an other and second nature outside of God and side by side with Him, is an indispensable prerequisite for the accomplishment of the Incarnation without any change in or transmutation of the Divine nature.
>
> What is created is outside of God, but is united with Him. The Fathers of the fourth century, moved by the Arian controversy to define the concept of creation in a clear and precise manner, stressed above all else the heterogeneity of the created and

---

133. Basil, *THS*, 50–52.
134. Basil, *THS*, 51–52; also (16.38) 62–64.
135. See similarly Basil, *HEX* (1.7), 289–90.
136. Turner, *Roots of Science*, 92.

the Creator in counter distinction to the "consubstantiality" of generation; and they corrected this heterogeneity with the dependence of creation upon the will and volition.[137]

Furthermore, Basil will not have the waters above and below the heavens (Gen 1:6–7) understood as

> a figure to denote spiritual and incorporeal powers. In the higher regions, above the firmament, dwell the better; in the lower regions, earth and matter are the dwelling place of the malignant . . . although however, waters above the heaven are invited to give glory to the Lord of the Universe, do not let us think of them as intelligent beings; the heavens are not alive because they "declare the glory of God," nor the firmament a sensible thing because "it sheweth forth His handiwork," . . . this is only a figure, accepted as such by enlightened minds, to complete the glory of the Creator . . . Besides the singer of the Psalms does not reject the deeps which our inventors of allegories rank in the divisions of evil; he admits them to the universal choir of creation, and the deeps sing in their language a harmonious hymn to the glory of the Creator. (*HEX*, 3.9)

Nor is the darkness on the face of the deep a reference to evil powers or personifications in perpetual struggle with God (*HEX*, 2.4). Evil itself "is not a living animated essence; it is the condition of the soul opposed to virtue, developed in the careless on account of their falling away from good" (*HEX*, 2.4). Even the creation of the sun follows the appearance of green herbs upon the earth, "in order that those who live in ignorance of God may not consider the sun as the origin . . . or as the maker of all that grows out of the earth" (*HEX*, 6.2).

The whole purpose of creation is to point beyond itself. Firstly, by its beauty and its provision for life it awakens in us thanksgiving and praise to God, and secondly, it gets us thinking beyond creation and of eternity. Thus, in a complex exposition of the significance of the expression "one day," Basil relates the periodicity of each day to the periodicity of each week and concludes, "such is also the character of eternity, to revolve upon itself and to end nowhere" (*HEX*, 2.8). The week of course begins again on the eighth day, and this is

---

137. Florovsky, "Creation and Creaturehood," 540. Incidentally, this observation regarding the centrality of divine volition in the thinking of the Eastern Fathers also contradicts White's contention that voluntarism is a peculiarly Western conception.

in order that you may carry your thoughts forward towards a future life, that Scripture marks by the word "one" the day which is the type of eternity, the first fruits of days, the contemporary of light, the holy Lord's day honored by the Resurrection of our Lord. And the evening and the morning were one day. (*HEX*, 2.8)[138]

Not only the week, but the day also is divided into the seven hours of prayer, "none of which should be overlooked by those who have freely chosen to live in watchfulness to the glory of God and his Christ" (*BLR*, 37.5).[139] Writing to Bishop Optimus, Basil again references the seventh day as one of Sabbath and Jubilee, noting that "scripture continually assigns seven as the number of remission of sins," and that, after the seventh day,

> a new life began over again . . . these things are types of this present life, which revolves in seven days and passes by, wherein punishments of slighter sins are inflicted, according to the loving care of our good Lord, to save us from being delivered to punishment in the age that has no end.[140]

Thus, Basil's creation must be understood eschatologically, a dimension which according to Silvas "played an important part in Fourth Century asceticism."[141] Exemplifying the harmony of style and substance which Kustas identifies as shaping Basil's rhetoric, the eschatological vision of restoration is not merely taught; by this periodicity it is actually built into the creation.[142]

Although it has no share in the divine nature, nature is sustained by the divine Word and enlivened by the divine Spirit. Alongside and above human beings are other angelic and reasonable creatures who both guide and keep a watchful accountability, as also do the irrational elements of the material creation. Human beings in fact live within a highly constrained network of relationships, all of which function for God's purposes. This is no mere materiality available to humanity for whatever

---

138. See also Basil, *HEX* (1.3), 286; and a similar argument in *THS* (27.66), 100–101.

139. Basil, *BLR*, 247.

140. Basil, "Letter to Optimus," 297.

141. Silvas, *Asketikon*, 160, note 25. See also Chryssavgis, "Christian Orthodoxy," 2–3.

142. Kustas, "Rhetorical Tradition," see 230, 241, 247, 252.

rapacious plans we may conceive. Nature as creation exists not for our ends but for God's.

Humanity in Basil's Nature

Only in light of all the foregoing should we read a statement that could otherwise raise anxiety levels. Basil suggests that, far exceeding any of the blessings we may receive in creation,

> there is something we cannot pass over even if we wished to . . . and this one thing so great of which I speak is that God made man in his image and likeness (cf. Gen 1:26–27) and deemed man worthy of knowledge of himself and adorned him with reason beyond that of all animals and provided for his delight the ineffable beauties of paradise and appointed him ruler of all things upon the earth. (*BLR*, 2.41–44)[143]

Humanity thus completes creation yet remains an integral part of the whole. "Scripture depicts to us the supreme artist, praising each one of his works; soon, when His work is complete, He will accord well deserved praise to the whole together" (*HEX*, 3.10). Creation as beauty is a sign that creation exists not as an indifferent material resource for human consumption, but as the divine means to draw the human heart and mind towards God. What their creation as reasonable beings in the image and likeness of God allows for humanity is an active participation in the pursuit of the knowledge of God. We are not merely observers nor consumers. Thus, at the beginning of Homily 6 Basil likens his listeners to the crowd at the games, who so join in that "each one there should not only be a spectator of the athletes, but be, in a certain measure, a true athlete himself" (*HEX*, 6.1). This is a theory of knowledge that requires each one to bring personal light, commitment to a struggle, love, preparation, wonder at beauty, and humility. With such a disposition, then they will discover

> that you are formed of earth, but the work of God's hands; much weaker than the brute, but ordained to command beings without reason or soul; inferior as regards natural advantages, but, thanks to the privilege of reason, capable of raising yourself to heaven. (*HEX*, 6.1)

---

143. Basil, *BLR*, 168–69.

Thus we find that the capacity to command is not a concrete attribute, but something entered into only as one lives this life of committed seeking. Furthermore, this capacity is enabled, not in order to dominate other creatures but in order to raise ourselves to the contemplation of God. If entering into this form of existence depends upon seeking in a certain disposition of heart then it may be lost, and this of course is what happened. But, as the eucharistic narrative in *The Longer Responses* explains it, this loss has been redeemed by Christ and we are being remade (*BLR*, 2.45–57).[144] Even so, we are not to see the incarnation as only a post-lapsarian rescue mission. Chryssavgis describes the Cappadocian's position thus:

> A part of the original creative plan, the Incarnation of the Word of God is not perceived simply as a result of human failure but in fact constitutes an essential and natural characteristic of God. In this respect, the Incarnation is to be seen as related to the *creation* of the entire world and not limited to the *creation* of humanity. Thus, Gregory of Nyssa (c.395) describes the mystery of Incarnation as a normative, and not an exceptional movement in the relationship between God and the world. Thus Christ appears as the center and focus of all things (cf. Col 3:10–11), revealing the original beauty and restoring the ultimate purpose of the world.[145]

This restoration in us is no easy task, and the Prologue to the *Longer Responses* is clear that the whole manner of life must be one of continual repentance as a remaking of one's mind (*BLR*, "Prologue" 1–17).[146] Then, those for whom reason is awakened are enabled to engage in the praise of God in a manner uniquely fitted to their nature. Aided by the rest of creation and adding their own rationality, they complete creation's praise, but only in fellowship with the whole creation. And thus is begun the fulfillment of the first commandment, that we should love God.

This mutual fellowship in praise finds glorious and repentant expression in a prayer Scully attributes to Basil:

> O God:
> Enlarge within us the sense of fellowship with all living things,
> Our brothers and sisters the animals,

---

144. Basil, *BLR*, 170–71.
145. Chryssavgis, "Christian Orthodoxy," 2.
146. Basil, *BLR*, 153–60.

> To whom in common with us
> You have given this earth as home.
>
> We remember with shame
> That in the past we have exercised the high dominion of man
> With ruthless cruelty
> So that the voice of the earth,
> which should have risen to you in song,
> has turned into a groan of travail.
>
> May we realize that all these creatures
> Also live for themselves and for you, not for us alone.
> They too have the goodness of life as we do,
> And serve you better in their way, than we do in ours living it.[147]

To be made in God's image and likeness is the great grace but it does not, for Basil, confer any rights or freedom to use creation however we may please—as the prayer above so well acknowledges. Rather, "we are all the possessions of our Creator; we all share the rank of slave" (*THS*, 20.51).[148] This identity as servants becomes a recurring theme, but the obedience it calls for need not be servile. Obedience may arise from fear, greed, or love—and it is the latter that is in the character of those who, having received the Spirit know themselves to be the children of God (*BLR*, "Prologue" 3).[149] Christ made himself present upon earth in the guise of a servant, and this is the form of the new humanity in him—most especially in any holding positions of power or authority.

> The definition of Christianity is this: the imitation of Christ in the measure of his Incarnation according to the duty of each one's calling . . . For if the Lord was not ashamed of ministering to his own servants, but was willing to wait on the earth and clay that he had fashioned into man—*for I am in the midst of you, he says, as one who serves* (Luke 22:27)—how ought we to act towards those of equal honor with us? (*BLR*, 43.9-2)[150]

---

147. Scully, *Dominion*, 13. Scully attributes this prayer to Basil without a specific reference. Since completion of this book, controversy has arisen over whether the prayer comes from Basil or from a more recent time.

148. Basil, *THS*, 80.

149. Basil, *BLR*, 156–57; see also *BLR*, 157, note 10.

150. Basil, *BLR*, 255.

Furthermore, Diane Butler-Bass argues that this call to servanthood extends beyond human beings. Tracing the influence of Macrina, she suggests that

> human beings and "irrational animals" share common gifts from God, the ability to perceive and passions. What separates human animals from "irrational" ones is the capacity of free will, part of human ability to discern and choose. Thus humans are given the responsibility to care for animals, as irrational animals are subject to human free will.[151]

All this remaking in Christ is in order that by serving we may love our neighbors, and indeed the two loves are for Basil inextricably entwined (*BLR*, 3.58–69).[152] Consequently, the appointment as "ruler over all things," is only to enable this end. To love our neighbors is not one among a number of commands, but an essential element in the fulfillment of our creaturely nature. We are social animals and, as noted earlier, we may even learn from animals how this may be pursued.

> Now who does not know that man is a domesticated and sociable animal, not a solitary and wild one? Nothing is more characteristic of our nature that we have fellowship with one another, need one another and love our own kind. Since the Lord himself gave us the seeds of these things in anticipation, he therefore seeks fruit from them, and as the testimony of our love for him, he accepts our love for our neighbors. (*BLR*, 3.58–63)[153]

But for us, unlike the animals, this will not happen by instinct only. It requires also the exercise and the reconstitution of our reason. It is this sociality, integral to our created humanity, which leads Basil to promote the necessity of the communal life.

Humanity in Communal Life

Basil had observed the monks of Egypt, and although impressed by much that he saw, recognized that the oft preferred solitary life was quite counter to both our creation as social beings and the gospel call to communion. The whole of *Longer Responses*, chapter 7, is an exposition of

---

151. Butler Bass, "Michael Vick Versus Gregory of Nyssa."
152. Basil, *BLR*, 172–73.
153. Basil, *BLR*, 172.

the necessity of a communal life. Far more reasons are elucidated than we need to cover here but some are: The solitary life fails to recognize that our very survival involves dependence upon others, and this is a gift of God (*BLR*, 7.2–4);[154] and solitariness is also contrary to the law of love (*BLR*, 7.5),[155] "for neither are the hungry fed nor the naked clothed" (*BLR*, 7.8).[156] Thus the life to be pursued is the one modeled in the first communities described in the Book of Acts. Even more importantly, the communal life is the sign of the hope to which we are called (*BLR*, 7.9),[157] and it is the living expression of both the servant and high priestly ministries of Christ (*BLR*, 7.34–36).[158]

We love our neighbors by the provision we make for them through our work. And they do likewise for us because in Basil's conception we never work for ourselves alone and give away the surplus—it is the community through its leaders that ensures that each receives what they need. "The worker's purpose is not to minister to his own need by his own labors, but to fulfill the command of the Lord who said: 'I was hungry and you gave me food (Matt 25:35)'" (*BLR*, 42.1–2).[159] Although each is assigned to their own tasks, care of tools is seen as both a personal and a communal responsibility, so that no craft may appear as unimportant and no sense of private proprietorship develop (*BLR*, 41.2).[160] Basil's vision is not one of work dominating nature. Rather it is another element in renunciation, as one works not according to personal preference but communal direction (*BLR*, 42.1).[161] And the food produced and hospitality offered must also be simple, sustainable, and locally sourced (*BLR*, 19.19–22).[162]

All foods are good for Basil and are to be received with thanksgiving (*BLR*, 18).[163] Abstinence from certain foods, or the pursuit of intemperate pleasure with food, both indicate heretical tendencies—either questioning the goodness of creation or turning our minds from the quest for

154. Basil, *BLR*, 181.
155. Basil, *BLR*, 181.
156. Basil, *BLR*, 182.
157. Basil, *BLR*, 182.
158. Basil, *BLR*, 185.
159. Basil, *BLR*, 253–54.
160. Basil, *BLR*, 252–53.
161. Basil, *BLR*, 251.
162. Basil, *BLR*, 215.
163. Basil, *BLR*, 211–12.

fellowship with God (*BLR*, 16.1–25; 18; 19.1).[164] Abstinence from meat may be the exception, as we have earlier noted Berkman's observation that for Basil meat eating involved a sacrifice which had been surpassed by Christ and was contrary to the relations proper to the new creation.[165] Nevertheless, Basil is adamant that no strict rule can be drawn because of the great diversity of individual needs and conditions (*BLR*, 19.1–7).[166]

The appropriateness of different kinds of work depends upon local conditions. Generally, those tasks are preferred which safeguard communal peace, are not difficult to resource or sell, and which meet real needs not the demands of luxury or excess—"Agriculture is the best, since of its nature it provides the necessities of life and it preserves farmers from much wandering about or running hither and thither" (*BLR*, 38).[167]

Agriculture is "one of the arts bestowed on us by God to supply for the infirmity of nature . . . because what sprouts of itself from the earth is not sufficient to relieve our needs," (*BLR*, 55.1)[168]—and weaving, building, some metalwork, and medicine are others. The *Longer Responses* concludes with an unusually long section on the nature and role of medicine. Medicine is a gift of God, both for the body and, "as a pattern for the healing of the soul" (*BLR*, 55.1).[169] By it we are enabled to engage still more deeply with the wonder of creation, for

> not a single thing is useless. One serves as food to some animal; medicine has found in another a relief for one of our maladies . . . [hellebore, monkshood, mandrake and juice of the poppy—plants known to be poisonous, are mentioned] . . . These plants, then, instead of making you accuse the Creator, give you a new subject for gratitude. (*HEX*, 5.4)

Indeed it is proper that we care for the body so that we may properly serve the commandments of God.[170]

> It follows that we must neither avoid the art [i.e., medicine] completely [which manifests a contentious spirit], nor place all our hopes in it . . . all the same, it seems to me, the art contributes in

---

164. Basil, *BLR*, 205–8, 211, 212.
165. Berkman, "Consumption of Animals," 179.
166. Basil *BLR*, 212–13.
167. Basil, *BLR*, 248–49.
168. Basil, *BLR*, 265.
169. Basil, *BLR*, 265.
170. Basil, *BLR*, 214.

> no small measure towards self-control, for I see that it cuts out luxury and condemns satiety and banishes as unsuitable a rich diet and superfluous preparations of condiments. For the most part it calls want the mother of health, so in this respect, too, its counsels are not without use to us. (*BLR*, 55.3)[171]

> Let us arrange all things . . . fulfilling the commandment of the Apostle who said: "Whether you eat or drink, or whatever you do, do it all to the glory of God (1 Cor. 10:31)." (*BLR*, 55.5)[172]

Thus we see that whether in his general knowledge of nature, or his thinking about agriculture or medicine, Basil's understanding of human power is not at all directed towards the domination of nature; even where there is active engagement with nature it is for ascetic ends.

Basil continues developing the tradition that marries work and prayer. There are set times when work must be set aside, and he details scriptural warrant for all the canonical hours of prayer (*BLR*, 37.3–5).[173] These are especially valuable in cultivating a disposition of thanksgiving, because each has been chosen for "its own special reminder of benefits received from God" (*BLR*, 37.3).[174] But in addition to the set times

> for prayer and psalmody . . . every time is suitable; so . . . we praise God with the tongue . . . while we employ our hands at work, but if not, then in the heart. In this way we fulfill prayer even in the midst of work, giving thanks to him who gave both strength of hand to work and cleverness of mind to acquire the skill and also bestowed the material with which to work, both in the tools we use and in what is requisite for the crafts we practice, whatever they happen to be. And we pray that the work of our hands may be directed to the goal of being well pleasing to God. (*BLR*, 37.2)[175]

Thus all of life and all the gifts of creation are offered to God in thanksgiving, while in the same action the mind is being transformed.

---

171. Basil, *BLR*, 267.
172. Basil, *BLR*, 269.
173. Basil, *BLR*, 245–47.
174. Basil, *BLR*, 245.
175. Basil, *BLR*, 244–45.

Basil and the Ecumenical Creed

Along with his brother Gregory of Nyssa, and his friend (until being prevailed upon by Basil to become a bishop) Gregory of Nazianzus, Basil became one of that theological triumvirate known as the Cappadocian Fathers. Theirs was a politically astute and pastorally wise exposition of Nicene orthodoxy, which clarified the issues around the nature of Christ by addressing the question of the nature of the Holy Spirit (*THS*, 7–10).[176] Consequently, two years after Basil's death, the Council of Constantinople expanded the earlier Nicene statement, "We believe in the Holy Spirit," to confess, "We believe in the Holy Spirit, the Lord, the Giver of Life, who proceeds from the Father; who with the Father and the Son is worshipped and glorified" (*THS*, 7).[177] Basil thus became a key theological influence throughout the whole church, in the West as much as the East. Furthermore, "the *Hexaemeron* was paraphrased by Ambrose in 389, and an elegant Latin translation by Eustathius appeared around the turn of the fifth century. Basil's work was also known by Augustine, Cassiodorus, and the Venerable Bede."[178]

Basil heads Bede's list of those who have inspired and informed his own commentary on Genesis,[179] and Calvin Kendall's footnotes indicate Bede's constant recourse to the *Hexaemeron*. Besides being explicitly recommended as reading by Benedict in the final chapter of his *Rule*, Basil's *Rules* also were widely used throughout the west until as late as the tenth century.[180] J. M. Wallace-Hadrill notes that between 600 and 750 thirteen popes were Greek-speaking Easterners and "the Rule of Basil displaced that of St Benedict in many a Roman monastery."[181] Thus, not only his general influence in the ecumenical creed but also his specific teaching emphases became widespread and valued in the regions of the western church, and White's contention of a deep divide between eastern and western spiritualities is again called into question.

In his account of the history of science, Christopher Kaiser attributes to Basil the coherent formulation of three principal themes: "the comprehensibility of the world, the unity of heaven and earth, and the

---

176. Basil, *THS*, 7–10.
177. Basil, *THS*, 7.
178. Kaiser, *History of Science*, 21.
179. Bede, *Genesis*, 65. See further, Bischoff and Lapidge, *Commentaries*, 206–7.
180. Lawrence, *Medieval Monasticism*, 58.
181. Wallace-Hadrill, *Barbarian West*, 62.

relative autonomy of nature."[182] In addition, he notes "the liturgical concern for time and the regulation of monastic life as vehicles for the sense of regularity in the rhythms of the cosmos."[183] Further, Basil's interest in medicine, having found a theological synthesis between the miraculous and the natural (*BLR*, 55.1–5),[184] "gave rise to the Christian traditions of medical science and technology in the middle ages."[185] These developments lie open to White's charges concerning the impacts of Christian desacralization of the world, and Kaiser himself recognizes developments after the tenth century which begin to accord with White's judgments.[186] But for Basil, and in the monasticism which he inspired, any such powers are entirely about cultivating a life of awestruck thanksgiving, a disciplined simplicity of life, loving service of others, and purity of mind devoted to the loving pursuit of God.

A School for the Lord's Service: On Benedict and the Benedictines

About the year 500 a student in Rome, Benedict from Nursia, troubled by the licentiousness of his contemporaries and the general social decay around him, dropped out of his studies and took to a cave in the hills to pursue the life of a hermit monk. His desire was simply to seek God.[187] Below him literally and behind him figuratively lay a land devastated by both the long decay of the Roman Empire and one hundred years of Barbarian invasions. Historians of the period display a disturbing degree of unanimity in describing the social and environmental devastation, not only of the Italian Peninsula but of the European lands generally. Concluding a truly harrowing catalogue, Cuthbert Butler writes, "the picture is one of decay, disorganization, and confusion perhaps without parallel in history."[188] Yet Benedict would in time emerge from his hermit's cave with a renewed vision for community, and the movement that subsequently developed would become a source of healing and stability in that

---

182. Kaiser, *History of Science*, 34.

183. Kaiser, *History of Science*, 34–35.

184. Basil, *BLR*, 264–69.

185. Kaiser, *History of Science*, 34–35; on Basil's contribution to medicine and medical care, see also Turner, *Roots of Science*, 90, 113–14.

186. Kaiser, *History of Science*, 50–51.

187. Butler, *Monachism*, 8.

188. Butler, *Monachism*, 3. See also Fumagalli, *Landscapes of Fear*, 16–20.

troubled world. Nevertheless, in a statement with which he clearly agrees, Workman quotes Montalembert, "I firmly believe that he never dreamed of regenerating anything but his own soul."[189] The contrary argument of this section will be that, whatever may have been Benedict's concerns for his own soul, he had come to see that he would not be saved in isolation nor would he be saved apart from the earth upon which he and his monastic communities depended.

Others began to gather around him and initially he organized them into twelve monasteries of twelve members each. In response to opposition from local clergy, about 525 he took a small group and shifted south to Monte Cassino where they established the center that for the next fifteen hundred years would function, in myth and memory if not always in fact,[190] as the emotional and spiritual well-spring of the movement which was soon to develop. Here Benedict engaged in an act that for White and others symbolizes the Christian environmental history of Europe—he cut down the ancient grove of Apollo and turned the temple into a chapel of Saint Martin.

Subsequently, about 540, he compiled the *Rule* by which all future Benedictine life would be guided. Its goal was "to establish a school for the Lord's service, in which there shall be nothing harsh or oppressive."[191] The community would be in the nature of a family under a father's care,[192] and its members would be bound, not to an ascetic's stone but to one another, by "the chains of Christ."[193]

A twenty-first-century reader is probably disturbed by the provisions Benedict makes for disciplinary beatings—sometimes even of children, and perhaps bemused that such beatings are regarded as lesser punishments than periods of excommunication. This school seems harsh and oppressive yet it quickly drew members. Its austerities were no worse, and perhaps sometimes easier, than those endured by many—especially among the peasantry;[194] the security enabled by the common life was con-

---

189. Workman, *Monastic Ideal*, 12.

190. Butler, *Monachism*, 355–56 and note 1. See also Davidson, *Public Faith*, 322–24.

191. White, "Prologue," *Rule of Benedict*, 9.

192. White, "Prologue," *Rule of Benedict*, 7, 11–12; see also Workman, *Monastic Ideal*, 147; and Butler, *Monachism*, 28.

193. Workman, *Monastic Ideal*, 148.

194. Butler, *Monachism*, 32.

siderably greater than that of peasant subsistence;[195] the expectation of celibacy was not as burdensome as might be imagined given the allusion Peter Brown has somewhere made to the truly sinister demands made by marriage in the ancient world, upon the bodies of young people; poverty, pestilence, and appalling rates of infant and maternal mortality did little to make the married state an attractive life option;[196] but "amid the debris of classical civilization, in a world grown violent, barbarous, and unpredictable, Benedict's monastery offered an enclave of peace and order."[197] None of which means that his monks were not genuinely seeking God—the decay of the world must have made that quest seem one of the most rational of undertakings; nor that there were not significant costs and disciplines involved;[198] nor that his communities floated above the troubles of the times—"the years 537–542 were a time of misery for the Italian peoples that baffles description: the entire country went out of cultivation, and famine, starvation, and pestilence raged throughout the land,"[199] and in 577 Cassino itself was burned during the Lombard invasion. Yet some kind of alternative vision had been awakened, some more creative fire had begun to burn, and within two hundred years of Benedict's death his Order "had swarmed like bees into every land of the West . . . At one time the total number of Benedictine foundations in Western Europe is said to have been not less than fifteen thousand."[200]

The Community of the Benedictine Rule

The *Rule* describes a monastery which is "a unit, completely self-contained and self-sufficient, both economically and constitutionally."[201] Benedict himself wished that "the monastery should be arranged in such a way that everything necessary—in other words, water, the mill, the garden and the various crafts practiced—should be inside the monastery, so

---

195. Lawrence, *Medieval Monasticism*, 28.
196. Fumagalli, *Landscapes*, 23–30, for a general survey of conditions.
197. Lawrence, *Medieval Monasticism*, 38.
198. White, *Rule of Benedict*, 85–86.
199. Butler, *Monachism*, 5. See also Fumagalli, *Landscapes*, 20–21.
200. Workman, *Monastic Ideal*, 145.
201. Knowles, *Monastic Order*, 4.

that the monks do not need to go wandering outside for that is not at all good for their souls."²⁰² Thus,

> economically and materially it contained within its walls and fields all the necessaries of life and the means of converting them to man's use; living upon its own fields and exercising its own crafts, it was perfectly adapted to exist through and survive all the changes of the invasions; economically and administratively a unit, it escaped all the dangers of dismemberment short of total destruction.²⁰³

In contemporary parlance it was a model of environmental sustainability.

Furthermore, drawing into its fold all classes and conditions of people the community was a microcosm of the world, or hopefully of the world to come.²⁰⁴ In a world of endemic and brutal violence "many monks and priests rejected [violence] entirely, devoting themselves to a life of peace,"²⁰⁵ and many of the aristocracy, grown weary of constant resort to violence, retreated to the monastery as the place to pursue an alternative form of life.²⁰⁶ But the subsequent history, so frequently involving the accumulation of estates, tenants, servile workers, wealth, patronage and power, continually sees this model undermined, until such times as new reform movements develop.

Although Benedict himself imagined communities quite cut off from the surrounding world, this rarely turned out to be the case. The monasteries always served to model alternative ways of life, and these were often attempted, even by those who for any number of reasons did not embark upon a completely "regular" life.²⁰⁷ They soon became the main means of missionary expansion or centers of pastoral care in regions nominally Christian. As the only centers of learning across vast swathes of Europe, they also became centers of education and administrative capability for those attempting to establish some kind of civil order. Thus, to a degree far beyond what their numbers might imply, monasticism—and Benedictine monasticism especially, became a key

---

202. White, *Rule of Benedict*, 97.
203. Knowles, *Monastic Order*, 9.
204. Workman, *Monastic Ideal*, 156–57.
205. Fumagalli, *Landscapes*, 41.
206. Fumagalli, *Landscapes*, 59–65.
207. Dunn, *Emergence of Monasticism*, 201–2.

cultural influence, sometimes subservient to the civil power but often representing an alternative vision of how things should and could be.

Benedict's *Rule* appears to lack the theological integration which is the beauty of Basil's. There are rules but nothing of the narrative concerning creation, Christ, or the significance of this new community. Dunn notes that the only reference to the communal life of the Jerusalem church, so important for Basil and Augustine, does not appear until chapter 33 and then only in respect of property.[208] Similarly, although brotherly love makes it into the list of "Tools for Good Works" in chapter four,[209] it provides no overarching framework for the *Rule*.[210] Rather the focus is much more on the formational potential and the communal necessity of obedience.[211] Workman sees this emphasis on law as constituting its great appeal to the essentially pragmatic Roman world—"the *Rule* is instinct with the Roman genius for organization and solidarity,"[212] and it may also be that such a mix of authority and stability was the most important gift to offer in the degenerate situation Benedict was writing for.[213]

Esther de Waal, however, wishes to see this obedience rooted in an essential quality of listening. "Listen" is the very first word with which the *Rule* begins, and by this means obedience is connected to the call of Christ, the word of Scripture (which Benedict draws upon constantly), humility, and contemplative silence. This, for her, provides the theological integration.

> Benedict's spirituality is all about listening and the totality of listening. It begins with listening to the Word itself, for it is that which shapes and judges us. Just as Benedict himself is totally fed, directed, energized by the scriptures, he expects the same for us. We are to listen to the rule . . . the voice of the community, the father and the brothers, the mother and the sisters.[214]

She extrapolates to include "listening to the world"—which may be an excellent discipline but is not one of Benedict's requirements in his chapter on obedience. The section concludes, "it is only when I remind myself

---

208. Dunn, *Emergence of Monasticism*, 117–20.
209. White, *Rule of Benedict*, 17.
210. White, *Rule of Benedict*, xi–xii.
211. White, "Prologue," *Rule of Benedict*, 7–10, 17–20.
212. Workman, *Monastic Ideal*, 147.
213. Knowles, *Monastic Order*, 9.
214. de Waal, *Life-Giving Way*, 41–42.

that obedience is *ob-audiens*, listening intently to God rather than listening to my own self, that what Benedict is telling me ... is not impossible, for it is a response of love to love."[215] One can listen for Christ by listening in obedience to one's abbot, for in Benedict's vision the abbot is Christ's representative.[216] By that obedience we begin to participate with Christ in the repair of Adam's primal dis-obedience.[217] Nevertheless, we must read between the lines and in the subsequent tradition when attempting to identify any Benedictine theology of nature and the place of humanity in relation to that nature.

Nature in the Benedictine Vision

A first reading might suggest that there is no nature in the Benedictine vision. There is nothing of Basil's interest in plants, animals, or processes, nor of his theological reflection on the significance of beauty. The doctrine of the Word in creation, so central in other patristic writers, and in the contests with Gnosticism and Arianism, seems quite absent from Benedict. Even the contemplative life, following the teaching of John Cassian, is primarily focused on the meditative study of Scripture. Nature, if we may call it that, is, however, recognized in the bodily needs of human beings. These are not a cause of disdain in Benedict. He orders for adequate sleep,[218] and makes no provision for the antipathy to sleep witnessed in some of the Desert Fathers. Similarly he makes clear the abbot's responsibility of tenderness to the struggling and recalcitrant,[219] the importance of generosity with discernment in the cellarer,[220] flexibility for each different type and condition of person,[221] extra rations for those with special work responsibilities,[222] special care for the sick,[223] the young, and the aged,[224] and a generous and interesting daily provision of

---

215. de Waal, *Life-Giving Way*, 43.
216. White, *Rule of Benedict*, 13.
217. White, *Rule of Benedict*, 19–20. See also Lawrence, *Medieval Monasticism*, 29.
218. White, *Rule of Benedict*, 43.
219. White, *Rule of Benedict*, 48.
220. White, *Rule of Benedict*, 52–53.
221. White, *Rule of Benedict*, 56.
222. White, *Rule of Benedict*, 57–58.
223. White, *Rule of Benedict*, 59.
224. White, *Rule of Benedict*, 60.

food and drink.[225] Nature as the body is a necessary and accepted part of Benedict's spirituality. Ambrose Zenner finds all these provisions deliberately integrated as part of Benedict's vision of peace, and suggests he is following an Augustinian conviction that there is peace in observance of the laws of nature.[226] Thus this asceticism is not destructive but disciplined.

> The rule not only allows but actually encourages me to see my body as worthy of care and nurture, and to be honored as one element of the whole balance of body, mind, and spirit, playing its part in the daily rhythm of work, study, and prayer which Benedict establishes as the way to fullness of our humanity.[227]

Nevertheless, this body bears a fallen humanity, which will constantly seek to indulge the body and distract its focus and energies from the pursuit of God. We must therefore be disciplined and that is the whole point of all ascetic practice[228]—and also the potential root of the antipathy to the body that appears repeatedly in the tradition.[229]

Alongside these recognitions of the needs of the body as nature, Benedict also recognizes the importance of accommodating life to the rhythm of the seasons. In chapters 8 to 10, he provides for changes to the order of daily prayer according to the time of year,[230] and similarly with regard to meal times,[231] the hours of daily labor,[232] and the need for appropriate clothing.[233] Despite the complete absence of reference to other creatures nor any suggestion that humans have a place of "dominion" in all this, there appears to be no distinction drawn between humanity and nature. Humans are neither the enemy of nature nor the entirety of nature, but they are that part of nature that needs to be reoriented to God and remade in Christ.

When, however, one engages in a deeper re-reading of the *Rule* it reveals a remarkable engagement with nature beyond human beings, rather

---

225. White, *Rule of Benedict*, 62–63.
226. Zenner, "Saint Benedict's Peace," 59.
227. de Waal, *Life-Giving Way*, xiv; see also De Vogue, *Commentary*, 234–35.
228. White, *Rule of Benedict*, 33.
229. Fumagalli, *Landscapes*, 165–69.
230. White, *Rule of Benedict*, 27–29.
231. White, *Rule of Benedict*, 64.
232. White, *Rule of Benedict*, 72–73.
233. White, *Rule of Benedict*, 81–82.

like a Narnian wardrobe or a Chinese box. All commentators recognize the centrality for Benedict of "the work of God," that is the life of prayer and praise.[234] Through chapters 9 to 18 Benedict carefully outlines an order of prayer that will see the whole Psalter sung during the course of one week. There are seven "hours" during the day and the night office as well. Significantly from our point of view, some psalms are used not once but every day. Always they will sing Psalm 3—a night prayer for deliverance, and 95—an affirmation that not only the singers but the whole creation, are God's. Every day at Lauds they sing of the blessings of creation in Psalm 67, and join their praise with that of the whole creation in Psalms 148 to 150. Thus, although creation goes unmentioned in the *Rule*, it is the *Rule* that draws the community into a constant engagement with creation in the totality of body, mind, and heart at worship.

In addition to the daily round of Psalms, the *Rule* also provides for the singing during Vespers of "one of the Ambrosian hymns."[235] Albert Kleber points out that these are based on Ambrose's *Hexaemeron*, and each day's hymn is a meditation on one day of creation.[236] The singers' prayer is that the creative work of God in the world will be replicated in some aspect of their own spiritual re-creation. The Hymn for day six recognizes that humans have power over the other creatures also created on that day, but as Kleber observes,

> it is senseless, in fact sacrilegious, for man to become proud because he begins to understand and apply the forces and laws of nature . . . God has made and adapted all things unto this purpose; by his work, man merely becomes the beneficiary of God's generosity to him.[237]

Equally significant is the recognition that whatever powers the humans have they have been corrupted and are at constant risk of being misused. The prayer is that while they may tame animals they will also tame their own inner wildness, and while fruit from the earth provides for their sustenance they may produce in their own lives the fruit of peace.[238] Benedict astutely arranges his material so that the hymns for Saturday—the day of Sabbath rest and the gathering of the whole creation

---

234. White, *Rule of Benedict*, 66. See also Knowles, *Monastic Order*, 5.
235. White, *Rule of Benedict*, 28.
236. Kleber, "Hymns," 171–87.
237. Kleber, "Hymns," 184.
238. Kleber, "Hymns," 183–85.

in praise—are also the hymns for Sunday—the first day of creation and the day of the Lord's resurrection, the beginning of the new creation.

> Throughout this hymn there is no longer any thought of sin and its consequences as there was in the other Vesper hymns. Now the toils and fears of the workday week are over, and the children of God are happy to have entered upon their Sabbath rest and joy, a type as well as an anticipation of the eternal Sabbath in the beatific vision of God.[239]

Thus the rhythm of life in the monastic community revolves around sharing in the praise of all creation, and that praise anticipates the renewal of creation signified in the Sabbath. This praise is not a spiritual activity squeezed into the busyness of the secular day, rather it infuses the whole day, is the framework into which all else fits, and by which all of life is offered to God. Time itself is sanctified by the recurring rhythm of the daily and weekly hours of prayer, "according to the sacred number seven,"[240] and by the skillful association of particular psalms with particular periods of the day.[241]

On Nature and Time

The sanctification of time is a central theme in the monastic engagement with creation. The need to understand and predict the seasons was vital to a properly ordered life and this was achieved, not by imposing a purely human construct upon creation, but by identifying those rhythms that the creator had built into the creation. Thus, about two hundred years after Benedict, as the movement reached some of its most prolific flowering in distant Northumbria,[242] Bede carefully calculated *The Reckoning of Time*. Bede recognized three ways of reckoning time; it may be either according to nature, or custom, or authority. This authority is itself twofold. It is either human authority—seen for example in holding Olympics in a cycle of four years, or divine authority, seen when "the Lord in the law commands that the Sabbath be kept on the seventh day."[243] He further recognizes that custom makes inaccurate calculations of the courses of

---

239. Kleber, "Hymns," 187.
240. White, *Rule of Benedict*, 36.
241. White, *Rule of Benedict*, 36, 39, and also 115.
242. Knowles, *Monastic Order*, 23 and note 5.
243. Bede, *Reckoning of Time*, 13.

the sun and moon, but "with nature as our guide we discover"[244] solar, lunar, embolismic, nineteen-year lunar cycles, and planetary movements through the zodiac. "This nature was created by the one true God when he commanded that the stars which he had set in the heavens should be the signs of seasons, days, and years; it is not, as the folly of the pagans asserts, a creating goddess, one amongst many."[245]

Faith Wallis suggests that Bede finds a new role for nature, "no longer the governing deity of the lower world, nature is now God's law and instruction to His creation. Natural time was 'hard-wired' into the heavens on the fourth day of Creation."[246] Furthermore, Bede finds parallels between the week of creation and six other kinds of week in Scripture, "all of which, if I am not mistaken, point to a single end: that is they urge us to hope for endless peace in the grace of the Holy Spirit when all good works are accomplished,"[247] and this is the age of the Sabbath.

Bede's obsession with time in nature is focused in his desire to correctly calculate the date of Easter. We have noted Benedict's flexible accommodation of monastic life to the passage of the seasons, but Donato Ogliari demonstrates that this flexibility circulates around the centrality of Easter.[248] Calvin Kendall quotes Benedicta Ward, "'Easter was not an arbitrary date but the pivot of the whole cosmos, the central moment when reality was revealed in the face of Jesus Christ' . . . better than any of his contemporaries Bede knew the technical details of the *computus*, and Easter was for him both the starting point of history and the core of theology. He was passionately committed to its correct calculation."[249] Faith Wallis recognizes the sacramental significance of this concern: "The correct computation of Easter is, in his view, sacramental. It is a union of a sign with the reality it effects: Observing the Paschal season is not meaningless, for it is fitting that by means of it the world's salvation both be symbolized, and actually come to pass."[250]

These sabbatical and paschal realities are written into nature and the processes of creation. The point of all Bede's researches and computations

---

244. Bede, *Reckoning of Time*, 13. See also Bede, *Genesis*, 83–84.

245. Bede, *Reckoning of Time*, 14.

246. Bede, *Reckoning of Time*, 266.

247. Bede, *Reckoning of Time*, 32.

248. Ogliari, "Tempus Monasticum," 44–46. See also Böckmann, "Manual Labor; Part II," 283.

249. Bede, *Genesis*, 32.

250. Bede, *Reckoning of Time*, 274.

is not to rule over nature, but to properly discern and fit into what God has established. Not outside or over nature will human beings seek God and pursue their divine calling, but within nature, according to its sabbatical and paschal rhythms of time.[251] It can hardly be stressed too much that this vision sees nothing of nature handed over to human beings, but is entirely about human beings fulfilling their calling within the constraints of nature as God has established it.

On Space and Place

As with the sanctification of time in the monastic vision, so also with the sanctification of space. In his actions at the grove of Apollo Benedict was not secularizing but re-sacralizing the sacred space. The newly emergent monastic communities moved into the haunted forests to rebuild the ancient ruins. Theirs was a ministry of restoration, rather than a mission of domination.[252] If not initially, certainly eventually, Gregory's commission to Augustine in his Benedictine mission to Britain was not so much to destroy but to transform and sanctify the pagan cultic places.[253] Randon Jerris has explored the sanctification of space in a study of the landscape in the region of Churraetia.[254] The earliest Christian sites are found within the secure confines of Roman towns, and show no indication of being anything other than private initiatives lacking systematic or official organization.[255] After the withdrawal of Roman governance however, and during the confident expansion of Christian pastoral care, a new and apparently systematic dynamic appears. In the mountainous regions numbers of churches are built on the sites of much earlier pagan astronomical cult megaliths. Many of these are aligned to the sunrise at special dates in the agricultural year, before, after, or upon the winter or summer solstice, or to the sunrise on particular saints' days.[256] Bede likewise had identified the importance of the equinoxes.[257] Natural features such as mountaintops that had earlier featured in the pagan astronomical mapping are

---

251. Bede, *Genesis*, 96, and notes 122 and 123.
252. Fumagalli, *Landscapes*, 15–16.
253. Bede, *History*, 86. See also Davidson, *Public Faith*, 385.
254. Jerris, "Cult Lines," 85–108.
255. Jerris, "Cult Lines," 88.
256. Jerris, "Cult Lines," 95–98.
257. Bede, *Genesis*, 33–34, 83–84.

also claimed for the Christian faith by being renamed. In all this, Jerris identifies not the piecemeal appropriation of individual sites for Christian worship, but the establishment of "a network of monuments that embraced and thereby Christianized the landscape."[258] Time and space are inextricably entwined in this development.

What Bishops and Benedictines were doing in Bavaria paralleled what Bede was doing in Northumbria, and can probably also be witnessed in Brittany and southern England.[259] This is not the de-sacralization of the land, but it is certainly a re-sacralizing—this time according to a story that was believed to have universal significance and to embrace the whole creation. Randon suggests that "ultimately Christianity succeeded because it acknowledged the dependency of the people in these agricultural communities on the cycles of the natural world."[260] Given what we have seen of the monastic desire to establish the cycles of the natural world, the connections Jerris identifies should be regarded as being made happily rather than reluctantly. Further, we could argue that in sacralizing the land by an orientation towards Christ a less environmentally threatening conception was being developed, compared to that in which a pagan fertility cult is focused upon providing rich harvests and the accumulation of personal wealth.

On the Forests and Their Animals

This world of sacred time and sacred land represented God's providential ordering of creation. Much more ambiguous, however, were animals and the forests in which they lived. While some modern writers appear to romanticize the great forests of early medieval Europe, Fumagalli offers a more realistic account. After centuries of overexploitation, wars, dislocations and massive plague-induced depopulation,

> land once intensively settled and cultivated everywhere, from the wide lower valleys of the Alps and Appennines to the foothills and plains close to the towns, continued to revert to forest, marsh and moor. Even the towns, inside their crumbling walls, became overgrown and generally had an increasingly rural aspect as cultivated land dwindled into insignificance in

---

258. Jerris, "Cult Lines," 99.
259. Jerris, "Cult Lines," 99.
260. Jerris, "Cult Lines," 98.

comparison with the great areas of wilderness. Towns and villages were swallowed up by the advancing wilderness, and their ruins, choked by vegetation, were to be found everywhere until eventually monks began to reuse them as building material for their churches and monasteries.[261]

Pagan peoples lived with as much fear of being swallowed by these forests as did Christians,[262] but churchmen, he observes, were especially troubled by such desolation because, being educated, they knew that it had not always been so. In addition to these always encroaching forests of reversion there were also the vast *solitudines*—forests and wetlands that had never known cultivation or habitation, and were the domain of bandits, wild animals, and the occasional hermit.[263] The overwhelming disposition he identifies is one of vulnerability and fear. Thus, of the seventh to the twelfth centuries, Georges Duby writes,

> the level of material civilization remained so low that the main point of economic life is to be found in the struggle that man had to wage against natural forces day by day in order to survive. The fight was arduous, for he wielded ineffectual weapons and the power of nature overawed him.[264]

This is the context for the stories involving the destruction of the ancient pagan groves. In this light, the widespread veneration of trees[265] may not be a sign of sylvan idyll but of constant fear—fear so great that it extended to the practice of human sacrifice.[266] It is too easy for contemporary academics, protected by all the wealth and technologies of modernity, to make judgments upon people struggling barely to survive, slowly adopting and adapting a new vision of their place in such an inhospitable world.

> In the heart of the ancient, empty forests, countless small bands of monks led a life no different from that of the peasants who ventured into the forests to clear land for cultivation. Little by little, their combined efforts made inroads into, and eventually

---

261. Fumagalli, *Landscapes*, 15.
262. Fumagalli, *Landscapes*, 7.
263. Fumagalli, *Landscapes*, 15.
264. Duby, *Early Growth*, 5.
265. Fumagalli, *Landscapes*, 6–7.
266. Fumagalli, *Landscapes*, 12.

erased, the great forests which had covered almost all of Europe in the early Middle Ages.[267]

These changes did not however obliterate the forests, but rather created a mixed landscape of forest tracts, wetlands, and cultivations which, properly managed, provided a wide range of possibilities for farming, a wide diversity of resources, and still enough wild places for monks and hermits to find space for prayer and revelation.[268] In this "silvo-pastoral" economy some animals would be herded, while other wild ones would still roam the forest remnants. Duby argues that forests held sway over the whole natural landscape well into the twelfth century. Even at the abbey of St Germaine-des-Pres, an area "where agricultural endeavor had probably made greater progress than anywhere else . . . woodland still covered two-fifths of the estate"[269] at the beginning of the ninth century.

Bede seems aware of both beauty and menace in the forests. Commenting on Genesis 1:11–13—the earth bringing forth green plants and trees, he writes,

> it is clear . . . that the adornment of the world was accomplished in springtime, for that is the time when green plants usually appear on earth and trees are usually loaded with fruits. Likewise, it should be noted that the first shoots of the plants and trees did not appear from seed, but from the earth.[270]

This, according to Jones, is "Bede's ode to spring and creation," and further recognition that nature for him is God's created world.[271] In the subsequent exposition of the second creation story in Genesis 2 he is clear, both that this paradise is a real geographical location, somewhere "in this earth which we inhabit,"[272] and that

> poisonous plants were created for the punishment and for the torment of mortals. And it should be noted in regard to sin that we became mortals after sin. Men are mocked by barren trees, so that they may understand how shameful it is to be without the fruit of good works in the field of God . . . and so that they may fear that God may forsake them because they neglect the

267. Fumagalli, *Landscapes*, 21.
268. Fumagalli, *Landscapes*, 21–22.
269. Duby, *Early Growth*, 5.
270. Bede, *Genesis*, 79–80.
271. Bede, *Genesis*, 80, note 51.
272. Bede, *Genesis*, 113.

barren trees in their fields and do not apply any cultivation to them. Therefore, before the sin of man it is not written that the earth brought forth anything except crops of food and fruitful trees; but after sin we see that many wild and barren things spring up.[273]

In this account Bede alternates between literal and figurative readings of the text. Thus nature is not itself evil, but in the purpose of God elements of nature have taken on a menacing aspect, both in order to constantly remind humanity of its sin and thereby call us back to faithfulness, and in order to require of humanity a faithful cultivation of the earth and thereby discover the faithfulness of God. Bede also differs from Basil—for whom the poisonous plants had always been present but often useful for other creatures if not for humans, and only problematical for those who, due to their fallen loss of reason, no longer live appropriately and observantly in the world.

Towards the end of the period under review William of Aquitaine consulted with Abbot Berno regarding his desire to establish a monastery. Berno saw possibilities in the richly wooded valley of Cluny but William objected on the grounds that these woods were his favorite hunting grounds. "'Which will serve you better at the judgement, O Duke,' asked Berno, 'the prayers of monks or the baying of hounds?'"[274] By such tales we are reminded that the forests frequently served utilitarian purposes— the wealth and pleasure of powerful elites,[275] and while a monastic presence might see them removed, it might also see them retained either as a means of support or to ensure a degree of seclusion for the contemplative life. In fact, monks valued forests for a wider range of reasons than did secular lords, and Ellen Arnold suggests that flexible use of forest terminology was "useful to monks who did not want to construct either a single view of forested landscapes or an artificial divide between their own spiritual and secular uses of the natural world."[276]

It is a commonplace in contemporary literature regarding relations between humans and animals that the classical Christian position is presented as one of a fixed gulf between humans and animals, with humans established in the place of domination—a position articulated by Joyce

273. Bede, *Genesis*, 135.
274. Lawrence, *Medieval Monasticism*, 84.
275. Gies and Gies, *Technology and Invention*, 6.
276. Arnold, "Engineering Miracles," 497, note 3.

Salisbury, for example, in *The Beast Within: Animals in the Middle Ages*. She argues that the classical Christian position was "that humans and animals were qualitatively different (Augustine's view),"[277] and that in attempting to distinguish Christianity from paganism "the earliest church fathers rejected ... species ambiguity and established a principal of qualitative difference between humans and animals."[278] Consequently,

> the main principle defining animals was their perceived lack of intellect, "reason." Ambrose in the fourth century defined the unbreachable difference between the two species by claiming that humans have reason and animals are irrational. Augustine, too, confidently expressed humans' superiority to "brute animals" because humans are "rational creatures."[279]

While not dismissing her case entirely, I would argue that she has missed important nuances in the patristic tradition. As we have seen, Augustine did distinguish between humans and animals on the basis of rationality, but he also recognized that this rationality was not a concrete possession—rather it was a quality of life to be enjoyed when one was rightly orientated towards God. Therefore it could and would be lost when one turned away from God, and in that case one would become as the animals. Furthermore, part of the right exercise of rationality involved appropriate care for the wellbeing of the non-rational creatures. Basil had argued similarly, and in the Benedictine monastic tradition so too did Bede,

> there is no doubt that man was made in the image of God chiefly in the respect in which he surpasses the irrational creatures— that is to say, he was created capable of reason, by which means he could properly govern each and every created thing in the world and enjoy the knowledge of the One who created all things. Having been placed in this position of dignity, if he does not understand that he should behave well, he will be put in the same class with those same irrational animals over which he was exalted, just as the psalmist declares.[280]

Furthermore, despite the differences there may be between humans and other animals, Bede also recognizes their common creation on the same

---

277. Salisbury, *Beast Within*, 2. See also Page, "Fellowship," 102.
278. Salisbury, *Beast Within*, 4.
279. Salisbury, *Beast Within*, 5.
280. Bede, *Genesis*, 91–92.

day, suggests that the blessing pronounced upon human fertility is intended also to embrace all other animals,[281] and of Gen 1:27 writes that the man and woman are animals, but "unlike the other animals" in their particular bond of love, rather than rationality.[282]

The relationship with animals is complex. "Man does not still rule over all living creatures, for after he would not submit himself to his Creator he lost dominion over those whom the Creator had subjected to his jurisdiction."[283] Again we observe the elements of covenant and qualification in the understanding of dominion. Some animals are believed to have been created for the use of humankind,[284] while others are always wild and untamed. These, according to Salisbury's reading of Ambrose and Isidore, belong in the control of God.[285] Bede further distinguishes between human and other animals by drawing a double meaning out of Gen 1:21—"every living and moving creature." By taking moving to also mean mutable, he argues that humanity could have remained immutable had they kept the commandment, but "the other living creatures were made immediately in such a way that either they would die as nourishment for others or they would perish in their declining age from lack of the same."[286] Thus it appears that, for Bede, wild and even predatory nature is not something in need of human management or transformation, but is nature as God has created it. Yet there are apparent contradictions in Bede for a few verses below, in reflecting upon the provision of green plants for the nourishment of all living creatures (Gen 1:29–30), he writes,

> here it is clear that before the sin of man earth produced nothing harmful—no poisonous plant, no unfruitful tree. Since it is plainly said that every plant and all trees were given to men and to birds and to all the living creatures of the earth for food, it is clear that those birds did not live by stealing the food of weaker animals, nor did the wolf search out an ambush around the sheepfold, nor was the dust the serpent's food, but all things in harmony fed upon the green plants and the fruits of the trees.[287]

281. Bede, *Genesis*, 89.
282. Bede, *Genesis*, 92.
283. Bede, *Genesis*, 94.
284. Bede, *Genesis*, 88.
285. Salisbury, *Beast Within*, 14. See also Bede, *Genesis*, 88.
286. Bede, *Genesis*, 87.
287. Bede, *Genesis*, 94.

Throughout the history of interpretation, the disastrous impact of the fall appears as a constant refrain, but exactly how this rupture has impacted upon wild nature—those parts of creation outside of direct human influence, seems to be a matter of uncertainty, even for the same author within the same book! From the vast literature that now exists on the relations between humans and animals, the best that can be said in summary is that there is ambiguity regarding animals.

> A consequence of the intimate relationship with nature (characteristic of the early Middle Ages), was that animals were seen as the most authentic and forceful expression of nature, and at the same time as emblematic of the arcane forces which lay behind the natural order. Dogs, for instance, were held to exemplify the virtues of courage and faithfulness.[288]

But how an animal was perceived also depended upon one's own interest, "the wolf, for example, which for the aristocracy represented strength and courage, in clerical eyes stood for the negative aspects of those characteristics, violence and force."[289] Nor did such perceptions necessarily issue in consistency of behavior towards the animals concerned. The aristocracy still mounted hunting campaigns and "Charlemagne had appointed *luparii*, men who were employed specifically to hunt wolves."[290] On the other hand, in the presence of a saintly figure, wild animals could prove benign or even helpful. Thus, Paul the Deacon's great-grandfather was led to safety through the forest by a wolf.[291]

Fumagalli argues that as the medieval became the early modern world, "fear increased, as familiarity with the environment, the countryside, bodies and the animal and plant world diminished. This break has always been seen most clearly in the towns . . . the city stood in stark opposition to the countryside."[292]

Such fear also became increasingly "supernaturalised."[293] Salisbury however surveys the same medieval millennium convinced that "thinkers moved from the idea that humans and animals were qualitatively different (Augustine's view) to a notion that we have more in common

---

288. Fumagalli, *Landscapes*, 140–41.
289. Fumagalli, *Landscapes*, 142.
290. Fumagalli, *Landscapes*, 136.
291. Fumagalli, *Landscapes*, 16. See also Bede, *Genesis*, 94 and note 113.
292. Fumagalli, *Landscapes*, 1.
293. Fumagalli, *Landscapes*, 810.

with animals than we like to admit (Gerald of Wales' view.)"[294] As we have seen, Augustine's is a more nuanced position than Salisbury recognizes. And Gerald's in fact represents an ancient view of the instability of nature, common in the Celtic world, and not indicative of any new consciousness of human-animal commonalities.[295] Just as ambiguous as the animals are the positions taken by those who write about them. Commonalities between humans and animals were acknowledged in all the patristic and monastic writers we have considered. Equally, they also identified significant differences, and surely these are most clearly evident in the ability to write and publish books in which it is argued that the differences are largely imaginary!

Humanity in the Benedictine World of Nature

According to the divinely ordained rhythms of creation, the monks—and all who choose to join them will gather throughout the day in worship and in that worship will be reminded of their participation in praise with the rest of creation. Along with the worship they will also spend significant hours each day at manual work. This blend is a key characteristic of the Benedictine life and is the context for all reflection upon the role of human beings within the world of nature.

Work as Worship

Benedict's instructions on Daily Manual Labor begin by observing that the cellarer must regard "all the tools and utensils of the monastery as sacred vessels of the altar."[296] To adopt this particular metaphor is to declare, not simply that all tasks are important for the community life but that all are consecrated to the worship of God. Esther de Waal finds in this instruction liberation from the dualism

> that believes that the spiritual was of infinitely greater worth than the material, that God was much more interested in souls

---

294. Salisbury, *Beast Within*, 2.

295. Cahill, *How the Irish Saved Civilization*, 128–29. One could equally well read Gerald's story, of an illicit lover who turns into a repulsive hairy creature, as a perfect example of Augustine's understanding of the likely fate of those who neglect to live in God-given rationality—they become as the animals.

296. de Waal, *Life-Giving Way*, 103.

> than in bodies, that the saying of prayers was of far greater concern to him than the handling of the tools of my daily life . . . a split between the sacred and profane . . . such a dichotomy is not to be found in Benedict.[297]

In the Benedictine vision we do not offer to God some portion of wealth, in hope that such an offering will sanctify activity that is otherwise servile, profane or even unjust. All work must be done in obedience before God, in the obedience of Christ and for God's glory. There is nothing here of some sphere of human endeavor independent of the call of Christ and the purpose of God. Furthermore, Judith Sutera observes that,

> this image of the sacred vessels is reminiscent of Zech 14:20–21 where the prophet announces that, "every pot in Jerusalem and Judah shall be holy to the Lord of Hosts." . . . Thus Benedict evokes an eschatological image; all vessels have become holy in the already/not yet Kingdom, the new Jerusalem which the monastery symbolizes.[298]

David Stubbs sees this passage in Zechariah as central to the eschatological vision of the temple as both presence and foretaste of heaven on Earth,[299] and this further strengthens the case that the monastic community regarded itself in the same way.

As all life is consecrated, so daily manual labor is good for the soul.[300] To this end Benedict lays down slightly over six hours each day, with the encouragement not to be despondent when they have to gather the harvest themselves "because it is when they live by the work of their hands, like our fathers and the apostles, that they are truly monks."[301] Butler summarizes the impact of such a vision of human work: "in the condition of Italy at the time the best contribution to the work of the world that they could have made was the bringing of the devastated land under cultivation once more, and also the asserting the dignity of labour as the work of free men."[302]

The invitation to freely associate in a life of common labor represents a socialist vision about which Workman, with all the passion of

---

297. de Waal, *Life-Giving Way*, 104.
298. Sutera, "Stewardship and the Kingdom," 353.
299. Stubbs, "Protestant Eucharistic Imagination," 6.
300. White, *Rule of Benedict*, 72.
301. White, *Rule of Benedict*, 72.
302. Butler, *Monachism*, 373.

a late nineteenth-century Methodist, waxes lyrical; and which he contrasts with the rapaciousness of individualistic modern capitalism.[303] In such a revaluation of work Gies and Gies[304] and Sonnlechner[305] all find an impetus that undermined the old Roman institutions of slavery, and thereby the old latifundian estates, and thus contributed to a new social order.[306] It drew together theoretical and practical skills in a way that had rarely happened before—and which was always at risk of abandonment when monasteries became homes to the aristocracy.[307] Thus Lynn White, Jr. writes of the Benedictine monk being "the first to get dirt under his fingernails,"[308] and Rene Dubos, "for the first time in the history of human institutions, the Benedictine abbey created a way of life in which practical and theoretical skills could be embodied in the same person."[309] That Benedict should describe his school as the Lord's workshop and the spiritual life as a craft using tools,[310] further accentuates the sense that labor of the hands was as important as labor of the mind in his vision of an integrated life. Böckmann contrasts Benedict at this point with the *Rule of the Master*—which appears dismissive of the earth, and of any spiritual value being found in field labor, suggesting that Benedict demonstrates a commitment to field work, "as in no other ancient Rule."[311]

Nevertheless, Böckmann and de Waal both note that "On the Daily Manual Labor" is a title that misrepresents the concerns of chapter 48, for a great deal of it is devoted to the mental and contemplative work of *Lectio*.[312] Thus, although Benedict does place high value on manual labor, "one only labours as necessary,"[313] and *lectio* is every bit as important. De Vogue further observes that,

---

303. Workman, *Monastic Ideal*, 154–58.

304. Gies and Gies, *Technology and Invention*, 36, 44.

305. Sonnlechner, "Establishment of New Units," 22.

306. Böckmann, "Manual Labor; Part I," 150. See also Workman, *Monastic Ideal*, 156–57.

307. Gies and Gies, *Technology and Invention*, 10. See also Workman, *Monastic Ideal*, 156–57.

308. White, in McGinn, "Steward of Creation," 170.

309. Dubos, "Franciscan Versus Benedictine," 57.

310 White, *Rule of Benedict*, 18.

311. Böckmann, "Manual Labor; Part II," 265.

312. Böckmann, "Manual Labor; Part II," 253; and de Waal, *Life-Giving Way*, 142.

313. Böckmann, "Manual Labor; Part I," 159.

the best hours of the day are reserved to *lectio*. Moreover, although reading properly so-called occupies only a limited time, it is prolonged during the other occupations by the exercise of "meditation"... thus the entire day rings with the divine Word. The part assigned to it seems secondary, but is in fact limitless.[314]

Clearly this has significance for both informing and limiting the environmental impact of the Benedictine ethic.

This positive evaluation of work in the Benedictine tradition is widely recognized as one of the most influential contributions made to the formation of the medieval, and ultimately the modern world.[315] By providing a divine orientation and religious blessing upon work it also represents one of the most ambiguous elements in the evaluation of the monastic and Christian environmental impact. Nevertheless, this need not necessarily be destructive if the field-work involves care for and engagement with the earth.

Benedictine Farming

Two aspects of monastic engagement with the earth merit particular attention. Firstly, in respect to farming: One of the primary Benedictine values was stability—commitment to a particular place,[316] and McGinn suggests that "a large part of the success the Benedictines enjoyed in their agricultural efforts doubtless comes from the persistence with which they clung to places—even difficult and inhospitable places—in order to be faithful to this central injunction of the Rule."[317]

Knowles argues that "the monasteries were among the first to introduce new methods into the exploitation of their property,"[318] and critical for this was the common ownership of land. Freed from the burden of multiple claims and fragmentation by inheritance, monasteries were able to organize their land use and labor into a more "scientific" system.[319] Farming for self-sufficiency rather than for profit on the market created

---

314. De Vogue, *Commentary*, 242.

315. Workman, *Monastic Ideal*, 154–58. See also Ovitt, *Restoration of Perfection*, 11.

316. White, *Rule of Benedict*, 85–86.

317. McGinn, "Steward of Creation," 175.

318. Knowles, *Monastic Order*, 441.

319. Knowles, *Monastic Order*, 443.

a different orientation to the land and a new set of priorities.[320] Thus, Arnold observes that there is a contrast "between the short-term mentality of secular lords and the long-term, corporate mentality of monastic lords."[321] Furthermore, Sonnlechner suggests that,

> Europe, in contrast to China and the Islamic world, developed an agro-ecological land-use system which integrated cattle pasturing into husbandry, thereby solving the problem of adequate fertilization of fields . . . this mixed farming . . . was conceived not only as a social and economic structure, but also as an ecological reality within which elements are combined functionally. The *mansus* must be understood as a highly self-sustaining unit of land use.[322]

Dunn notes that the monastery at Bobbio was "a centre of agricultural production as well as of evangelization . . . Bobbio's monks and those who lived in its *cellae* brought a degree of technical expertise to the regions in which they were settled—for example in the manufacture and use of the plough."[323]

She also cites sources suggesting considerable openness to, and engagement with, the surrounding communities,[324] which enhances the likelihood that monastic farming practices were shared with others. This may strengthen White's argument regarding the development of the heavy plough.[325] But Rene Dubos observes (in a 1969 reply to White) that "the monks learned to manage the land in such a manner that it supplied them with food and clothing, and in such a manner that it retained its productivity despite intensive cultivation."[326] This, he argues, was because "Benedictine monasteries had to apply, although empirically, ecological principles so as to remain self-supporting and viable . . . they demonstrate that transforming of the land, when intelligently carried out, is not destructive but, instead, can be a creative art."[327]

---

320. Gies and Gies, *Technology and Invention*, 44.
321. Arnold, "Engineering Miracles," 491.
322. Sonnlechner, "Establishment of New Units," 46–47.
323. Dunn, *Emergence of Monasticism*, 184.
324. Dunn, *Emergence of Monasticism*, 184.
325. White, "Historical Roots," 1205.
326. Dubos, "Theology of the Earth," 47.
327. Dubos, "Theology of the Earth," 48–49.

Paradoxically this remains true only as long as the monks remain working. As monasteries became drawn into royal patronage, public service, and highly liturgical lives, so monks worked less and increased their land holdings, leading to both dependence and demands upon tenants, and greatly increased demands upon lands which they no longer worked themselves. Thus, under Benedict of Aniane—and central to the monastic role in the Carolingian empire, "agricultural work was explicitly recognized as extraordinary for monks . . . and a considerable addition was made to the liturgical prayer of the Rule . . . a great and undesirable development."[328] This was not generally the situation beyond the Carolingian empire, but it received further impetus through the later reforms and widespread influence of Cluny.[329] "Work . . . had been gradually ceremonialized, and this is in itself an indication that it had become exceptional."[330]

Correction to these trends occurred with the reforms of the Cistercians. In pursuit of the original vision liturgical activity was much reduced and manual field-work reinstated as an essential element of monastic life, along with more time for private devotion. The centrality of the Sabbath was recognized in that "on Sundays and some fifty other days during the year no manual work was done by the choir monks"[331] (a state of affairs that matches employment conditions in New Zealand for most of the second half of twentieth century!) Yet, despite the desire to break with the worldly entanglements that he saw emasculating the true Benedictine spirit, Bernard still recognized a social element to monasticism: "with cares for the temporal good of our neighbour; we apply ourselves . . . more to promote the peace of earth than the glory of heaven."[332]

More than any other reform movement, Cistercians are recognized for their impact upon agricultural practice. Colin Platt argues that "Scientific agriculture began with the Cistercians . . . and it is to their initiative that we owe . . . the first establishment of many of those great farms

---

328. Knowles, *Monastic Order*, 27. See also Lawrence, *Medieval Monasticism*, 80–81.

329. Knowles, *Monastic Order*, 29–30. See also Dunn, *Emergence of Monasticism*, 208.

330. Knowles, *Monastic Order*, 467.

331. Knowles, *Monastic Order*, 212.

332. Butler, *Monachism*, 102.

on the hills and on the flood-plains of our rivers that have survived intact as units to this day."³³³

That any such holdings should have survived intact for five to eight hundred years (from any time that must pre-date Henry's dissolution of the English monasteries) indicates that, by accident or design, the original founders had established something approaching an ecologically sustainable operation.

In a comprehensive study of Cistercian farming in Southern France, Constance Hoffman Berman explores numerous initiatives in land-care that not only sustained the health of the earth but which also, in some cases, clearly correct the received wisdom of rapacious domination. She demonstrates that expansion was "not by pioneering new land but by managing existing land in new ways."³³⁴ "In general abbeys seem to have been more anxious to preserve forests than to cut them down."³³⁵ "Forest was managed, selectively cut . . . protected, perhaps even replaced,"³³⁶ and "concessions for forest use forbid clearance or conversion to arable land."³³⁷ Ownership fragmentation, she argues, was in some areas so advanced as to make land valueless and unfarmable.³³⁸ But the Cistercian consolidation and communal life allowed a better matching of land to appropriate use, movement of labor between granges, more constancy of work, protective "buffers" from natural events, and flexibility to rest and even to retire land from agricultural production.³³⁹ The ability to run livestock and to practice transhumance and haymaking actually reduced the pressure of need to expand onto wasteland or forest, unlike the situation for many peasants.³⁴⁰

The Cistercians initially rejected any gifts that entailed tenancies, tithes, or other ties of social or political obligation.³⁴¹ To work their lands they developed instead an order of lay brothers, or *conversi*, who, "unlike peasants who were often on the edge of starvation, were healthier and consistently better fed. This probably made them not only more efficient,

333. Platt, *Monastic Grange*, 13.
334. Berman, "Medieval Agriculture," 8.
335. Berman, "Medieval Agriculture," 11.
336. Berman, "Medieval Agriculture," 14.
337. Berman, "Medieval Agriculture," 97–98.
338. Berman, "Medieval Agriculture," 20–21.
339. Berman, "Medieval Agriculture," 74–78.
340. Berman, "Medieval Agriculture," 92.
341. Duby, *Early Growth*, 219.

more innovative, and less lethargic, but more productive."[342] They also found themselves modeling and being copied in both communal organization and agricultural practice.[343]

All this however meant that the order quickly became exceptionally wealthy and therefore powerful, soon seduced away from its early simplicity and increasingly the focus of widespread resentment for its economic hegemony, which often extended to the banishment and dispossession of peasant tenants whose lands they had acquired.[344] Berman, while acknowledging this dynamic, also recognizes that for many, the opportunity to sell their fragmented holdings to a monastery opened up a whole new range of freedoms and possibilities.[345] For the monks, stability and prayer issued in a connection with the land which must be viewed positively, for

> these were men who knew the land intimately because they had been born there; they were concerned with agricultural cultivation and land management because such activities were part of their praise of God. They also undoubtedly worked more effectively on that land than their peasant predecessors, because they were well fed.[346]

Benedictine Water Management

A second significant element of the monastic environmental impact concerns the appropriation of water. Large areas of northern Italy and north-western Europe were a world of water. In the early middle ages many great rivers emptied, not directly into the sea, but into vast deltas, marshes, swamps, and estuaries. On the one hand, these functioned as huge sponges to soak up and dissipate flood waters and provide habitat for innumerable food-stocks of wildlife, fish, and waterfowl, but on the other hand they made homes and villages vulnerable, farming difficult,

---

342. Berman, "Medieval Agriculture," 81, see also note 81.

343. Berman, "Medieval Agriculture," 120–21. Van Bath, *Agrarian History*, 153–55, on the other hand, appears dismissive of any suggestions the Cistercians contributed anything innovative to European agriculture.

344. Knowles, *Monastic Order*, 348–51. See also Workman, *Monastic Ideal*, 244–46; Duby, *Early Growth*, 220–21; Lawrence, *Medieval Monasticism*, 198–99.

345. Berman, "Medieval Agriculture," 119–20.

346. Berman, "Medieval Agriculture," 127.

land communication almost impossible, and provided a ready retreat for bandits of all kinds.[347]

Such a geography appeared to confirm the received biblical cosmology with its waters beneath and waters above (Gen 1:6–10). For Bede these waters constitute one of the four elements from which all else is made.[348] Furthermore, these waters had once destroyed the world by flood and even now were only held in check by the grace of God. Every natural event served as a reminder of what could be! Bede expends a somewhat tortuous thirty-eight pages on the flood, and variously identifies the waters with baptism, the temptations that assail the baptized, and as a reminder of the last judgment.[349] Pagan mythologies also invested springs, wells, and streams with divinities—some at least of which were associated with fertility rites and not all of which were necessarily benign. In addition, "Medieval Christianity associated water with spiritual fertility, healing and religious conversion."[350] Jeremy Cohen would add, with natural human fertility as well.[351] In such a world, to be able to exercise control of the waters signified spiritual power—engineering skill was but its means.

Ellen Arnold, in a study of seventh-century monastic missionary activity in the Ardennes, demonstrates the monastic appropriation of water to missional goals. One account, for example, concerns St Remacle (a seventh-century monastic bishop) who was noted not for cutting down trees but for cleansing a spring that was "fit for human purposes, but polluted by pagan error, and subject to demonic infestation."[352] After prayer and appropriate ritual, the appropriation of the spring for the Christian faith was demonstrated by "channeling the spring through a lead pipe, controlling the resource and marking the new Christian control of the landscape."[353] Another similar story demonstrates that the evangelist's intervention made the spring into a reliable rather than erratic water source.[354] Following such actions a monastic center was frequently es-

---

347. Fumagalli, *Landscapes*, 105–7.
348. Bede, *Genesis*, 70.
349. Bede, *Genesis*, 171–209.
350. Arnold, "Engineering Miracles," 478.
351. Cohen, *"Be Fertile and Increase,"* 83–84.
352. Arnold, "Engineering Miracles," 478.
353. Arnold, "Engineering Miracles," 478.
354. Arnold, "Engineering Miracles," 485.

tablished and the site became a place of healing and pilgrimage. The monastic community extended its power in the land by engineering flood control or irrigation canals, and eventually even the construction of mill ponds, water races, and water mills. In a world of erratic flooding, unstable streams, and non-absorbent soils, such ability to exercise some kind of control was received as both blessing and sign of spiritual approval. Not all was economic exploitation however. Other stories make clear that sites of such miracles were explicitly preserved from cultivation, and unhappy could be the consequences for those who failed to respect such restraints![355] Arnold summarizes her study thus:

> springs became associated with the healing and transformative power of evangelising saints. The conversion of the waters stood for the conversion of the wider Ardennes, and the monastically engineered water systems represented the power of the monks who were the successors of the saints. Miracle stories linked the mundane and the miraculous, the natural and the super-natural.[356]

Whatever may have been the benefits, and relatively benign impacts, of relatively small-scale engineering interventions, eventually they became a major feature of the late medieval landscape with much more mixed results. Fumagalli recounts a history of cultivation extended into marshlands and floodplains, drained by ditches and protected by levees.[357] But as deforestation increased, run-off rates in the headwaters and floods downstream increased pressure upon now-constrained rivers, and when the banks did break, the damage was all the greater.

> The environment could only be manipulated so far. It is no coincidence that probably the worst floods to occur in the whole recorded history of the Po have been the deluges of the last hundred years or so, when the development of agriculture in the region has entailed the virtual elimination marshes and high-water beds along the central section of the river.[358]

---

355. Arnold, "Engineering Miracles," 485.

356. Arnold, "Engineering Miracles," 496. See also Short, *History of Religious Architecture*, 114.

357. Fumagalli, *Landscapes*, 104–15.

358. Fumagalli, *Landscapes*, 111.

Benedictine Study

Work in the Benedictine monastery involved not only manual labor but also study. It is in the context of such study that we may explore Benedictine reflection upon the biblical ideas concerning "the image of God" and "dominion over the earth." However, as we have seen with nature so too with these particular aspects of human identity, Benedict in the *Rule* says nothing at all. Even for subsequent commentators these are not passages that seem to elicit much attention—unlike the intense interest shown by patristic writers.

In 668 Theodore of Tarsus was consecrated Archbishop of Canterbury. With his Benedictine colleagues Abbot Hadrian and Benedict Biscop (an English monk later to become founding Abbot of the outstanding monasteries at Wearmouth and Jarrow), he then journeyed from Rome and was installed at Canterbury in May 669. Between them, Theodore and Hadrian "represented one of the most brilliant moments in European scholarship between the fall of Rome and the rise of the universities."[359] Their significance for this study lies firstly in their Greek origins—Latin was for them a second language[360] and (to the degree that they needed it among their Anglo-Saxon flock) Old English a third! In the lands farthest west, they were vigorous exponents of Greek learning, especially in regard to medicine and Antiochene literal interpretation.[361] Again White's contention of deep separations between East and West are shown to be vastly overstated.

Secondly, in their teaching ministry they addressed Genesis 1 and their commentary remains in student notes, which unfortunately means in a fragmentary form. Of Genesis 1:26 two comments appear:

> 28—*To our image* (1:26): that is, that man should be king of terrestrial beings, as is God of all beings. And likewise for us: that is we shall be uncorrupt like Him after the resurrection, as John says;[362] and subsequently, "31 *Let us make man to our im-*

---

359. Bischoff and Lapidge, *Commentaries*, 4.
360. Bischoff and Lapidge, *Commentaries*, 294.
361. Bischoff and Lapidge, *Commentaries*, 249.
362. Bischoff and Lapidge, *Commentaries*, 438, the editors regard this as a reference to John Chrysostom, "on man's superior role on earth in order that he may inherit the kingdom of heaven with Christ."

age (1:26): that is, let us make man with a soul, as subsequently when the text says 'breathed.'"[363]

This breath, they go on to explain, was the gift of the Holy Spirit which Adam lost through sin but which Christ has restored, "as when he breathed into the apostles, saying, 'Receive ye the Holy Ghost.'"[364] The commentary says nothing more about humanity exercising any kind of rule, nor anything about Adam's work, either before or after the fall. Christological interpretation remains a key strategy and the focus all appears to be upon anticipation of resurrection life. And just as with the creation of all things in the twinkling of an eye, "likewise is the resurrection thought to be of all things at once,"[365] which, given the subsequent interest they show in animals, could suggest an expectation that the resurrection will indeed incorporate all created beings.

Bede's commentary is much more extensive. Within his first page he identifies Christ as the one in whom "were all things created in heaven and on earth,"[366] he alerts his readers to the dangers associated with allegorical interpretation, and finds the angels filling the whole creation with praise. That human beings will have a place of honor in this creation is clear. On Gen 1:11–13 he writes of all things coming forth from the earth in perfect shape, as also will "man himself, for whom all things were made on earth."[367] Then, of Gen 1:25c, he writes, "after the habitation of the earth had been made and adorned, it remained for the inhabitor and lord of all things himself to be created, for whose sake all things were ordained; and this follows."[368] What actually follows is extensively detailed commentary: Humankind are like all other creatures in being created according to their own particular class, but unlike all others they are also the subject of a unique divine deliberation,

> so that it would truly seem that he was formed as a rational creature . . . He is formed from the earth as if by study, and he is raised up by the breath of the Creator through the power of the vital Spirit, evidently so that he who was made in the image of

---

363. Bischoff and Lapidge, *Commentaries*, 309.
364. Bischoff and Lapidge, *Commentaries*, 309.
365. Bischoff and Lapidge, *Commentaries*, 365.
366. Bede, *Genesis*, 68–69.
367. Bede, *Genesis*, 80.
368. Bede, *Genesis*, 89.

the Creator would exist not by a word of command but by the dignity of an action.[369]

This action was trinitarian and involved the first revelation of this doctrine concerning the nature of God. Finally, there is an exposition of the nature of the fall and the restoration of humanity by Christ who is the new man. He then quotes from Augustine, Ovid, and the Apostle Paul (truly covering his bases!), to clarify the nature of the difference between humans and other animals. It's all in the posture. "And while all other animals, face down, look at the earth, He gave to man an uplifted face, and ordered him to view the heavens and raise his upright countenance to the stars."[370]

Then he addresses the commission to exercise dominion.

> There is no doubt that man was made in the image of God chiefly in the respect in which he surpasses the irrational creatures—that is to say, he was created capable of reason, by which means he could both properly govern each and every created thing in the world and enjoy the knowledge of the One who created all things.[371]

There follows the earlier referenced assertion that this dignity may be lost if one does not live rightly with God. Nevertheless, the whole section is pregnant with a notion of human primacy which some would describe as speciesism. The earth is the human home and humans are in some way lords of the household. Therefore, it is even more important to note, firstly that this dignity is to ensure good governance of all non-rational creatures (a good householder will not abuse their own estate), and secondly, it is to enable the conscious enjoyment of God. Again, there is nothing about taking power, control, or domination. Thirdly, since the Genesis text repeats itself at 1:27—"God created man in his own image, in the image of God he created him," Bede argues that this is in order to impress upon us the true nature of our human hope,

> lest we who walk in the image of God be needlessly disquieted, amassing treasure in the uncertainty of riches. But rather let us wait for the Lord, thirsting for the time when we may come and

---

369. Bede, *Genesis*, 89.
370. Bede, *Genesis*, 90–91.
371. Bede, *Genesis*, 91.

appear before his face, certain that when he appears we will be like to him, because we will see him as he is.[372]

It would be hard to imagine a clearer statement that, for Bede, image and dominion are nothing at all to do with domination or taking the resources of the earth for one's own aggrandizement. Rather, precisely because in Christ we may bear this image, we need not and must not consume the earth or its creatures, because ours is a spiritual not a merely material nature, and fullness of life is to be found in the contemplation of God.

Following Bede, Aelfric also addressed himself to the opening chapter of Genesis. He too finds rich christological and trinitarian references in the opening verses,[373] recognizes the significance of the sun, moon, and stars for measuring times and seasons and calculating Easter,[374] and comments upon air having mass, the earth and other bodies being globes—"which not all will believe," and the praise of God by the waters not being in words but through the manifestation within them of God's power.[375] Most importantly for our purposes, he is clear that the whole creation exists for the glory and praise of God,

> it was always from the beginning in his everlasting design that he would make all this world and all the earth by his own might, for his own praise, as we now see that all creatures praise their Creator, except the wretched men who despise him, and refuse to praise him nor do they regard him.[376]

In such a vision we do not even have the role of helping creation in its praise, but merely of being part of the choir. Of domination or use for any ends of our own there is no mention at all. As long as the human beings obeyed their creator they were able to live in happiness with all other creatures. He seems to suggest that fierce beasts were always so, but not, prior to the fall, a problem for human-kind, and indeed, before that time, even the lice, gnats, and fleas, "reverenced him greatly"![377]

---

372. Bede, *Genesis*, 92.
373. Aelfric, *Old English Hexameron*, 35–37.
374. Aelfric, *Old English Hexameron*, 42–43, 50.
375. Aelfric, *Old English Hexameron*, 44–46.
376. Aelfric, *Old English Hexameron*, 63.
377. Aelfric, *Old English Hexameron*, 65–68.

CONCLUSIONS

Throughout the whole monastic tradition that we have examined, the world of nature is affirmed as the creation of God. No longer itself divine, it nevertheless remains sacred as dependent creation, as the revelation of God's glory and beauty, and as the place of God's action. Even the passage of the seasons proclaims the central truths of the gospel. Sometimes by its order and beauty, nature functions as our partner in praise. At other times, when humans suffer or are overwhelmed by the world of nature, we are reminded of our fallen state, perhaps punished for our foolishness and called back to obedient trust. Thus, the human experience of nature will frequently be an ambiguous one. But never is nature mere materiality, handed over to dominant humanity for our use as we please. Such a vision of nature as mere resource represents all that is sinful and idolatrous in our condition—looking to consume the earth when rather we should be being consumed by the beauty of God, encountered in the beauty of creation.

Nevertheless, human beings have been placed in a privileged place in the world of nature. All of nature supports our life and we are commissioned by God, on the one hand to exercise the power of rationality to seek God in the contemplative life, and on the other hand to demonstrate the divine concern for creatures by the exercise of good governance over all those who are subject to us. The contemplative life includes engagement with the world of nature in quietness, in study, in field work, in loving service of others and in worship. This whole life is shaped by the liturgy of the hours, and this in turn is shaped by the days of creation. All is orientated around the Sabbath rest. Here is signified hope for all creation, and the monastic community exists as a sign in the world of this future already present. Its life is a foretaste of the healing of creation and the restoration that has been made present in Christ, and is offered to all who will listen and follow him.

But, despite this vision, the snake still lurks in the garden and the impacts of the fall are never far away. We have noted how quickly the Cistercian renewal became cause for revulsion, how easily the new community could become an aristocrat's means for maintaining the old order, and how discipline of the body could become deeply destructive. Dominion could readily be appropriated as domination. Workman summarizes the monastic paradox,

> for eight hundred years after Benedict men tried to achieve the impossible, to attain simplicity and poverty by renunciation, through means of an organization that must inevitably produce wealth . . . in time a commercial spirit invaded the monastery, and wealth and splendour produced the inevitable decay.[378]

It is beyond the scope of this study to explore whether such decay could have been avoided by the better maintenance of a missionary spirit and a sense of identity in service of the world, rather than withdrawal from it. Nevertheless, what the next millennium would show is that the abandonment of the contemplative vision would truly see the Earth given over to those who saw it as resource to be battled with, dominated, and consumed.

Frances and Joseph Gies suggest that both Augustine and Bede promoted visions of a pre-lapsarian harmony between humanity and all other creatures, followed by post-lapsarian tensions, exploitation, and greed—which may yet be healed through the salvation in Christ. But the fall of reason has meant the end of human governance for the common good. "Nevertheless, Medieval theologians' interpretation of the Creation and Fall revealed a God-ordained world dominated by human beings, whose role in respect to nature, however, was not exploitation but stewardship and cooperation."[379] How that vision was affirmed but also began to unravel is the subject of the next chapter.

---

378. Workman, *Monastic Ideal*, 224, 246.
379. Gies and Gies, *Technology and Invention*, 6–7.

7

At the Turning of the Ages: Reviewing White's Account of the First Millennium, and Previewing the Second

INTRODUCTION

As the Cistercian movement mutated from its initial simplicity into one of the great landowners and powerbrokers of the medieval age, completely new forms of monastic renunciation were appearing on the scene in the form of the mendicant friars. In contrast to the Benedictine vision of withdrawal, they tended to be based in the newly developing cities with their new profit-driven economies,[1] and rather than committing to enclosed stability, their inspiration lay in their poverty-stricken mobility. Highly likely it was that travelling preachers would find themselves caught out under the stars, feeding on the remains of other's meals, warming themselves at a roadside fire, or even having to decide how to respond to the interest of a passing wolf. Such a one was Francis, and it was Francis whom White idealized and nominated as the patron saint of ecologists.[2]

---

1. Fumagalli, *Landscapes*, 198, also 146. See also Gies and Gies, *Technology and Invention*, 105–237.

2. White, "Historical Roots," 1207.

We thus come to a watershed in both social and theological history. This is an appropriate time to identify some key themes from the period under review, and attempt some assessment of the strengths and weaknesses of White's case against Christian orthodoxy up until the time of Francis. We also look ahead to other developments largely unacknowledged by White.

The patristic and monastic periods, especially in the late seventh century, are characterized by White through the use of dramatic and triumphalistic language:

> The new plows attack the land with such violence . . . man's relationship to the soil is profoundly changed . . . formerly part of nature; now he is the exploiter. The Western tradition is one of ruthlessness . . . of an exploitive attitude . . . the new Frankish calendars show man coercing the world . . . Man and nature are two things and man is the master . . . no item in the physical creation had any purpose save to serve man's purposes . . . there was established a dualism of man and nature. Pagan animism was destroyed and thus it became possible to exploit nature in a mood of indifference to the feelings of natural objects . . . old inhibitions to the exploitation of nature crumbled . . . we are superior to nature, contemptuous of it, willing to use it for our slightest whim . . . Christianity bears a huge burden of guilt.[3]

This, as noted earlier, has become the received wisdom of the Western academy. However, apart from one passing and superficial reference to Irenaeus,[4] White makes no mention at all of any of the writers or movements we have reviewed in the preceding five chapters![5] Despite his acknowledged role, as an historian of medieval technology, in overturning the modernist conceit of the middle-ages as the dark ages,[6] in this paper he demonstrates almost complete indifference to the huge and complex edifice of medieval theology. This is a serious oversight, for patristic and early medieval theology, far from being speculative, was

---

3. White, "Historical Roots," 1205–6. I am also informed that among New Zealand Maori, the traditional (i.e., pre-European contact) names for the months described the agricultural or hunting activity pursued at that time of the year, a form of naming White complained about in the eighth-century Frankish calendars as being a recent Christian innovation.

4. White, "Historical Roots," 1205.

5. McGrath, *Re-enchantment*, 32–36, also notes White's failure, except for a passing misrepresentation, to engage at all with the traditions of Celtic spirituality.

6. Gies and Gies, *Technology and Invention*, 3–5.

essentially pastoral—devoted to exposition of the gospel and to enabling theologically-informed discipleship arising from the life of Christ. It is also a serious oversight because for White, at least in this paper, ideas are everything. Frances and Joseph Gies[7] and George Ovitt[8] are among those who have critiqued White for a failure to acknowledge the impacts of other factors—such as the inheritance of the Roman Empire (whose relentlessly straight lines and massive engineering works constitute a commitment to conquest of nature far more ideological than anything produced by Christian theologians), or gradual population growth, or socio-political changes, or climatic change, or the simple struggle to survive in the developments he writes about. Nor does he ponder the possibility that ideas such as human dominion were "discovered" after the event, and offered as accounts or even justifications for developments that had been driven by quite different forces. But for White the idea is the origin of everything, yet those who were producing, promoting and debating the ideas of the medieval centuries remain utterly unengaged by him!

THE "PSYCHIC REVOLUTION" OF CHRISTIANITY

If we accept as a working hypothesis White's assertion that "the victory of Christianity over paganism was the greatest psychic revolution in the history of our culture"[9] (while recognizing that the victory was not then, and even less now, nearly as complete as White might suggest or Christians might hope), we can identify at least three elements in our sources that contribute to this psychic revolution.

Creation *Ex Nihilo*

Firstly the doctrine of creation *ex nihilo*, common to all our sources, posits a completely new conception of the relation between God and the world. God has not been caught in an eternal struggle to impose a divine will upon eternal but recalcitrant—even essentially evil—matter. Rather, all that is arises from the divine command "let be," is an expression of the divine Word, is adorned by the Spirit, and utterly dependent for

---

7. Gies and Gies, *Technology and Invention*, 14–16, 40–41.
8. Ovitt, *Restoration of Perfection*, 16, 40, 165–66.
9. White, "Historical Roots," 1205.

continued existence upon the divine determination to sustain it. All that is is held in this divine love, and has been brought to being in order to enjoy and participate in this love. Such radical contingency makes all of life a gift, and places human beings in exactly the same position of dependence as all other created things. It is this dependence upon God, and the possibilities which may arise from this divine purpose in creation, that make creation "good." The struggles we have traced with paganism, Manichaeism, and Gnosticism, right back to Marcion (or even to the writers of the Johannine letters, and Paul to the Colossians), are all one struggle to assert the divine origin, goodness, and value in the divine purpose of *ALL* created things, and not the human only. White slides too easily and superficially into his claim that "man shares, in great measure, God's transcendence of nature [and thus] Christianity . . . established a dualism of man and nature,"[10] but as we have seen, humanity shares nothing of God's transcendence of nature and has neither brought to being nor sustains anything. Rather, the human beings are utterly embedded in nature, subject to all its processes, and as dependent as any other creature.

Paulos Gregorios, in a review of various uses of the term "nature," notes that "the Hebrew tradition . . . has no word at all for what we call nature . . . no notion of something 'out there' which they [i.e., humans] were to set about 'desacralizing' and then dominating,"[11] and he continues,

> it is clear in Gregory of Nyssa, who laid the foundations for later Christian reflection on the subject, that the basic distinction for patristic literature is not between humanity and the non-human part of creation, but between "He who truly is" (ὁ ὄντος ὤν) and "the things which merely exist" (τὰ πάντα). The two do not share the same mode of being, and to apply verbs like "is" or "exist" in the same sense to both God and the creation seems to Gregory to be disastrous.[12]

The only dualism is that between God and creation, and even that distinction is not strictly dualistic because contingent creation is entirely an ongoing act of the sustaining divine grace.

In contrast, White grieves the loss of a divinized universe where "every tree, every spring, every stream, every hill had its own *genius loci*,

---

10. White, "Historical Roots," 1205.
11. Gregorios, *Human Presence*, 19. See also Rusmussen, "Symbols to Live By," 175.
12. Gregorios, *Human Presence*, 24.

its guardian spirit," all of whom were in constant need of being placated.[13] And they could be placated—at a cost! Our foray into historical geography has demonstrated that such divinization provides no assured protection for the natural world. The need to honor gods or ancestors could lead to devastating environmental consequences and Athanasius, who shows some interest in geography, also explored the deleterious impacts of honoring the creation as if it was divine.

Furthermore, if the natural world is divine, what of the human beings? Are we also part of the natural world? Are we also divine? If not, are we to conceive of ourselves as slaves of the gods, as in the Babylonian mythologies—the cannon-fodder for their heavenly battles and therefore not at all accountable for any damage that may occur in the course of their scrapping? Or if we are divine, are we not yet another participant in the anarchic story of wild loves and angry conflicts that characterizes the history of the gods, with no accountability elsewhere for our desire to be victorious in our particular battles? The patristic writers were conscious of these issues but White shows no awareness of them at all.

Finally, the divinized universe with its many free spirits is totally opaque to the development of any kind of science.[14] But in patristic theology it was the Word of God who sustained and ordered the whole creation, and it was in the contemplation (not the manipulation!) of this Word in creation that we humans could find the right ordering of our own existence. Furthermore, since we as much as everything else are all formed and sustained by the same divine Word, we may, as Irenaeus recognized, have some confidence in our processes of thinking about, engaging, and knowing the world in which we live. Thus as White rightly acknowledges, until well into the modern era, the motivation of most science was actually the enhancement of worship![15] Given the eventual unhappy marriage of science and technology which White describes, some may well see this as a bad thing and desire a re-divinized universe. But the science that can be abused is also the science that has opened to us the wonder of life, the delicacy of our ecological inter-relations, and—perhaps most importantly at this point of the argument, the information that confronts us with the facts of our ecologic crisis. Without

---

13. White, "Historical Roots," 1205.
14. Turner, *Roots of Science*, 31–33, 116.
15. White, "Historical Roots," 1206. See also Ovitt, *Restoration*, 44–45.

this science we would probably still have our crisis, but in all likelihood very little awareness of it, nor language with which to discuss it.

The Incarnation of the Word

A second significant element in the "psychic revolution" is the doctrine of the incarnation of the Word. Turner states,

> for Athanasius and the Council of Nicaea, the divine and the human, the heavenly realm and this world, were not opposed to or separated from one another. In fact they inter-penetrated without losing their distinctive identity; how to describe this was the problem and . . . for this purpose Athanasius developed his doctrine of inter-penetration in the form of co-inherence, described in the Greek term "perichoresis," with its suggestion of three equal figures dancing linked in a circle—perichoresis is now a technical term in recent revived study of the Trinity.[16]

Such inter-penetration involves a real relationship. The Word which was already present sustaining creation, now becomes visible as part of the creation. The essential goodness of creation is demonstrated in that in the incarnation creation becomes the vehicle of divine self-disclosure. The Arian alternative, in which Jesus is not God incarnate, is, according to Turner, "another form of the classic Greek dualism of time and eternity, with rationality existing only in the latter. On this view there could be no science in the sense of rational understanding of the material and temporal world, which was both irrational and ephemeral."[17]

Thus the incarnation affirms the existence in relationship of both the divine and the creation, and it affirms the creation as a means of expressing and encountering the divine. But that the divine should become incarnate as a human being does, for some modern critics, raise the specter of speciesism. Why should the humans be so especially privileged?[18] Here we come closest to ideas which no doubt can issue in dominationist understandings of human identity. Yet even these were to some extent anticipated by patristic writers.

The divine becomes incarnate in a human being because it is human beings who bear the image which allows the possibility of rational,

---

16. Turner, *Roots of Science*, 89–90. See also McGrath, *Christian Theology*, 298–300.
17. Turner, *Roots of Science*, 89.
18. Smith, *Environmental Ethics*, 5–18.

contemplative engagement with the divine. This does not however set humanity apart from the rest of creation. Rather, humanity constitutes the completion of creation. By their particular dominion human beings have, on the one hand, a particular role in articulating the praise of the whole creation; and on the other hand, a particular responsibility of governance for the well-being of all other creatures. This is power nevertheless, and we have witnessed repeatedly in our sources the concern to see the incarnation understood in terms of humility and service—this is how the Lord comes among us and this is the life to which we are called. In all patristic theology the incarnation provides both model and enabling of what it means for us to live as human beings. It is the model for our dominion. In this respect Francis is of particular significance, for part of his influence lay in his re-presentation of the incarnation as a sign of the humility of God. It was among the poor and as one of them that Christ had come among us.

The divine also becomes incarnate in the human being because it is the human beings who have fallen, become disorientated, corrupted their desires, lost their capacity for proper contemplative living, begun to worship the creation rather than the creator, and abuse their place in relation to other creatures. It is the human creatures who are in need of the salvation through re-creation that is offered through the whole series of events that constitutes the incarnation. But it is not the humans in isolation from the rest of creation who need this salvation. Precisely because they are an integral part of the whole creation, human sinfulness destructively impacts upon the rest of creation. Other things may not themselves be fallen but they are certainly now fallen upon!

An academic historian may understandably choke on the challenge of having to write about human sinfulness, especially when doing it as a suspect outsider in a prestigious scientific journal. But had White paid more attention to Athanasius's expose of myth-making and idolatry or to Augustine's on the psychology of desire, he could have used modern categories to engage more thoroughly with the dynamic he was attempting to address, and more honestly with the thinking of those he was too simplistically criticizing.

The doctrine of the incarnation also exposes weaknesses in White's arguments regarding the differences between the Eastern and Western theological traditions. We have repeatedly contested White's assertion that the contemplative life characterizes the Eastern tradition while the West is marked by voluntarist impulses. If the contemplative life par excellence is the eremitic life, we should note that Benedict made specific provision for it while Basil specifically prohibited it! Furthermore, while Augustine eulogized the contemplative life many would argue that his most enduring, and most baneful, legacy to Western Christianity is his unrelenting critique of the capacities of the human will. It is rather the Eastern theologians who find a higher place for the operation of the human will, and this arises from their being more hospitable to the Dyothelite position in the controversy regarding the two wills in the incarnate Christ. John Cassian had earlier attempted a similar *via media* in the dispute between Augustine and Pelagius, but his position had been rejected in the West by those—Augustinians, who dismissed it as "semi-Pelagian." Nevertheless, Eastern theological influence continued to be injected into the Western church through the monastic movement, and the key issue for us is that a higher evaluation of the role of the will is associated, not with a drive to dominate the Earth but with the cultivation of the contemplative life.[19]

Such a life includes gardening or other manual work by which one partners with divine providence in the procurement of life's necessities, but its essential asceticism is intended to orientate it away from self-centeredness, greed, or the lust for power/domination. Thus John Zizioulas encapsulates the whole tradition, observing that asceticism is not about hostility to nature but about "the breaking of one's own selfish will so that the individual with his or her desires to dominate the external world and use it for their own satisfaction might learn not to make the individual the center of creation."[20]

The Resurrection of Jesus

A third element in the "psychic revolution" is the impact of the message concerning the resurrection of Jesus. Bede's story of Edwin's council of chiefs and the bird's flight through the winter banqueting hall[21] is a clear indication that at a popular level the resurrection provided people with some new confidence in the face of death. (And perhaps new fears too, since there was also the possibility of a judgment to come!) Poorly formed, ill-informed, and even superstitious it may have been,

---

19. Yule, "Orthodox Spirituality," 15–16. See also Davidson, *Public Faith*, 234–37; and Gregorios, *Human Presence*, 68–71.

20. Zizioulas, "Priest of Creation," 279.

21. Bede, *History*, 124.

but nevertheless there was some realization that in the resurrection, the future was beginning to be present now, and this had implications for the materiality of creation. Thus it was that the bodies of especially saintly individuals, like Cuthbert, were found not to be subject to decay.[22] This, according to Anestis Keselopoulus—who draws here on a rich tradition,

> is the realization of the great potentiality given to matter and the body by the fact of Christ's Transfiguration on Mount Tabor, where His divine glory was manifested in and through His body . . . a potential which defines . . . incorruption not simply as something "to come," but as something already inaugurated and being realized.[23]

Thus the resurrection embodies hope for the restoration of all creation. It does not however imply the notions of "progress" which White also finds environmentally deleterious.[24] Our sources have read Genesis 1 in many different ways and found differing layers of meaning, but the idea of constant improvement through time is not one of them. More frequently, the sixth day—the last age before the divine sabbath, was regarded as the age of decay—precisely because of the fall of humanity, the darkening of our minds, and the silencing of our praise. Renewal does not come by some progressive process, but by the sheer grace of the divine intervention in Jesus Christ, central to all of which was the resurrection.

Nevertheless, as with un-corrupt bodies so with living persons, the resurrection may be anticipated in this present life. This as we have seen is central to the monastic vision. The community exists as a present sign of the world to come. Under the discipline and with the support of a monastic Rule, a believer may begin to put on the life of Christ, the contemplative life may be renewed and with it one's sense of proper connection with the rest of creation. Idolatrous and lustful/greedy demands upon the Earth will be confronted and begin to change. For some, even the pre-lapsarian and eschatological peaceable relationships with animals will become present experience.[25] The theological significance of vegetarianism is a theme throughout our sources, with huge implications

---

22. Bede, *History*, 260; see also the sections on Fursey, 171–72, and Etheldreda, 234–36.

23. Keselópoulos, *Man and the Environment*, 46–47.

24. White, "Historical Roots," 1205.

25. Similar claims, better attested, are recorded in the remarkable early twentieth-century life of the mystic, ascetic, itinerate preacher—the Indian Christian Sadhu, Sundar Singh. See Davey, *Sadhu Sundar Singh*, 88, 108–10.

for the life of animals. Yet White completely ignores this vast tradition of asceticism that, for good and ill, was such a central feature of pre-modern life and spirituality both within and outside the monasteries. Is it possible to honestly assess the patristic and medieval periods without engaging with these most formative impulses?

Furthermore, just as the apocalyptic vision foresees the whole redeemed creation gathered in praise before the throne of God, so the central task of the monastic community is to foreshadow that praise now. By the offering of manual work, prayer, study, and the Psalms all of creation is presented in this worship. This creation however, like the human beings within it, is also in need of transformation and these monastic communities are also in need of support. Consequently, the world will not remain unchanged as it is offered back to God. Nevertheless, we have noted that the monastic impact upon the land was generally more beneficial than that of the former empire and even of contemporary peasants and aristocrats, for this creation was not a matter of indifference in our life before God. This vision of the centrality of praise also goes unmentioned by White, yet it constitutes a radically different view of the relationship between humanity and the rest of creation than that which he proposes.

ON HUMAN POWER AND SINFULNESS

The more one compares White's account of the first millennium with the most influential theologians and movements of the time, the more superficial and tendentious it appears. And yet there remains an uneasy suspicion that somehow he is right! Even if they are not necessarily destructive every one of these distinctive christian elements is vulnerable to becoming destructive. A universe which is not divine but is sustained by the divine Word can easily become a universe from which God is totally absent, with the ordering power of the Word reconceived as nothing more than impersonal mechanistic processes. A humanity with a distinct role in creation by virtue of its "dominion" can easily be reconceived as a humanity that is separate from the rest of creation, with a freedom to dominate and use its powers in whatever way its appetites may desire. Such appetites may well include an appetite for monastic or patronly glory, under the cover of raising a resource-consuming abbey to the glory of God! The more distant God is conceived as being, the more susceptible the creation is to such domination. Conversely, if God has chosen to become part of creation within a human person, how much more susceptible are humans to the conceit that they alone are special in all creation. If the life of humanity is orientated towards an eschatological fulfillment, how easy it is to develop a mindset that "nothing can stop progress" and thereby justify whatever forms of excess, or consumption, or political oppression may characterize any particular economy. And if the eschaton is conceived as the end of creation, the non-human elements may well be devalued—as in some of the ascetic excesses we have observed, or greedily consumed as being of no eternal account anyway.

None of these are the necessary outcomes of Christian orthodoxy, but they are real outcomes nonetheless. Which raises the question—how one speaks of human sinfulness in the context of academic discourse? Despite the insights of Athanasius and Augustine this was not an issue White chose to address. Gregorios however argues that the roots of

> the tendency to view nature as purely an object to be known and used for our own purposes . . . are not to be sought in any theology of dominion over nature . . . but in the historical phenomenon of the expansion of the West . . . Could we not ask whether greed—sometimes naked, sometimes clothed in highly moral terminology, but always acquisitive—was not one of the factors that led Europe to expand . . . to colonise . . . to exploit . . . to accumulate . . . to make possible the growth of science and technology in the West.[26]

Note that he does not see the expansion of the West arising from its science and technology, but rather, its science and technology arising from its greed. Ovitt draws similar conclusions in relation to a medieval scheme to blockade the Red Sea against Arab traders which was he says, "premature,"[27] and the Irish and Viking expeditions to North America, which were "fruitless because Europe was not ready to discover America, which it did not yet need."[28] That is, despite the idea or experience, no action followed because expansionist greed or imperialist lust had not yet seen a use, created a need, or developed a market for the potential resources. Such ideas lay dormant, in this account, until the pressure of greed or acquisitiveness provided the energy needed to pursue them.

---

26. Gregorios, *Human Presence*, 15.
27. Ovitt, *Restoration*, 167.
28. Ovitt, *Restoration*, 106.

This in turn is a reminder that science has its own motives, interests, and drivers, which may be far from "pure."

However, Gregorios does not stop here. Writing as an Indian, an Eastern Orthodox Metropolitan based in Delhi, outside both the theological and cultural traditions of the West, he continues,

> even from the perspective of both eastern theology and the exploited two-thirds world, it is impossible to dissociate oneself from western Christianity and western culture and society and to brand "them" alone as responsible for our current crisis . . . Greed and aggression are by no means limited to the latter; the need to overcome them is as acute in the two-thirds world as in the West. In fact, our efforts to eradicate poverty and to usher in a just society are frustrated mainly by our own insatiable greed and group aggressiveness among ourselves.[29]

NEW DEVELOPMENTS IN THE SECOND MILLENNIUM

Quite apart from his failure to acknowledge some of the dark corners of human motivation, White also fails to pay any attention at all to the impacts of overtly pagan or aggressively secularist intellectual developments during the Renaissance and subsequent Enlightenment. Gregorios and Bauckham both note, for example, the popularity of the rebellious friar Giordano Bruno who, while "re-divinizing" the world also promoted the divinized humanity, possessed of limitless power to overcome the laws of nature and remake the earth according to its own desires.[30] Such a vision of human power, potential and domination may well characterize the modern world, but Bruno was clear that this involved rejection of any orthodox Christian understanding of the relationship between God and the creation.

Turner surveys key scientific thinkers through the sixteenth to eighteenth centuries, identifying a mix of christian devotion or deviation in some, and deliberate appropriation of pre-christian cosmologies in others.[31] He clearly demonstrates the re-emergence of a deep-seated dualism in the cosmology of modernity, which is clearly at odds with the

---

29. Gregorios, *Human Presence*, 15.

30. Gregorios, *Human Presence*, 32–34. See also Bauckham, "Modern Domination," 34–36.

31. Turner, *Frames of Mind*, 181–201.

cosmology of the Genesis narrative, Jewish thinking, and the theological tradition we have reviewed.[32]

Protestant Biblical Interpretation

Peter Harrison explores significant changes in biblical interpretation consequent upon the Reformation, but notes that the new "literalism" by no means necessitated a more domineering attitude: "early modern discussions of dominion are less to do with the exercise of a tyrannical authority . . . than about attempting to undo the damage wrought by human sin . . . dominion is about redemption . . . the restoration of the Earth to its original and 'natural' condition."[33]

Luther nibbles repeatedly at our key passage. We are, for example, like the beasts in needing and enjoying physical pleasure and refreshment (no negativity there), but also like God, which is, "an indication of another and better life than the physical."[34] Nevertheless, the *imago* is so lost as to be merely a matter of speculation. It is not something to be exercised or striven for because "we are speaking about something unknown."[35] However, apparently uncomfortable with such agnosticism, he subsequently suggests that dominion involved the full knowledge of nature as "completely engulfed by the goodness and justice of God."[36] But now, "we retain the title but have almost entirely lost the substance, and even then it is exercised only through industry, skill . . . cunning and deceit."[37] Our first parents on the other hand, "would have made use of the creatures only for the admiration of God and for a holy joy which is unknown to us . . . to amuse himself with the animals . . . to work and to guard, cultivate and watch."[38] Against all this sadness and loss he argues that the gospel has brought some restoration of the image, and this is

---

32. Turner, *Roots of Science*, 127–33; note too the cosmological diagram inside the back cover, opposite 205. See also Gunton, *Triune Creator*, 126–34.
33. Harrison, "Having Dominion," 27.
34. Pelikan, *Luther's Works*, 56–57.
35. Pelikan, *Luther's Works*, 62–63.
36. Pelikan, *Luther's Works*, 66.
37. Pelikan, *Luther's Works*, 67.
38. Pelikan, *Luther's Works*, 71.

seen not in any new power to dominate the world, but in the awakening of "the hope of eternal life by faith."[39]

Calvin, like Luther, recognizes that the *imago* has been corrupted by the fall, but is less pessimistic about what may transpire in us now. Adam "had right judgement, had affections in harmony with reason, had all his senses sound and well-regulated, and truly excelled in everything good. Thus the chief seat of the Divine Image was in his mind and heart."[40] Nothing needed to be taken in hand, for Adam's descendants as well as Adam himself are,

> the end for which all things were created; namely that none of the conveniences and necessaries of life might be wanting to man . . . he furnished the world with all things needful, and even with an immense profusion of wealth, before he formed man. Thus man was rich before he was born.[41]

In the presence of such generosity, such profusion of life, there is no call for greed or domination. The whole Earth may function to support our lives, but it exists to glorify God. We too are called to live in such a spirit, precisely because we are so provided for, and so amazed by what we witness in creation. Thus, even the ensuing command to subdue the earth is to be exercised within limits, "it is of great importance that we touch nothing of God's bounty but what we know he has permitted us to do . . . in the use of his gifts, we are to exercise ourselves in meditating on his goodness and paternal care."[42] He recognizes that "God cherishes and propagates all creatures . . . and is the bountiful Father of a family . . . all interconnected."[43] In this respect Calvin can be seen to stand much more within the monastic than the modern tradition!

Perhaps more than any we have studied so far, he directly addresses attitudes to land-ownership and use, and recognizes that it lies within our powers to make a difference to the health of the land. We possess in order to take care, with frugal and moderate use.

> Let him who possesses a field . . . endeavour to hand it down to posterity as he received it, or even better cultivated. Let him so feed on its fruits, that he neither dissipates it by luxury, nor

---

39. Pelikan, *Luther's Works*, 64.
40. Calvin, *Genesis*, 95.
41. Calvin, *Genesis*, 96.
42. Calvin, *Genesis*, 98–99.
43. Calvin, *Genesis*, 103–5.

permits it to be marred by or ruined by neglect . . . let every one regard himself as the steward of God in all things which he possesses. Then he will neither conduct himself dissolutely, nor corrupt by abuse those things which God requires to be preserved.[44]

Here we have one of the earliest uses of the concept of "stewardship" in understanding human responsibility for the Earth.[45] Likewise in the *Institutes*, "we are the stewards of everything God has conferred on us by which we are able to help our neighbour, and are required to render account of our stewardship. Moreover, the only right stewardship is that which is tested by the rule of love" (III.vi.5).[46]

He continues, arguing that the "First Fruits" of Exod 23:19, and 22:29 are not the only part of our goods to be given, but they stand as a sign and recognition that all we have and do is to be sanctified to God's purpose.

Nevertheless, Calvin can be read in different ways, and John Passmore also uses the *Institutes* to demonstrate that Calvin stands within what he, Passmore, calls the despotic tradition.[47] But such differing accounts must be seen in the context of Calvin's over-riding theological concern that everything exists for the glory of God. In case Calvin should be suspected of making the world too much the human possession, Randall Zachman draws attention to his central conviction that "the world is founded to be the theatre of divine glory."[48] Among others, he uses the metaphors of mirror, representation, theatre, living image, clothing, school, and silent proclamation, and argues that the Sabbath is given for the contemplation of God in creation—if we don't get to engage in such contemplation the rest of the week. Zachman also outlines what he calls Calvin's "systematic ecology," progressing through the heavens, the atmosphere, the wilderness, life—including the human life of Christ, and

---

44. Calvin, *Genesis*, 125.

45. Passmore, *Man's Responsibility*, 29–30, shows no awareness at all of this passage in his ascerbic dismissal of arguments that there is a tradition of stewardship in Christian attitudes to nature, earlier and other than in a quotation from Sir Matthew Hale, "a passage so often quoted in this connexion that one has good reason for suspecting that it would be embarrassing to ask for another example."

46. Calvin, *Institutes*, 695.

47. Passmore, *Man's Responsibility*, 13.

48 The following paragraph based on notes from a public lecture: Zachman, "Calvin's Ecology."

the sea, all of which is intended to awaken in us wonder, gratitude, and a sense of our own finitude. In writing of wilderness Calvin referred to Job, and thereby touches on the question whether the original "natural" condition (mentioned above by Peter Harrison) included the wild places and animals that Paul Santmire, for example, identifies as a key theme in the creation theology of the book of Job. Here we encounter a wilderness "untouched by the divine curse. The world of nature as God sees it and partners with it in his own ways."[49] It would seem that for Calvin wilderness remains a necessary part of the world, untouched by human activity, reminding us of our place in the scheme of things, and yet another sign of the glory of God.

Meanwhile, struggling to survive (Calvin's) persecution, those on the so-called Radical wing of the Reformation were also reflecting upon human responsibility for the land.

> This idea, that ownership is nothing more than stewardship and that he who possesses must answer both to God and to his fellow man, led the Anabaptists to a sort of "Christian Conservationism," the idea that a man must use the resources of the earth in such a way as not to deprive later generations of what is rightly theirs. Moreover, it was felt that the government has an assignment in this matter, must keep men from stripping the earth bare, as it were.[50]

By the end of the sixteenth century, Anabaptist communities who had found refuge as estate tenants, and were freed from the constraints of conservative village communes, were recognized for their especially innovative farming. They were the first to (re)introduce nitrogen-fixing leguminous crops to European agriculture, and later to experiment with sowing lime and gypsum. As a result, their own holdings were vastly improved in terms of both productivity, and general health and appearance. By the mid-eighteenth century they were credited with having initiated an agricultural revolution.[51]

All this represented much more than merely economic survival. Stuart Murray explores how, "eschatology was one of the more colourful aspects of Anabaptist theology . . . for early Anabaptists, their communities

---

49. Santmire, "Partnership with Nature," 265.

50. Verduin, *Reformers and Their Stepchildren*, 232, note h. Note also, contra Passmore above, that these Anabaptist sources explicitly speak of stewardship, not ownership, as early as 1529.

51. Stinner et al., "Forage legumes," 233–48.

were signs of hope,"[52] and they were, "committed to cultivating portions of the earth, as well as communities of Christian disciples, in preparation for the kingdom of God."[53]

For the English Puritan Francis Bacon (1561–1626), nothing was to remain immune to the human touch! Bauckham has reviewed Bacon's thinking and influence in some detail,[54] and finds him in many ways to mirror Bruno's promethean humanism, except that Bacon recognized that to master nature it was necessary to understand nature.

> Man is but the servant and interpreter of nature: what he does and what he knows is only what he has observed of nature's order . . . for the chain of causes cannot by any force be loosed or broken, nor can nature be commanded except by being obeyed. And so those twin objects, human Knowledge and human Power, do really meet in one.[55]

For Bacon, such a marriage of knowledge and power was motivated by love of humanity, and represented "my only earthly wish, namely to stretch the deplorably narrow limits of man's dominion over the universe to their promised bounds."[56] He conceived this work in theological terms as an *instauration*, being an explicit reference to Solomon's building of the temple.[57] Such a project was necessary because,

> Man by his Fall fell at the same time from his state of innocency and from his dominion over creation. Both of these losses can in this life be in some part repaired; the former by religion and faith, the latter by arts and sciences.[58]

That the losses could be so divided, and that some could be repaired without the influence of religion and faith constitutes a radically new departure for Christian theology. Bacon can hardly have imagined what he was letting out of the cage, but this of course is a manifesto for all subsequent secularization, and the development of a form of science in

---

52. Murray, *Naked Anabaptist*, 115.
53. Murray, *Naked Anabaptist*, 156.
54. Bauckham, "Modern Domination," 37–42. For an even more comprehensive review, which takes greater account than we have of the impact of Rene Descarte, see Turner, *Frames of Mind*, 181–203.
55. Francis Bacon, in Bauckham, "Modern Domination," 39.
56. Francis Bacon, in Bauckham, "Modern Domination," 37.
57. Ball, "Making Stuff," 299.
58. Francis Bacon, in Bauckham, "Modern Domination," 37.

which any morality, humility, or humanity has been excised from its inner logic.[59] Thus, Philip Ball observes, "the disturbing aspect of Bacon's scientific writings is often not so much what they consider possible, but how readily he assumes that humankind has the wisdom to handle such power."[60] Bauckham's assessment is that,

> the value of nature has become purely utilitarian; the notion that all creatures exist for the glory of God and thereby assist humanity's contemplation of God has disappeared in favour of nature's usefulness for practical human need. Despite the continued reference to God the Creator, this is the point at which Western attitudes to nature become exclusively anthropocentric rather than theocentric. It made little practical difference when atheistic scientists eventually took their place alongside believing scientists in the Baconian tradition.[61]

Thomas Traherne (1636–1674) was one to benefit from this newly emerging division of knowledge. But, troubled by it, he described the wonders learned at university, "as *aliena*, which we ought to have studied as our enjoyments . . . [but] we knew not for what end . . . and so erred in the manner . . . It is not sufficient for us to study the most excellent things unless we do it in the most excellent of manners."[62]

And that, he maintains, should be a burning desire for the glory of God. He suggested there were

> two worlds. One made by God, the other by men. That made by God was great and beautiful. Before the fall it was Adam's joy and the Temple of his Glory. That made by man is a Babel of Confusions: Inverted Riches, Pomps and Vanities, brought in by

---

59. This is NOT a claim that all scientists are immoral, arrogant, or inhumane. Some are, some are not, but the method itself excludes any such considerations.

Disturbing accounts, not only of the subsequent technological use, but also the actual research practice, of a completely amoral scientific enterprise, are provided in Scully, *Dominion* (see e.g., "Sinning Bravely," 375). Similar observations could be made about the "science" of economics, wealth creation and consumption: see, for example, Harris, *Kingfisher's Fire*, 165; or for the promethean motivations of those—atheists all, who in the 1940s developed the atomic bomb, see McGrath, *Re-enchantment*, 96.

60. Ball, "Making Stuff," 317.

61. Bauckham, "Modern Domination," 40.

62. Traherne, *Centuries*, (3.36–39). A theological account of this alienation of knowledge, and how it may be repaired, is provided in Gunton, *Enlightenment and Alienation*.

Sin. Give all (saith Thomas A Kempis) for all. Leave the one that you may enjoy the other.[63]

In a kind of Protestant monasticism, he committed to a simple clerical life in the country, where he lived with, "ten pounds a year . . . leather clothes . . . bread and water . . . I have had all things plentifully provided for me . . . through this blessing I live a free and kingly life as if the world was turned again into Eden, or much more, as it is at this day."[64]

In this context, and contrary to his contemporaries who were beginning busily to set about the task of mending the world, he claimed to have discovered that "all things were well in their proper places, I alone was out of frame and had need to be mended . . . I was withdrawn from all endeavours of altering and mending outward things. They lay so well, methought, they could not be mended: but I must be mended to enjoy them."[65]

That he was not alone in this sense of reverence before creation we may infer from a complaint by Robert Boyle that,

> the veneration wherewith men are imbued for what they call nature has been a discouraging impediment to the empire of man over the inferior creatures of God: for many have not only looked upon it, as an impossible thing to compass, but as something of impious (sic) to attempt.[66]

Almost a century after Traherne, Matthew Henry began his monumental *Commentary on the Whole Bible*. He likens the creation in Genesis 1 to "a palace made ready,"[67] and by the subsequent dominion, man "is, as it were, God's representative or vice-roy upon earth . . . his government of himself by the freedom of his will has in it more of God's image than his government of the creatures."[68] This honor is upon man in order that "he might find himself the more strongly obliged to bring honor to his maker."[69] Similarly the command of Gen 2 not to eat of the tree, was also part of a covenant, so that "when God had given man a dominion over

---

63. Traherne, *Centuries*, (1:7).
64. Traherne, *Centuries*, (3:46).
65. Traherne, *Centuries*, (3:60).
66. Boyle, in Passmore, *Man's Responsibility*, 11.
67. Henry, *Commentary*, 10.
68. Henry, *Commentary*, 10.
69. Henry, *Commentary*, 11.

the creatures, he would let him know that still he himself was under the government of his Creator."[70]

Repeatedly Henry reminds his readers that whatever God has provided for humankind has also been equally provided for the sustenance of all other creatures, and this divine provision and ordering is yet another reason for our quiet trust and thankful praise. With his Puritan and patristic forbears, Henry also recognizes that this dominion has been "largely lost in the fall but by God's providence enough continues as is necessary to the safety and support of their lives."[71] He also values simplicity of life, perhaps already anticipating the economics of consumerism that would characterize the industrial revolution, in the dawning of which he lived.

> The better we can accommodate ourselves to plain things, and the less we indulge ourselves with those artificial delights which have been invented to gratify man's pride and luxury, the nearer we approach to a state of innocency. Nature is content with a little and that which is most natural, grace with less, but lust with nothing.[72]

That Adam in Gen 2 was made outside the garden and then placed within it was indicative of a grace, not a right,[73] and thus, "all boasting was hereby forever excluded."[74] In describing the work to be pursued in the garden, he notes that it was from the beginning (i.e., before the fall) a divine requirement, it may include all "secular" employments—and that of the husbandman is especially ancient and honorable because,

> nature, even in its primitive state, left room for improvements of art and industry. It was a calling fit for a state of innocency, making provision for life, not for lust, and giving man an opportunity of admiring the creator and acknowledging his providence: while his hands were about his trees his heart might be with his God.[75]

Thus, as late as the mid-eighteenth century, for this influential writer the relationship between nature and humanity still closely reflects that

70. Henry, *Commentary*, 17.
71. Henry, *Commentary*, 11.
72. Henry, *Commentary*, 14.
73. Henry, *Commentary*, 16.
74. Henry, *Commentary*, 16.
75. Henry, *Commentary*, 17.

expounded by Basil, and the exercise of dominion and the pursuit of work is still recognized as to be practiced within the goals of a contemplative life.

Bauckham observes that "without the Baconian desacralization of nature, a scientific enterprise would have been possible, but not the actual scientific and technological enterprise of aggressive domination of nature that has been so significant a feature of modern Western history."[76]

Harold Turner, following Michael Polanyi, draws similar conclusions in his discussion of "the pragmatic theory of truth." "The great Kant," he says,

> was simply wrong in his understanding of science (he absolutized Newton), of art, morality and religion. As a result his meditations during his precisely-timed daily walks in Konigsberg could share in William Temple's evaluation of Descartes' solitary meditations—as equally disastrous for Europe, and beyond.[77]

Interpreting White's Heretics

Nevertheless, despite these many alternative voices, White casually gathers Marxism, and post-Christian modernity, along with Islam, into the same grab-bag as being Christian heresies—all equally unhappily tinctured by what he regards as the one Christian vision of the relationship between humanity and the world of nature.[78] If these are in fact to be regarded as Christian heresies the critical theological question is, how are they so? Does their alleged heresy actually lie in their conception of the nature of the relationship between God and creation? If so, we have an issue that is critical, rather than incidental, to our whole discussion.

We have established that central to the tradition are convictions that creation exists for the glory of God, not for human consumption; that humanity exists within creation, not above or outside it—even while having a unique mode of existence; and that there are life-ways that are appropriate to this human situation, and others that are not. Alister McGrath's survey of the Enlightenment rejection of Christian theology—in which he interrogates the period's enthusiasm for the myth of Prometheus, and its indifference to the cautionary tale of Pandora; and his review of Lenin

---

76. Bauckham, "Modern Domination," 40–41.
77. Turner, *Frames of Mind*, 209.
78. White, "Historical Roots," 1205, 1206.

and Stalin's New Economic Policy—makes this point with considerable clarity,

> White was absolutely right to stress how the imperative to "dominate nature" is central to our present ecological crisis. Yet he signally failed to discern its importance within the secularised worldview of the Enlightenment, to which Stalin is heir . . . White insists that Marxism is merely a "Judaeo-Christian heresy," failing to note how it incorporates the central themes of the Enlightenment precisely where these repudiate the central themes of the Christian faith.[79]

That heresy may in fact affect these relationships White himself acknowledges, in his enthusiasm for the heroic heretic of his choosing, Francis of Assisi. But, although White wants Francis as a heretic,[80] it is doubtful that he is, or indeed ever was. Therefore, I propose to conclude this chapter with a brief review of the ecological possibilities embodied in the different lifestyles adopted by Francis and Benedict.

In proposing Francis as the patron saint for ecologists, White suggested that,

the key to an understanding of Francis is his belief in the virtue of humility—not merely for the individual but for man as a species. Francis tried to depose man from his monarchy over creation and set up a democracy of all God's creatures . . . now they are Brother Ant and Sister Fire, praising the Creator in their own ways as Brother Man does in his.[81]

All our sources have urged the necessity of humility, and it is an integral feature of Benedict's *Rule*. It may not be so clear that they have urged humility in relation to other creatures, but nevertheless it is in some sense necessitated by virtue of being an utterly dependent creature, and it is certainly present among the Desert Fathers. How there may be a democracy of such creatures is much harder to imagine, and probably would end in disastrous outcomes for all of them but the humans. How would the animals describe, protect, or advocate for their interests? How and where would they exercise their democratic "rights"? When over-ruled by human self-interest, to whom would they appeal, and on what grounds, given that this possibility always lies at the heart of all democratic systems? Matthew Scully, despite—or perhaps because of, his

---

79. McGrath, *Re-enchantment*, 91.
80. White, "Historical Roots," 1205, 1206.
81. White, "Historical Roots," 1205–6.

passionate advocacy for animals, recognizes the dangerous weaknesses of such political analogies when applied to the relations between humanity and the rest of creation. The fact is, as we have argued previously, humans have a unique power in the world. Because it is unique it cannot be understood, exercised or moderated by resort to the democratic categories of equality. Rather, we must employ theological categories to understand this power.

In urging Francis's recognition of a partnership in praise, White is on stronger ground. But this too is not new. That each element praises the Creator in its own unique way is present in Basil, and all our sources are agreed that the whole creation exists in praise and for the glory of God. White suggests that Francis's

> view of nature and man rested on a unique sort of pan-psychism of all things animate and inanimate, designed for the glorification of their transcendent Creator, who, in the ultimate gesture of cosmic humility, assumed flesh, lay helpless in a manger, and hung dying on a scaffold.[82]

We have previously noted that both Basil and Augustine recognized that animals possessed souls, although they did not see such souls as sharing human rationality. Scully demonstrates that many of those characteristics which once had been regarded as uniquely human may also be observed in animals. Nevertheless, as he also observes, the differences in capacity are so vast that human beings still remain in a unique position of power. Even with such new awareness, it would be difficult to demonstrate that animals also engage in the conscious, rational, loving contemplation of God. But, from a theological point of view, all that is necessary is to assert that, as God's creatures, all animals have their own life before God (even if it is hidden from us) and our human responsibility is to participate with them as members of the choir, and to ensure—as best we can, that their contribution to the hymn is not silenced. And why, as Scully so movingly reminds us, should we not show mercy?

Francis of Assisi

Jan Boesema has examined all of Francis's references to nature, creatures, or the natural world. He concludes that Francis

---

82. White, "Historical Roots," 1207.

preached humility and taught the whole of creation to glorify and praise its maker. What he did *not* preach, though, was the equality of all creatures, let alone some form of "ecocentrism." What does emerge from the *Canticle* . . . is a profound sense of solidarity and communion with the whole creation.[83]

This apparent affinity with the natural world is, he believes, what has given rise to the many stories engaging Francis with nature.[84] Nevertheless, most of these show Francis exercising some form of dominance over animals, often to convert them from destructive or morally reprehensible behavior, and thus to signify the restoration of creation.[85] Francis's few direct sayings indicate no sense of a unique relationship with nature, but are concerned only to illustrate or to exhort.[86] Indeed, one version of the Canticle

has an unambiguous though indirect human focus: "For every creature proclaims, 'God made me for your sake, O man.'" This is not the kind of remark one would expect from the St. Francis posited by White and others. In the modern literature on the saint this passage is quoted remarkably rarely.[87]

In all this, Boesema finds Francis to be thoroughly within the orthodox and received monastic traditions.

With Francis there is anything but equality among the creatures of the earth: he addresses them with authority, and they obey. He feels at one with the whole of creation, but there is an anthropocentric ring about it all . . . Over and against White, we can say that "with Francis, *nothing* is different": in absolutely no way does he differ from our conventional image of a saint.[88]

Precisely because Francis engaged animals as moral agents, Boesema argues that it is utterly inappropriate to promote him as the Patron saint of ecologists.[89] Even the "hybrid" ecology that has emerged in the Deep Green movement is foreign to Francis, "the attitude of St. Francis towards

83. Boersema, "Francis of Assisi," 64.
84. Boersema, "Francis of Assisi," 65.
85. Boersema, "Francis of Assisi," 69.
86. Boersema, "Francis of Assisi," 63.
87. Boersema, "Francis of Assisi," 62.
88. Boersema, "Francis of Assisi," 71. The italicized contrast is drawn with White, 1207.
89. Boersema, "Francis of Assisi," 71–72.

nature is not only worlds apart from the outlook of traditional ecologists, but also very different from that of deep ecologists. For ecologists of whatever variety, then, Francis is not an appropriate patron."[90]

Nevertheless, as we shall see shortly, there is support for the idea that Francis be enlisted as the patron for Environmentalists.

Perhaps Francis's most radical departure was in relation to the life of poverty, and Boersema suggests that it was not in his attitude to creatures, but in his poverty that Francis was most at risk of being branded heretical and politically subversive.[91] Yet it was not his poverty as such which was new, but rather his peculiar vision of poverty. This involved total identification with Jesus through identification with the most abjectly poor, to be pursued within the world rather than by conventual withdrawal, and without the supports of a community working the land or otherwise endowed.[92] Such poverty is also inseparable from his experience of sickness, disability, and constant pain.[93] This central feature of Francis's spirituality is unmentioned by White, and numerous authors have recognized with G. K. Chesterton (writing in the 1920s!), that in much of the modern enthusiasm, "his ascetical theology [is] ignored or dismissed as a contemporary accident."[94] Leonardo Boff explores Francis's poverty in relation to contemporary political and economic conditions, and also identifies elements within the Franciscan vision that carry ecological or environmental significance.[95] Poverty as an ascetic virtue

> translates into an ecological mentality, responsible for all the goods of nature and culture, for a sober and anticonsumeristic life, in the face of a society of production for production's sake and consumerism for consumerism's sake . . . this poverty is a challenge to materialism and opens the doors to alternative solutions to consumer society.[96]

It is in this sense that we can concur with Boersema's suggestion that Francis could be adopted as a patron for environmentalists, even if not

---

90. Boersema, "Francis of Assisi," 74.
91. Boersema, "Francis of Assisi," 55–56.
92. Boff, *Saint Francis*, 64–80. See also von Galli, *Living Our Future*, 70–71.
93. Cunningham, *Brother Francis*, 9.
94. Chesterton, *St. Francis of Assisi*, 8. See also Cunningham, *Brother Francis*, ix–xix.
95. Boff, *Saint Francis*, 59–64.
96. Boff, *Saint Francis*, 63.

ecologists. Integrating these and other elements of poverty, Boff identifies in Francis the primacy of love over a form of analytic rationality that has banished

> other legitimate avenues to the real, those described as Pathos, sympathy, or Eros, fraternal communication and tenderness. This whole dimension will be marked and even denounced as disturbing to scientific objectivity . . . at the beginning of the modern revolution, nature was separated from the emotional and archetypal life of people; it stopped being one of the great sources of the symbolic and sacramental dimensions of life, losing its therapeutic and humanizing functions.[97]

Significantly, this Eros—which Boff believes Francis held to be primary, he also identifies with Augustine's conception of desire for God.[98] And he also congratulates Pascal, at the dawn of the scientific era, for recognizing "that feeling also is a form of knowledge, but more comprehensive and enveloping than reason . . . the primary axioms of thought are intuited by the heart and that it is the heart that determines the premises for all possible knowledge of the real."[99]

It is life in the primacy of love that enables Francis's deep and joyous sense of connectedness with all things. And it is the absence, or the repression, of this love which leads to modern alienation, the subjugation of the poor by the powerful, and the development of a form of consumerist economics that knows no end for itself—"What does one do after having won the battle of hunger, having satisfied one's needs to the point of nausea? Having reduced the point of existence to the satisfying of these needs, once they are met one does not know what else to do."[100]

While his thinking is completely at home in the received tradition, it may be argued that the spirituality of Francis does serve to cultivate a sense of loving engagement, of belonging, with the rest of creation, that may not have been so strongly *felt* within some earlier aspects of the tradition. But it has subsequently become integral to a long history

---

97. Boff, *Saint Francis*, 6–7; for the extended argument see 17–47. See also, Zizioulas, "Preserving God's Creation" (12:1, 1989), 1.

98. Boff, *Saint Francis*, 12.

99. Boff, *Saint Francis*, 10.

100. Boff, *Saint Francis*, 7.

of Western thought and feeling.[101] Whether this is theologically robust enough to address the issues of our ecologic crisis is another question.

To feel a deep sense of affinity with brother sun, sister moon, or mother earth does not in itself answer questions about how we are to live with them. Rene Dubos has described Francis's attitude as "romantic and unworldly,"[102] and notes that the Earth which Francis loved had already been deeply altered by human activity—including, one may add, his own building! Thus, Dubos argues,

> Benedict of Nursia, who was certainly as good a Christian as Francis of Assisi, can be regarded as a patron saint of those who believe that true conservation means not only protecting nature against human misbehaviour but also developing human activities which favour a creative, harmonious relationship between man and nature.[103]

Dubos suggests that the Benedictine *Rule* is inspired more by the second chapter of Genesis than by the first, and here, "man is placed in the Garden of Eden not as a master but rather in a spirit of stewardship."[104] Thus,

> throughout the history of the Benedictine order, its monks have actively intervened in nature—as farmers, builders, and scholars. They have brought about profound transformations of soil, water, fauna, and flora, but in such a wise manner that their management of nature has proved compatible in most cases with the maintenance of environmental quality. To this extent, Saint Benedict is much more relevant than Saint Francis to human life in the modern world, and to the human condition in general.[105]

The Benedictine *Rule* is directed to developing an integrated life: worship, work, study, and prayer are all provided for, in a life of stability, within a community. Francis allowed that his friars might work, but actually preferred that they identify with the poor by a life of begging. Quite apart from the question whether, or to what degree, Jesus lived like this and urged his followers to do likewise, the ecological issue centers around

---

101. Dubos, *God Within*, 161–62.
102. Dubos, *God Within*, 167.
103. Dubos, *God Within*, 168.
104. Dubos, *God Within*, 169. If this is true, the tradition of stewardship may be seen as reaching a full millennium further back than has been otherwise recognized.
105. Dubos, *God Within*, 169; see also 170–71.

the means by which that which is begged has been produced. Whether in 1210 or 2012, no matter how profitable the work, or how generous the gift, if it has been generated through unjust or environmentally disastrous activity the question confronts us whether such an approach to life is sufficiently integrated to provide a fruitful way to the future?

Dubos is not however advocating that all should be altered. He argues the necessity of conservation because we do not know how much environmental change the Earth, or any particular ecosystem, can actually bear before collapsing. Further, bio-diversity is a protection against the risks associated with simplified systems or monocultures, and diversity also provides the base for future biological flourishing. But,

> above and beyond the economic and ecological reasons for conservation, there are aesthetic and moral ones which are even more compelling . . . our separation from the rest of natural world leaves us with a subconscious feeling that we must retain some contact with wilderness and with as wide a range of living things as possible. The national parks contribute a value that transcends economic considerations and may play a role similar to that of Stonehenge, the pyramids, Greek temples, Roman ruins, Gothic cathedrals . . . or the holy sites of various religions . . . saving marshlands and redwoods does not need biological justification any more than does opposing callousness and vandalism. The cult of wilderness is not a luxury; it is a necessary protection of humanized nature and for the preservation of mental health.[106]

Even the preservation of wilderness for the sake of the creatures which live there is a matter of human initiative and human management. Conservation is the discipline of subjugating our wants to the needs of other creatures, and thereby showing that we are able to care—or, as Scully reminds us, to show mercy.

CONCLUSIONS

We have explored "the greatest psychic revolution in the history of our culture,"[107] and observed that key affirmations of creation *ex nihilo*, the incarnation and the resurrection all affirm intimate divine engagement with creation, rather than indifference. The realm of materiality is a vital

---

106. Dubos, *God Within*, 164–67.
107. White, "Historical Roots," 1205.

component within the purposes of God. Nevertheless, Athanasian and Augustinian accounts of human sinfulness recognize a constant risk of misuse of human power, and of creation. Thus the conversion of attitudes and behavior is central to their account of the gospel.

Progressing from the medieval to modern eras, we also observed diverging attitudes in relation to the exercise of power within creation. Bacon's separation of religion and faith from the arts and sciences opened a door for secularizing and desacralizing developments which have had disastrous consequences. Others, better integrating the new learning with humility, developed ideas about careful stewardship and even the healing of creation.

There is no escaping the reality of our unique power. Francis was uneasy with power and seemed always to try and avoid it. The Benedictine vision recognizes power—both its real dangers and its wonderful possibilities, and within an integrated life invites us to live our power well. Power is lordship, and in the next chapter we come to evaluate this power christologically, in the teaching and ministry, and ultimately the resurrection of Jesus.

8

With Christ in the Care of Creation—Part One: Human Dominion and the Resurrected Lord

WE COME NOW TO draw together the diverse elements of this study, which originated in an interrogation of Lynn White's widely influential account of the roots of our ecologic crisis. In this chapter we shall review key aspects of White's thesis in relation to the study thus far. Then, in response to the New Testament proclamation of Jesus' resurrection, we will introduce a christological account of human dominion, exploring the confessions that Jesus is Lord, the image of God, and the incarnate Word. In the final chapter we shall examine the resurrection as vindication of three aspects of Jesus' ministry—his proclamation of the kingdom of God, and his claims in relation to the Sabbath and the Sanctuary. Thereafter we shall draw our final conclusions.

Within a wider ambit of historical geography, we have noted significant, indeed dramatic, environmental degradation in contexts untouched by the biblical stories. We have also explored how the concept of dominion, as it appears in the Genesis material, must be understood as a theological protest against the divinized imperialism of ancient Mesopotamian civilizations. In Genesis 1 all humanity is established as an ambassadorial representative of God, and the associated dominion consists in referring the creation to its maker. Thus the Sabbath, not the creation of human beings, is the high point and goal of the creation story. In Genesis 2 the human beings are charged with serving and caring for the garden. Whatever may be their subsequent appropriations, neither of these stories are inherently dominationist, nor destructive. Indeed, the Jewish heritage was relatively environmentally benign in comparison to that of its various imperial neighbors. Failure to acknowledge any of this represents a serious weakness in White's case. Nor are these lacunae repaired in White's account of the environmental impact of emerging Christianity.

Patristic theologians who wrote extensively on creation, and the place of humanity within creation, go unmentioned by White. Those we have engaged recognize a key role for humanity within creation. As bearers of the divine image—a relational conception that is entirely dependent upon remaining orientated towards God, humanity must, on the one hand, cultivate a contemplative life with God. On the other hand, the same contemplative existence is to enable good governance over other creatures, and this finds its primary expression in the referral of all creatures to their Creator. Thus worship is central to the human calling upon Earth.

While he makes some passing references to Christian monasticism, key themes arising from its ascetic theology, stability in place, and the quest for Christ in all creation, are all ignored by White. And, perhaps most seriously of all, the whole intellectual transformation associated with the Renaissance and Enlightenment also remains unexamined, except for a superficial suggestion that some of their elements are Christian heresies, and therefore (curiously) Christian orthodoxy must bear tarring with their brush. Francis of Assisi, also named among the heretics, is promoted by White to be the patron saint of ecologists. We have explored elements of Francis's spirituality which have helped generate a sense of connection with the Earth and sympathy with animals. But we have also noted some romantic elements in White's assessment which fail to engage with many of the human and environmental issues involved in living in the world as it is.

In all this there is a sense in which White was attempting a theological—or at least religious, account of the environmental impact of Western Christianity, but failed to bring adequate theological resources to the task. Such a theological evaluation is vital for two reasons. Firstly, at the heart of Christian faith is the conviction that in Jesus Christ we encounter both true divinity and true humanity, and thus questions about the divine relationship with the Earth and the proper human presence in the world, must be addressed in the light of this Christ. Secondly, the Bible can be read, and its images appropriated, in many different and sometimes conflicting ways. But the central theological question is whether either White or those who are the objects of his ire, have read the Bible theologically, in the light of Christ. For it is Christ who the earliest witnesses, and their successors, believed was both the subject and key to all the Scriptures. It is this essential theological task that we will attempt to address by a christological evaluation of the idea of human dominion over creation. How does Christology inform our understanding of the human place, and exercise of human power, in creation?

CHRISTOLOGY AND HUMAN DOMINION

Jewish accounts of creation, some deeply impacted by experiences of enslavement and exile, recognize that creation is good in the purposes of God, but still in need of being brought to completion, liberation, or restoration. Messianic hopes of a healing for the world constitute an integrating thread through much of the Old Testament tradition. Thus, the tradition itself yearns to be read in a messianic or christological light.[1] Such christological readings are also eschatological. Recognizing the incompleteness of the world, they see creation as an unfolding divine project, and look to its end as the only place from which it can be properly understood.

Central to the emerging Christian account of creation was the confession, received as "Good News," that the messianic hopes had begun their fulfillment in Jesus, and that his resurrection confirmed him as Messiah/Christ and represented the definitive divine initiative for the restoration of creation. The resurrection is the end, and therefore all reality must now be read in its light, and in the light of the Christ who has been resurrected. The divine engagement with the world, exemplified in Jesus' resurrection, led soon to the early Christian debates about the nature of God's presence in Christ, and the nature of creation as a possible vehicle for divine self-disclosure. These questions are central to the patristic period. A crucial contribution by patristic theology to christian faith involved developing a robust doctrine of the Trinity.

1. Knight, *Christ the Center*, 31–49.

Therefore, we begin, in Section 1, with an account of the significance of trinitarian theology for addressing questions about both the presence of God and the place of humanity within creation. The Genesis stories are central to patristic and monastic accounts of the world. Much more than in Jewish tradition, the fallenness of humanity and the despoliation of the Earth become central themes. Yet this is accompanied by a most vigorous assertion of the goodness of creation, the dignity of humanity, and the centrality of creation in the purposes of God. These affirmations are crucial to the patristic theological enterprise, and the ultimate ground for this certainty lies in the whole complex of events that constitute the life and person of Jesus Christ. Thus, all patristic accounts of creation and humanity are deeply christological. Section 2 addresses issues arising from the earliest confessional and doxological affirmations. What does it mean for the Earth, and for humanity in Christ, that resurrection reveals Jesus as Lord, as the image of God, and as the incarnate Word of God?

The Trinitarian God with Two Hands Entangled in the World

All our sources in the patristic and monastic traditions have conceived the image of God and its associated dominion as a dynamic quality, only present in humanity to the degree that human beings live orientated towards God. *Imago* is a function of relationality, a gift sustained only by life in right relationship. In such a conception the exercise of dominion consisted in contemplation of the Word in relation to God, and good governance by the wisdom of the Word in relation to one's own life and world. Although humanity may have some unique capacities within the world of creatures, we are established inextricably as part of that world, sharing in all its animal qualities and its utter dependence upon the sustaining and enlivening actions of the Word and Spirit of God. This thoroughly relational understanding can properly be regarded as an ecological model of human existence, and Jürgen Moltmann is one of many who have unashamedly grounded such an understanding within an orthodox doctrine of the Trinity.

> We need to rediscover the triune God. However dogmatic, orthodox, and old fashioned it sounds, it is nevertheless true. Simply hearing the name "of the Father, of the Son, and of the Holy Spirit" already imparts this sense of the divine mystery as wonderful community. The triune God is not the lonely, unloved ruler in heaven, who subjects everything in dominion,

> but a communal God rich in relationships: "God is love." Father, Son, and Holy Spirit live *together* and *for each other* and *in each other* in the highest and most perfect community of love one can imagine: "I am in the Father, the Father is in me, I and the Father are one," says Jesus. If this is true, then it is not through domination and subjection, but through community and life-promoting mutuality that one corresponds to this triune God. Not the human as a lonely subject, but the human in community is God's true likeness on earth. Not the single parts, but the creation-community as a whole is what reflects God's wisdom and beauty.[2]

Furthermore, this Triune God does not sit "above" the world merely to be modeled by human beings. By the ordering presence of the Word, and life-giving action of the Spirit (Irenaeus's conception of "the two hands"), God is intimately involved within the creation, and human community and mutuality is not so much a copying of the divine life, but a participation with it.

We have observed however, that since the Renaissance, and particularly in the development of Modernity, the *imago* was increasingly conceived as a concrete possession, a rationality possessed by all human beings, to be exercised for power over creation rather than in the contemplation of God. For such as Luther and Calvin this capacity was corrupted by the fall to the degree that if not unrecognizable it was certainly seriously impaired, but for those more heterodox it represented an untrammelled power to conquer the Earth. Thus, was the modern scientific/technological project unleashed upon the world, and in close association with it a Deistic conception of God—alone, disconnected from the world, and reconstructed to be devoid of any trinitarian mystery or relationality. As Moltmann, again, describes it, any humanity framed in the image of this kind of God will indeed practice a totally disengaged, objectifying, domination of the world.

> Since the Renaissance, God has always been understood one-sidedly as "The Almighty." *Omnipotence* has been valued as the superior characteristic of godliness. God is the Lord and the world is God's property to do with whatever God wills. God is the *absolute subject* and the world is the *passive object* of God's dominion. As God's likeness on earth, humans must understand themselves correspondingly as a subject, namely, as the subject

---

2. Moltmann, "Reconciliation," 119.

of knowledge and will, and the world as their passive object to be conquered. It is only through domination over the earth that humanity can correspond to God, the Lord of the world. Just as God is the Lord and owner of the whole world, so humans must work to become lords and owners of the earth and of themselves.[3]

Such a conception may appear to concede White's claims, but as we have earlier demonstrated, this is not the God, nor the humanity, of the trinitarian traditions of Christian orthodoxy.

Alister McGrath's survey of Enlightenment modernity reveals the degree to which Deistic, and eventually atheistic, conceptions were focused on liberating humanity from all constraints of either God or nature. McGrath, rather more optimistically than Bauckham, wants to present Francis Bacon as one who still recognized that, even within his project, there remained some divinely imposed limits upon human activity.[4] But having reviewed the impact of Feuerbach, Marx, and Freud he continues,

> did not these approaches point inescapably to the conclusion that, since humanity created God, humanity was God? Having dethroned God, was humanity—perhaps for the first time in its history—in a position to ascend to the throne of nature, which previous generations had naively assumed to be occupied by God? No obstacles now remained to the mastery of nature.[5]

"It was," he writes, "no accident that deicide lies at the heart of the Enlightenment project of conquering nature. Only when God has been eliminated can humanity do what it pleases."[6] Yet this central and defining feature of Modernity does not even appear on the horizon of White's assessment of our ecologic crisis!

To reclaim a trinitarian understanding of the relations between God, the world, and humanity within that world, is to reclaim an ecological understanding of the place of humanity within the Earth community. This requires also the reclamation of an ecological understanding of the nature of our knowledge. John Zizioulas reminds us that,

> humanity does not always behave rationally and cannot be made to behave so . . . there are other forces . . . areas other

---

3. Moltmann, "Reconciliation," 118.
4. McGrath, *Re-enchantment*, 59–61.
5. McGrath, *Re-enchantment*, 63–64.
6. McGrath, *Re-enchantment*, 61.

> than the ethical—that is, the rational prescription of behavior
> . . . all that in the pre-Enlightenment world used to belong to
> the mythological, the imaginative, the sacred. We did our best
> in the post-Enlightenment world to destroy . . . the understand-
> ing of the world in which we live as a mysterious, sacred reality
> broader than the human mind can grasp or contain, a "cosmic
> liturgy" as the seventh-century Greek Father St Maximus the
> Confessor would describe the world.[7]

Such reclamation involves, not simply a restoration of trinitarian as against deistic theology, but also a reconciliation of alienated humanity in all its relationships. McGrath also affirms the necessity of trinitarian theology for addressing the deep problem of nature's ambiguities.

> A Trinitarian natural theology brings to the observation and
> interpretation of nature an understanding of God that is deeply
> shaped by the revelational and soteriological implications of the
> cross. A Trinitarian engagement with nature is already marked
> with the sign of the cross and is thus especially attentive to the
> problem of suffering in nature.[8]

Thus the healing of ecological relationships cannot be conceived apart from the restoration achieved in Jesus Christ and offered in the gospel. Self-centered, self-referential, isolationist, and domineering humanity must be born again into a new mode of existence, a participation in the life of Christ with its essentially trinitarian character. No matter how intensely personal, and even hidden/private, are the operations of the Holy Spirit in awakening the faith which pursues this transformation, its trinitarian character means that conversion to Christ is conversion into communal existence, into the fellowship of Christ's body—the church, and into an ecological mode of existence. For New Testament writers, such a rebirth is signified in baptism. So for Paul, we die and are buried with Christ in baptism and are raised with him to live a new life (see Rom 6:3–4; 8:10–11; Col 2:12; and similarly 1 Cor 6:14), and 2 Peter 1:3 has us, "born anew into a living hope through the resurrection of Jesus Christ from the dead" (cf. John 3:3–8 and 1 Peter 3:21–22). Furthermore, in case there be any doubt about these resurrection claims, the outpouring of the Spirit is seen as a living demonstration of its truth (Acts 2:16–17, 33, 38). We shall explore this further below in the section

---

7. Zizioulas, "Preserving God's Creation" (12:1, 1989), 1. See also Boff, *Saint Francis*, 10; and Gunton, *Promise of Trinitarian Theology*, 53.

8. McGrath, *Fine-Tuned Universe*, 80.

on resurrection as the presence of the kingdom that is to come. Suffice here to note that the event of Jesus' resurrection is intimately associated with our ongoing experience of new life in the power of the Holy Spirit. The Spirit by whom Christ was raised from death (Rom 1:4; Eph 1:20), is the same Spirit at work in us to awaken faith, transform life, be a promise of hope for the healing of creation, and enable a participation now in the ministry of Christ. Whoever is in Christ has become a new creation, and this reconciling initiative of God through Christ now involves us in the same work of reconciliation (2 Cor. 5:17–18).

> To the nearness of the end which began with Jesus' resurrection belongs, as well, the early Christian conviction that the same Spirit of God by which Jesus had been raised now already dwells in the Christians. In early Christianity the Spirit had eschatological significance. The word designated nothing else than the presence of the resurrection life in Christians.[9]

Thus the resurrection of Jesus is central to the reconstitution of true humanity, and key to a christological evaluation of all ideas about human dominion over creation.

Resurrection and Reality

The resurrection of Jesus is crucial in the earliest apostolic proclamation, for understanding all his significance, "this Jesus, whom you crucified, God has raised from death and thereby shown him to be Lord and Messiah" (cf. Acts 2:36). James Dunn argues that,

> in interpreting what they saw as "the resurrection of Jesus," the first disciples were affirming that what had happened to Jesus afforded an insight into reality which was determinative for how reality itself should be seen . . . the resurrection of Jesus was not so much a historical fact as a foundational fact or meta-fact, the interpretative insight into reality which enables discernment of the relative importance and unimportance of all other facts.[10]

Richard B. Hays argues similarly, "this is the historical event in the light of which all our history must be interpreted anew . . . to make such a

---

9. Pannenberg, *Jesus: God and Man*, 67. See also Dunn, *Jesus Remembered*, 694–96, 869–72.

10. Dunn, *Jesus Remembered*, 878.

claim is to make an assertion that redefines reality."[11] Resurrection is not simply another in a series of events, but something that transforms the very nature of all creation, and our ways of viewing creation.

It was in light of the resurrection that the earliest church attributed divine titles to Jesus (e.g., Acts 2:36; 2 Cor 4:4–5; Phil 2:11; Col 1:15–20; Rom 1:3–4; Heb 1:1–3; Mark 1:1; John 20:28, and the whole Johannine emphasis on Jesus being the Word incarnate).[12] Of these references, Colossians, Hebrews, and John all explicitly connect Christ's resurrection with his role in creation. "There is little doubt," suggests Colin Gunton, "that a major impulse for the development of a christological and pneumatological treatment of creation came from the resurrection of Jesus from the dead."[13] Such a redefinition of reality was central to the monastic ordering of life—as we observed in the way Benedict, and Bede even more, read all creation in the light of Easter. There are three significant aspects for us.

Resurrection and Lordship as Service

The earliest attribution of divinity to Jesus was encapsulated in the confession, "Jesus is Lord." On the one hand it claims for Jesus a title by which the whole Old Testament tradition spoke of God (e.g., Gen 2; 13:4; Exod 20:7; Deut 6:4, 10:17–21; Dan 2:47; and multiple acclamations in the psalms). Michael Gorman also notes the political implications of the confession: "its simultaneously creedal and counter-imperial character, rooted in the confession that 'Jesus [not Caesar] is Lord.'"[14] On the other hand, this confession brings us to the heart of our study, for it claims exclusively for Jesus the lordship, or dominion, that might otherwise be allowed to all humanity (Rev 1:5–6; Rom 14:9; 1 Cor 8:5–6; 2 Cor 4:4–6; Eph 1:20–22; Phil 2:6–11; Col 1:15–20). Jesus is consistently portrayed as showing this lordship to be of a servant nature. At the culmination of his ministry, at the Last Supper, both Luke and John have Jesus explicitly teaching (Luke 22:27), or enacting (John 13:1–15), that his lordship is one of service, and his followers are to exercise whatever power

11. Hays, *Moral Vision*, 165–66.

12. Dunn, *Jesus Remembered*, 761–62, concludes that, apart from references to "The Son of Man," Jesus did not claim titles but fulfilled roles, and from those actions, deductions may be made regarding his own self understanding.

13. Gunton, *Triune Creator*, 23.

14. Gorman, *Cruciform God*, 12.

they have in the same way (see also Matt 20:24–28, 23:11; Mark 9:35 and 10:42–45). The Johannine story of the foot washing (John 13:1–17) begins with an extended reflection upon Jesus' identity and self-knowledge (John 13:1–5), suggesting that such service is in no way to be regarded as servile, but as a free gift expressive of both Jesus' deepest identity with the Father and his loving purpose for the restoration of all things.[15] Here we encounter the great paradox of the gospel: the creator becomes subject to creation, the Lord becomes the servant, the host becomes the meal that is to be eaten. So having earlier taken, blessed, broken, and distributed the bread (John 6:11; cf. Luke 22:19–20; Matt 26:26–29; Mark 14:22–25; 1 Cor 11:23–26), Jesus proceeds to present himself as the living bread of life upon whom all must feed if they would enter into fullness of life (John 6:30–51).[16]

The practice of servanthood is frequently associated with the practice of hospitality, and by these actions Jesus extends his Father's divine hospitality to the disciples. The image is anticipated at the wedding in Cana (John 2:1–11) and is taken up again in John 14:1–5, and 21:9–14. We have already seen Genesis 1 portrayed as an offer of divine hospitality, Isaiah's visions of the New Creation are couched in terms of God's hospitality (Isaiah 25:6, 55:1, 58:14)—including towards all the animal kingdom (Isaiah 65:17–25), and Irenaeus's eucharistic theology of creation also recognizes the centrality of this image (*AH*, 5.2:2–3). Creation as the hospitality of God is explored by Colin Gunton,[17] Robert Jenson,[18] and Norman Wirzba[19]—all of them drawing on ideas in Augustine and John of Damascus that in creating God has made room for creation. Murray Rae, following proposals by Udo Schnelle, M. Girard, Joseph A. Grassi, and John Marsh, locates the feeding of the crowd in John 6 as being central to the structure of John's Gospel and in it we see

---

15. Brown, *John*, 564, who also specifically notes Jewish sources that foot washing was not required of a Jewish slave/servant. See also Morris, *John*, 544, who suggests that the deliberation is enhanced by the act occurring in the middle of the meal, not upon arrival, when the feet would normally be washed; and Ridderbos, *John*, 459.

16. Jeremias, *Eucharistic Words*, 90 and 136, argues that John was fully conversant with the Synoptic and Pauline accounts of the words and actions of institution, but relocated them to John 6 for his own particular theological reasons.

17. Gunton, *Christ and Creation*, 75.

18. Jenson, "Doctrine of Creation," 24.

19. Wirzba, "Mark 10," 147.

Jesus' bountiful replenishment of the fruits of land and sea, a renewal, that is, of God's blessing of the earth . . . the recreation of the conditions of abundant blessing that were evident at the completion of God's work in creation. There is also the suggestion of the heavenly feast hosted by the Lord himself and marking the fulfillment of the purposes of God.[20]

Of this event C. K. Barrett also notes its eschatological and eucharistic significance, and sees Jesus portrayed "as the dispenser of life."[21] Dunn similarly suggests, "such an event might well recall the manna miracle of Israel's wilderness wanderings or evoke the prophetic hope of a fruitful desert in the age to come."[22] In keeping with the hospitable table theme, Stephen Verney and J. Ramsey Michaels both note the unusual usage of *anapesein*, "as if reclining at a table,"[23] like the disciples at the supper, in describing the people present for the meal. Herman Ridderbos notes the differing kinds of service that may be involved, contrasting foot washing—as truly servile, with that of table-service, which involves waiting upon guests (Luke 12:37, 17:8).[24] In these Johannine stories Jesus engages in both.

Central therefore to any reflection upon the human place in creation must be the realization that we are here as guests. The responsibility of being a guest includes "trying to be sensitive to strange households, learning complex codes and risking new food and drink. Ideally, habitual hospitality gives rise to trust and friendship in which new exchanges can plumb the depths of similarity, difference, and suffering."[25] What is not appropriate, even for those who may find themselves fearful of the strange company with whom they share the table, is that they trash the place of welcome or abuse the other guests! In confronting issues of fear and hospitality Scott Bader-Saye invokes the trinitarian language of *perichoresis* as, literally, an image of "dancing around."

> The coordinated motion gains its beauty from the elegant interweaving of difference. Here in the very life of God is the condition of possibility for a difference that does not become

---

20. Rae, "Testimony of Works," 303–4.
21. Barrett, *St. John*, 226–30.
22. Dunn, *Jesus Remembered*, 646.
23. Verney, *Water into Wine*, 79; Michaels, *Gospel of John*, 347.
24. Ridderbos, *John*, 454.
25. Bader-Saye, *Following Jesus*, 111.

> competitive, an otherness that does not provoke a struggle for ascendancy. Rather, difference can be held together in a unity of purpose, in an eternal dance of love in which we are all invited to participate . . . as we welcome the difference of the stranger, we take up the challenge of asking how the dance might be extended to incorporate the new steps this stranger brings us.[26]

Although strange to Reformed and Evangelical Protestantism, with traditions of worship based almost entirely upon sitting and listening, the vision of the dance relates very closely to that of the "Cosmic liturgy" espoused earlier by Zizioulas. To recognize ourselves as guests of this kind will open up quite new conceptions of the human relationship with the rest of the Earth community. We are here as dancing partners, none can properly move without the others. Whatever leadership we may have in the dance, it is in order that those we lead may joyfully fulfill their moves also.

The end of the foot-washing story is that those who have been so welcomed, and received such ministry, will now extend that to others. But, they cannot give who have not first received, and it is in this light we read the account of Peter's refusal to accept Jesus' ministry. This is a complex encounter but at its heart, as William Temple reminds us, lies the uncomfortable truth that,

> we are ready, perhaps, to be humble before God; but we do not want Him to be humble in His dealings with us . . . man's humility does not begin with the giving of service; it begins with the readiness to receive it. For there can be much pride and condescension in our giving of service . . . but to accept service is to acknowledge a measure of dependence.[27]

Thus we are here not only as guests, who could conceivably have brought gifts of exchange, but also as dependents, who bring nothing to the table but their invitations, and their need for the host's washing of welcome. On the other hand, to the degree that we do practice the servant-hood enjoined by Jesus, we are also representing the host. Servant-hood therefore involves commitment to the wellbeing of all the other guests.

Temple continues by noting "the danger of virtue that has its origin in the action of our deliberate will rather than as an impulse of love."[28]

---

26. Bader-Saye, *Following Jesus*, 109–10.
27. Temple, *Readings*, 209–10.
28. Temple, *Readings*, 209–10.

The relevance of this observation lies in its connection with the debate we have already explored regarding the place, significance, and power of human will. McGrath reminds us, it is in the theoreticians of the Enlightenment with their uncompromising rejection of christian faith, that the unrestrained "will to power" is most vigorously pursued. But Jesus, as we have noted above, is acting in freedom, and it is all an expression of his love (John 13:1). This contrast between will and power, and an ethos of love, is further recognized by Lesslie Newbigin when exploring this exchange as,

> a sign of the subversion of all human power and authority which took place when Jesus was crucified by the decision of the "powers" that rule this present age. In that act the wisdom of this world was shown to be folly, and the "powers" of this world were disarmed (Col 2:15) . . . The natural man makes gods in his own image, and the supreme God will be one who stands at the summit of the chain of command. How can the natural man recognize the supreme God in the stooping figure of a slave clad only in a loincloth?[29]

Discussing Jesus' death on the cross as the paradigm of faithfulness, Hays writes, "the New Testament writers consistently employ the pattern of the cross precisely to call those who possess power and privilege to *surrender* it for the sake of the weak (see, e.g., Mark 10:42–45, Rom 15:1–3, 1 Cor 8:1—11:1)."[30] Where could there be a clearer recognition that lordship and dominion in Christ involves a radically new assessment of the nature and exercise of human power?

To imagine that such a radical re-orientation of human power can simply be willed is of course self-contradictory. Hence the need for Peter and all who come after him to receive the washing that only Jesus can offer (John 13:8–10, cf. 3:5). Leopold Sabourin suggests the full implications, and a priestly reference, in this washing, by relating it to the ritual washings prescribed in Exodus 29:4 (cf. Lev 8:6, Exod 40:29; Lev 16:4).[31] This washing immediately follows the introductory note that "Jesus knew that his hour had now come" (John 13:1), and is in fact an expression of what "the hour" is about. Rae explores connections between the chiastic

---

29. Newbigin, *Light Has Come*, 168.
30. Hays, *Moral Vision*, 197.
31. Sabourin, *Priesthood*, 145.

arrangement of John's signs, and Jesus' hour upon the cross.[32] The first sign (John 2:1–11) involved the water of purification being transformed into the wine of joy—indicative of Old Testament anticipations of the kingdom of God.[33] Newbigin notes, "the water removes uncleanness but does not give the fullness of joy. What the law cannot supply Jesus will give—in superabundance . . . the 'new wine' of the kingdom of God (Mark 2:22). It is an act of the overflowing majesty of the Creator."[34]

At this point however, "his hour had not yet come" (John 2:4). But the final sign, Jesus' death on the cross and resurrection, is his hour, and again it involves an outpouring, this time of blood and water (John 19:32–34).

> Blood and water, water and wine. John is telling us of the transformation from old life to new, from the blandness of water to the richness of wine. Is it new life we want? In linking the first sign to the seventh John is telling us how we may have it. The new creation comes about because of the work of Jesus, brought to its climax on the cross.[35]

Newbigin stresses that this account of blood and water is not given as casual, passing information, but rather is pregnant with theological significance. Within the materiality of creation, it affirms that "Jesus is dead . . . but this death is itself the source of life. The dying of Jesus—truly in the flesh, is the means by which the life-giving and cleansing power of God is released into the life of the world."[36] Furthermore, we are reminded of the recurring use of the image of water in John, and elsewhere, to speak of the life-giving gift of the Holy Spirit, "water is a symbol both of cleansing and of giving life."[37] Thus, to experience Jesus' servant ministry is to become subject to a process of transformation, at the heart of which is humility.

Finally, in case this servant-hood be regarded as only a temporary aberration, the Lucan parable of the returning Lord (Luke 12:35–38) portrays the master as maintaining a servant role even in the time of his return. Ridderbos, suggesting that the emphasis of the foot washing

---

32. Rae, "Testimony of Works," 303–7.
33. Rae, "Testimony of Works," 307.
34. Newbigin, *Light Has Come*, 27–28.
35. Rae, "Testimony of Works," 308.
36. Newbigin, *Light Has Come*, 258.
37. Newbigin, *Light Has Come*, 258.

story is not on the cleansing of impurity, but on the servant-hood, argues that Jesus is concerned "to present himself... for all time to come in the form of a servant,"[38] and Morris, commenting on verse 14, argues that the reading "because I am your Lord" is to be preferred over "although I am your Lord,"[39] as Jesus' expressed motivation—it is integral to his lordship, not an unusual departure. Similarly, discussing Christ's descent to servant-hood, Michael Gorman, drawing on an impressive list of sources, suggests that Phil 2:6–11 is "Paul's master story." At its heart is the phrase, *en morphē theou hyparchōn*, which, he argues, bears a double translation, "one concessive and one causative: '*although* he was in the form of God' and '*because* he was in the form of God'" [my italics].[40] In Ephesians 4 Paul appropriates the victory language of Psalm 68:18 to describe the triumphant Christ distributing gifts, as a victor might to his retainers. But unlike the imperial gifts of titles, lands, and influence, the gifts of Christ are tasks of service; the same contrast with imperial practice is drawn by Jesus in Luke 22. Thus, here, in servant-hood, is a christologically definitive indication of the character of God.

A servant may also be a steward of the master's goods, and therefore the relationship between servant-hood and stewardship invites further exploration. Stewardship has become the paradigm through which many people, who wish to be responsible in their ways of living, understand the practice of dominion. But there are some difficulties. Clare Palmer, for example, explores two models of stewardship, "the feudal perception, where God the master leaves man in charge of his estate, and also the (mid 20th Century) financial perception, where God, the owner of financial resources, puts them in the trust of humanity, the investor, to use for him as best it can."[41]

Palmer contends that both models suffer from theological, political, and ecological problems: God—the absentee landlord/owner, is excluded from this world; this particular "model" of the relationship often takes on an absolute character—frustrating consideration of other conceptions; the term is drawn from a politico-social order which, for some commendable reasons, we now reject, and therefore its use risks legitimizing unjust global power relations. James Nash, likewise, recognizes that

---

38. Ridderbos, *John*, 460.
39. Morris, *John*, 551, note 36.
40. Gorman, *Cruciform God*, 9–11.
41. Palmer, "Stewardship: A Case Study," 68.

because of its association with certain economic theories, stewardship is a negative idea for many, conveying "the notion of anthropocentric and instrumental management of the biosphere as humanly owned 'property' and 'resources.'"[42] It also risks separating humanity from the natural world and encourages a conception of the world as "resources" to be mined or managed, but without the humility to recognize significant limits upon the human capacity to manage the world. James Lovelock is at particular pains to demonstrate that the limitations of our knowledge make the concept of stewardship misleadingly dangerous, "it requires us to be wise enough to regulate the environment for the common good and to be better at doing this than the evolved system that has kept the Earth fit for life for nearly four billion years."[43] The heart of these objections is that the role of the steward is to serve an absentee landlord—not unlike Moltmann's account above of a Deistic conception of God, and there is little sense, either of serving the wellbeing of the estate for itself, or of any deeply interdependent relationship of belonging.

But these objections need not necessarily hold, and other commentators conceive stewardship more positively.[44] In both Calvin and the Anabaptists we have noted conceptions of stewardship in which creation is the place of God's presence and glory, and Earth-care is deeply conditioned by the priority of love. Lovelock may be correct in his concern about how little we really know of the operations of the Earth, but given the reality of human power, and that nothing is untouched by human influence in the Earth, appropriate forms of stewardship need to be articulated.

Drawing the foregoing together we may say that servant-hood as disclosed in Christ expresses a disposition of love that finds security of identity in relation with the heavenly Father, not in any ability to exercise power over others. While orientated to the well-being of the other it also recognizes its own radical dependence, and therefore its ministry of hospitality is something both given and received with humility. This mutual hospitality seeks the nurture, restoration and healing of all those with whom the table is shared. In this respect Lovelock's proposal that we need to develop the concept and practice of being "planetary physicians"[45] is

---

42. Nash, *Loving Nature*, 107.

43. Lovelock, "Fallible Stewardship," 108.

44. See Dubos, "Franciscan Versus Benedictine," 56–59; Attfield, "Environmental Sensitivity," 76–91; Black, "Dominion of Man," 92–96.

45. Lovelock, "Fallible Stewardship," 109.

particularly congruent with the ministry of Jesus. All this arises from participation in the death of Christ, described by New Testament writers as washing or baptism, and signifying not only forgiveness, nor even reception of the Spirit of life, but also the pursuit of reconciliation through a radically new way of using one's power or responding to one's enemies. Nevertheless, the question remains whether such servant-hood can characterize our dealings with the wider world of nature, or is it confined merely to our dealings with other human beings?

Although from another source than the P material which is our primary focus, Genesis 2:15 has for most of history been read as an explication of Genesis 1:26, and envisaged that the man had been placed in the garden "to serve and to guard it." Can the doctrine of creation *ex nihilo* be regarded as an expression of the servant nature of God? What Jesus enacts as servant for the disciples is actually indicative of something done for the whole creation. By the ordering Word and enlivening Spirit, God is always in a disposition of self-giving towards creation, always acting for the creation's well-being and adornment, and yet always leaving the creation with sufficient freedom that this sustenance can be abused or ignored.[46] Bader-Saye cites David Ford:

> A theology under the sign of hospitality is formed through its generous welcome to others—theologies, traditions, disciplines, and spheres of life. It has the host's responsibilities for homemaking, the hard work of preparation, and the vulnerability of courteously offering something while having little control over its reception.[47]

Such an outcome is always the risk of servant-hood. Judas was among those who received the foot washing (John 13:20–30), as also were Peter—the denier, and all those disciples who apparently ran away. In some sense this is recognized throughout John's Gospel by the reminder that "the Word came to his own realm, yet, although the world was brought into being by him, the world [for the most part] did not recognize him" (John 1:10–11), and indeed eventually rejected him by death on a cross. The same dynamic is expressed in the Philippian hymn (Phil 2:5–11) and a little less explicitly in Col 1:15–22. The centrality of Isaiah's "servant songs" in Christian reflection upon Jesus also places servant-hood—and

---

46. See Ward, "Cosmos and Kenosis," 152–66.
47. Ford, in Bader-Saye, *Following Jesus*, 111.

the experience of ignorance, misunderstanding, rejection, and redemptive suffering, squarely at the center of notions about Christ's lordship.[48]

That the Lord of creation is found to be the servant of creation is critical for understanding our human participation with Christ in the exercise of dominion. To be the servant of creation can be conceived in two ways. The servant who is obedient *to* creation, is one who works in accord with the operations of the *logos* as they may be discerned within nature. The same servant, in obedience *for* creation, is partnering in Christ's priestly activity to the world on behalf of God, and to God on behalf of the world.

Of God's ongoing involvement with the world, Gunton writes,

> from Christology and pneumatology together flow those further aspects of the doctrine which are indicated by words like, "conservation," "preservation," "providence," and "redemption." The first two of those expressions refer to God's continuing upholding of and care for his creation . . . the latter expressions have a more forward-looking orientation, and refer to the forms of action by which God provides for the needs of the creation and enables it to achieve the end that was purposed for it from the beginning.[49]

In none of these activities can humanity take a truly initiatory role. Any attempt to do so would involve attempting to usurp the place of God in sustaining the world. But by being granted a role in the governance of the world, we are invited to participate in the care and redemption of the Earth, in accordance with the servant lordship of Christ.

Resurrection and the Restoration of the Image of God

Although not the first or only "sign," Jesus' resurrection provided the ultimate ground for the faith that God had indeed been present in Christ,[50] and thus for a developing doctrine of the incarnation. In the incarnation we see God's intimate engagement with creation. God chooses to become subject to all the constraints of materiality and it is within those constraints that God's being is revealed and purposes achieved (John 1:1–18;

---

48. See Carson, *Divine Sovereignty*, 133–35.
49. Gunton, *Triune Creator*, 10.
50. Pannenberg, *Jesus: God and Man*, 69.

Rom 1:1-6; 2 Cor 4:4-6, 5:17-20; Phil 2:6-11; Col 1:15-20; Heb 1:1-4, 2:9, 17-18). Gunton suggests that,

> the distinctive place of the human creation cannot be understood apart from christology. Genesis makes the human race both the crown of, and uniquely responsible for, the shape that creation takes. By speaking of Jesus Christ as the true image of God, the New Testament shows that this responsibility is realized only in and through him.[51]

Thus, for example, Psalm 8—which in its evocations of human likeness to God (v. 5), and dominion over all other creatures (v. 6-8), is the Old Testament passage most similar to Genesis 1—is appropriated by the writer of Hebrews for entirely christological purposes (Heb 2:5-9). In both Romans 5 and 1 Cor 15 Paul contrasts the trespass and death that have come through Adam with the righteousness and resurrection that have come through Christ. Both John 1:18 and Phil 2:6 imply, while Heb 1:1-5 and Colossians 1:15 are explicit, that Jesus Christ uniquely is the image of God. Therefore, it is by the incarnation, in Jesus Christ, that the true image of God is restored to humanity. But what does this mean for human living?

We have already encountered the wealth of Old Testament scholarship that regards the image as indicative of God's ownership of, and claim upon, the world. The image is present in the world in order to refer away from itself and towards the one who it represents. But as the image of the trinitarian God this is not merely an imprint but an essentially relational identity. As with the sovereign's image on a coin, it in no way indicates the sovereign's absence or distance from their realm, and unlike the sovereign's image on a coin, this image involves a responsive, responsible partner, who has a role in making things happen. Thus Richard Middleton, in his monumental study, affirms,

> *Imago Dei* refers to humanity's office and role as God's earthly delegates . . . In Gen 1:26-28, that task is understood as the exercise of significant power over the earth and its nonhuman creatures (likely including the agricultural cultivation of the land and the domestication of animals—which together constitute the minimal historical requirements for organized human society or culture). Imaging God thus involves representing and

---

51. Gunton, *Triune Creator*, 12.

perhaps extending in some way God's rule on earth through the ordinary communal practices of human sociopolitical life.[52]

The Earth is subsequently seen to be God's artistic, architectonic, creation—an artful world, for the benefit of creatures. The whole Earth is in fact a temple, with humanity therein as image, "to represent and mediate the divine presence on earth."[53] We have previously noted those ancient readings in which humanity was understood as having such a priestly role. Within the cosmic sanctuary of God's world, human beings act

> as priests of creation, actively mediating divine blessing to the nonhuman world and—in a post-fall situation—interceding on behalf of a groaning creation until that day when heaven and earth are redemptively transformed to fulfil God's purposes for justice and shalom . . . [corresponding] in important respects to Israel's vocation as a "royal priesthood" among the nations (Exodus 19:6).[54]

The royal priesthood of humanity represents the rule of God in the world. "Humans," says Middleton, "exercise their fundamental vocation of transforming the world by the historical agency granted them at creation."[55] And transform the world we have! But to what degree has it been in conformity with the image of God revealed in the humanity of Jesus Christ? Drawing on James Dunn's discussion of Philippians 2, Keith Ward concludes that Jesus "showed what the image of God truly is by serving others."[56] Despite its valuable comprehensiveness, and some hints in that direction, Middleton's work nowhere addresses a christological account of this *imago*. Such an account is vital, for without it human rule can—and has, become despotic, destructive, and—even within the human community, discriminatory, and all the while claiming theological justification. But christologically conceived, such rule is one of service for the whole household of the Earth. Similarly, the Kingship of God as exhibited in Christ is in most respects the antithesis of that exercised by the kings of this world. Middleton recognizes something of this in his account of social context and the "counter-imperial" democratization of

52. Middleton, *Liberating Image*, 60.
53. Middleton, *Liberating Image*, 87.
54. Middleton, *Liberating Image*, 89–90.
55. Middleton, *Liberating Image*, 217.
56. Ward, "Cosmos and Kenosis," 161.

the *imago* in Genesis 1.[57] Our own elucidation of the kingdom of God, as inaugurated by Jesus, will be found in the next chapter.

As the *imago* of Genesis 1 democratizes royal power, so too it democratizes priesthood. Humans no longer "need institutional mediation of God's presence by either kings or priests . . . but are themselves priests of the creator of heaven and earth."[58] Rhetoric about the priesthood of the believer "articulates what we might call the redemptive restoration of the fundamental priesthood of humanity as *imago Dei*, after its distortion or diminution by sin."[59] But how is it restored? Democratized priesthood has, in the evangelical protestant, and post-christian world, largely become privatized religion, characterized by modernist individualism, highly fragmented and fragmenting, and generally lacking any sense of priestly intercession for the world.[60] It lies with Torrance and others, rather than Middleton, to remind us that as Christ is the authentic image of God in the world, so authentic human priesthood is only practiced when by the Holy Spirit his image is restored in us, and we become participants in Christ's priesthood.

This priesthood is not, in the first instance, a judicial mediation between enemies. Rather, it is the means by which God who is not creation nevertheless encounters creation. The image, thus conceived, never exists for itself alone. Its presence indicates two parties to a relationship, each worthy of its own recognition. Creation is thus a potential covenant partner for God. Therefore, even humanity's establishment as image upon Earth is recognition of creation as being a worthy partner for relationship with God.[61] And this is through God's Word. William Countryman,[62] Leopold Sabourin,[63] and Thomas Torrance[64] all note the central significance of the Word of God in the biblical practice of priesthood, reminding us

---

57. Middleton, *Liberating Image*, 93–209.

58. Middleton, *Liberating Image*, 207.

59. Middleton, *Liberating Image*, 207.

60. Middleton and others are correct to identify Genesis 1 as "ideology critique," but constant use of the term "democratisation" suggests they might themselves have been captured by the political rhetoric of modernity and contemporary North America.

61. For a much more comprehensive account of the relationship between creation and covenant, see Barth, *Church Dogmatics*, III.1 Section 41.

62. Countryman, *Border of the Holy*, 3–12, 48–53.

63. Sabourin, *Priesthood*, 101, 150–155.

64. Torrance, *Royal Priesthood*, 1–9.

again that *imago* is essentially relational and not merely imprint. Stephen Edmondson notes that even in Calvin—whose account of priesthood is overwhelmingly focused upon expiatory sacrifice, Christ is mediator eternally, not merely after the fall, so that "mediation is at the heart of all God's activity toward us . . . the Word from the beginning had fulfilled this office of mediator."[65] Thus, in Gregorios's conception,

> Humanity has a special vocation as the priest of creation, as the mediator through whom God manifests himself to creation and redeems it. But this does not make humanity totally discontinuous with creation, since a priest has to be part of the people he represents. Christ has become part of creation, and in his created body he lifted up the creation to God, and humankind must participate in this eternal priesthood of Christ.[66]

This humanity is defined "by its original model, namely the divine Logos himself who became the Son of Man . . . The measure of our conformity to Jesus Christ is the measure in which we are human."[67] Humanity, or humanity as renewed in Christ, thus stands on the boundary between the creator and the creation, enabling the interpenetration of the two. This is the language of *perichoresis*,[68] which we have already seen used in relation to hospitable dancing partners. To the degree that humanity bears the image of divinity, this is not in order to lord over or denigrate the rest of creation, but rather to mediate creation's divinization; a process which Gregorios wryly observes, "seems to be in particular contrast with current trends which see the role of humanity as 'de-divinizing' the cosmos."[69] That creation and divinity are interpenetrated is central to any trinitarian account of the relationship, but Gregorios's proposed "divinization" may be his Scylla to the Charybdis of denigration, and ends up potentially depriving creation of its own authentic existence. Perhaps preferable, yet out of the same Orthodox tradition, is Zizioulas's argument that the superiority of humanity in creation lies in our ability to create events of communion. We need to revalue priesthood as characterized by "'offering,' in the sense of opening up particular beings

---

65. Edmondson, *Calvin's Christology*, 32.

66. Gregorios, *Human Presence*, 85.

67. Gregorios, *Human Presence*, 75.

68. Gregorios, *Human Presence*, 78.

69. Gregorios, *Human Presence*, 68. See also Ward, "Cosmos and Kenosis," 164–66.

to a transcending relatedness with the 'other'—an idea more or less corresponding to that of *love* in its deepest sense."[70]

William Countryman conceives priesthood as *Living on the Border of the Holy*. For him, the Old Testament sacrificial system is not about payment of debts, but "sacramental images of the boundary: death and life, gain and loss, of risk, of approaching the unapproachable, of surrender. They were also images of the bridging of that boundary—of life in communion."[71] Priesthood that arises from the Word is one devoted to unveiling secrets, rather than keeping them hidden.[72] It is directed to revealing the depths and full significance of life,[73] including our limitations and our sinfulness. It is thus about revealing the significance of everyday life—of the profane, and in this sense is related to Middleton's account of human socio-political life.[74] In fact, all of life is found to be "Holy," and priesthood is about a particular quality of engagement with the world. Jesus' priesthood is the supreme expression of this. His incarnation is "God's act of reaching across the boundary to meet us."[75] His birth into a non-priestly tribe, his movement among the unclean, and his identification with Melchizedek by the writer of Hebrews, all indicate both the fulfillment, and the redemption from sinful misuse, of the priesthood that belongs to all humanity.[76] Following Gustav Aulen, Countryman argues that in the earliest Christian theologies, even the sacrifice of the cross shows God "working in Jesus to give a gift, to bring freedom and new life, to turn back the ravages of sin and death."[77] In taking on the name of David, Jesus was, says George Knight, "taking on himself his calling to be Saviour not just of David but of the whole array of sinful human beings. In this way he revealed that he was the true image of God, for saving, forgiving love and recreative passion is at the heart of God."[78]

From the common priesthood—and not vice versa, is derived a sacramental priesthood. "The purpose of the institutional priesthood was to serve the royal priesthood, and the purpose of the royal priesthood, that

---

70. Zizioulas, "Preserving God's Creation" (12:1, 1989), 2.
71. Countryman, *Border of the Holy*, 56.
72. Countryman, *Border of the Holy*, 3–7.
73. Countryman, *Border of the Holy*, 9–11.
74. Middleton, *Liberating Image*, 60.
75. Countryman, *Border of the Holy*, 60.
76. Countryman, *Border of the Holy*, 47.
77. Countryman, *Border of the Holy*, 55.
78. Knight, *Christ the Center*, 43.

is of Israel as a kingdom of priests, was to serve God's saving purpose for all nations. So with the Christian Church."[79]

Without sacraments, "there is a real danger that people lose sight of their shared priesthood amid the everyday pre-occupations of life. What is everywhere is hard to see anywhere. The sacrament refocuses attention on the almost unnoticed pervasiveness of grace."[80] Old Testament sacramental ministry "shadowed forth the danger and the cost of our approach to God—and also its bountifulness, for most sacrifices culminated in a sacred banquet."[81] The Eucharist is the banquet of Christ's priesthood. Here, the common things of the Earth become God's means of encounter with us, as the Earth became such a means in the incarnation.

Ziziuolas explores this sacramental aspect of creation at length. His argument is that, central to all the ancient liturgies is "the *lifting up of the gifts of bread and wine to the Creator father* . . . this attaches at least equal centrality . . . to man's act as the priest of creation . . . both terms—*Anaphora* and *Eucharistia*, have to do with man's priestly action as representative of creation."[82] This contrasts with later Western conceptions, where creation disappeared from the liturgical consciousness, and the emphasis became "a memorial service of the sacrifice of Christ and a means of grace for the nourishment of the (intellectual) *soul*."[83] The significance of this is as follows: By virtue of creation *ex nihilo*, creation is forever confronted with the threat of dissolution into nothingness, experienced within creation as death.[84] To survive, creation must somehow transcend itself, and this occurs when it is referred beyond itself to God, its creator. This referral is the role of humanity in its freedom.[85] Robert Jenson suggests that to hear the Word at the source of all priesthood is to be taken into the conversational life of the Trinity, "those who are thus addressed are God's human creatures; and to be actually human is then to respond in prayer."[86] Thus, doxological prayer becomes the defining characteristic of humanity. Humanity in its freedom can refer creation to

---

79. Torrance, *Royal Priesthood*, 81.
80. Countryman, *Border of the Holy*, 44.
81. Countryman, *Border of the Holy*, 44.
82. Zizioulas, "Preserving God's Creation" (12:2, 1989), 4.
83. Zizioulas, "Preserving God's Creation" (12:2, 1989), 3.
84. Zizioulas, "Preserving God's Creation" (12:2, 1989), 44; and (13:1, 1990), 1, 3.
85. Zizioulas, "Preserving God's Creation" (12:2, 1989), 44–45; (13:1, 1990), 1, 3.
86. Jenson, *Large Catechism*, 21.

its creator in a doxological attitude, or towards humanity in a utilitarian attitude. This was the choice at the Enlightenment and is a key factor in the world's current ecological crisis.[87] Of course such a misuse of freedom, and misdirection of creation, long precedes the Enlightenment. But what humanity in Adam has failed to do, humanity in Christ has done.

> We believe . . . that in the person of Christ the world possesses its Priest of Creation, the model of man's proper relation to the natural world.
>
> On the basis of this belief, we form a community which takes from this creation certain elements (the bread and the wine) which we offer to God with the solemn declaration "Thine own of thine own we offer unto Thee," thus recognizing that creation does not belong to us but to God, who is its only "owner." By so doing we believe that creation is brought into relation with God and not only is it treated with the reverence that befits what belongs to God, but it is also liberated from its natural limitations and is transformed into a bearer of life. We believe that in doing this "in Christ" we, like Christ, act as priests of creation. When we receive these elements back, after having referred them to God, we believe that because of this reference to God we can take them back and consume them no longer as death but as life. Creation acquires for us in this way a sacredness which is not inherent in its nature but "acquired" in and through Man's free exercise of his *imago Dei*.[88]

Creation thus acquires sacredness when the sacramental elements are passed through human hands.[89] This dynamic must hold good for every element of creation that passes through human hands. Middleton has reminded us that the priestly ministry involves all the activities of daily life. Countryman similarly demonstrates the priestly nature of parenting and child-hood, mentoring, education, politics, management, the arts, and friendship.[90] In all the manifold ways that creation passes through our hands, does our work suggest that we are holding something sacred—something of that stuff which God has chosen as "a place for my name to dwell"? Does all this work issue in communion among all

---

87. Zizioulas, "Preserving God's Creation" (13:1, 1990), 1.
88. Zizioulas, "Preserving God's Creation" (13:1, 1990), 5.
89. Zizioulas, "Preserving God's Creation" (13:1, 1990), 4.
90. Countryman, *Border of the Holy*, 20–23.

Earth's creatures—or benefit only for a few? Does it minister healing? Can it be done as offering in prayer, and does it issue in thanksgiving—or in cries of pain and cries for justice? Only as it reflects the stewardship of the Lord's table,[91] can all other handling of creation be regarded as true stewardship. Here is the *ethos* of love which Zizioulas believes it is crucial to cultivate. This is the priestly vision of ordinary work so central to the Benedictine life. It is our failure to understand our existence in such priestly terms that leads to many of "the grave ills"[92] now confronting modern Western culture—including our contemptuousness towards the creation within which we have been placed to exercise priestly ministry.

My own years of pastoral experience suggest that for the overwhelming majority of Western Christians, priesthood is either relegated to one sacral person, who is deliberately kept apart from the common life of the rest (as in popular Catholicism), or it is completely privatized (we are each our own priests), or it is simply an idea so alien as to be for the most part ignored or even beyond consciousness. Yet, since it is crucial to any conception of our bearing the image of God, it is also crucial that there be a renewal of priestly consciousness. Without it we live here either claiming unbridled power over the Earth, or denying our significance by resort to the deceits of a reductive science, which Berry caricatures as "nothing buttery."[93]

The constitutive identity and primary life-calling of human beings made in God's image, as narrated in Genesis 1, is both understood and restored in Jesus Christ. His priesthood is both God's means of engagement with creation, and ours of response to God. Such engagement means, on the one hand, that creation is not a matter of indifference or neglect. But, on the other hand, nor is creation so totally absorbed into God as to lose its own identity as creation—that is, as a significant other, a loved partner. Priesthood, as experienced in Christ, is about communion, and creation is to be both honored and enjoyed as a partner in that communion.

The ultimate end of Christ's priesthood is the reconciliation of all things to God the Father. Priesthood thus has an eschatological orientation which is most fully articulated in the vision of heavenly worship—overwhelmingly in the Revelation to John. There, among many other things, the heavenly Council sings,

---

91. Torrance, *Royal Priesthood*, 77.
92. Countryman, *Border of the Holy*, 67–69.
93. Berry, *God and the Biologist*, 23–25.

> "You are worthy, our Lord and God,
> To receive glory and honor and power,
> For you created all things,
> And by your will they existed and were created." (Rev 4:11, NRSV)

Somewhat more evocatively, the translators of the Authorized Version have it that "for Your pleasure they are created." In Revelation 5:13 it is not only the heavenly Council but, "every creature in heaven and on earth and under the earth and in the sea, and all that is in them, singing,

> 'To the one seated on the throne
> And to the Lamb
> Be blessing and honor and glory and might
> Forever and ever! . . . Amen!'"(NRSV)

That every creature is together in this praise is itself a sign of the redemption of creation, for the wolf here, as in Isaiah 11, is no longer interested in eating the lamb! Among this great company are the redeemed of Jesus Christ who have been made, "a kingdom, priests serving his God and Father, to whom be glory and dominion forever and ever" (Rev 1:6, NRSV). However believers participate in the Priesthood of Christ, it is with him on behalf of all living creatures.

Resurrection and the Incarnation of the Word of God

In John 1 and Hebrews 1, and especially in the patristic writers we have explored, the Word of God which has become incarnate in Jesus Christ by the power of the Holy Spirit is the same Word by whom all things were created, and are even now held in being. We have noted the centrality of the Word to the human priestly identity as image of God, but the incarnation of the Word in creation is significant in three further ways.

INCARNATION AND RESTORATION OF THE CONTEMPLATIVE LIFE

Athanasius saw that fullness of human life involved the contemplation of the Word in creation, and this included the presentation of the Word to us through our senses (*DI*, 16). Basil, similarly, identified the contemplation of beauty in creation as a calling critical for cultivating life with God and being truly human. Augustine had recognized (contrary to his earlier Platonic traditions) that this contemplative life properly included such activities as gardening, for by them was enabled "a conversation" with the natural world. A similar understanding was elucidated in the monastic tradition by Bede. We have also followed Harold Turner's argument that Basil's understanding of the Word in creation constituted a de-divinizing of creation which allowed for the development of investigative science. Philosopher Scott Olsen identifies the *Logos* of John's Gospel with the divine Ratio by which Plato discerned the relationship of the one and the many throughout the Cosmos—subsequently described as the Golden Ratio/Section.[94] "Concerning the Logos (ratio or word), at the start of St. John's Gospel, 1:1, we read 'In the beginning was the Logos, and the Logos was with God and the Logos was God.' The only ratio that is simultaneously one and with one is the golden section."[95] His elucidation of the manifold ways this ratio occurs in nature, and its use in Christian architecture, thus provides a further focus for the contemplation of the Word/Logos in creation. That all such "listening" to creation has immediate practical outcomes is demonstrated in this description of approaches to farming practice:

> An apt witness to the nurturing responsiveness of stewardship comes from the reflections of careful farmers. Fred and Janet Kirschenmann, who raise organic grains in North Dakota, observe that the Genesis responsibilities "to service and take care" of the earth involve long-term attachments to a small plots. The wisdom to cultivate creation's goodness comes slowly, over generations of working with a place. Richard Thompson, who believed "that God would teach me how to farm" and turned to the Bible to find out, felt called by the Spirit away from chemicals toward more natural ways of farming. His "biblically based" farming techniques now require understanding his land and animals much better. Wendell Berry, from the Kentucky hills, writes that stewardship as a form of love means knowing how to "use knowledge and tools in a particular place with good long-term results." Larry and Carolyn Olson, small-scale Minnesota farmers, say that faithful land care means learning its soil by "asking a lot of questions and being close to the earth."[96]

---

94. Olsen, *Golden Section*, 1–6.

95. Olsen, *Golden Section*, 34.

96. Jenkins, *Ecologies of Grace*, 87–88. See also Pollan, *Omnivore's Dilemma*, 123–33, and 185–238, for a similar, more extensive account of attentiveness.

Similarly, "Farming God's Way" is an approach to conservation agriculture developed in Africa. By attentiveness to natural processes in the ordering of creation—which are regarded as God's providential ordering, rather than by following traditional animistic practices; but equally concerned to avoid enslavement to multi-national seed and petro-chemical interests, the movement is lifting its practitioners out of poverty without the cost of environmental degeneration.[97]

The attentiveness exemplified by all these practitioners is a remarkable contemporary reprise of the commitments we observed in monastic accounts of the relationship between humanity and the land. It connects also with Rene Dubos's suggestion that land may have a "vocation." Such questioning and listening requires the embodied presence of human listeners, but these are the ones banished from the land by new forms of industrialized agriculture,

> cleared of "surplus" farmers and their scaled, attentive stewardship, despotic and destructive practices of industrial agriculture take over the land. That supposed surplus watches over the land, embodying grace by maintaining love's knowledge of earth in the skilled, responsive practices of nurturing a particular place.[98]

Ironically, not only does industrialized agriculture banish human "listeners" from its world, so too does its antithesis—those ideologies which have come to regard humanity as the enemy of nature and therefore to be excluded from those places which are to be preserved as authentic. This, despite the recognition that humanity is as much a part of the natural history of the Earth as every other creature.

The contemplation of the Word in creation is a necessary element for growth in Christ, and science provides one important means for enabling this contemplation. "We learn how the world works by being informed by the best science,"[99] and this in turn informs a better obedience. Such study, according to Richard Foster, is one of the most necessary Spiritual Disciplines if we are to undergo transformation into the likeness

---

97. Goodwin, unpublished address at Faith and Development Symposium, University of Otago, Aug 2010. See also "'Farming God's Way' in Zimbabwe"; Wibberley, "Framework for Sustainable Agriculture," 130–33; and Hodson, "Creative Harmony: Isaiah's Vision," 169–77.

98. Jenkins, *Ecologies of Grace*, 87–88. See also Berry, *Recollected Essays*, 215.

99. Bouma-Prediger, *Beauty of the Earth*, 176.

of Christ.[100] Science does not, however, supplant all other elements in the contemplative life, for it is the incarnate Christ, witnessed in the Scriptures, who remains the definitive revelation of the Word of God, and it is in that christological light that all attempts to "read" the Word must take place.[101] Science is not immune to the corrupting influence of human sinfulness and the distortions that trouble the groaning creation. Boff, McGrath, Scully, and Zizioulas have all already alerted us to the oppressive and destructive outcomes arising from those forms of science which claim to be the sole arbiter of all knowledge, goodness and truth—for example, the dehumanized "science" of industrial agriculture,[102] or the technological excesses of modern militarism and consumerism. Nevertheless, suitably humbled science can provide a way of listening for the Word in creation, a way of identifying the order and beauty of creation which inspires wonder, informs life, and elicits our thankful praise; and also a way of identifying the disorder in creation, and in our human handling of creation, which may call for the reordering of our lives. Science that enables a better service of the other is a science that properly reflects a christological vision of servant dominion. Science that seeks knowledge only in order to dominate and technologically control for human advantage does indeed invite the strictures of White and others—including Christian theologians as far back at least as Calvin or Traherne.

Originating in similar convictions about the ordering Word and the adorning Spirit, and in similar contemplative impulses, a similar role in Christian formation can also be conceived for the arts and architecture. We have previously encountered the idea of the temple as a model of the whole creation, and Psalms 48, 84, 87 and 122 invite meditation upon the built world itself. Basil argued the importance of the contemplation of beauty in creation. Gunton quotes John of Damascus—in his defense of icons, against those he considered to be Manichaean, that, although the Godhead cannot be imaged,

> when God is seen in the flesh conversing with men (i.e., in Jesus), I make an image of the God whom I see. I do not worship matter; I worship the Creator of matter who became matter for

---

100. Foster, *Celebration of Discipline*, 66, 73–76.

101. This is not a claim that scientists must become subject to theologians, but a recognition of the inadequacy of the reductionism that Berry calls "nothing buttery" in *God and the Biologist*, 21–25. See also Begbie, *Voicing Creation's Praise*, 144–46.

102. Pollan, *Omnivore's Dilemma*, 218–19.

my sake, who wills to take his abode in matter; who worked out my salvation through matter (1:16).[103]

In contrast to this, Gunton recounts a western history of uncertainty and ambiguity concerning the arts as a sign of the goodness of creation, or as a way of conveying truth about God or humanity in the world. This uncertainty is ubiquitous and in no way confined to Christian faith, but by a trinitarian account of God's engagement with the world it may be healed.[104] Jeremy Begbie is one who recognizes that to be truthful—and thus truly redemptive, the arts must engage with the pain and disorder of the world, as much as with its beauty. Thus,

> the distorted portraits of Francis Bacon affect us and horrify us only because we recognize them as brutally fragmented pictures of human beings. To describe modern art as "meaningless" is thus crude and inaccurate . . . Put in theological terms, a "No" of protest in art may well echo God's rejection of all that corrupts his world, but it will never be sufficient on its own. The Christian confession is that God's "No" yields its true meaning only in the light of his "Yes," his unconditional love towards creation, a "Yes" which has found its supreme enactment in the resurrection of Christ from the dead.
>
> In the resurrection too we are reminded that redemption not only achieves the exposure and rejection of evil, but the transformation of that which has been distorted, a renewal of what is disordered.[105]

Such "listening" and creative engagement is also a necessary element in discerning what constitutes appropriate or inappropriate architecture and building. Opening a door, which again we cannot go through in this thesis, Sigurd Bergmann writes,

> reflecting on theological criteria for built environments implies . . . a commitment to contributing to an environment that is worth living in for all human and other beings. A theological aesthetics of architecture always implies also an ethics of a just and sustainable environment for all to live in.[106]

---

103. John of Damascus, *On the Divine Images*, cited in Gunton, *Triune Creator*, 232.

104. Gunton, *Triune Creator*, 228–34.

105. Begbie, *Voicing Creation's Praise*, 214.

106. Bergmann, "God's Here and Now," 14.

Here—and literally in regard of building, is another example of the stewardship of all that passes through human hands. This is an increasingly important issue as the world's population becomes increasingly gathered in cities, and even what little "wild nature" remains, only does so by virtue of rigorous legislative protection and management. The contemplative life will necessarily be one that is nurtured in conversation with human creativity.

What is "heard" in the contemplation of creation becomes a word to be proclaimed when it is integrated into all else that Christ the Word would reveal about the nature and purpose of creation. It may be a word of wonder, but it may be a word of warning—and in the present climate increasingly is. Foster outlines the importance of the contemplative life—including, specifically, meditation on creation, for the development of a sense of the prophetic significance of things.[107] The world may grow darker yet, and we may feel singularly ineffective, but this aspect of our calling is not to power, but to faithfulness in prophetic proclamation.

Referring to Augustine's reflections on beauty, harmony, friendship, and desire in *Confessions* (II.10), William Cavanaugh writes,

> for St. Augustine, the constant renewing of desire is a condition of being creatures in time. Desire is not simply a negative; our desires are what get us out of bed in the morning. We desire because we live. The problem is that our desires continue to light on objects that fail to satisfy, objects on the lower end of the scale of being that, if cut off from the source of their being, quickly dissolve into nothing. The solution to the restlessness of desire is to cultivate a desire for God, the eternal, in whom our hearts will find rest.[108]

He continues, exploring the irony that consumer culture does recognize that particular material things cannot satisfy; however,

> rather than turning away from material things and toward God, in consumer culture we plunge ever more deeply into the world of things . . . pleasure is not in possessing objects but in their pursuit . . . it is not the desire for any one thing in particular, but the pleasure of stoking desire itself, that makes malls into the new cathedrals of Western culture. The dynamic is not an inordinate attachment to material things, but an irony and

---

107. Foster, *Celebration of Discipline*, 29–30.
108. Cavanaugh, *Being Consumed*, 90.

detachment from all things . . . the daily erotics of desire that keeps the individual in pursuit of novelty.[109]

In a wide-ranging analysis of the mimetic social and biological components in this process, John Naish reports,

> brain scans . . . show how the dopamine neurotransmitter gets released in waves as shoppers first see a product and then ponder buying it. But dopamine is all about the hunt here, not the trophy. It is only the anticipation, rather than the buying itself, that squirts dopamine around our skulls. And the effect is only fleeting. Once you've sealed the deal, the chemical high flattens out within minutes, often leaving a sense of regret that shop-owners call "buyer's remorse."[110]

He quotes marketing guru Victor Lebow, writing in 1950,

> our enormously productive economy demands that we make consumption a way of life, that we convert the buying and use of goods into rituals, that we seek our spiritual satisfaction, our ego satisfaction, in consumption . . . we need things consumed, burned up, worn out replaced, and discarded at an ever increasing rate.[111]

Noteworthy here is that consumerism is driven not by human need, but by a deliberately generated excess of supply. And noteworthy too is the promotion of consumerism in the language of Christian discipleship and spirituality. Indeed, not only material objects, but relationships, and religious experiences at worship, are also subject to this dynamic.[112] "Consumerism," writes Cavanaugh, "is an important subject for theology because it is a spiritual disposition, a way of looking at the world around us that is deeply formative."[113]

To the degree that we could find beauty and contemplative possibilities in particular things we would affirm material creation, and consumerist economics would almost certainly grind to a halt.[114] To the degree that we fail in this, we assault creation by making endless and excessive

---

109. Cavanaugh, *Being Consumed*, 91.

110. Naish, *Enough*, 83.

111. Naish, *Enough*, 206. See also Cavanaugh, on "Libido Dominandi," in *Being Consumed*, 15–24, and "the organized creation of dissatisfaction," 46.

112. Brueggemann, *Land*, 174–5,

113. Cavanaugh, *Being Consumed*, 35, and 47–53.

114. Naish, *Enough*, 104.

demands that creation is unable to fulfill. This is so, not only in relation to the truth that we "cannot live on bread alone, but need every word that God speaks" (Matt 4:4), but also that the planet Earth simply cannot sustain the consumerist demands of the wealthy minority, much less those demands when they are promoted as the good of the whole human race.[115] Samuel Alexander suggests that,

> western society is, at last, rich enough to be truly free, free from material want; although . . . not many people seem willing to accept that this is so. Is it because the prospect of freedom is terrifying? Perhaps it is terrifying because, once we recognize the sufficiency of our material situations . . . we are forced to give an answer to that great question of what to *do* with the radical freedom that material sufficiency provides . . . But rather than facing the ultimate human question, many people today seem to have climbed or fallen upon a consumerist treadmill, and become enslaved, consciously or unconsciously, to a lifestyle in which too much consumption is never enough.[116]

Because what is "heard" and "seen" in the contemplative life described above is the personally engaging Word of divine love, and because this relation of *logikos* is the true goal of human existence, the renewal of contemplative life is crucially necessary to confront the destructive impacts of contemporary consumerism. But it is also necessary for an appropriate environmentalism. Peter Harris, co-founder of the conservation organization A Rocha, observes,

> the environmental movement has been perceived as judgmental and angry, claiming moral high ground and issuing rules with disapproval . . . studies have shown one of the marker personality traits among environmentalists is anxiety. The Christian approach is very different: it is celebratory and grateful and hopeful.[117]

---

115. Blair, "Energy and Environment," 103–25. See also Dyer, "Time to Redefine," 11.

116. Alexander, *Voluntary Simplicity*, 2.

117. Crouch, "Joyful Environmentalists," 30.

Incarnation and the Non-human Creation

The doctrine of the incarnation raises the question whether the whole of the material creation is incorporated into its blessing or only the human beings. The continuity of humanity with the rest of creation is recognized in the biblical sources by virtue of a common creation on the same day as other animals (Gen 1:24–31),[118] or by a shared participation in the divine "breath of life" (Gen 2:7, cf. Gen 6:17, 7:15, 7:22; Ps 104:29–30),[119] or by formation from the same earth (Gen 2:7, 2:19). Mark Brett argues that human continuity with the non-human creation is exemplified by the fact of divine imperatives to the creatures of sea and air, and the Earth itself, as well as to humans, and that in Genesis 9 (also part of the P document), God's first covenant is made with all creatures.[120] He further suggests that the genealogical introduction to the creation story in Genesis 2—"these are the generations of the heavens and the earth," indicates that "the human is equivalent to the animals in that they are all part of a kinship group which descends from the land . . . the land is the parent."[121] Prophetic visions, or psalms of praise for the salvation of God, incorporate the land, the forests and the animals, alongside the people (e.g., Psalms 65, 72, 85, 96, 98, 104, 147; Isaiah 11:1–10; 35, 42:1–10; 65:17–25; Hosea 2:18; Joel 2:18–27; Amos 9:11–15; Micah 4:1–5).

Murray Rae, with his sources already mentioned, argues that the whole structure of John's Gospel—both the linguistic parallels between the prologue and Genesis 1, and especially the chiastic arrangement of the seven signs, is an allusion to the creation story. The intention is to demonstrate not only that Jesus is the incarnation of the Word through whom all things were created, but also that in him the work of creation continues, and the work of the restoration, renewal and fulfillment of creation takes place. "Each of the pairs [of signs]," he suggests, "is concerned unmistakably with the redemptive transformation of the old creation and the ushering in of the new."[122] Thus, the healings by Jesus are not only for individuals, but are actually the first-fruits of a healing for all creation. Paul in Romans 8:18–24 sees the whole groaning creation as the eventual beneficiary of the liberation of the children of God, and his account of

---

118. Westermann, *Genesis*, 25.
119. Anderson, *Creation to New Creation*, 149.
120. Brett, *Genesis*, 27.
121. Brett, *Genesis*, 30–31.
122. Rae, "Testimony of Works," 304. See also Brown, *John*, 23.

resurrection in 1 Corinthians 15 also envisages that in Christ *all things* will be restored to God the Father. A similar hope is articulated in Ephesians 1:10 and Colossians 1:15–20. In all these cases it is the restoration of *all things* that constitutes the completion of the work of Christ, but humanity is especially implicated, as participants by the Holy Spirit, and witnesses to the restoration that is yet to be completed.

Athanasius's whole case for the incarnation depends upon the body being an integral part of the material creation, and not in any way distinct from it (*DI*, 1.16–17). We have previously taken issue with both Gunton and Zizioulas regarding their critical dismissal of Augustine on the matter of salvation including the non-human creation, and have seen that the general position of the patristic theologians is that all that was created will also be recreated; and we have addressed the complaint that the incarnation somehow represents a form of "speciesism." Christ's incarnation/resurrection can also be seen to incorporate the whole creation when understood in the light of both evolutionary theory, and field theory. Graeme Finlay, for example, demonstrates the genetic commonalities that humans share with other primates, by a series of family trees that are uncannily similar to those constructed by biblical textual critics.[123] Other researchers propose that human mitochondria actually incorporate our earliest bacterial ancestors;[124] and the human body itself is a symbiotic community, unable to survive apart from the presence within it of other living creatures—for example, the micro-organisms of the digestive tract. In its physics, chemistry and biology the human body is incorporated in every way into the rest of creation. To deny that the incarnation incorporates the entirety of creation is actually to deny the reality of the incarnation.

The Incarnation, Particularity, and Place

That God could be definitively revealed in a Jewish male, living in a remote corner of the Roman Empire, and who died by crucifixion, has from the beginning been regarded as scandalous nonsense (1 Cor 1:20–25; Acts 17:32). Yet this is the definitive sign of God's commitment to, and engagement with, the material world—something which both Irenaeus's

---

123. Finlay, *God's Books*, 14–28. See also Berry, *God and the Biologist*, 29–31.
124. Ruby et al., "Microbiology."

and Augustine's interlocutors found incomprehensible. Dietrich Bonhoeffer writes,

> there is [only] one place where God and the reality of the world are reconciled with each other . . . at which it is possible to fix one's eyes on God and the world together . . . it does not lie somewhere . . . in the realm of ideas. It lies in the midst of history . . . in Jesus Christ.[125]

But this "place"—Jesus, is also formed and seen in a particular place. "To be human," writes Tim Gorringe, "is to be placed, to exist in relation to physical structures, both to shape them and to be shaped by them . . . enfleshment is incurably particular."[126] Thus there is a developing interest in the significance of particular places in the Gospels, and of Jesus' movements between them—"History demanded geography."[127] So inextricable is this connection with the land that Torrance writes,

> the Word of God . . . physically implicated with Israel in the very stuff of its earthly being and behavior . . . involved itself in the concrete actuality of its existence in time and space . . . we cannot detach the Old Testament Scriptures from the land any more than from the people of Israel. When separated [they] become an abstract ethical religion, largely bereft of the all-important priestly and redemptive tradition and characterized by a serious loss of relevance in space and time.[128]

This contrasts with "dualist frameworks which want to peel away from divine revelation what we tend to regard as its transient physical clothing."[129]

Knight, reflecting on the temple as model of the Earth, suggests that Israel has been located in this particular place to "practice on this model . . . and pick up skills of householding for God and his creation."[130] Given all that we have considered of the incarnation incorporating all creation, this "householding" must be extended beyond human communities, to biological and ecological ones also. Brueggemann argues that land might be, "*the central theme* of biblical faith,"[131] with significance precisely in re-

---

125. Bonhoeffer, *Ethics*, 82.
126. Gorringe, "Preface," 7–8.
127. Davies, *Gospel and the Land*, 366.
128. Torrance, *Mediation*, 25–26.
129. Torrance, *Mediation*, 25.
130. Knight, *Eschatological Economy*, 51.
131. Brueggemann, *Land*, 3.

lation to the rootlessness of the modern world. He contrasts the notion of "space"—as a realm of emptiness and detachment, with that of "place" as, "space that has historical meanings, where some things have happened that are now remembered and that provide continuity and identity across the generations."[132] Cavanaugh demonstrates that one impact of economic globalization is the loss of identification with real people and their lives, and another is the abandonment, the loss, of all sense of place.[133] Vast monocultures, established with little regard for local environmental conditions, and sustained only by massive applications of chemicals (and frequently violence also), contribute to soil depletion, bio-diversity loss, ecological devastation, and the displacement of peoples and loss of their particular cultural contributions to the song of creation's praise. Precisely in the refusal to recognize the unique value of every place, the globalized world has become an inhospitable place for many.

Even before the writing of the Gospels, the church recognized that to become a follower did not entail also becoming a Palestinian Jew. Beginning with John's Gospel and Hebrews, and tracing the theme through art and literature, Davies identifies "a sacramental process, that is, the process of reaching the truth by the frank acceptance of the actual conditions of life and making these a 'gate to heaven' . . . such 'sacramentalism' could find holy space everywhere."[134] Bergmann, similarly, "is not the earthly and historical Christ pictured in the Gospel as a modern nomad, an opponent of the guardians of the sacred sites, a restless walker strolling around trying to set up an alternative sacred geography where all that is created shall be holy?"[135] In these accounts, the incarnation has expanded the holy significance of the land "Israel" to include all land. This is not romanticism, for just as in Israel the incarnate Christ needed to exercise a ministry of healing, and was ultimately rejected by the guardians of the land (and his crucifixion constituted a pollution of the land), so all other land will also be subject to the same struggle for the appearing of the kingdom.[136] Nevertheless, the incarnation has revealed all places, as they are, as places of meeting, and of divine significance. Thus the householding of creation, anticipated by Knight, is opened up as a real possibility. We

132. Brueggemann, *Land*, 4. See also Lilburne, *Sense of Place*, 89–110.
133. Cavanaugh, *Being Consumed*, 39–44. See also Leach, *Country of Exiles*, 3–30, 173–77.
134. Davies, *Gospel and the Land*, 367.
135. Bergmann, "God's Here and Now," 10.
136. Brueggemann, *Land*, 169–72.

have explored a history of such "householding" in monastic understandings of the land and farming, in Anabaptist approaches to Earth-care, and in many contemporary attempts to "listen" for the Word in creation. Particularity of "place" is also a key element in the "Ecosophy" articulated in the Deep Ecology of Arne Naess, for whom, "all ecosophies must be envisioned from a concrete locale . . . familiar to the philosopher and with which she or he has a personal relationship."[137]

CONCLUSIONS

In this chapter we have begun a christological account of human dominion and elucidated the New Testament proclamation of the risen Christ as Servant Lord, image of God, and incarnate Word. We see that God is in no way distanced from the world of creation but intimately involved, constantly sustaining, ordering and promoting the flourishing of life. Equally, we see the nature of true human dominion. It involves us in serving the well-being of all creatures; in relating to them as partners in praise, and as their priestly advocate; and in a life of contemplative listening for the Word in creation, ordering our lives according to this *logikos*, and making prophetic declaration of all that we hear—which is both judgment and Good News. We have noted that resurrection also constituted a divine vindication of Jesus, in the face of his rejection. In the next chapter we shall explore the theme of vindication in relation to key, and controversial, elements in Jesus' ministry—his proclamation of the kingdom of God, and his claims to authority over the Sabbath and the Sanctuary. Grounded as they all are in the particularities of Jesus' life and place, we shall examine their profound implications for living our human dominion.

---

137. Smith, *Environmental Ethics*, 6. See also de Steiguer, *Origins*, 185–201. Deep Ecology demands a more intensive critique than we can offer in this study, but its convictions regarding the meditative life, the importance of place, inter-relationships, and values beyond the merely utilitarian are all congruent with the christological vision we have been developing.

9

With Christ in the Care of Creation—Part Two: Resurrection and the Vindication of Jesus

IN THIS FINAL CHAPTER we change key from the doxological affirmations of Jesus as Lord, image of God, and divine Word, to examine the resurrection as vindication of specific aspects of Jesus' ministry, which also have a bearing on the nature of human dominion. Central to Jesus' mission was his proclamation of the kingdom of God. We address the claim that Jesus' resurrection was God's vindication of this proclamation, and thereby God's future has broken into the present order of things, and the kingdom of God—the healing of creation, has begun. We explore what the kingdom means in terms of hope, and hopeful living, for the earth. Finally, we argue that vindication of Jesus' proclamation of the kingdom involves vindication of his particular accounts of the Sabbath and the Sanctuary. These also provide a basis for a christologically informed environmentalism, and have a formative role in the contemporary practice of discipleship. With these materials we draw our conclusions.

The resurrection is the sign that "God himself has confirmed the pre-Easter activity of Jesus."[1] It is God's vindication of Jesus, and the dynamic of vindication is a recurring feature of the preaching recorded

---

1. Pannenburg, *Jesus: God and Man*, 67–68.

in Acts where we frequently read, "you killed him . . . but God raised him from death." It was the resurrection that clarified the puzzlement, or answered the objections, recorded by the Gospel writers, expressed in such questions as "who is this?" or "where does he get such authority?" or "by what authority?"[2] So too, accounts of Jesus predicting his death also predict resurrection as vindication (Matt 16:21, 28; 20:17–19; Mark 8:31; 9:10; Luke 9:21; 18:31–34). We have seen through John's Gospel the significance of Jesus' acts of power, as signs of the restoration, reconciliation, or fulfillment of creation. In the synoptic traditions also, such acts are seen as signs of the presence of the awaited kingdom of God.

RESURRECTION AS VINDICATION FOR JESUS' PROCLAMATION OF THE KINGDOM OF GOD

In the context of Israel's eschatological hopes, the resurrection was the sign that in Jesus the end of this age, and the in-breaking of the life of the age to come, had arrived: "if Jesus has been raised, then the end of the world has begun."[3] Dunn examines three categories by which the earliest community could have spoken of what happened to Jesus,[4] and identifies the particular significance of the category of "resurrection." It involved the body,[5] and it really did indicate the end of this age and the arrival of God's final judgment and kingdom.

> The probability is . . . that any hope of resurrection entertained by Jesus for himself was hope to share in the final resurrection . . . the possibility is quite strong that Jesus saw the climax to his mission as the climax to God's eschatological purpose. Jesus (and his disciples) would suffer the final tribulation through which God's kingly purpose would achieve its goal; the kingdom would come. His death would introduce that final climactic period, to be followed shortly ("after three days"?) by the general resurrection, the implementation of the new covenant, and the coming of the kingdom.[6]

---

2. Gunton, *Triune Creator*, 22. See also Dunn, *Jesus Remembered*, 892.
3. Pannenberg, *Jesus: God and Man*, 67, 226.
4. Dunn, *Jesus Remembered*, 866–70.
5. Dunn, *Jesus Remembered*, 835, 872.
6. Dunn, *Jesus Remembered*, 824. See also Wright, *Victory of God*, 215.

That this general resurrection did not occur in quite this manner does not seem to have been a deep problem for the first Christians. From the beginning this was their proclamation.[7] Tom Wright writes of,

> that tension between present realization and future hope which is so utterly characteristic of early Christianity . . . what we find across the board . . . is a firm belief in the presentness of the kingdom, *alongside* an equally firm belief in its futurity, these two positions being held together within a redefined apocalyptic schema . . . [in which] the crucified and risen Jesus has turned out to be the central character in the apocalyptic drama.[8]

Furthermore, "the point of the present kingdom is that it is the first-fruits of the future kingdom; and the future kingdom involves the abolition, not of space, time, or the cosmos itself, but rather of that which threatens space, time, and creation, namely, sin and death."[9] The theology of the kingdom remains Jewish and monotheistic, but its vision has expanded, "in terms of a redeemed humanity and cosmos, rather than in terms simply of Israel and her national hope."[10] That the resurrection was true of Jesus alone simply strengthened the case that it was in *him* that the kingdom of God had arrived. Nevertheless, hope was not located entirely over the eschatological horizon.

The first believers' experience of Jesus' lordship was in their experience of the Holy Spirit. From the beginning theirs was a mission involving both proclamation—that in Jesus, who is God's Messiah, everything had been transformed—and the establishment of communities whose life-ways were intended to reflect the nature of God's new order. But this presence of the Spirit is not a fully realized eschatology. The Spirit is the "down payment" (Eph 1:14), both in anticipation and also in present participation, closely associated with the idea of Christ as the "first fruits" (1 Cor 15:20), or the "firstborn from the dead" (Col 1:18; Rom 8:29; Rev 1:5). Those who have entered upon this life in the Spirit now live according to the Spirit (Rom 8:1–11), while still sharing in the groaning of creation as they await the final liberation, "the redemption of our bodies" (Rom 8:17–24). Such active waiting is characterized by Torrance as utterly trinitarian,

---

7. Dunn, *Jesus Remembered*, 868, 872, 875.
8. Wright, *Victory of God*, 217–18.
9. Wright, *Victory of God*, 218.
10. Wright, *Victory of God*, 218.

> the church has its existence and mission between the penultimate event and the ultimate event, that is, in "the last times" that are fully inaugurated by the descent of the Spirit (Acts 2:17), for it is through the Creator Spirit that the saving work of Christ is actualized in the Church as redemption (*apolutrosis*, Eph. 1:7, 14; 4:30) reaching out to the *parousia*, demanding and pressing toward the redemption of the body (*soma*, Romans 8:23), and indeed the whole creation . . . remember the inseparable relation in the Bible between *RUACH* and *DABAR*, *pneuma* and *logos*, where the basic conception is of the living Breath of God uttering the Word, so that reception of the Spirit is through the Word.[11]

Hans Küng is reputed to have encapsulated such a vision of redemption in the aphorism, "the Kingdom of God is Creation healed."[12] This element is also recognized by Rae in addressing the Johannine account of the gift of the Holy Spirit (John 20:21–23). Not only does Jesus' breathing of the Spirit re-enact the life-giving act of God in Genesis 2:7 but,

> because of the inspiration of the Spirit, we are told, those who believe will also do the works that Jesus does (14:12). The pattern of new creation is to be continued in the church because the Son has given his Spirit for the continuation of his work. As a further mark of the new creation, the disciples receive from the risen Christ the authority to forgive sins (20:23) in addition to the Spirit. The exercise of that authority, in the name of Christ, is the redemptive extension of God's creative work. It is the overcoming of darkness and release from bondage to the way of sin and death.[13]

Such an integrative vision has immense pastoral implications. No longer do believers need to live with constant, and often manipulative, anxiety about the presence or absence of particular miraculous works, rather, they become partners in a whole movement towards the renewal of creation. Such a participation in the life-giving work of Christ by the Spirit is the fruit of obedient faith. The obedience integral to the first sign, at Cana (John 2:5–8), establishes a pattern to be carried through to the end. So, having shown the disciples his hands and side, Jesus

---

11. Torrance, *Royal Priesthood*, 23.

12. D. C. K. Watson, in a presentation on church life in the charismatic renewal, Knox Church, Dunedin, 1985.

13. Rae, "Testimony of Works," 299.

commissions them—"'As the Father has sent me, so I send you (John 20:21b).' The disciples may have a share in the new creation wrought by Christ. They may have new life. But it is made clear to them at the last that the new creation comes by following the way of Christ."[14] This is the way of costly self-giving, of servanthood, and also of participation in the work of new creation.

To live in resurrection hope in no way means living in indifferent disconnection from the present pain or longing of the world, but to live by a prayerful, patient, active obedience to the future that has been revealed in Jesus' resurrection. Pannenburg's account of the eschatological reality of Jesus' resurrection is applied to the believer in terms of a lived radical openness to God's future, and a radical re-evaluation of priorities.[15] In an observation particularly germane to issues explored in this study, he writes,

> even though openness for always new possibilities belongs constitutively to the anthropological structure of the human being, it can be shaken: as it was once hidden in *the bondage of ancient man to a sacral order of the world*, so it can once more atrophy, for example, in *the conformity of a technically perfectly organized consumer society* if it loses its creative power. (my italics)[16]

Gregorios also imagines an alternative future to the one posited by narrowly conceived scientific/technological/commercial interests.

> Our whole culture . . . [is] training us to be transcendent-vision-blind. Science is not as objective a system of knowledge as we once thought it was. It is an option we have chosen . . . Are we going to project the future entirely and exclusively in terms of the limited possibilities of our science and technology, or are we prepared to conceive a future in which the full potential of human existence is taken into account? Are Christians not to have an understanding of the meaning of existence that shatters the fetters of time and death, and liberates us to envision and to create a future that is more than the product of scientific-technological creativity?[17]

---

14. Rae, "Testimony of Works," 309–10.
15. Pannenburg, *Jesus: God and Man*, 225–27.
16. Pannenburg, *Jesus: God and Man*, 227.
17. Gregorios, *Human Presence*, 95.

Such an eschatological orientation places us in a position of uncertainty as well as hope. We can never be utterly sure that the vision we have is in complete alignment with the ultimate purpose of God. We can be relatively certain that the knowledge we have is seen in a glass darkly, and only a little of all there is to be known. In this respect science, when itself humbled, and with its constant questing, ought to help maintain an attitude of both humility and openness—as much in biblical interpretation as in environmental activism. Such humility invites us to prudent and precautionary positions, rather than dismissive ebullience, especially in relation to the unknowns associated with global environmental changes. But the eschatological orientation of the uncertainty of our knowledge also requires that we never settle for either the fears or the complacency of the present order of things.

The kingdom may appear as a muted theme in the New Testament outside the Gospels. But this view fails to recognize the eschatological kingdom significance of the resurrection glory of Christ and the activity of the Holy Spirit, nor that the kingdom remains the context in which New Testament writers address particular concerns about the gospel, the church or Christian lifestyle (e.g., Acts 1:3, 6–8; 14:22; 20:25; 28:23, 31; Rom 14:17; 1 Cor 6:9; 15:24–25; Eph 5:5; Col 1:13; 1 Thess 2:12; Rev 1:5–9).[18] Seen in this light, the community of the Spirit is a living sign of the new creation, and the restoration of all things in Jesus Christ is the integrating heart of its witness to the gospel. Thus, both a hopeful future for material creation, and the proper nature of human belonging within that creation are to be discerned in the resurrection, when seen as the in-breaking of God's eschatological future.

Of course, not all have always seen it so, as witnessed in the patristic, especially Irenaean, conflict with Gnosticism, or Augustine's with Manichaeism. In the modern era, forms of piety influenced by the Dispensationalism articulated by J. N. Darby have been notoriously influential in providing a justification for otherworldliness in personal discipleship, and neglect of creation in proclamation and common life.[19] Steven Bouma-Prediger recounts the case of James Watt, President Ronald Reagan's Secretary of the Interior:

---

18. Wright, *Victory of God*, 663–70, includes an appendix, "Kingdom of God in Early Christian Literature," which covers five small font pages for the Gospels and Acts, and a further twenty references from the Pauline corpus, nineteen from the rest of the New Testament, and twenty-five from other early Christian and related literature.

19. Murray, *Puritan Hope*, 187–206, esp. 197–206.

> In response to a question during a discussion (on February 5th, 1981) with a committee of the House of Representatives as to why his agency was acting contrary to its expressed mandate, Watt, a devout Christian, said, "I do not know how many future generations we can count on before the Lord returns." In other words, since Jesus is coming back soon, and since when Jesus returns everything will be destroyed, why care about the earth?[20]

Berry quotes M. Northcott, addressing the same issue, "The premillennialist scorns all efforts to correct the ills of society for to inaugurate any programme of social betterment or to set the church as a whole upon an upward course would be to thwart the divine purpose and to delay the advent of Christ."[21]

Perhaps Watt, and to a lesser degree Darby (who was a scholar and linguist), can be understood—even if not forgiven, on account of the translation they had received of 2 Peter 3:10. The last clause of the verse reads, in the Authorized Version (KJV), "the earth also and the works that are therein shall be burned up." Such a fate for the Earth is widely promoted in certain genre of recent Christian literature.[22] After referencing numerous translations, generally in a similar vein, Bouma-Prediger retorts,

> this verse represents perhaps the most egregious mistranslation in the entire New Testament. The Greek verb in question here is *heurethesetai,* from *heureskein,* "to find," and from which we get the English expression "eureka." In other words, the text states that after a refiner's fire of purification (v.7), the new earth will be *found,* not burned up. The earth will be discovered, not destroyed . . . the text rightly rendered speaks of a basic continuity rather than discontinuity of this world with the next.[23]

Stephen Pattemore also exposes this mistranslation with the even more radical observation that the verse speaks of the heavens being destroyed, while the Earth is disclosed for what God has always intended it to be.[24] But, as Bouma-Prediger further argues, even if the Earth is ultimately to

---

20. Bouma-Prediger, *Beauty of the Earth,* 71–72. Numerous others have also referenced this encounter.

21. Berry, "Stewardship: A Default Position?" 2.

22. See Lindsey and Carlson, *Late Great Planet Earth*; see also Tim LaHaye's Left Behind series.

23. Bouma-Prediger, *Beauty of the Earth,* 77.

24. Pattemore, "Apocalypse: An Environmental Impact Report."

be destroyed, it absolutely does not follow that we should destructively exploit it now. Peter Harris argues similarly,

> you do what you do because you believe it pleases the living God, who is the Creator and whose handiwork this is . . . I don't think there is any guarantee we will save the planet. I don't think the Bible gives us much reassurance about that. But I do believe it gives God tremendous pleasure when his people do what they were created to do, which is care for what he made.[25]

To articulate hope, not primarily as a desire located entirely in an unseen, uncertain future, but as an orientation to present living, occasioned by the Earth's experience of resurrection, is a strange but significant contribution to current environmental discussions. James Lovelock appears to offer only counsels of despair in his assessments that we are long past the time when anything can be done to prevent runaway global warming.[26] Others have suggested that the only future for the human race lies in migration to a suitably hospitable planet in another galaxy! (The resource consumption, global conflicts, and accumulation of privilege, wealth and power by a few, to enable such a project positively beggars belief!) Of course, neither of these possibilities involves the dissolution of creation, and both could conceivably be way-stations in God's painful struggle with the human race. But neither can they be claimed by the Dispensationalist as signs that the end is near. Most significantly, they eviscerate hopeful living *on and for the Earth*, and in that respect do not represent an option for Christians.

That the resurrection constitutes the in-breaking of God's future is also a reminder that in creation God is involved in time, and creation is in fact a "project" being drawn towards a consummation. Thus Paul in 1 Cor 15 describes a process moving from the resurrection of Jesus, as the "first-fruits," to the final consummation of all things. Similarly, our transformation into the image of Christ by the Lord who is the Spirit, is also presented by Paul as an ongoing project (2 Cor 3:17–18). Irenaeus and Augustine (with a little less comfort about God's engagement with time), also see creation as a project being brought to its fulfillment.[27]

---

25. Crouch, "Joyful Environmentalists," 30.
26. Lovelock, "Fallible Stewardship," 108–9.
27. Gunton, *Triune Creator*, 187–190. See also Ward, "Cosmos and Kenosis," 152–66.

The passage of time raises some particular questions, for it is abundantly clear in the geological record that much of what God has brought to being no longer exists, and if God is the author of so many extinctions why should a few more bother us?[28] The whole range of theological traditions we have examined has seen the unfolding of creation as a preparation for the coming of humankind. God has brought about a world fit for humanity, and as the dramatic Stephen Spielberg movie portrayed it, the Jurassic certainly was not! The dynamic nature of creation is such that constant change is in the nature of things—as we have already seen recognized by Augustine in his reflections upon measure, number, and weight. But it is *this* world in which we have been appointed to exercise dominion, this particular complex of life and planetary conditions in which human beings have appeared, and in which we are called to *image* God, exercise care and grow up into human fullness, and this world that inspires the praise and love of God. What is disturbingly new in the era of the Anthropocene,[29] and especially since the mid-eighteenth century, is that these rates of change, and the more serious associated loss of biodiversity, far exceed the rates of change and loss that may be observed in previous eras. The human does represent something new in the history of the Earth. The time of humanity requires of us responsibilities of care and a consciousness of other creatures that none of our forerunners appears to have had, and, most importantly of all, the conscious orientation of all of life towards the glory of God. This is the nature of *logikos*. To (re)discover the humanity necessary for this calling requires that we die with Christ and be raised to participate in a servant lordship in the power of the Holy Spirit of life.

Christ's resurrection is, most crucially, the ultimate sign of victory over death, "the last enemy." It was in these terms that it was proclaimed by the early church (Acts 2:24–36; 3:13–16; 4:8–12; 10:36–43; 17:30–32; 1 Cor 15:12–58; Eph 1:20–23; Col 1:18; 1 Thess 4:14–18; Heb 2:14–15; 1 Peter 1:3–5; Rev 1:5, 17–18; 21:4). Such a victory represents a total reconfiguration of the processes of life as we know it. But despite the victory of Christ over death, we still live in the presence of death. Predation is still necessary and life is still enabled by death. These are the only ecologies we know. We groan, along with the rest of creation (Rom 8:22–24),

---

28. While advocating conservation initiatives over the years I have regularly had this put to me as a reason for indifference to the conservation of threatened species.

29. Flannery, *Weather Makers*, 64–68.

and we grieve, though "not as those who have no hope" (1 Thess 4:13).[30] But as Moule reminded us, it is possible to live obediently in resurrection hope, while still living within the ecological processes of decay. Here most painfully we encounter the tension between the already and the not yet of the kingdom of God. This situation introduces all manner of conundrums and ambiguities into the actuality of living in the light of God's future. To protect many vulnerable indigenous New Zealand species from the threat of extinction by introduced predators, it still appears necessary to use the agents of death—traps and poisons. Or, to maintain reasonable integrity in the whole New Zealand environment—its biodiversity, forests, soil and water conservation, and erosion control—it is necessary to hunt and kill introduced browsing animals. Such hunting can require a deep attentiveness to the processes of the Earth. It is the antithesis of the kind of "hunting" described by Scully that requires little skill but large amounts of money, and is most often focused on killing animals that pose no threat to environmental well-being, and are already endangered species.[31] A similar ambiguity attends the malaria-carrying mosquito, or the Guinea Worm, for example, whose hideously painful, parasitic presence requires a human host. Not even the deepest green advocates of animal rights are found offering themselves for this task, and agencies that have come to regard environmental care and conservation as part of their development brief, nevertheless work diligently for the eradication of these particular species![32]

Such eco-ethical challenges are common to all, not only the christian theologian. But christian theology will seek its answer by engaging the question, "what actions best serve the flourishing of life as it is offered to us in Jesus Christ?" As we have already argued, fullness of life does not consist in the exercise of individualized power, but in participation in the trinitarian ecology revealed in Jesus. A world that is ecologically rich is a world in keeping with the profligacy of God, that promotes possibilities for life, and that urges us to join in praise as we are uniquely able. Whether it be birds singing to claim territory or animals fighting to gather mates, even the most basic biological processes are fulfilling the divine command to "be fruitful and multiply" (Gen 1:22). Like Basil's predatory fish, these creatures are saying "yes" to the divine command

---

30. See Moule, *Man and Nature*, 9–20.
31. Scully, *Dominion*, 47–87.
32. Tearfund, "Help Eradicate a Nasty Parasite."

in their aggressive claim to life. But a world that has become ecologically impoverished is not one that inspires or enables these things. Those forms of life that elicit no inspiration, and deal only sickness, impoverishment and death, are not forms that engender hope for the coming of the reign of life in all its fullness. Despite all that we need to affirm of ecological/relational existence as revealed in Jesus, some of the clearest signs in his ministry of the presence of the kingdom were his works of healing to overcome disease and exclusion from the human community. Yet, as we have also seen, these were signs of restoration and healing for the whole Earth.

RESURRECTION AS VINDICATION OF JESUS' CLAIMS OVER SANCTUARY AND SABBATH

In addressing what features as a central controversy in the Gospels, we note some elements of Jesus' context. Heather Mckay has surveyed the intertestamental literature,[33] and observes that although there is a wide range of attitudes developing towards the Sabbath it is generally held in increasingly high regard as a holy day. So, for example, Judith's Sabbath is not a fast but a blessing and its joys are not confined to that one day, but are anticipated in the preceding days (Judith 8:6). The special qualities of Sabbath impact on normal time and there is the sense of the future breaking into the present. In 1 Maccabees 2, unhappy experience and subsequent communal discussion, lead to a decision that profaning the Sabbath by fighting is appropriate in order to secure a better future for the Sabbath. Apart from such an exception however, Sabbath observance becomes the subject of increasingly detailed prescription. Ritual washings are introduced. The Dead Sea Scrolls indicate a community highly conscious of the need to keep a tightly regulated Sabbath, in which restrictions on work are also extended to restrictions upon thought. Here, perhaps for the first time, are clear indications of prayers and songs developed for Sabbath liturgies of common people—if those who lived at Qumran could ever be described as "common people!" The book of Jubilees builds on all this in widening the application of the death penalty for breaches of the Sabbath. Following VanderKam, McKay suggests that in Jubilees keeping proper Sabbath "has the power to influence the cosmic harmony on behalf of Israel, and perhaps . . . has influence over God

---

33. McKay, *Sabbath and Synagogue*, 44–60.

himself."³⁴ Here again, the nature and power of the Sabbath impacts upon the week of ordinary time. Nevertheless, despite the many prohibitions, what they must do on the Sabbath is, "eat, drink, bless the Creator and be satisfied, rest and refrain from all work."³⁵ All these sources increasingly view Sabbath as a sign of Jewish identity, its faithful observance necessary for their national well-being, and for some at least, "a privilege not open to Gentiles."³⁶

We have already noted the significance of the Sabbath in completing the creation story, the tradition that the creation so formed was mirrored in the sanctuary, and that the human beings were placed here to fulfill a priestly role. In the Gospels all these traditions quickly become focused in the person of Jesus. At the Passover festival Jesus takes authority over the temple in John's account of the cleansing (John 2:13–22), and the idea is introduced that the authentic temple is "the temple of his body" (John 2:21). In John 5, the healing of the paralytic at the pool is the occasion for an extensive reflection on Jesus' authority over the Sabbath and his claim that this authority is grounded in his own intimacy with the Father (John 5:17–22).

The synoptic writers also focus Sabbath and Sanctuary significance upon Jesus. Luke's account has Jesus' public ministry begin in the Synagogue at Nazareth, with the claim that Isaiah's messianic proclamation of a Jubilee has finally found its fulfillment in the person of Jesus (Luke 4:16–21). On the Sabbath he announces the Jubilee Sabbath. He expands on the theme with two stories of God's generosity to non-Israelites (Luke 4:25–27; cf. 1 Kings 17:1–16 and 2 Kings 5:1–14), thus giving the first intimation that his vision of the kingdom extends beyond the bounds of racial and political Israel.³⁷ Moltmann recognizes that Protestant theologies and dogmatics have generally read Jesus' Sabbath teaching in terms of opposition to Jewish law, whereas his use of the Sabbath proclamation in Luke 4 "is the proclamation of the imminent kingdom of God, whose unparalleled closeness he authenticates through the signs of the messianic age."³⁸ Neither Mark nor Matthew place this incident in Nazareth at the beginning of the ministry, nor do they make reference to this Isaiah

---

34. McKay, *Sabbath and Synagogue*, 57.
35. McKay, *Sabbath and Synagogue*, 58.
36. McKay, *Sabbath and Synagogue*, 59 and note 48.
37. Lowery, *Sabbath and Jubilee*, 138–39. See also Brueggemann, *Land*, 162.
38. Moltmann, *God in Creation*, 291.

passage. But they both have Jesus coming into Galilee, newly empowered by the Spirit and proclaiming the arrival of the kingdom of God. Matthew prefaces this with another reference from Isaiah, and Mark, in a slightly longer announcement than Matthew's, is pregnant with messianic implications in speaking of "the good news of God," and the time of "fulfillment" (Matt 4:13–17; Mark 1:14–15). Thus they gather to Jesus all the eschatological significance that had become attached to the Sabbath. Similarly, the claim, already announced by John the Baptist, that Jesus is the agent of the Holy Spirit suggests that the encounter previously associated with the Sanctuary may now be mediated by Jesus (Matt 3:11; Mark 1:8; Luke 3:16), and that in him the "new age of the Spirit," anticipated in the Sabbath, has dawned.

Mark 2 and 3 introduce three contentious issues that will focus the question of who Jesus is and what is the nature of his authority. They concern the authority to forgive sins (Mark 2:1–12), to extend the circle of God's welcome to outsiders (13–17), and to reinterpret the laws regarding the Sabbath (2:23—3:6). A fourth contentious issue is implied within this dispute regarding the Sabbath: the particular illustration Jesus uses, of David taking and sharing the sacred bread from the sanctuary (2:25–26), suggests that while staking his claim to authority over the Sabbath he is also making a claim to authority in the Sanctuary. In any event, what Jesus does clearly state is firstly, that "The Sabbath was made for humankind, and not humankind for the Sabbath," and secondly, that "The Son of Man is Lord even of the Sabbath" (Mark 2:27–28). Richard Lowery argues that by running the two observations together as he does, Jesus is actually identifying the lordship of the Son of Man, with the lordship of all humanity.

> The title is grounded in Jesus' role as representative human, a role especially revealed in his rejection, suffering, and death (Mark 8:31; 9:12; 14:21, 41) . . . As "the human being," Jesus participates fully in the humanity of all people. The "authority of the human being" is the authority of Jesus, but it is also the authority of all human beings.[39]

In his much more comprehensive and nuanced account, James Dunn also suggests, "in response to criticism of his disciples, Jesus was remembered as defending their action as appropriate to the lordship which God had

---

39. Lowery, *Sabbath and Jubilee*, 125.

given to humankind (or Israel) over all his creation."[40] Thus while he promotes a generous, life-giving understanding of the Sabbath in contrast to one that he considered to be characterized by "hardness of heart" (Mark 3:5), it is nonetheless a Sabbath under his lordship and one which will enable human beings to properly exercise their lordship.

Matthew 12 repeats the same two stories with the addition of the reminders that "priests in the temple break the Sabbath" (12:5), and that God "desires mercy rather than sacrifice" (12:7), the example of rescuing a sheep in trouble (12:11-12), and—again indicating a parallel claim to authority in the sanctuary, the observation that "something greater than the temple is here" (12:6). Also repeated is the claim that "The Son of Man is Lord of the Sabbath" (12:8). Hays thus argues,

> the Christological claim that Jesus is greater than the Temple and that therefore those who serve him are, like priests in the Temple, not subject to the ordinary restrictions on Sabbath activity is an extraordinarily bold—and some would say nearly blasphemous—assertion; in the aftermath of the Temple's destruction it takes on a specially freighted import. To this Christological argument is coupled once again an appeal to the Hosea text: the "hermeneutic of mercy" supplants or relativizes the Law's specific commandments (cf. Exod. 34:21).[41]

Luke also recounts these two stories, with their special claims to authority, at chapter 6:1-11. At chapter 13:10-17 he tells of the healing of the crippled woman and has Jesus declaring that such works of liberation are not simply allowed, but are especially appropriate on the Sabbath. The reference to Abraham (13:16), suggests that he sees such works of healing liberation as a fulfillment of the covenantal promises right back to the beginning. Luke 14:1-6 recounts another Sabbath healing, similar in some respects to that in Matthew 12, but with the examples of need used by Jesus being this time, that of a child or an ox fallen into a well. The claim to authority common to all the other accounts is not repeated in words, but in action, and his critics are silent.

In all three synoptic Gospels Jesus makes an explicit claim to be "Lord of the Sabbath," and in each case with it there is a very strong hint of a claim to a similar authority in the Sanctuary. Any doubt is banished toward the end when all three have him entering the temple and clearing

---

40. Dunn, *Jesus Remembered*, 741.
41. Hays, *Moral Vision*, 100.

it of the traders and money exchangers (Matt 21:12; Mark 11:15; Luke 19:45). In all three, Jesus justifies his action by a conflated quotation of Isaiah 56:7 and Jeremiah 7:11, claiming that the commercial activities have overwhelmed the temple's function as a house of prayer. Mark's quote includes additional words from Isaiah that the house of prayer should be, "for all nations" (11:17). Matthew seamlessly adds a note about the blind and lame coming to Jesus to be cured (21:14). This is quickly followed by the question about his authority to do such things (Matt 21:23-27; Mark 11:27-33; Luke 20:1-8). Subsequently in all three Synoptics, the charges against Jesus and the subsequent taunting make no reference to Sabbath breaking but do confront his perceived attitude to the temple and his alleged messianic claims (Matt 26:61-65; 27:39-44; Mark 14:58-64; 15:29-32; Luke 22:66-71; 23:35-39). The inseparable relation between temple and Sabbath is explored in Knight's extensive account of the ways in which the temple is understood to represent the whole creation under the rule of God, and the role of humanity within it. The temple is "the throne where God invites the Son to sit with him, to declare that the labour of creation is done, and that people may no longer force one another to work. The Sabbath is here, and all things in the completed creation are very good."[42]

Dunn, exploring Sabbath issues as expressing an intra-Jewish debate about the relationship between law-keeping and covenant identity, argues that,

> Jesus had a high regard for the Sabbath as a gift from God. To be noted is that neither episode [Mark 2:23-28; 3:1-5] even suggests the abolition or abandonment of the Sabbath. The question under debate is not *whether* the Sabbath should be observed, but *how* it should be observed . . . Jesus refuses to make the Sabbath a test case of obedience to God, a distinctive mark of God's people . . . rather he presses . . . to fundamental issues: that the Sabbath was made for human beings, not human beings for the Sabbath, and that at no time, however sacred, can it be wrong to do good or save life.[43]

He also wonders whether there might be "an eschatological note and/or echo of the Genesis provision of the Sabbath for creation (as well as for God), for humankind at the end of the age as for Adam at the beginning?"

---

42. Knight, *Eschatological Economy*, 150.
43. Dunn, *Jesus Remembered*, 568-69.

But, "if so, it is not obvious."⁴⁴ In his account of Jesus' relationship with the Sabbath, Ben Witherington is willing to chance more;

> Jesus' point of view seems to be that human beings do not exist for the sake of the law, but rather the converse. The function of the Sabbath is to restore and renew creation to its full capacity, just as leaving the land fallow for a sabbatical year might do . . . this meant that at least some of the old rules no longer applied, for a new situation was dawning, a divine dominion was breaking in through the ministry of Jesus.⁴⁵

He quotes Robert Banks, "Sabbath is not only a day upon which it is appropriate to heal, it is the day on which one must do so . . . [Jesus'] practice is a direct consequence of his understanding of his mission."⁴⁶

Tom Wright suggests that Jesus' proclamation did not involve rejection of Jewish hopes, but a radical reinterpretation of them, declaring an alternative to the national zeal for distinctiveness that was leading the nation to ruin, was increasingly violent, and had lost sight of the call to be light for the world.⁴⁷ All the controversial Sabbath activities of Jesus are intimations of the coming kingdom of God, but we quote at length Wright's account of two Lukan Sabbath stories,

> The emphasis falls . . . on Jesus' mission to restore Israel: this daughter of Abraham, whom the satan bound for eighteen years, is to be loosed from her bond on the Sabbath. Here Jesus is portrayed as taking up and transforming the great theme of Sabbath as release from work, bringing into immediate presence and sharp focus the theme of Sabbath as rest after trouble, as redemption after slavery. Jesus was claiming that Israel's longing—for a great Sabbath day when all her enemies would be put to shame, and she herself would rejoice at God's release—was being fulfilled in him . . . the Sabbath day was the most appropriate day [for her healing], because that day celebrated release from captivity, from bondage, as well as from work.⁴⁸

He continues, noting the connections Jesus drew between the woman's bondage and that of all Israel, and the great Sabbath which he himself

---

44. Dunn, *Jesus Remembered*, 569, note 116.
45. Witherington, *Christology of Jesus*, 68-69.
46. Banks, in Witherington, *Christology of Jesus*, 69.
47. Wright, *Victory of God*, 389. See also Davies, *Gospel and the Land*, 352-53.
48. Wright, *Victory of God*, 394. See also Lowery, *Sabbath and Jubilee*, 134-35.

was inaugurating, and concludes, "such a claim was felt as a threat, not to petty legalism, but to the whole normal perception of the coming kingdom of god."[49] Indeed, Jesus "had not come to rehabilitate the symbol of the holy land, but to subsume it within a different fulfillment of the kingdom, which would embrace the whole creation."[50]

Lowery also recognizes that the disputes are not about whether, but how, the Sabbath should be kept. He suggests the Pharisees interpret the grain-plucking incident through the lens of the Exodus 34 prohibition on work. But for Jesus,

> the more fitting association, is the gleaning tradition (Lev. 19:9–10; 23:22; Deut. 24:19–21; Ruth 2), and the Sabbath and Sabbath-year laws in Exodus 23:9–12, which ground seventh day and seventh year in economic support for the resident alien . . . Jesus' disciples pluck grain, not as householders who own the crop and have the right to sell it, but as the economically vulnerable who have a God-given right to take what they need to survive.[51]

In this light, the example of David in the sanctuary is to be read within the gleaning and Sabbath-year traditions.[52] The Lord's Prayer (Matt 6:9–15; Luke 11:2–4) also is structured around Sabbath-manna and Sabbath-release themes,[53] and so too the parable of the rich fool (Luke 12:16–21).[54] "Fundamentally misunderstanding the nature of his miraculous bounty, the rich fool fails to trust that God will continue to provide necessary sustenance. His fear breeds greed, which causes him to hoard what is graciously given for the common good."[55] Jonathan Sacks, describing a Jewish ethical tradition concerning the responsibilities attaching to wealth—especially job creation, writes, "conspicuous consumption was frowned upon, and periodically banned through local 'sumptuary laws.' Wealth was a divine blessing, and therefore it carried with it an obligation to use it for the benefit of the whole community."[56]

49. Wright, *Victory of God*, 395.
50. Wright, *Victory of God*, 446.
51. Lowery, *Sabbath and Jubilee*, 128.
52. Lowery, *Sabbath and Jubilee*, 128–30.
53. Lowery, *Sabbath and Jubilee*, 139–40.
54. Lowery, *Sabbath and Jubilee*, 140–42.
55. Lowery, *Sabbath and Jubilee*, 143.
56. Sacks, "Morals and Markets," 44.

Thus we see, Jesus does not abandon but rather appropriates a comprehensive vision of the Sabbath as the definitive sign of the kingdom. It is a Sabbath that exemplifies the generosity of God, is directed towards the proper flourishing of all, and which embraces the needy of the world, the land, and indeed the whole creation. Hays and Lowery each see Jesus' Sabbath vision as both expressing and transforming some already existing traditions of Jewish orthodoxy.[57] Therefore we are reminded that even the Sabbath of the kingdom is grounded in and draws upon the concrete realities of daily life in the world. In this Sabbath Jesus provides the model for kingdom living between the already and the not yet, and the means in which (but only within which) humanity may exercise its proper lordship in creation. In the provisionality of this eschatological orientation towards God's future, this christological Sabbath has a dynamic character about it which will enable different expressions in different times and places. How we are to live our dominion must be construed within this Sabbath framework. This vision of Sabbath, which is inseparable from elements of Jesus' own self-understanding, is vindicated in the resurrection of Jesus. So Wright concludes,

> if he [Jesus] was an eschatological prophet/Messiah, announcing the kingdom and dying to bring it about, the resurrection would declare that he had in principle succeeded in his task, and that his earlier redefinitions of the coming kingdom had pointed to a further task awaiting his followers, that of implementing what he had achieved . . . they would be people with a task, not just an idea.[58]

LIVING THE SABBATH OF THE KINGDOM

The Sabbath as "Rest"

For Jesus, Sabbath is still about rest that enables the contemplation of God and the restoration of life in fellowship with God. Simply to stop, for the duration of a day, is a radical relativization of the culture of work that has become despotic in contemporary society. It is perhaps the most radical, yet accessible, counter-cultural act of witness in which members of the christian community could engage. Sacks notes that the Sabbath

---

57. Hays, *Moral Vision*, 99–100; Lowery, *Sabbath and Jubilee*, 131–32.
58. Wright, *Victory of God*, 662.

was largely unintelligible, even suspect, to non-Jews in the ancient world, but at its heart, then and now, was

> the idea that there are important truths about the human condition that cannot be accounted for in terms of work or economics. The Sabbath is the day on which we neither work nor employ others to do our work, on which we neither buy nor sell, in which all manipulation of nature for creative ends is forbidden, in which all hierarchies of power or wealth are suspended . . . in which we stop making a living and learn instead simply how to live.[59]

Such a Sabbath is much more than merely "taking a break," for, unlike taking a break, it structures a rhythm to life, is received rather than taken, and it is inspired by the inseparable theological affirmations that this God is both bountiful creator and self-giving Redeemer. "Taking a break" can in fact be regarded as yet another extension of the consumerist mentality, in which something more is *taken*, at one's own whim, for one's own personal satisfaction. Nor is such a break from work to be regarded as a Sabbath if its goal is primarily to reflect upon how work may be made more profitable or efficient.

Our ancient sources,[60] and Jesus himself, would appear to agree that one element of this resting involved the enjoyment of the creator's good gifts. Those with whom Jesus came into conflict, and more recent forms of Sabbattarianism, are better known for the avoidance of such enjoyment, and it may well be that the value of the Sabbath as a source of life has been eviscerated by such austerity. That God was "pleased" with the work suggests that God also takes pleasure in the creation. Others note that in Genesis 2:9 "the trees are for enjoyment . . . and Genesis places the aesthetic before the utilitarian."[61] However, enjoyment of the creator's good gifts can so easily become a religiously legitimized form of consumerism, even idolatry—"serving the creature, rather than the creator" (Rom 1:25), that the resting and enjoyment of Sabbath cannot be pursued apart from their being located within the spiritual disciplines of the contemplative life, foremost among them being thankfulness. The Desert Fathers' communal gatherings, Augustine's gardening, Calvin's Sabbath for meditation upon creation, or Matthew Henry's Adam "with his hands

---

59. Sacks, "Markets and Morals," 45–46.
60. McKay, *Sabbath and Synagogue*, 56–58.
61. Prance, "Thoughts on Sustainability," 72.

about his trees, while his heart was with his God,"⁶² all open up possibilities for such an engagement. But inadequate attention to the disciplines of the contemplative life lead Richard Foster to observe that, in contrast to times past, "today there is an abysmal ignorance of the most simple and practical aspects of nearly all the classic Spiritual Disciplines."⁶³ These too must be renewed if the enjoyment of Sabbath is not to become mere indulgence, and the resting of Sabbath not crushing boredom.

The writer of Hebrews 4 appropriated the image of Sabbath rest to describe the salvation achieved by Christ, and we have seen that patristic theologians enthusiastically adopted the same metaphor. This may appear to have nothing to do with Sabbath practice, Christian environmentalism, or a christological reading of human dominion. It is in fact a vital antidote to the message of secular salvation through the endless pursuit of things, from which there is never any rest. "Many of society's richest people now think it's cool to be overstretched . . . 'Busyness, and not leisure, is now the badge of honour.'"⁶⁴ New Zealanders who have employment are now working twenty percent more hours than they did in the 1960s, despite the remarkable increase in labor-saving devices. Naish quotes similar figures for the United Kingdom.⁶⁵ Yet, in both cases, other research suggests that such increases in hours of work are not matched by similar increases in personal well-being—indeed the opposite is often the case.

> Not only have measures of wellbeing and happiness ceased to rise with economic growth but, as affluent societies have grown richer, there have been long-term rises in rates of anxiety, depression and numerous other social problems. The populations of rich countries have got to the end of a long historical journey.⁶⁶

But there may be deep fearful resistance to acknowledging that. Cavanaugh, noting Augustine's reflections on the need of an appropriate goal for desire, writes that,

> to desire with no good other than the desire itself is to desire arbitrarily. To desire with no *telos*, no connection to the objective

---

62. Henry, *Commentary*, 17.
63. Foster, *Celebration of Discipline*, 3.
64. Naish, *Enough*, 114.
65. Naish, *Enough*, 113.
66. Wilkinson and Pickett, *Spirit Level*, 6; and see (Fig.1.2), 9.

> end of desire, is to desire nothing and to become nothing . . .
> A person buys something—anything—trying to fill the empty
> shrine . . . with no objective ends to guide the search, her search
> is literally endless.[67]

But to "rest" in Christ is to enter into the end, the goal, of our existence. It is to enter into all those things of Christ which we have outlined in this and the preceding chapter. It is to receive back our true identity, and at least to begin the journey into liberation from the burden of finding our identity in our works and our status in the appearances we present to others,[68] and from the destructive dynamics of an economics that has no sense of Christ's Sabbath vision in its treatment of the world. Hauerwas captures the connections between Christology, the kingdom and the Sabbath,

> Jesus is nothing less than the embodiment of God's Sabbath as a
> reality for all people. Jesus proclaims peace as a real alternative,
> because he has made it possible to rest—to have confidence that
> our lives are in God's hands. No longer is the Sabbath one day,
> but the form of life of a people on the move. God's kingdom,
> God's peace, is a movement of those who have found the con-
> fidence through the life of Jesus to make their lives a constant
> worship of God.[69]

This is serenity, "the Augustinian heart finally resting—at home—in God."[70]

Sabbath as Recognition of the Abundant Provision of God

Rest is called for because God has established all that is needed. So certain is this, that even God can rest! The salvation in Christ is the fullness of such provision, for in Christ by the Holy Spirit we are reconciled and given God's own self. This provision is to be lived in the world in recognition of all the other provisions that are made for us. Indeed, in light of all we have already affirmed of the presence of Christ in creation, it is not really appropriate to draw a distinction between two kinds of provision. Thus, Richard Foster references Col 1:17—Christ as the integrator

---

67. Cavanaugh, *Being Consumed*, 14–15.
68. Naish, *Enough*, 106–8.
69. Hauerwas, *Peaceable Kingdom*, 87.
70. Bouma-Prediger, *Beauty of the Earth*, 153.

of creation, in demonstrating the paradoxical abundance of provision encountered in fasting.[71]

We have previously explored the suggestion that Jesus' feeding of the crowd in John 6 represented the hospitality of God and the fulfillment of creation. In the Synoptics, although the eucharistic words are not recorded, Jesus' actions are described in a detail that is always the same and anticipates those at the last supper—taking, blessing with thanksgiving, breaking, and distributing (Matt 14:19, 15:35; Mark 6:41, 8:6; Luke 9:16, cf. Matt 26:26–27; Mark 14:22–23; Luke 22:19–20; 1 Cor 11:23–25; and also Luke 24:30). In two other accounts of meals—with Levi (Mark 2 and Luke 5), and Zacchaeus (Luke 19), although eucharistic words or actions are unmentioned, Jesus explicitly presents the events as experiences of the hospitality and salvation of God. In the temptation regarding bread (Matt 4:4, cf. Luke 5:4), Jesus' response assumes the trustworthiness of the provision of God. The urging that his hearers consider the birds of the air and lilies of the field (Matt 6:26–28) is likewise an invitation to believe that the basic disposition of the world is one of provision.

This fullness of provision is also exemplified in the Lord's Prayer. Jeremias argues that the prayer for daily bread is properly understood as, "our bread for tomorrow, give us today,"[72] and that this is not simply a request for each day's provision, but for the bread of "the great Tomorrow, the final consummation . . . the bread of life."[73] This is not, however, to draw any distinction between "earthly" and "heavenly" bread, for in the new eschatological community of the kingdom, which is the Sabbath and within which context this prayer is being prayed, all earthly things are hallowed. "Every meal his disciples had with him was a usual eating and drinking, and yet it was more: a meal of salvation, a messianic meal, image and anticipation of the meal at the consummation, because he was master of the house."[74] Thus, in summarizing the Sabbath Bouma-Prediger writes, "God is a gracious homemaker and the earth is our home . . . God is a homemaker, showing hospitality to an increasingly diverse range of creaturely inhabitants."[75]

---

71. Foster, *Celebration of Discipline*, 56.
72. Jeremias, *Prayers*, 100.
73. Jeremias, *Prayers*, 100–101.
74. Jeremias, *Prayers*, 102.
75. Bouma-Prediger, *Beauty of the Earth*, 96.

Zizioulas stresses that "all ancient Eucharistic liturgies began … with thanksgiving for *creation* in the first place, and only afterwards for redemption through Christ."[76] It is this configuration that in fact gives rise to the very name of the celebration—*eucharist*. Here we recognize the fullness of provision that is embodied in such a sacramental understanding. Within such abundance of provision, rather than in fear, and restless, unending, dis-satisfaction, we are free to truly enjoy the world in trust, thankfulness and simplicity.

As the sign of abundant provision, Sabbath is the reminder that God has established an Earth set up to provide for all creatures. Part of the fullness of provision is, for human beings, the provision of work. Whether it be the work of representation—as in Genesis 1, or of husbandry—as in Genesis 2, in both cases it involves a sharing in the work of Christ the Word. And in both cases it is this christological reference that determines what is appropriate work and what is not. Work is the means by which humanity is able to transform the provision of the Earth into food, clothing, shelter, and objects of beauty and exchange—all those things that support life, and are gathered up and offered in thanksgiving. But equally, and this is a tragically neglected theme, it is also the means by which human beings may participate in ensuring that fullness of provision functions for the flourishing of all other creatures also. They too live under the same blessing of fruitfulness, but are—or may be, in some sense subject to human power in their freedom to fulfill it. Thus Mark Brett suggests that Genesis 2:4–5 places the needs of the land before those of the human, observing that "the word for 'work' is otherwise most commonly translated as 'serve,' in the sense of 'work for,'" and that 2:15 is best translated "to serve it and take care of it."[77]

Nevertheless, as already noted, central to the meaning of Sabbath is that there are limits to work. It must not be endless or rapacious, for such work is a denial of the abundance of God. Rather, it must produce enough to enable thanksgiving and common life. This is the lesson for Israel in the desert. Even in the place of perceived threat, to take more than enough is to distrust and then to experience waste and decay. The only manna that did not decay was that which was set aside in the sanctuary as a permanent, communal reminder of the trustworthy provision of God (Exod 16:32–35). We have previously noted the unrealistic and

---

76. Zizioulas, "Preserving God's Creation" (12:1, 1989), 4.
77. Brett, *Genesis*, 30.

unsustainable nature of the contemporary economics of endless growth. John's account of the feeding in the wilderness concludes with a simple instruction, "gather up the fragments left over, so that nothing may be lost" (John 6:12), a reminder if we need one, that even in the presence of the creative Lord of life, the overwhelming abundance of God is never to be squandered. Then follows an extended reflection connecting Jesus with the manna in the wilderness. Thus, we can recognize with Lowery that Sabbath provides us with "an ethic of social solidarity, abundance and self-restraint."[78]

Sabbath as the Economics of Ecological Sustainability

Despite our living in a world of abundant provision, that provision does not always fall equally nor adequately to all. Hence the need for deliberate provision for the poor, for work, and, as Sacks has reminded us—noting its high value in Jewish spirituality, for job creation. We have seen Jesus' adoption of the gleaning tradition in relation to the Sabbath. The Sabbath year of debt release was yet another means of controlling excessive wealth and alleviating undue poverty. Lowery explores issues of international indebtedness, and the negative impact of excessive interest repayments upon every measure of well-being in the countries concerned.[79] Sabbath is the biblical reminder that debts can be unjustly imposed, and debt burdens must have limits. Indeed, most debt would not be burdensome were it not for the application of compounding interest—a device which the Bible frequently constrains (Exod 22; Lev 25; Deut 23—24; Matt 5:42), and sometimes curses (Ezek 18:13, 22:12), and the church prohibited until at least the twelfth century. Sabbath provision for the release of slaves also required the provision of resources by which a person could re-establish their own economic viability (Deut 15:12-15). In all these cases Sabbath release was to enable constructive participation in the community life, by the enabling of free work. Thus, Sacks argues, "the ideal society envisaged by the prophets is one in which each person is able to sit 'underneath his own vine and fig tree'"[80] (see e.g., Joel 2:22; Micah 4:4; Zech 3:10), enjoying and disposing of the fruits of their own labor. Such personal economic viability, he argues, was a

---

78. Lowery, *Sabbath and Jubilee*, 1–5.
79. Lowery, *Sabbath and Jubilee*, 149–51.
80. Sacks, "Markets and Morals," 42.

revolutionary development in the ancient world, against the tendency of rulers to regard property and people as their own possession.[81] It also relates seamlessly to the democratization/generalization of human dominion in Genesis 1, and thereby opens up realms of responsibility to common people that were otherwise inconceivable. Despite its vision of economic independence and free work this is far removed from a "Free market," for the whole Sabbath system operates deliberately to restrain excesses of wealth and power, and to ensure the maintenance of some kind of equilibrium. While in the ancient world it may have functioned to limit the power of kings, in the modern world it is a vision necessary to address the hegemonic activities of international capital and corporations.

Sabbath was a gift equally to animals as to their owners (Exod 23:12; Lev 25:3–7). Given that animals were overwhelmingly the main source of energy in the ancient world, such a restriction is a further indication that Sabbath represents a limit on economic activity. An owner could conceivably rest while oxen continued to trample out the corn, but not where this kind of Sabbath is practiced. Meanwhile, the gleaning provision also extended to the wellbeing of the wild animals (Exod 23:10–11; Lev 25:3–7). Further, Sabbath year was intended to provide rest even for the land (Exod 23:10–11; Lev 25:3–7). The writer of 2 Chronicles declared that the seventy years of exile in Babylon were in order for the land to make up for the Sabbaths which it had been denied (2 Chron 36:21, cf. Lev 26:34–35). The ultimate Sabbath, expressed in the Jubilee year, required not only the release of debts, but the return of lands to their original tribal inheritors (Lev 25:8–17). This was primarily in order to remind people that the land could not be privatized, because it is the Lord's and they live upon it as "aliens and tenants" (Lev 25:23). Lowery sees this as another attempt to mitigate the impacts of Royal ideologies, serving "as a check on the long-term concentration of wealth in the hands of a rich few."[82]

Rest for the land should not create anxiety, because the whole Sabbath vision is based upon the assurance of the provision and trustworthiness of God and the need for people to remember their vulnerability and redemption from their national origins in slavery (Lev 25:38, 42, 55). But some aspects of it might create anxiety for, as Lowery observes, to take land out of cultivation for two years at a Jubilee could result in national

---

81. Sacks, "Markets and Morals," 42.
82. Lowery, *Sabbath and Jubilee*, 68.

disaster,[83] prefiguring the situation in which Benedict began his ministry! Lowery argues that these particular regulations are utopian and deliberately intended not to be anthropocentric.[84] Rather, what we have is a theological statement about creation, located within the ordered creation story, reminding of the generous provision of God, and promoting an alternative vision to that of unrestrained demands upon others and the Earth. Just as Jesus recognized a wide variety of Sabbath practice—the concern always being that it should bring life, not death, so the vision and intention of Jubilee can be adopted and adapted, without the necessity of submitting to all of its specific provisions. Whether such a comprehensive social and economic Sabbath was ever attempted in Israel is highly uncertain, but it was this comprehensive vision of Sabbath which Jesus appropriated in inaugurating his ministry in Luke 4.

Although much has rightly been made of the significance of Jewish conceptions of linear time,[85] it is equally important to recognize the importance of Sabbath time. Sabbath time establishes rhythms to the world and to living, and sets limits within which human activity takes place. In this sense it represents a counter-vision to the contemporary market economics that imagines the possibility of access to endless resources, for never ending consumption and growth, where there is no rest. Furthermore, such seasonality is recognized, not only by the Sabbath, but also by the establishment of the heavenly lights (Gen 1:14). Sabbath is built into creation, and it is a truth of nature that we are to learn to live within its limits and the rhythms of life. This was well recognized in monastic theologies, but Promethean enthusiasms have seen it almost completely abandoned in the modern world. Nevertheless, recent science again asserts that all life upon Earth is lived within delicately established parameters. Much of McGrath's *Fine-Tuned Universe* is devoted to exploring the significance of "anthropic phenomena."

> Sir Martin Rees . . . has argued that the emergence of human life in the aftermath of the big bang is governed by a mere six numbers, each of which is so precisely determined that a miniscule variation in any one would have made both our universe and human life, as we know them, impossible. Roger Penrose

---

83. Lowery, *Sabbath and Jubilee*, 60.

84. Lowery, *Sabbath and Jubilee*, 60–62.

85. See Cahill, *Gifts of the Jews*, 5, 128–32; Turner, *Roots of Science*, 65–70, 82; Sacks, "Markets and Morals," 44.

also speaks of an "extraordinary degree of precision (or 'fine-tuning')" required for life.[86]

These constants are of the stuff of the universe and utterly impervious to human interference. But there are others, more delicate, unique to the Earth, and it may well be that to flout them is to invite disaster. The most discussed concerns the level of carbon dioxide (CO_2) in the Earth's atmosphere above which atmospheric heating could run out of control, destructively impacting all life on Earth. This figure is largely within human influence and is rising steadily to dangerous levels, almost entirely due to the prodigious burning of fossil fuels to meet the energy demands of the world's wealthiest economies, and secondarily to the loss of vast tropical forests which have hitherto served to soak up large quantities of carbon.[87] Of course, while it lies within human power to alter levels of CO_2 within the Earth's atmosphere, it does not lie with us to alter the inexorability of the physics.

> Physics has set an immutable bottom line on life as we know it on this planet . . . Any value for carbon dioxide (CO_2) in the atmosphere greater than 350 parts per million is not compatible "with the planet on which civilization developed and to which life on earth is adapted." That bottom line won't change: above 350 and, sooner or later, the ice caps melt, sea levels rise, hydrological cycles are thrown off kilter, and so on.[88]

It is beyond the scope of this study to explore anthropogenic climate change in detail. The critical point is that life on Earth is lived within limits. As the ancient biblical writers recognized that humanity could "trespass" its limits (see Genesis 6–9), so we must not dismiss the likelihood of doing the same in the modern world!

Refusal to accept life within limits is not only driving environmental decay, but also increasing injustice. Flannery reviews the serious agricultural impacts in Sub-Saharan Africa associated with anthropogenic global warming, generated by activities in places far distant from their worst effects. Through a combination of rising sea-surface temperatures in the Indian Ocean and local cooling in Europe—due to industrial-dust-induced "global dimming," together weakening the monsoon, "the Sahelian climate shift is emblematic of the situation faced by the world as

---

86. McGrath, *Fine-Tuned Universe*, 85.
87. McKibben, "Remember This."
88. McKibben, "Physics of Copenhagen."

a whole . . . so big is the climate shift that it could influence the climate of the entire planet."[89] David Lobell and colleagues demonstrate measurable decline in the Earth's grain crop production and food availability, in direct relation to warming induced climate changes. "At the global scale, maize and wheat exhibited negative impacts for several major producers and global net loss of 3.8% and 5.5% relative to what would have been achieved without the climate trends in 1980–2008."[90] Further exacerbating this negative impact upon the world's poorest, "the estimated changes in crop production excluding and including CO_2 fertilization . . . translate into average commodity price increases of 18.9% and 6.4%."[91] Furthermore, as climate change generates rising sea levels so millions of people, and whole island nations, are already being inundated.[92] Yet it is by no means clear that those nations which have generated the greenhouse warming are at all open to welcoming the stranger, who comes in the guise of a climate refugee.

Sustainability is the expression most commonly used to speak of this ability to live within limits. Drawing on Herman Daly, Clare Hammond offers three rules that define throughput sustainability:

> For a *renewable resource*—soil, water, forest, fish—the sustainable rate of use can be no greater than the rate of regeneration . . . For a *non-renewable resource*—fossil fuel, high-grade mineral ore, fossil groundwater—the sustainable rate of use can be no greater than the rate at which a renewable resource, used sustainably, can be substituted for it . . . For a *pollutant* the sustainable rate of emission can be no greater than the rate at which the pollutant can be recycled, absorbed, or rendered harmless by the environment.[93]

Jesus' account of Sabbath provides the model of life for the witness of the disciple community—the church. The kingdom of God, to which we bear witness, is both a future hope and a present reality, and may thus find expression in the present materiality of the creation. The first call upon the disciple community is to bear witness, not to attempt to establish the kingdom by the tactics of an unredeemed politics. Nevertheless,

---

89. Flannery, *Weather Makers*, 126.
90. Lobell et al., "Climate Trends," 2.
91. Lobell et al., "Climate Trends," 2–3.
92. *Just Change*, 10. See also Flannery, *Weather Makers*, 286–89.
93. Hammond, "Limits to Growth," 6.

if those who bear witness to the kingdom are unable to demonstrate an alternative economics, serious questions must be raised about the validity of the message that is proclaimed. Indeed, if the Earth is constitutionally incapable of bearing the life of the kingdom, the whole biblical, patristic, and monastic theological confrontation with Gnosticism and Manichaeism is probably shown to have been mistaken. Conversely, if this community can demonstrate models of sustainable living, the message of the kingdom cannot be lightly dismissed. A key question then is how the Sabbath vision relates to actual experience of poverty and Earth-care in the world. Is the Sabbath vision of sustainability, itself sustainable? Although not drawing explicitly upon Sabbath sources, this is precisely the issue addressed by Gregorios when he issues an urgent call for new models of experimental community, addressing the present crisis but living by the light of the gospel of Christ.

> From such a community, new reflection and new patterns of living may emerge which could have a prophetic role in the world. For it is the *energeia* of God in Christ that should be available to us as both existence and grace, as we conscientiously seek to follow him, the captain of our salvation who has gone before us.[94]

Wilkinson and Pickett address the challenging question whether consumption and carbon emissions can be reduced while maintaining adequate quality of life. Using research into infant mortality, and other research based on the United Nations Human Development Index, they show that,

> scarcely a single country combines a quality of life . . . with an ecological footprint which is globally sustainable. Cuba is the only one which does so. Despite its much lower income levels, its life expectancy and infant mortality rates are almost identical to those in the United States. That at least one country manages to combine acceptable living standards with a sustainable economy, proves that it can be done.[95]

This is especially significant given Cuba's relative lack of the best environmental technologies, and its long experience of economic sanction by the United States, but it has been achieved through its "cold-turkey"

---

94. Gregorios, *Human Presence*, 103.
95. Wilkinson and Pickett, *Spirit Level*, 217; see also figures (15.1) and (15.2).

withdrawal from petroleum dependence following the collapse of the Soviet Union.[96]

Michael Pollan's account of management-intensive grazing convincingly explores the possibility of ecologically sustainable agriculture. The operation he describes is integrated—recognizing the value to the farming practice of wild-lands as much as pasture. Based on natural complexity rather than industrial simplification, it requires no outside inputs of chemicals or antibiotics, taxpayer subsidies or exceptions to environmental legislation. It produces nothing by way of waste or pollution. Everything is recycled within the natural system. And its levels of food productivity easily match those of industrialized agriculture.[97] Furthermore, like African conservation farmers, some of its key practitioners do it for explicitly theological reasons.[98]

Ecologically sustainable agriculture is a real possibility. William McDonough and Michael Braungart address the even more fraught issues of sustainable manufacturing and urban design, in their book *Cradle to Cradle: Remaking the Way We Make Things*. As with sustainable agriculture, central to their conception is the recognition that in nature there is no waste. A tree produces thousands of blossoms in order to create another tree, yet its abundance is not considered wasteful but safe, beautiful, and highly effective. Waste equals food, everything is part of a "nutrient stream,"[99] and human design processes should also be working within such a paradigm. Products might be designed so that, after their useful life, they provide nourishment for something new—either as "biological nutrients" that safely re-enter the environment or as "technical nutrients" that circulate within closed-loop industrial cycles, without being "downcycled" into low-grade uses (as most "recyclables" now are). They contrast the values of "eco-efficiency" with the practice of "eco-effectiveness," suggesting that "Eco-effective design considers . . . What is the entire system—cultural, commercial, ecological—of which this made thing, and way of making things, will be a part?"[100] Conversely, efficiency, they suggest, may extend the period of resource depletion[101]

---

96. Morgan, *Power of Community*.
97. Pollan, *Omnivore's Dilemma*, 185–225.
98. Pollan, *Omnivore's Dilemma*, 125, 203, 215, 233.
99. McDonough and Braungart, *Cradle to Cradle*, 92–93, 104–9.
100. McDonough and Braungart, *Cradle to Cradle*, 81.
101. McDonough and Braungart, *Cradle to Cradle*, 155.

but it is reductive and no fun, "an efficient world is not one we envision as delightful... In contrast to nature, it is downright parsimonious."[102] But, following the example of natural systems—recognizing that trees or ants, put back as well as take,

> we can follow their cue to a more inspiring engagement—a partnership—with nature... Instead of using nature as a mere tool for human purposes, we can strive to become tools of nature who serve its purposes too. We can celebrate the fecundity in the world, instead of perpetuating a way of thinking and making that eliminates it.[103]

Working with nature and serving its purposes is, as we have earlier suggested, to be *logikos*—responsive to the operations of the Word in creation. To celebrate the fecundity of the world is to enter into the joy of Sabbath with its joyful recognition of the generous, life-sustaining, provision of God.

CONCLUSIONS

With Christ in the Care of Creation—A Christology of Human Dominion

While the Bible tells stories and sings songs that delight in, or are sometimes terrified by, the living presence of God in the world, the patristic and monastic theologians systematically expound it. God is intimately involved in creation by the Word—who orders and sustains, and by the Spirit—who generates life and liberates for flourishing. Jesus Christ, himself generated by the Spirit, is the human incarnation of this Word, and as risen Lord is now the dispenser of the Spirit, who both renews the life of Christ within people—thus creating a renewed humanity, and also constantly renews life within creation—drawing all things on to their final consummation with Christ in God. Such intimate engagement by God with the Earth is a picture quite foreign to that painted by White, whose conception of humanity is similarly extracted from its intimate relational existence within the living body of the world. From the time of our first appearing humanity has been influencing and altering the Earth in ways quite unlike those of any other creature. We find ourselves able to concur

---

102. McDonough and Braungart, *Cradle to Cradle*, 65.
103. McDonough and Braungart, *Cradle to Cradle*, 156.

with White that human power over creation has been used to destructive effect in the world. But, unlike him, we observe dramatic environmental degradation in other contexts, quite untouched by the biblical stories involving human dominion, or by Christian faith. Human power cannot be denied. The question is always how we are to understand and properly exercise this power. At the heart of this thesis we argue that a christological account of human dominion will issue in an understanding of the human presence in the Earth that may be integrative, healing, and hopeful.

In exploring the earliest confession that "Jesus is Lord," we have seen that Christ's lordship is service, and such self-giving for the other is an attribute of God's own being. Those who have put on Christ have been baptized into this humility and participate in Christ's service of creation. Christ's lordship—or dominion—is experienced as hospitable service, nurturing the Earth as a place of welcome, provision, healing, and flourishing for all. Despite its brevity, this is perhaps the clearest element in a christological account of human dominion.

The confession of Jesus as the incarnation of the Word has implications in various directions. This Word is the divine self-expression, calling creation—and humanity within creation, into being, and simultaneously into relational existence. To contemplate the Word in creation is to engage in that for which we have been created, relationship with God. Jesus Christ as the definitive, personal, expression of the Word does not supplant creation but fulfills it, and thus becomes the interpretive key for all contemplation of creation. In patristic language, to be *logikos* is not merely to be rational, but to be deeply relational. To live in this relationality is the goal and end of all desire. It does not involve any rejection of material existence—the beauty and fecundity of the world is to be enjoyed more than ever. But it utterly transforms that desire without end which consumes the Earth yet knows neither satisfaction nor peace, and which is the hallmark of idolatry in every age and consumerist economics in the present age. Thus, the renewal of the contemplative life as relational existence is also vital to a christological understanding of the human place in the Earth.

Alongside the contemplative life as nurture of life with God in Christ, contemplation of the Word in creation also enables discernment how the service of the Earth may best take place. This too involves being *logikos*. In the cruciform fellowship of Christ, we read and listen to the Word in creation. We begin to learn a little of how the world works, and humbled by our ignorance and our sinful destructiveness, begin to take tentative steps towards the healing of some environments, and the transformation of others so that fullness of life—including human life, may be fostered. This vision of transformation is no license for exploitation, for it arises out of a renewed sensitivity to the whole Earth community, and its goal is the offering of a Christ-form of life to God in thanksgiving. These are motives and goals quite at odds with contemporary economics. But they are nevertheless *logikos*—they are true to the way things really are, unlike other ways of life, which as we have seen are now bringing the Earth to the point of environmental and societal collapse.

The confession of Jesus as the image of God embodies the ancient understanding of the image as the representative likeness, established to mediate a relationship between God and the world. In the biblical texts the whole Earth is God's temple, with the Jerusalem temple merely its model, and similarly, the whole human race is called to participate in this priesthood, as it is exercised by Christ, the high priest of creation. Thus this image is no mere imprint, but an essentially relational identity. The call to priestly existence is vital for understanding the relationship of humanity with the rest of the Earth community, and for proper exercise of the power held by humanity upon Earth. On one hand, it is to provide the words (or, more accurately, to echo Christ's words)—and some would add the melody, for the song of creation's praise; and to minister as stewards at the table of God, offering up all of life in thanksgiving and intercession. This in itself provides creation with an honor that merely utilitarian and instrumental accounts never can. On the other hand, it is to speak the word of God to creation, ministering reconciliation, healing, and communion. Advocacy for creation is thus central to sharing in the priestly ministry of Christ. This encapsulates Zizioulas's concern for love rather than mere will-power, and his suggestion that beneath a rational ethic, it is even more necessary to cultivate "an *ethos*. Not a programme, but an attitude and a mentality. Not a legislation, but a culture,"[104] within which people live and which shapes feelings and behavior at both conscious and unconscious levels.

These three confessional accounts—Servant Lord, priestly image, and sustaining Word, may all be accommodated within the classical model of Christ's offices—King, Priest, and Prophet. Thus, a christological account of human dominion over creation, such as we have here argued, is not a theological novelty so much as a drawing out of dormant

---

104. Zizioulas, "Preserving God's Creation" (13:1, 1990), 5.

seeds, or an opening of already vital buds. It does not so much call the church to construct some kind of new identity by following the fashions of the age, as remind it of the fullness of its life in Christ.

Finally, we have explored the implications for creation of Jesus' declaration of the presence of the kingdom of God and of his claims to lordship over the Sanctuary and the Sabbath. The kingdom is encountered in every one of Jesus' restorative or healing actions, but most definitively in his own resurrection. Here is the sign that creation is the subject of God's healing purpose, rather than indifference or abandonment. The gift of the Spirit enables participation in this new order, thus demonstrating that the kingdom hope of the healing of creation does not lie entirely over the eschatological horizon but may be entered into in this present time. Hope thereby takes on a two-directional character—calling to faith in God's future, but also demonstrating that creation in the present may bear the life of the age to come. Monastic movements have generally regarded their communities as signs of this new order, and within this category we could also include Anabaptist communities, which were often criticized by the magisterial Reformers for being a new form of monasticism![105] In our own day the emergence of a "new monasticism" witnesses to this hope, by its frequent symbiosis of contemplative living with care for the Earth, justice for the impoverished (with a particular emphasis on re-location to abandoned places—usually inner-cities), transformative mission, and congregational renewal.[106]

Jesus' account of the Sabbath provided the social embodiment of the kingdom vision, experienced as a communal event. Sabbath had functioned as the visible identifying feature of the Jewish community. To distinguish itself from Judaism the early Christian movement tended to abandon formal Sabbath practice. But it could never escape the inspiration, and Sabbath continued to function as a central component in both patristic theological reflection and monastic understandings of the ordering of time—and therefore of daily living. Sabbath has continually reasserted itself, currently by its significance for understanding human ecological living. A christological account of Sabbath recognizes the unity of the full provision of God; that is, the salvation in Christ is inextricable from fullness of life in creation. Sabbath thus bespeaks the profligacy of divine grace, expressed in the profligacy of the Earth. Such a

---

105. Murray, *Naked Anabaptist*, 100, and 186, note 3.

106. See Rutba House, *School(s) for Conversion*.

vision of fullness contrasts with the "mean world syndrome"[107] described by George Gerbner, or the "wasteland" which Michael Novak appears to celebrate in his apologia for individualism in the free market.[108] In the presence of such fullness our basic disposition may be one of resting. All that is necessary for life is provided, but this is life inextricably bound up in, and interdependent with, the life of all living creatures. Thus, even necessary and fulfilling work is a gift received, and is to serve the generous purposes of God. Sabbath is established for the well-being of the whole Earth community. Therefore, even while it celebrates the profligacy of the Earth, it provides for what we have recognized as sustainable models of living. It also calls for models of economic life that build community and facilitate just distribution of the gifts of creation, and it does not trust such outcomes simply to human self-interest and the operations of a disinterested "invisible hand."

Sabbath combines elements that are contemplative, communal, and eucharistic. A christological account recognizes that it is in Christ that we enter into the proper exercise of our human dominion. It is through Christ that we relate both to God and other creatures, and it is in his table fellowship that we experience our utter dependence, acknowledged in the basic disposition of thanksgiving. In his table fellowship we receive the life of God through the fruits of the Earth, and we serve blessing to the Earth by ministering to it the life of God, through Christ in the Spirit. Such a Sabbath is a celebration of resurrection as divine affirmation of creation and hope for human living.

Lordship as service of the well-being of creation, contemplation of the Word as listening to and speaking for creation, imaging God in creation by ministering communion, forming communities of hopeful kingdom living, and embodying that hope in Sabbath practices of sustainability—these are key elements in a christological evaluation of human dominion over creation, and provide the foundation for ethics that may be both sign and foretaste of the healing of creation.

---

107. Gerbner, https://web.archive.org/web/20110714063636/http://meanworldsyndrome.com/.

108. Novak, *Democratic Capitalism*, 54–55.

Bibliography

Aelfric. *The Old English Hexameron*. Translated and notes by S. J. Crawford. Hamburg: Henri Grand, 1921.

Alexander, Samuel, ed. *Voluntary Simplicity: The Poetic Alternative to Consumer Culture*. Whanganui, NZ: Stead and Daughters, 2009.

Alper, Loretta, et al. *The Mean World Syndrome: Media Violence & the Cultivation of Fear*. San Francisco: Kanopy Streaming, 2014.

Anderson, Atholl. "A Fragile Plenty: Pre-European Maori and the New Zealand Environment." In *Environmental Histories of New Zealand*, edited by Eric Pawson and Tom Brooking, 19–34. Melbourne: Oxford University Press, 2002.

———. *When All the Moa Ovens Grew Cold*. Dunedin: Otago Heritage, 1983.

Anderson, Bernard. *From Creation to New Creation: Old Testament Perspectives*. Minneapolis: Fortress, 1994.

Arnold, Ellen F. "Engineering Miracles: Water Control, Conversion and the Creation of a Religious Landscape in the Medieval Ardennes." *Environment and History* 13 (2007) 477–502.

Attfield, Robin. "Environmental Sensitivity and Critiques of Stewardship." In *Environmental Stewardship: Critical Perspectives, Past and Present*, edited by R. J. Berry, 76–91. London: T. & T. Clark, 2006.

Augustine. "Against Julian." In *Ancient Christian Commentary on Scripture: Genesis 1–11*, edited by Andrew Louth. Downers Grove: InterVarsity, 2001.

———. *Expositions on the Psalms*. Translated and edited by A. Cleveland Cox, in Nicene and Post-Nicene Fathers 4, edited by Philip Schaff. Grand Rapids: Eerdmans, 1888.

———. *The Trinity*. Introduction, translated, and notes by Edmund Hill. Brooklyn: New City, 1991.

Bader-Saye, Scott. *Following Jesus in a Culture of Fear*. Grand Rapids: Brazos, 2007.

Bahn, Paul, and John Flenley. *Easter Island, Earth Island*. London: Thames and Hudson, 1992.

Ball, Philip. "Making Stuff: From Bacon to Bakelite." In *Seeing Further: The Story of Science and the Royal Society*, edited by Bill Bryson, 295–319. London: Harper, 2010.

Barbour, Ian. *Earth Might Be Fair: Reflections on Ethics, Religion, and Ecology*. Englewood Cliffs, NJ: Prentice Hall, 1972.

———. *Western Man and Environmental Ethics: Attitudes towards Nature and Technology*. Reading, MA: Addison-Wesley, 1973.

Barr, James. "Man and Nature: The Ecological Controversy and the Old Testament." *Bulletin of the John Rylands University Library of Manchester* 55 (1972) 10–28.
Barrett, C. K. *The Gospel according to St. John*. London: SPCK, 1978.
Barth, Karl. *Church Dogmatics*. III.1 Section 41. Edited by Geoffrey Bromily and Thomas Torrance, translated by Harold Knight. Edinburgh: T. & T. Clark, 1958.
Barton, Stephen C. *Idolatry: False Worship in the Bible, Early Judaism and Christianity*. London: T. & T. Clark, 2007.
Bauckham, Richard, ed. *The Gospels for All Christians*. Grand Rapids: Eerdmans, 1998.
———. "Modern Domination of Nature: Historical Origins and Biblical Critique." In *Environmental Stewardship: Critical Perspectives, Past and Present*, edited by R. J. Berry, 32–50. London: T. & T. Clark, 2006.
Bauckham, Richard, and Carl Mosser, eds. *The Gospel of John and Christian Theology*. Grand Rapids: Eerdmans, 2008.
Beattie, James, and John Stenhouse. "Empire, Environment and Religion: God and Nature in Nineteenth-Century New Zealand." *Environment and History* 13 (2007) 413–46.
Bede. *A History of the English Church and People*. Translated and notes by Leo Sherley-Price. Harmondsworth: Penguin, 1955.
———. *On Genesis*. Translated, introduction and notes by Calvin B. Kendall. Liverpool: Liverpool University Press, 2008.
———. *The Reckoning of Time*. Translation and introduction by Faith Wallis. Liverpool: Liverpool University Press, 1999.
Begbie, Jeremy. *Voicing Creation's Praise: Towards a Theology of the Arts*. London: T. & T. Clark, 1991.
Behr, John. *Asceticism and Anthropology in Irenaeus and Clement*. Oxford: Oxford University Press, 2000.
Bergmann, Sigurd. "God's Here and Now in Built Environments." In *Theology in Built Environments: Exploring Religion, Architecture, and Design*, edited by Sigurd Bergmann, 9–22. New Brunswick, NJ: Transaction, 2009.
———. *Theology in Built Environments: Exploring Religion, Architecture, and Design*. New Brunswick, NJ: Transaction, 2009.
Berkman, John. "The Consumption of Animals and the Catholic Tradition." *Logos: A Journal of Catholic Thought and Culture* 7 (2004) 174–90.
Berlin, Adele, et al. *The Jewish Study Bible*. Oxford: Oxford University Press, 2004.
Berman, Constance Hoffman. "Medieval Agriculture, the Southern French Countryside, and the Cistercians: A Study of Forty-Three Monasteries." *Transactions of the American Philosophical Society* 76 (1986) i–xiv, 1–179.
Berry, R. J., ed. *Environmental Stewardship: Critical Perspectives, Past and Present*. London: T. & T. Clark, 2006.
———. *God and the Biologist*. Leicester: Apollos, 1996.
———. "Stewardship: A Default Position?" In *Environmental Stewardship: Critical Perspectives, Past and Presente*d, edited by R. J. Berry, 1–13. London: T. & T. Clark, 2006.
———, ed. *When Enough is Enough: A Christian Framework for Environmental Sustainability*. Nottingham: Apollos, 2007.
Berry, Wendell. *Recollected Essays, 1965–1980*. San Francisco: Northpoint, 1981.
Birch, Bruce C., ed. *A Theological Introduction to the Old Testament*. Nashville: Abingdon, 1999.

Bischoff, Bernhard, and Michael Lapidge, eds. *Biblical Commentaries from the Canterbury School of Theodore and Hadrian*. Cambridge: Cambridge University Press, 1994.
Black, John. "The Dominion of Man." In *Environmental Stewardship: Critical Perspectives, Past and Present*, edited by R. J. Berry, 92–96. London: T. & T. Clark, 2006.
———. *The Dominion of Man: The Search for Ecological Responsibility*. Edinburgh: Edinburgh University Press, 1970.
Blair, Ian. "Energy and Environment: the Ecological Debate." In *The Year 2000 AD*, edited by John Stott, 103–25. Basingstoke: Marshall, Morgan and Scott, 1983.
Böckmann, Aquinata. "RB 48: Of the Daily Manual Labor; Part I." *American Benedictine Review* 59 (2008) 141–66.
———. "RB 48: Of the Daily Manual Labor; Part II." *American Benedictine Review* 59 (2008) 253–90.
Boersema, Jan J. "Why is Francis of Assisi the Patron Saint of Ecologists?" *Science and Christian Belief* 14 (2002) 51–77.
Boff, Leonardo. *Saint Francis: A Model for Human Liberation*. Translated by John W. Diercksmeier. London: SCM, 1982.
Bonhoeffer, Dietrich. *Ethics*. Dietrich Bonhoeffer Works 6, edited by Clifford J. Green, translated by Reinhard Krauss et al. Minneapolis: Fortress, 2005.
Bouma-Prediger, Steve. *For the Beauty of the Earth: A Christian Vision for Creation Care*. Grand Rapids: Baker Academic, 2001.
Bratton, Susan Power. "Sea Sabbaths for Sea Stewards: Rest and Restoration for Marine Ecosystems." In *Environmental Stewardship: Critical Perspectives, Past and Present*, edited by R. J. Berry, 208–12. London: T. & T. Clark, 2006.
Brenner, Athalya, ed. *A Feminist Companion to Genesis*. Sheffield: Sheffield Academic, 1993.
Brett, Mark G. *Genesis: Procreation and the Politics of Identity*. New York: Routledge, 2000.
Brown, Peter. *Augustine of Hippo: A Biography*. New edition with epilogue. London: Faber and Faber, 2000.
———. *The Body and Society: Men, Women, and Sexual Renunciation in Early Christianity*. New York: Columbia University Press, 1988.
Brown, Raymond. *The Gospel according to John (XIII-XXI)*. Anchor Bible 29. Garden City, NY: Doubleday, 1970.
Brueggemann, Walter. *The Land: Place as Gift, Promise, and Challenge in Biblical Faith*. Minneapolis: Fortress, 2002.
Brunner, Emil. *Man in Revolt*. London: Lutterworth, 1939.
Bryson, Bill, ed. *Seeing Further: The Story of Science and the Royal Society*. London: Harper, 2010.
Burton-Christie, Douglas. *The Word in the Desert: Scripture and the Quest for Holiness in Early Christian Monasticism*. Oxford: Oxford University Press, 1993.
Butler, Cuthbert. *Benedictine Monachism*. 1924. Reprint, Cambridge: Speculum Historiale, 1961.
Butler Bass, Diana. "Michael Vick Versus Gregory of Nyssa." *Sojourners*, July 25, 2007.
Cahill, Thomas. *The Gifts of the Jews: How a Tribe of Desert Nomads Changed the Way Everyone Thinks and Feels*. New York: Nan A. Talese, 1998.

———. *How the Irish Saved Civilization: The Untold Story of Ireland's Heroic Role from the Fall of Rome to the Rise of Medieval Europe*. New York: Nan A. Talese, 1995.
Calvin, John. *Commentaries on the First Book of Moses Called Genesis*. Vol. 1. Translated by John King. Edinburgh: Calvin Translation Society, 1848.
———. *Institutes of the Christian Religion*. Edited by John T. McNeill, translated by Ford Lewis Battles. London: SCM, 1960.
Carson, D. A. *Divine Sovereignty and Human Responsibility: Biblical Perspectives in Tension*. London: Marshall Pickering/Harper Collins, 1994.
Cavanaugh, William T. *Being Consumed: Economics and Christian Desire*. Grand Rapids: Eerdmans, 2008.
Chesterton, G. K. *St. Francis of Assisi*. London: Hodder and Stoughton, 1923.
Chryssavgis, John. "Christian Orthodoxy." http://users.clas.ufl.edu/bron/pdf--christianity/Chryssavgis--Christian%20Orthodoxy.pdf.
———. "The Sacredness of Creation in the Sayings of the Desert Fathers." *Studia Patristica* 25 (1993) 350.
Clouse, R. G. "Millennium." *Evangelical Dictionary of Theology*, edited by Walter A. Elwell. Grand Rapids: Baker, 1984.
Cohen, Jeremy. *"Be Fertile and Increase. Fill the Earth and Master It": The Ancient and Medieval Career of a Biblical Text*. Ithaca, NY: Cornell University Press, 1989.
Countryman, Louis William. *Living on the Border of the Holy: Renewing the Priesthood of All*. Harrisburg, PA: Morehouse, 1999.
Cowan, James. *Journey to the Inner Mountain: In the Desert with Saint Antony*. London: Hodder and Stoughton, 2002.
Crouch, Andy. "The Joyful Environmentalists: Eugene Peterson and Peter Harris." *Christianity Today* 55 (2011). http://www.christianitytoday.com/ct/2011/june/joyfulenvironment.html.
Cumberland, Kenneth B. *Landmarks*. Surry Hills, NSW: Readers Digest, 1981.
Cunningham, Lawrence, ed. *Brother Francis: An Anthology of Writings by and about St. Francis of Assisi*. New York: Harper and Row, 1972.
Daley, Brian E. *The Hope of the Early Church: A Handbook of Patristic Eschatology*. Cambridge: Cambridge University Press, 1991.
Davey, Cyril J. *The Story of Sadhu Sundar Singh*. Chicago: Moody, 1963.
Davidson, Ivor. *A Public Faith: From Constantine to the Medieval World, AD 312–600*. Grand Rapids: Monarch, 2005.
Davies, D. R. *Thirty Minutes to Raise the Dead*. London: Canterbury, 1949.
Davies, W. D. *The Gospel and the Land*. Los Angeles: University of California Press, 1974.
Deane-Drummond, Celia. "Living from the Sabbath: Developing an Ecological Theology in the Context of Biodiversity." In *Biodiversity and Ecology as Interdisciplinary Challenge*, edited by Denis Edwards and Mark Worthing, 1–13. Adelaide: Australian Theological Forum, 2004.
Decarreaux, Jean. *Monks and Civilization: From the Barbarian Invasions to the Reign of Charlemagne*. London: Allen and Unwin, 1964.
Dembski, William A., et al., eds. *The Patristic Understanding of Creation*. Riesel, TX: Erasmus, 2008.
de Steiguer, J. Edward. *The Origins of Modern Environmental Thought*. Tucson: University of Arizona Press, 2006.

Devall, Bill, and George Sessions. *Deep Ecology: Living as if Nature Mattered*. Salt Lake City: Gibbs Smith, 1985.

De Vogue, Adalbert. *The Rule of Saint Benedict: A Doctrinal and Spiritual Commentary*. Kalamazoo: Cistercian, 1983.

de Waal, Esther. *A Life-Giving Way: A Commentary on the Rule of Saint Benedict*. London: Geoffrey Chapman, 1995.

Diamond, Jared. *Collapse: How Societies Choose to Fail or Succeed*. London: Penguin, 2005.

Djupe, Paul A., and Patrick Kieran Hunt. "Beyond the Lynn White Thesis: Congregational Effects on Environmental Concern." *Journal for the Scientific Study of Religion* 48 (2009) 670–86.

Dubos, Rene. "Franciscan Conservation Versus Benedictine Stewardship." In *Environmental Stewardship: Critical Perspective, Past and Present*, edited by R. J. Berry, 56–59. London: T. & T. Clark, 2006.

———. *A God Within*. New York: Charles Scribner's Sons, 1972.

———. "A Theology of the Earth." In *Western Man and Environmental Ethics: Attitudes towards Nature and Technology*, edited by Ian G. Barbour. Reading, MA: Addison-Wesley, 1973.

Duby, Georges. *The Early Growth of the European Economy*. Translated by Howard B. Clarke. London: Wiedenfeld and Nicolson, 1974.

Dunn, James D. G. *Jesus Remembered*. Grand Rapids: Eerdmans, 2003.

Dunn, Marilyn. *The Emergence of Monasticism*. Oxford: Blackwell, 2000.

Dyer, Gwynne. "Time to Redefine What it Means to be Rich." *Otago Daily Times* (Sept 20, 2010) 11.

Edmondson, Stephen. *Calvin's Christology*. Cambridge: Cambridge University Press, 2004.

Edwards, Denis, and Mark Worthing, eds. *Biodiversity and Ecology as Interdisciplinary Challenge*. Adelaide: Australian Theological Forum, 2004.

Ehrlich, Paul R., and Anne H. Ehrlich. *One with Nineveh: Politics, Consumption, and the Human Future*. Washington, DC: Island, 2004.

"'Farming God's Way' in Zimbabwe." *Touchstone*, Dec 2009, 8.

Farrow, Douglas. "St Irenaeus of Lyons: The Church and the World." *Pro Ecclesia* 4 (1995) 333–55.

Fedwick, Paul Jonathan, ed. *Basil of Caesarea: Christian, Humanist, Ascetic—A Sixteen-Hundredth Anniversary Symposium*. Vol. 1. Toronto: Pontifical Institute of Medieval Studies, 1981.

Finlay, Graeme. *God's Books: Genetics and Genesis*. Auckland: Telos, 2004.

Flannery, Tim. *The Future Eaters: An Ecological History of the Australasian Lands and People*. Sydney: Reed New Holland, 1994.

———. *The Weather Makers: The History and Future Impact of Climate Change*. Melbourne: Text, 2005.

Florovsky, Georges. "Creation and Creaturehood." In *The Patristic Understanding of Creation*, edited by William A. Dembski et al., 536–76. Riesel, TX: Erasmus, 2008.

Ford, David. *The Modern Theologians*. Malden, MA: Blackwell, 1997.

Foster, Richard. *Celebration of Discipline: The Path to Spiritual Growth*. 3rd ed. San Francisco: Harper Collins, 1998.

Fowl, Stephen E., ed. *The Theological Interpretation of Scripture*. Oxford: Blackwell, 1997.

Frend, W. H. C. *The Donatist Church*. Oxford: Oxford University Press, 1985.
Fumagalli, Vito. *Landscapes of Fear: Perceptions of Nature and the City in the Middle Ages*. Translated by Shayne Mitchell. Cambridge: Polity, 1994.
Galvin, Ray. *Christ and the Good Earth: An Introduction to Ecological Theology*. Auckland: Colcom, 1993.
Gies, Frances, and Joseph Gies. *Cathedral, Forge, and Waterwheel: Technology and Invention in the Middle Ages*. New York: Harper Collins, 1994.
Ginzberg, Louis. *The Legends of the Jews*. Vol. 1. Translated by Henrietta Szold. Baltimore: John Hopkins, 1998.
Glacken, Clarence J. *Traces on the Rhodian Shore: Nature and Culture in Western Thought from Ancient Times to the End of the Eighteenth Century*. Los Angeles: University of California Press, 1967.
Goodwin, Ruth. "Farming God's Way." Address at Faith and Development Symposium, University of Otago, August 2010.
Gorman, Michael J. *Inhabiting the Cruciform God: Kenosis, Justification, and Theosis in Paul's Narrative Soteriology*. Grand Rapids: Eerdmans, 2009.
Gorringe, Tim. "Preface." In *Theology in Built Environments: Exploring Religion, Architecture, and Design*, edited by Sigurd Bergmann, 7–8. New Brunswick, NJ: Transaction, 2009.
Gould, Graham. *The Desert Fathers on Monastic Community*. Oxford: Clarendon, 1993.
Grant, Robert M. *Irenaeus of Lyons*. New York: Routledge, 1997.
Gregorios, Paulos. *The Human Presence: An Orthodox View of Nature*. Geneva: World Council of Churches, 1978.
Gunton, Colin E. *Christ and Creation*. Carlisle: Paternoster, 1992.
———, ed. *The Doctrine of Creation*. Edinburgh: T. & T. Clark, 1997.
———. *Enlightenment and Alienation: An Essay towards a Trinitarian Theology*. Basingstoke: Marshall, Morgan and Scott, 1985.
———. *The Promise of Trinitarian Theology*. Edinburgh: T. & T. Clark, 1997.
———. *The Triune Creator*. Edinburgh: Edinburgh University Press, 1998.
Habel, Norman C. "Introducing Ecological Hermeneutics." In *Exploring Ecological Hermeneutics*, edited by Norman C. Habel and Peter Trudinger, 18. Atlanta: SBL, 2008.
Habel, Norman C., and Shirley Wurst, eds. *The Earth Story in Genesis*. Sheffield: Sheffield Academic, 2000.
Hall, Douglas John. *Imaging God: Dominion as Stewardship*. Grand Rapids: Eerdmans, 1986.
Hammond, Clare. "Limits to Growth." Draft preparatory document for Limits to Growth Conference, Victoria University of Wellington, Feb 18, 2011.
Harris, Peter. *Kingfisher's Fire: A Story of Hope for God's Earth*. Grand Rapids: Monarch, 2008.
Harrison, Carol. "Augustine and the Art of Gardening." In *Studies in Church History*, Vol. 37: *The Use and Abuse of Time in Christian History*, 13–33. Woodbridge, UK: The Ecclesiastical History Society, 2002.
———. *Augustine: Christian Truth and Fractured Humanity*. Oxford: Oxford University Press, 2000.
———. "Taking Creation for the Creator: Use and Enjoyment in Augustine's Theological Aesthetics." In *Idolatry: False Worship in the Bible, Early Judaism, and Christianity*, edited by Stephen C. Barton, 179–97. New York: T. & T. Clark, 2007.

Harrison, Peter. "Having Dominion: Genesis and the Mastery of Nature." In *Environmental Stewardship: Critical Perspectives, Past and Present*, edited by R. J. Berry, 17–31. London: T. & T. Clark, 2006.
Hartranft, Chester D. "An Introduction to the Anti-Donatist Writings." In Nicene and Post-Nicene Fathers 4, edited by Philip Schaff. Grand Rapids: Eerdmans, 1887.
Hauerwas, Stanley. *The Peaceable Kingdom: A Primer in Christian Ethics*. Notre Dame: University of Notre Dame Press, 1983.
Hays, Richard B. *The Moral Vision of the New Testament: Community, Cross, New Creation; A Contemporary Introduction to New Testament Ethics*. New York: HarperOne, 1996.
———. "Spirit, Church, Resurrection: The Third Article of the Creed as Hermeneutical Lens for Reading Romans." *Journal of Theological Interpretation* 5 (2011) 35–48.
Henry, Matthew. *Commentary on the Whole Bible*. Vol. 1, "Genesis to Deuteronomy." Christian Classics Ethereal Library, 2010. http://www.ccel.org/ccel/henry/mhc1.Gen.html.
Hodson, Margot R. "Creative Harmony: Isaiah's Vision of a Sustainable Future." In *When Enough is Enough: A Christian Framework for Environmental Sustainability*, edited by R. J. Berry, 169–77. Nottingham: Apollos, 2007.
Jacobsen, Thorkild. *The Treasures of Darkness: A History of Mesopotamian Religion*. New Haven: Yale University Press, 1976.
Jacobsen, Thorkild, and Robert M. Adams. "Salt and Silt in Ancient Mesopotamian Agriculture." *Science* 128 (1958) 1251–58.
Jenkins, Willis. *Ecologies of Grace: Environmental Ethics and Christian Theology*. Oxford: Oxford University Press, 2008.
Jenson, Robert W. "Aspects of a Doctrine of Creation." In *The Doctrine of Creation*, edited by Colin E. Gunton. Edinburgh: T. & T. Clark, 1997.
———. *A Large Catechism*. 2nd ed. Delhi, NY: American Lutheran Publicity Bureau, 1999.
Jeremias, Joachim. *The Eucharistic Words of Jesus*. London: SCM, 1966.
———. *The Prayers of Jesus*. London: SCM, 1967.
Jerris, Randon. "Cult Lines and Hellish Mountains: The Development of Sacred Landscapes in the Early Medieval Alps." *Journal of Medieval and Early Modern Studies* 32 (2002) 85–108.
Jónsson, Gunnlauger A. *The Image of God: Genesis 1:26–28 in a Century of Old Testament Research*. Lund: Almqvist and Wiksell, 1988.
Just Change: Critical Thinking on Global Issues; Going Under. Magazine. Issue 10 (Oct 2007). https://web.archive.org/web/20091003084208/http://www.dev-zone.org/justchange/documents/JC%20o_web.
Kaiser, Christopher B. *Creation and the History of Science*. London: Pickering, 1991.
Keller, Catherine. *Face of the Deep: A Theology of Becoming*. London: Routledge, 2003.
Keselópoulos, Anéstis G. *Man and the Environment: A Study of St. Symeon the New Theologian*. Crestwood, NY: St. Vladimir's Seminary, 2001.
Kirch, Patrick V., and Terry L. Hunt, eds. *Historical Ecology in the Pacific Islands: Prehistoric Environmental and Landscape Change*. New Haven: Yale University Press, 1997.
Kleber, Albert. "The Hymns at Weekly Vespers and the Week of Creation." *American Benedictine Review* 6 (1955) 171–87.

Knight, Douglas. *The Eschatological Economy: Time and the Hospitality of God.* Grand Rapids: Eerdmans, 2006.
Knight, George A. F. *A Christian Theology of the Old Testament.* London: SCM, 1959.
———. *Christ the Center.* Grand Rapids: Eerdmans, 1999.
Knowles, Dom David. *The Monastic Order in England.* 2nd ed. Cambridge: Cambridge University Press, 1966.
Kustas, George L. "Saint Basil and the Rhetorical Tradition." In *Basil Of Caesarea: Christian, Humanist, Ascetic; A Sixteen-Hundredth Anniversary Symposium 1*, edited by Paul Jonathan Fedwick, 221–79. Toronto: Pontifical Institute of Medieval Studies, 1981.
LaCugna, Catherine Mowry. *God for Us: The Trinity and Christian Life.* San Francisco: Harper, 1991.
Lawless, George. *Augustine of Hippo and His Monastic Rule.* Oxford: Clarendon, 1987.
Lawrence, C. H. *Medieval Monasticism: Forms of Religious Life in Western Europe in the Middle Ages.* 2nd ed. London: Longman, 1989.
Leach, William. *Country of Exiles: The Destruction of Place in American Life.* New York: Pantheon, 1999.
Lee, Bill. "Christian Conversations about Climate Change and Conservation." Paper presented at the South Island Ministry Conference, East Taieri Presbyterian Church, Dunedin, NZ, May 10, 2011.
Leopold, Aldo. *A Sand County Almanac: With Essays on Conservation from Round River.* New York: Ballantine, 1970.
Levenson, Jon D. "Genesis." In *The Jewish Study Bible*, edited by Adele Berlin et al. Oxford: Oxford University Press, 2004.
Lilburne, Geoffrey R. *A Sense of Place: A Christian Theology of the Land.* Nashville: Abingdon, 1989.
Lindsey, Hal, and Carole C. Carlson. *The Late Great Planet Earth.* Melbourne: S. John Bacon, 1972.
Lobell, David B., et al. "Climate Trends and Global Crop Production Since 1980." *Science Express*, May 5, 2011. https://science.sciencemag.org/content/333/6042/616.abstract.
Lohfink, Norbert. *Theology of the Pentateuch.* Edinburgh: T. & T. Clark, 1994.
Lovelock, James. "The Fallible Concept of Stewardship of the Earth." In *Environmental Stewardship: Critical Perspectives, Past and Present*, edited by R. J. Berry, 106–11. London: T. & T. Clark, 2006.
Louth, Andrew, ed. *Ancient Christian Commentary on Scripture.* Vol. 1, "Genesis 1–11." Downers Grove: InterVarsity, 2001.
Lowery, Richard H. *Sabbath and Jubilee.* St. Louis, MO: Chalice, 2000.
Lutz, Paul E., and H. Paul Santmire. *Ecological Renewal.* Philadelphia: Fortress, 1972.
Marsh, George Perkins. *Man and Nature.* Edited by David Lowenthal. Cambridge, MA: Belknap Press of Harvard University Press, 1965.
Matthews, Gareth B. *The Augustinian Tradition.* Berkeley: University of California Press, 1999.
McDonough, William, and Michael Braungart. *Cradle to Cradle: Remaking the Way We Make Things.* New York: North Point, 2002.
McFague, Sallie. *The Body of God: An Ecological Theology.* London: SCM, 1993.
McGinn, Bernard. "Benedict as Steward of Creation." *American Benedictine Review* 39 (1988) 161–76.

McGrath, Alister E. *Christian Theology: An Introduction*. 2nd ed. Malden, MA: Blackwell, 1997.

———. *A Fine-Tuned Universe: The Quest for God in Science and Theology*. Louisville: Westminster John Knox, 2010.

———. *The Re-enchantment of Nature: Science, Religion and the Human Sense of Wonder*. London: Hodder and Stoughton, 2002.

McHarg, Ian L. *Design with Nature*. Garden City, NY: Natural History, 1969.

McKay, Heather A. *Sabbath and Synagogue: The Question of Sabbath Worship in Ancient Judaism*. Leiden: Brill, 1994.

McKibben, Bill. "The Physics of Copenhagen: Why Politics-as-Usual May Mean the End of Civilization." http://www.tomdispatch.com/blog/175174/html.

———. "Remember This: 350 Parts Per Million." https://www.almendron.com/tribuna/remember-this-350-parts-per-million/.

Mead, Hirini Moko. *Tikanga Māori: Living by Māori Values*. Wellington: Huia, 2003.

Means, Richard L. "Why Worry about Nature?" In *Pollution and the Death of Man*, by Francis A. Schaeffer, 117–25. Wheaton, IL: Tyndale, 1970.

Michaels, J. Ramsey. *The Gospel of John*. Grand Rapids: Eerdmans, 2010.

Middleton, J. Richard. *The Liberating Image: The Imago Dei in Genesis 1*. Grand Rapids: Brazos, 2005.

Miller, Stephen M., and Robert V. Huber. *The Bible: A History*. Oxford: Lion Hudson, 2004.

Moltmann, Jürgen. *God in Creation: An Ecological Doctrine of Creation*. London: SCM, 1985.

———. "Reconciliation with Nature." *Word & World* 11 (1991) 117–23.

Montefiore, Hugh. *Can Man Survive?* Revised edition. Glasgow: Collins Fontana, 1970.

Morgan, Faith, dir. *The Power of Community: How Cuba Survived Peak Oil*. Video recording. Yellow Springs, OH: Community Service, 2006.

Morris, Leon. *The Gospel according to John, Revised*. Grand Rapids: Eerdmans, 1995.

Moule, C. F. D. *Man and Nature in the New Testament: Some Reflections on Biblical Ecology*. Philadelphia: Fortress, 1967.

Murray, Iain H. *The Puritan Hope: A Study in Revival and the Interpretation of Prophecy*. Edinburgh: Banner of Truth, 1971.

Murray, Stuart. *The Naked Anabaptist: The Bare Essentials of a Radical Faith*. Scottdale, PA: Herald, 2010.

Naish, John. *Enough: Breaking Free from the World of More*. London: Hodder and Stoughton, 2008.

Nash, James A. *Loving Nature: Ecological Integrity and Christian Responsibility*. Nashville: Abingdon, 1991.

Nash, Roderick. *The Rights of Nature: A History of Environmental Ethics*. Madison, WI: University of Wisconsin Press, 1989.

———. *Wilderness and the American Mind*. New Haven: Yale University Press, 1967.

Neilsen, Jan T. *Adam and Christ in the Theology of Irenaeus of Lyons: An Examination of the Function of the Adam-Christ Typology in the Adversus Haereses of Irenaeus, against the Background of the Gnosticism of His Time*. Assen: Van Gorcum, 1968.

Neville, Gwen Kennedy, and John H. Westerhoff, III. *Learning through Liturgy*. New York: Seabury, 1978.

Newbigin, Lesslie. *The Light Has Come: An Exposition of the Fourth Gospel*. Grand Rapids: Eerdmans, 1982.

Novak, Michael. *The Spirit of Democratic Capitalism*. New York: Simon and Schuster, 1982.
Oden, Thomas. "General Introduction." In *Ancient Christian Commentary on Scripture* 1, "Genesis 1–11," edited by Andrew Louth. Downers Grove: InterVarsity, 2001.
Ogliari, Donato. "Tempus Monasticum: Reflections on the Architecture of Time in the Rule of Saint Benedict." *American Benedictine Review* 59 (2008) 35–52.
Olsen, Scott. *The Golden Section: Nature's Greatest Secret*. New York: Walker, 2006.
Ovitt, George, Jr. *The Restoration of Perfection: Labor and Technology in Medieval Culture*. New Brunswick: Rutgers University Press, 1987.
Page, Ruth. "The Fellowship of All Creation." In *Environmental Stewardship: Critical Perspectives, Past and Present*, edited by R. J. Berry, 97–105.London: T. & T. Clark, 2006.
Palmer, Clare. "Stewardship: A Case Study in Environmental Ethics." In *Environmental Stewardship: Critical Perspectives, Past and Present*, edited by R. J. Berry, 63–75. London: T. & T. Clark, 2006.
Pannenberg, Wolfhart. *Jesus: God and Man*. Translated by Lewis L. Wilkins and Duane A. Priebe. London: SCM, 1968.
Park, Geoff. *Ngā Uruora: The Groves of Life; Ecology and History in a New Zealand Landscape*. Wellington: Victoria University Press, 1995.
Passmore, John. *Man's Responsibility for Nature*. London: Duckworth, 1974.
Pattemore, Stephen. "The Apocalypse: An Environmental Impact Report." Paper presented at Christianity, Crisis, and Conservation Conference, Auckland University, NZ, Feb 2005. Later published as "Translating the Eschaton: An Environmental Impact Report." *Journal of Biblical Text Research* 17 (2005) 94–107.
Patterson, John. *Exploring Maori Values*. Palmerston North, NZ: Dunmore, 1992.
Pawson, Eric, and Tom Brooking, eds. *Environmental Histories of New Zealand*. Melbourne: Oxford University Press, 2002.
Pelikan, Jaroslav. "Foreword." In *Augustine through the Ages: An Encyclopaedia*, edited by Allan Fitzgerald. Grand Rapids: Eerdmans, 1999.
———, ed. *Luther's Works*. Vol. 1, "Lectures on Genesis." St. Louis: Concordia, 1958.
Pettersen, Alvyn. *Athanasius and the Human Body*. Bristol: Bristol, 1990.
Platt, Colin. *The Monastic Grange in Medieval England: A Reassessment*. London: Macmillan, 1969.
Pollan, Michael. *The Omnivore's Dilemma: A Natural History of Four Meals*. London: Bloomsbury, 2006.
Ponting, Clive. *A Green History of the World: The Environment and the Collapse of Great Civilisations*. Harmondsworth: Penguin, 1991.
Prance, Ghillean T. "Thoughts on the Sustainability of the Non-human World." In *When Enough is Enough: A Christian Framework for Environmental Sustainability*, edited by R. J. Berry, 69–78. Nottingham: Apollos, 2007.
Quasten, Johannes. *Patrology*. Vol. 3. Utrect: Spectrum, 1960.
Rae, Murray. "The Testimony of Works in the Christology of John's Gospel." In *The Gospel of John and Christian Theology*, edited by Richard Bauckham and Carl Mosser. Grand Rapids: Eerdmans, 2008.
Rasmussen, Larry. "Symbols to Live By." In *Environmental Stewardship: Critical Perspectives, Past and Present*, edited by R.J Berry, 174–84. London: T. & T. Clark, 2006.
Reich, Charles A. *The Greening of America*. London: Allen Lane, 1971.

Reumann, John. "Intoduction." In *Man and Nature in the New Testament: Some Reflections on Biblical Ecology*, by C. F. D. Moule. Philadelphia: Fortress, 1967.
Ridderbos, Herman. *The Gospel of John: A Theological Commentary*. Translated by John Vriend. Grand Rapids: Eerdmans, 1997.
Roberts, Mere, et al. "Kaitiakitanga: Maori Perspectives on Conservation." *Pacific Conservation Biology* 2 (1995) 7–20.
Roszak, Theodore. *The Making of a Counter Culture: Reflections on the Technocratic Society and Its Youthful Opposition*. New York: Doubleday, 1969.
Ruby, Edwards, et al. "Microbiology. We Get by with a Little Help from Our (Little) Friends." *Science* 303 (2004) 1305–7.
Ruether, Rosemary Radford. *Gaia and God: An Ecofeminist Theology of Earth Healing*. San Francisco: Harper, 1992.
Russell, Bertrand. *A History of Western Philosophy and its Connection with Political and Social Circumstances from the Earliest Times to the Present Day*. London: Allen and Unwin, 1961.
Rutba House, ed. *School(s) for Conversion: 12 Marks of a New Monasticism*. Eugene, OR: Cascade, 2005.
Sabourin, Leopold. *Priesthood: A Comparative Study*. Leiden: Brill, 1973.
Sacks, Jonathan. "Morals and Markets." *Cutting Edge* 56 (2002) 41–47.
Salisbury, Joyce E. *The Beast Within: Animals in the Middle Ages*. New York: Routledge, 1994.
Santmire, Paul. *Brother Earth: Nature, God, and Ecology in Time of Crisis*. New York: Thomas Nelson, 1970.
———. "Partnership with Nature according to the Scriptures: Beyond the Theology of Stewardship." In *Environmental Stewardship: Critical Perspectives, Past and Present*, edited by R. J. Berry, 253–72. London: T. & T. Clark, 2006.
———. *The Travail of Nature: The Ambiguous Ecological Promise of Christian Theology*. Philadelphia: Fortress, 1985.
Sarna, Nahum M. *The JPS Torah Commentary: Genesis*. Philadelphia: Jewish Publication Society, 1989.
Scafi, Allessandro. *Mapping Paradise: A History of Heaven on Earth*. Chicago: University of Chicago Press, 2006.
Schaeffer, Francis A. *Pollution and the Death of Man: The Christian View of Ecology*. Wheaton, IL: Tyndale, 1970.
Schottroff, Luise. "The Creation Narrative: Genesis 1:1–2:4a." In *A Feminist Companion to Genesis*, edited by Athalya Brenner, 24–38. Sheffield: Sheffield Academic, 1993.
Scully, Matthew. *Dominion: The Power of Man, the Suffering of Animals, and the Call to Mercy*. New York: Saint Martin's, 2002.
Sharp, Andrew, ed. *The Journal of Jacob Roggeveen*. Oxford: Clarendon, 1970.
Short, Ernest. *A History of Religious Architecture*. London: Eyre and Spottiswoode, 1951.
Silvas, Anna M. *The Asketikon of Saint Basil the Great*. Oxford: Oxford University Press, 2005.
Simkins, Ronald A. *Creator and Creation: Nature in the Worldview of Ancient Israel*. Peabody, MA: Hendrickson, 1994.
Singer, Peter. *Animal Liberation*. New York: Harper Collins, 1975.
Sittler, Joseph. "A Theology for the Earth." In *Environmental Stewardship: Critical Perspectives, Past and Present*, edited by R. J. Berry, 51–55. London: T. & T. Clark, 2006.

Skinner, John. *A Critical and Exegetical Commentary on Genesis.* 2nd ed. International Critical Commentary. Edinburgh: T. & T. Clark, 1930.

Smetana, Cyril. "Augustinian Canons." In *Dictionary of the Middle Ages* 1, edited by Joseph R. Strayer. New York: Scribner, 1982.

———. "Augustinian Friars." In *Dictionary of the Middle Ages* 1, edited by Joseph R. Strayer. New York: Scribner, 1982.

Smith, James K. A. *Desiring the Kingdom: Worship, Worldview, and Cultural Formation.* Grand Rapids: Baker, 2009.

Smith, Pamela. *What Are They Saying about Environmental Ethics?* New York: Paulist, 1997.

Sonnlechner, Christoph. "The Establishment of New Units of Production in Carolingian Times: Making Early Medieval Sources Relevant for Environmental History." *Viator* 35 (2004) 21–48.

Southgate, Christopher. "Stewardship and Its Competitors: A Spectrum of Relationships between Humans and the Non-Human Creation." In *Environmental Stewardship: Critical Perspectives, Past and Present*, edited by R. J. Berry, 185–95. London: T. & T. Clark, 2006.

Steiner, Gary. *Anthropocentrism and Its Discontents: Animals and Their Moral Status in the History of Western Philosophy.* Pittsburgh: University of Pittsburgh Press, 2005.

Steinmetz, David C. "The Superiority of Pre-Critical Exegesis." In Fowl, *Theological Interpretation*, 26–38. Oxford: Blackwell, 1997.

Stinner, Deborah H., et al. "Forage Legumes and Cultural Sustainability: Lessons from History." *Agriculture, Ecosystems and Environment*, 40, Elsevier Science Publishers B.V., Amsterdam (1992) 233–48.

Stott, John, ed. *The Year 2000 AD.* Basingstoke: Marshall Morgan and Scott, 1983.

Stubbs, David. "The Temple and the Protestant Eucharistic Imagination." Open lecture, University of Otago, May 2010.

Stump, Eleonore, and Norman Kretzmann. *The Cambridge Companion to Augustine.* Cambridge: Cambridge University Press, 2001.

Sutera, Judith. "Stewardship and the Kingdom in RB 31–33." *American Benedictine Review* 41 (1990) 348–56.

Swanson, Robert N., ed. *The Use and Abuse of Time in Christian History.* Studies in Church History 37. Woodbridge, UK: Boydell, 2002.

Taft, Robert F. *The Liturgy of the Hours in East and West: The Origins of the Divine Office and Its Meaning for Today.* Collegeville, MN: Liturgical, 1986.

Tearfund. "Help Eradicate a Nasty Parasite." *Newsletter*, July 2009.

Temple, William. *Readings in St. John's Gospel.* London: Macmillan, 1952.

Thompson, Michael B. "The Holy Internet: Communication between Churches in the First Christian Generation." In *The Gospels for All Christians*, edited by Richard Bauckham, 24–38. Grand Rapids: Eerdmans, 1998.

Torrance, Thomas F. *The Mediation of Christ.* Grand Rapids: Eerdmanns, 1983.

———. *Royal Priesthood.* Scottish Journal of Theology Occasional Papers 3. Edinburgh: Oliver and Boyd, 1955.

———. *Space, Time and Resurrection.* Edinburgh: T. & T. Clark, 1998.

Traherne, Thomas. *Centuries of Meditations.* London: Private, 1908.

Turner, Harold W. *Frames of Mind: A Public Philosophy for Religion and Cultures.* Auckland: DeepSight Trust, 2001.

———. *The Roots of Science: An Investigative Journey through the World's Religions.* Auckland: DeepSight Trust, 1998.
Van Bath, Slicher. *The Agrarian History of Western Europe: A.D. 500–1850.* Translated by Olive Ordish. London: Edward Arnold, 1963.
Van Bavel, Tarsicius. "The Creator and the Integrity of Creation in the Fathers of the Church, Especially in Saint Augustine." *Augustinian Studies* 21 (1990) 1–33.
Verduin, Leonard. *The Reformers and Their Stepchildren.* Grand Rapids: Eerdmans, 1964.
Verney, Stephen. *Water into Wine: an Introduction to John's Gospel.* London: Darton, Longman and Todd, 1995.
von Galli, Mario. *Living Our Future: Francis of Assisi and the Church Tomorrow.* Translated by Maureen Sullivan and John Drury. Chicago: Franciscan Herald, 1972.
von Rad, Gerhard. *Genesis: A Commentary.* London: SCM, 1963.
Wallace-Hadrill, John M. *The Barbarian West 400–1000.* London: Hutchinson, 1966.
Ward, Benedicta, trans. *The Sayings of the Desert Fathers.* London: Mowbrays, 1975.
Ward, Keith. "Cosmos and Kenosis." In *The Work of Love: Creation as Kenosis*, edited by John Polkinghorne, 152–66. Cambridge, UK: Eerdmans, 2001.
Westermann, Claus. *Genesis 1–11: A Commentary.* Minneapolis: Augsburg, 1984.
———. *Genesis: A Practical Commentary.* Translated by David E. Green. Grand Rapids: Eerdmans, 1987.
White, Carolinne. *The Rule of Benedict.* London: Penguin, 2008
White, Lynn, Jr. "The Historical Roots of Our Ecologic Crisis." *Science* 155 (1967) 1203–7.
———. *Medieval Religion and Technology: Collected Essays.* Berkeley: University of California Press, 1978.
———. *Medieval Technology and Social Change.* Oxford: Oxford University Press, 1962.
Whitney, Elspeth. "Lynn White, Ecotheology, and History." *Environmental Ethics* 15 (1993) 151–69.
Wibberley, John. "A Framework for Sustainable Agriculture." In *When Enough is Enough: A Christian Framework for Environmental Sustainability*, edited by R. J. Berry, 125–36. Nottingham: Apollos, 2007.
Wilkinson, Loren, ed. *Earthkeeping: Christian Stewardship of Natural Resources.* Grand Rapids: Eerdmans, 1980.
Wilkinson, Richard, and Kate Pickett. *The Spirit Level: Why More Equal Societies Almost Always Do Better.* London: Allen Lane, 2009.
Williams, Rowan D. "'Good for Nothing'? Augustine on Creation." *Augustinian Studies* 25 (1994) 9–24.
Wingren, Gustaf. *Man and the Incarnation: A Study in the Biblical Theology of Irenaeus.* Translated by Ross Mackenzie. Eugene, OR: Wipf & Stock, 2004.
Wirzba, Norman. "Mark 10: Care for the Plot of God's Earth Given to Us along with Support of Our Local Economies." In *School(s) for Conversion: 12 Marks of a New Monasticism*, edited by The Rutba House, 137–48. Eugene, OR: Cascade, 2005.
Witherington, Ben. *The Christology of Jesus.* Minneapolis: Augsburg Fortress, 1990.
Workman, Herbert B. *The Evolution of the Monastic Ideal.* 2nd ed. London: Epworth, 1927.
Wright, N. T. *Jesus and the Victory of God.* Minneapolis: Fortress, 1996.

Wynne, Graeme. "Destruction under the Guise of Improvement? The Forest, 1840–1920." In *Environmental Histories of New Zealand*, edited by Eric Pawson and Tom Brooking, 100–16. Melbourne: Oxford University Press, 2002.

Yule, Robert M. "Orthodox Spirituality: An Outline of Its Characteristic Features." *Latimer* 73 (1981) 12–21.

Zachman, Randall. "Calvin's Ecology." Public lecture delivered at Knox Presbyterian Church, Dunedin, August 2009.

Zenner, Ambrose. "Saint Benedict's Peace." *American Benedictine Review* 5 (1954) 45–73.

Zizioulas, John D. "Preserving God's Creation: Three Lectures on Theology and Ecology." *King's Theological Review* 12:1 (1989) 1–5.

———. "Preserving God's Creation: Three Lectures on Theology and Ecology." *King's Theological Review* 12:2 (1989) 41–45.

———. "Preserving God's Creation: Three Lectures on Theology and Ecology." *King's Theological Review* 13 (1990) 1–5.

———. "Priest of Creation." In *Environmental Stewardship: Critical Perspectives, Past and Present*, edited by R. J. Berry, 273–90. London: T. & T. Clark, 2006.

Zumkeller, Adolar. *Augustine's Ideal of the Religious Life*. New York: Fordham University Press, 1986.

Author/Name Index

Adams, Robert M., 34
Aelfric, 196
Alexander, Samuel, 261
Anderson, Athol, 31, 32
Anderson, Bernard, 42, 45–47, 36, 37, 40, 262
Arnold, Ellen F., 179, 187, 191, 192
Athanasius, 2, 69–88, 104, 132, 134, 136, 138, 140, 146, 203, 204, 205, 209, 254, 263
Attfield, Robin, 243
Augustine of Hippo, 2, 26, 80, 83, 90–132, 134, 143, 146, 147, 160, 164, 169, 175, 180, 182, 183, 195, 198, 205, 206, 209, 221, 224, 237, 255, 259, 263, 264, 272, 274, 275, 285, 286
Bader-Saye, Scott, 238–39, 244
Bahn, Paul, 29–31, 35
Ball, Philip, 215, 216
Banks, Robert, 282
Barbour, Ian, 18
Barr, James, 19, 20, 21
Barrett, C. K., 238
Barth, Karl, 19, 248
Basil the Great (a.k.a. of Caesarea), 2, 133, 142, 147, 148–65, 169, 170, 172, 179, 180, 206, 219, 221, 254, 255, 257, 276

Bath, Slicher Van, 190
Bauckham, Richard, 39, 45, 46, 210, 215, 216, 219, 233
Bavel, Tarsicius Van, 110, 114–15, 116
Beattie, James, 8, 9
Bede, Venerable, 25, 91, 164, 173–76, 178–82, 191, 194–96, 198, 206, 207, 236, 255
Begbie, Jeremy, 257, 258
Behr, John, 54, 55, 56, 57, 61, 66, 67, 68
Benedict of Aniane, 188
Benedict of Nursia, 16, 133, 141, 143, 146, 148, 150, 164, 165–98, 206, 220, 225, 236, 292
Bergmann, Sigurd, 258, 265
Berkman, John, 141, 142, 162
Berman, Constance Hoffman, 189, 190
Bernard of Clairvaux, 188
Berno, Abbot, 179
Berry, R. J., 11, 23, 253, 263, 273
Berry, Wendell, 255, 256
Birch, Bruce C., 37
Bischoff, Bernhard, 165, 193, 194
Biscop, Benedict, 193
Black, John, 21, 32, 243
Blair, Ian, 261
Böckmann, Aquinata, 174, 185

Boersema, Jan J., 222, 223
Boff, Leonardo, 223, 224, 234, 257
Bonhoeffer, Dietrich, 264
Bouma-Prediger, Steve, 246, 273, 287, 288
Boyle, Robert, 217
Bratton, Susan Power, 26
Braungart, Michael, 296, 297
Brenner, Athalya, 23
Brett, Mark G., 24, 262, 289
Brooking, Tom, 9
Brown, Peter, 90, 91, 92, 93, 94, 95, 120, 122, 123, 167
Brown, Raymond, 237, 262
Brueggemann, Walter, 6, 59, 260, 264, 265, 278
Brunner, Emil, 67
Bruno, Giordano, 210, 215
Bryson, Bill, 303, 305
Burton-Christie, Douglas, 143, 144
Butler Bass, Diana, 150, 160
Butler, Cuthbert, 133, 146, 165, 166, 167

Cahill, Thomas, 183, 292
Caird, G. B., 14
Calvin, John, 212–14, 232, 243, 249, 257, 285
Carlson, Carole C., 273
Carson, D. A., 245
Cassian, John, 170, 206
Cavanaugh, William T., 121, 259, 260, 265, 286, 287
Charlemagne, 182
Chesterton, G. K., 223
Chryssavgis, John, 136, 137, 138, 143, 156, 158
Clouse, R. G., 145, 146
Cohen, Jeremy, 191
Countryman, Louis William, 248, 250, 251, 252, 253
Cowan, James, 83
Crouch, Andy, 261, 274
Cumberland, Kenneth B., 32
Cunningham, Lawrence, 223
Cuthbert, Saint, 207

Daley, Brian E., 124, 125

Daly, Herman, 294
Davey, Cyril J., 207
Davidson, Ivor, 90, 94, 124, 132, 134, 140, 141, 146, 166, 175, 206
Davies, D. R., 11
Davies, W. D., 264, 265, 282
de Steiguer, J. Edward, 5, 6, 8, 266
De Vogue, Adalbert, 171, 185, 186
de Waal, Esther, 169, 170, 171, 183, 184, 185
Deane-Drummond, Celia, 24, 26
Decarreaux, Jean, 140
Diamond, Jared, 28
Djupe, Paul A., 16
Dubos, Rene, 16, 185, 187, 225, 226, 243, 256
Duby, Georges, 177, 178, 189, 190
Dunn, James D. G., 235, 236, 238, 247, 268, 269, 279, 280, 281, 282
Dunn, Marilyn, 132, 133, 134, 135, 136, 140, 141, 142, 146, 147, 148, 149, 150, 168, 169, 187, 188
Dyer, Gwynne, 261

Edmondson, Stephen, 249
Edwin, King, 206
Ehrlich, Anne H., 33, 34
Ehrlich, Paul R., 33, 34
Emerson, Ralph Waldo, 6, 17
Emmelia, 149

Farrow, Douglas, 60
Fedwick, Paul Jonathan, 149
Feuerbach, Ludwig, 233
Finlay, Graeme, 263
Flannery, Tim, 7, 275, 293, 294
Flenley, John, 29, 30, 31, 35
Florovsky, Georges, 154, 155
Ford, David, 244
Foster, Richard, 256–57, 259, 286, 287, 288
Fowl, Stephen E., 24, 25
Francis of Assisi, 3, 12, 13, 16, 18, 153, 199, 200, 205, 220, 221–27, 229
Frend, W. H. C., 93
Fumagalli, Vito, 165, 167, 168, 171, 175, 176, 177, 178, 182, 191, 192, 199

Galli, Mario von, 223
Galvin, Ray, 7, 19
Gerald of Wales, 183
Gies, Frances, 179, 185, 187, 198, 199, 200, 201
Gies, Joseph, 179, 185, 187, 198, 199, 200, 201
Ginzberg, Louis, 45, 46
Glacken, Clarence, 9, 10, 11
Goodwin, Ruth, 256
Gorman, Michael J., 236, 242
Gorringe, Tim, 264
Gould, Graham, 134, 135, 144, 146
Grant, Robert M., 48, 49, 51, 65
Gregorios, Paulos, 22, 202, 206, 209, 210, 249, 271, 295
Gregory of Nyssa, 149, 158, 164, 202
Gunton, Colin E., 48, 60, 92, 100, 101, 211, 216, 234, 236, 237, 245, 246, 257, 258, 263, 268, 274
Guthrie-Smith, W. H., 9

Habel, Norman C., 24
Hadrian, Abbot, 193
Hall, Douglas John, 23, 26-27
Hammond, Clare, 294
Harris, Peter,, 16, 261, 274
Harrison, Carol, 93, 94, 95, 101, 115, 116, 117, 120, 121, 122, 127
Harrison, Peter, 16, 26, 63, 112, 211
Hartranft, Chester D., 93
Hauerwas, Stanley, 287
Hays, Richard B., 25, 236, 240, 280, 284
Henry, Matthew, 217-18, 285-86
Hodson, Margot R., 256
Huber, Robert V., 38, 44
Hunt, Patrick Kieran, 16
Hunt, Terry L., 30, 31

Irenaeus of Lyons, 2, 16, 27, 48-68, 69, 100, 101, 200, 203, 232, 237, 263, 274

Jacobsen, Thorkild, 33, 34
Jenkins, Willis, 12, 255, 256
Jenson, Robert W., 237, 251
Jeremias, Joachim, 237, 288
Jerris, Randon, 175-176
Jónsson, Gunnlauger A., 36

Kaiser, Christopher B., 148, 164-65
Kant, Immanuel, 219
Keller, Catherine, 23
Kendall, Calvin, 164, 174
Keselópoulos, Anéstis G., 207
Kirch, Patrick V., 30, 31
Kirschenmann, Fred, 255
Kirschenmann, Janet, 255
Kleber, Albert, 172-173
Knight, Douglas, 39, 40, 43, 45, 264, 266, 281
Knight, George A. F., 36, 230, 250
Knowles, Dom David, 167-68, 169, 172, 173, 186, 188, 190
Kretzmann, Norman, 90
Kustas, George L., 150, 156

LaCugna, Catherine Mowry, 124
Lapidge, Michael, 165, 193, 194
Lawless, George, 113, 143, 147
Lawrence, C. H., 164, 167, 170, 179, 188, 190
Leach, William, 265
Lebow, Victor, 260
Lenin, Vladimir, 219
Leopold, Aldo, 5, 6
Levenson, Jon D., 36, 37
Lilburne, Geoffrey R., 265
Lindsey, Hal, 273
Lobell, David B., 294
Lohfink, Norbert, 36, 38, 44, 60-61
Louth, Andrew, 25, 26, 123
Lovelock, James, 243, 244, 274
Lowdermilk, Walter, 11
Lowery, Richard H., 278, 279, 282, 283, 284, 290-92
Lutz, Paul E., 18

Macrina, 149, 150, 160
Marsh, George Perkins, 7, 8, 9, 11
Marsh, John, 237
Marx, Karl, 233
Matthews, Gareth B., 90
Maximus the Confessor, Saint, 234

McDonough, William, 296, 297
McFague, Sallie, 23
McGinn, Bernard, 185, 186
McGrath, Alister E., 90, 200, 204, 216, 219, 220, 233, 234, 240, 257, 292–93
McHarg, Ian L., 15
McKay, Heather A., 38, 277, 278, 285
McKibben, Bill, 293
Mead, Hirini Moko, 35
Michaels, J. Ramsey, 238
Middleton, Richard, 24, 247, 248
  critiqued, 248, 250, 252
Miller, Stephen M., 38, 44
Moltmann, Jürgen, 40, 41, 43, 44, 231, 232, 233, 243, 278
Montefiore, Hugh, 14
Marduk, 33
Morgan, Faith, 296
Morris, Leon, 237, 242
Moule, C. F. D., 12, 13–14, 81, 276
Muir, John, 6, 7, 11
Murray, Iain H., 272
Murray, Stuart, 214, 215, 300

Naish, John, 260, 286, 287
Nash, James, 6, 242–243
Nash, Roderick, 5, 6, 7, 11, 14, 16, 19
Neilsen, Jan T., 49, 50, 65
Neville, Gwen Kennedy, 38
Newbigin, Lesslie, 240–41
Novak, Michael, 301

Oden, Thomas, 25
Ogliari, Donato, 174
Olsen, Scott, 255
Olson, Carolyn, 255
Olson, Larry, 255
Ovid, 195
Ovitt, George, Jr., 186, 201, 203, 209

Page, Ruth, 110, 180
Palmer, Clare, 242
Pandora, 219
Pannenberg, Wolfhart, 235, 245, 268
Park, Geoff, 7
Passmore, John, 213, 217
Pattemore, Stephen, 273

Patterson, John, 35
Paul the Deacon, 182
Pawson, Eric, 9
Pelagius, 93, 94, 206
Pelikan, Jaroslav, 90, 211, 212
Penrose, Roger, 292
Pettersen, Alvyn, 75–76, 79, 84
Pickett, Kate, 286, 295
Platt, Colin, 188–189
Polanyi, Michael, 219
Pollan, Michael, 255, 257, 296
Ponting, Clive, 16, 61
Prance, Ghillean T., 285
Prometheus, 215, 216, 219, 292
Quasten, Johannes, 69–70

Rad, Gerhard von,, 19, 42, 43, 46
Rae, Murray,, 237–38, 262, 241, 262, 270–71
Rasmussen, Larry, 42
Rees, Sir Martin, 292
Reich, Charles A., 15
Remacle, Saint, 191
Reumann, John, 12, 13
Ridderbos, Herman, 237, 238, 242
Roberts, Mere, 35
Roggeveen, Jacob, 30
Roszak, Theodore, 15
Ruether, Rosemary Radford, 23
Russell, Bertrand,, 90
Rutba House, 300

Sabourin, Leopold, 240, 248
Sacks, Jonathan, 283, 284–85, 290, 291, 292
Salisbury, Joyce E., 180, 181, 182, 183
Santmire, Paul, 6, 16, 17, 18, 19, 21, 22, 23, 26, 37, 46, 214
Sarna, Nahum M., 44
Schaeffer, Francis A., 16–17
Schottroff, Luise, 23, 24, 37, 59
Scully, Matthew, 158–159, 216, 221, 226, 257, 276
Sharp, Andrew, 30
Short, Ernest, 192
Silvas, Anna M., 134, 145, 147, 148, 149, 150, 151, 156
Simkins, Ronald A., 44, 45

Singer, Peter, 25
Singh, Sadhu Sundar, 207
Sittler, Joseph, 11, 12, 19
Skinner, John, 19
Smetana, Cyril, 128
Smith, James K. A., 38
Smith, Pamela, 204, 208
Sonnlechner, Christoph, 185, 187
Southgate, Christopher, 118
Stalin, Joseph, 219
Steigeur, Eduard de, 5, 6, 8, 166
Steiner, Gary, 25
Stenhouse, John, 8, 9
Stinner, Deborah H., 214
Stubbs, David, 184
Stump, Eleonore, 90
Sutera, Judith, 184

Taft, Robert F., 143
TEARFund, 276
Temple, William, 219, 239-40
Theodore of Tarsus, 193
Thomas a Kempis, 217
Thompson, Michael B., 49
Thompson, Richard, 255
Thomson, Robert, 73, 74, 77, 78
Thoreau, Henry David, 6, 17
Torrance, Thomas F., 82, 83, 248, 251, 253, 264, 265, 269-70
Travers, William, 9
Turner, Harold, 28, 154, 165, 203, 204, 210, 211, 215, 219, 255, 292

VanderKam, James, 277
Verduin, Leonard, 214
Verney, Stephen, 238

Wallace-Hadrill, John M., 164
Ward, Benedicta, 134, 135, 136, 137, 138, 139, 140, 141, 142, 143, 144, 145, 147, 174

Ward, Keith, 244, 247, 249, 274
Westerhoff, John H., III, 38
Westermann, Claus, 19, 20, 37, 38, 39, 41, 42, 43, 46, 47, 262
White, Carolinne, 141, 148, 166-73, 184-86
White, Lynn, Jr., 1-5, 7, 10, 11, 14-21, 25-27, 28-29, 36, 39, 46, 49, 50, 58, 63, 69, 85, 86, 89, 91, 97, 108, 112, 117, 128, 139, 185, 186, 187, 193, 199-203, 205, 207-10, 219-23, 226, 228-30, 233, 257, 297, 298
Whitney, Elspeth, 12, 15, 16, 19
Wibberley, John, 256
Wilkinson, Loren, 21, 22, 26, 286, 295
Wilkinson, Richard, 286, 295
William of Aquitaine, 179
Williams, Rowan D., 102, 104, 110
Wingren, Gustaf, 55, 56, 57, 61
Wirzba, Norman, 237
Witherington, Ben, 282
Workman, Herbert B., 132, 133, 134, 135, 136, 137, 140, 142, 145-46, 150, 166, 167, 168, 169, 184-85, 186, 190, 197-98
Wright, N. T., 268-69, 272, 282-83, 284
Wurst, Shirley, 24

Yule, Robert M., 206

Zachman, Randall, 213
Zenner, Ambrose, 171
Zizioulas, John D., 64, 118, 119, 125, 206, 233-34, 239, 250, 251, 252, 253, 257, 263, 289, 299
Zumkeller, Adolar, 116, 128

Subject Index

Africa
    and Donatism, 92–93
    and conservation agriculture, 256, 296
    and climate change, 293
agriculture/gardening, 8–9, 22, 34, 114–16, 128, 138–39, 162–63, 178–79, 185–90, 206, 213–14, 218, 255–256, 266, 289, 293, 296
    and contemplative 'listening', 130, 183–84, 255, 298
    conservation agriculture / "Farming God's Way", 255–56
    declining crop yields, 30, 34, 294
    industrialized agricultural critiqued, 13, 256, 294–96
Anabaptists (see also Agriculture), 214, 243
angels, 5, 52, 54, 61, 105–8, 130, 138, 153, 194
animals
    and peaceable relations, 58, 207
    as food / vegetarianism, 44, 142
    commonalities with and distinctions from human beings, 42, 67, 262–63
    provision for in Genesis, and Sabbath, 20, 42, 46
    worthy of ethical consideration / as moral agents, 13, 46–47, 222, 262
Animist/Animism (see also Divinization), 1, 2, 107, 200, 256
Anthropocene, 275
Apocalyptic/apocalypse, 208, 269, 273
Arius/Arianism, 70, 149, 154, 170

"Arts" and Architecture, 54, 247, 255–58
Ascetism/Ascetics/Ascetic, 61, 93, 132, 135, 142, 149
as positive engagement, 56, 83, 85, 112, 135, 137, 138, 140, 143, 147, 151, 162–163, 169–70, 171, 206, 223

Babylon/Babylonia / Babylonian, 23, 33, 36–37, 43, 45, 129, 203
Babylonian exile, 36–37, 43, 59, 230, 291
Bacon, Francis, 17, 215
    contribution to secularization, 215–16, 219, 227
    desacralization, 219
    optimistic about human use of power, 216
    science to serve human dominion / healing for creation, 215, 233
Bacon, Francis (artist), 258
Benedict of Nursia. *See* Monasticism
bio-diversity, 226, 265, 275

Calvin College (Grand Rapids, MI, USA), 21–22
Christological interpretation, 12, 15, 27, 37, 47
    central in patristic exegesis, 25, 84, 100, 119, 144, 195, 231
    neglected, 10, 247
    (see also Interpretation)

SUBJECT INDEX

Christology / Christological, 3, 27, 100, 101, 227, 228, 245, 249, 282, 289, 298, 299
  and human dominion, 230–66, 246, 266, 286, 297, 298
  and Jesus' resurrection, 235, 236, 267, 280
  and Sabbath/sanctuary, 280, 284, 287, 300, 301
  and science, 257
  and servanthood, 242, 247, 257
climate/weather, 275, 293–94
community
  as sign of hope/witness, 197, 207, 208, 272, 277, 284, 288, 295
  Christian community, 3, 56, 128–29, 252, 268, 272, 294
  Earth community, 24, 233, 239, 299, 301
  of Jewish faith, 40, 277, 283, 290, 300
  of the Trinity, 231–32, 233
  the body itself a community, 263 (*see also* Monasticism)
consumerist/consumerism (*see also* economics; debt), 77, 85, 121, 129, 218, 223, 257, 259, 260, 261, 271, 285, 298
contemplation/contemplative life, 75–76, 80, 85, 109, 127–29, 169, 170, 185, 205–6, 207, 229, 257, 261, 285, 286, 298, 300
  engaging creation, 23, 77, 83, 84, 88, 115, 117, 118, 128, 197, 203, 213, 254–55, 257, 259, 260, 266
  Platonic/Neo-Platonic conceptions, 123–24
covenant (*see also* Priesthood)
  and human dominion, 181
  and human failure, 26, 217
  and Sabbath, 40, 281
  New covenant and Jesus' resurrection, 268
  with Abraham, 280,
  with creation, 17, 248, 262
creation *ex-nihilo*, 17, 98, 105, 114, 121, 130, 201, 226, 251
  critiqued, 1, 23

expressing servant nature of God, 244
Cuba, 295

dance/*Perichoresis* (*see also* Trinitarianism), 204, 238–39, 249
debt/interest (*see also* Consumerism; Economics), 40, 250, 290, 291
Deep Green/Deep Ecology, 222, 266
deicide, 233
divinization/de-divinization/divinized/de-divinized, 2, 7, 27, 28, 35, 36, 61, 64, 67, 69, 72, 75, 86, 87, 108, 130, 154, 202, 203, 249
  as menace, 33, 72–73, 108, 176–77, 182, 202–3
divinized humanity, 210, 233

earth as 'mother', 154, 225
Earth Bible/eco justice principles, 24
Easter Island/*Rapanui*, 29–30, 35
  Moai, 29
economics (*see also* Consumerism; Debt), 121, 216, 218, 224, 260, 265, 287, 290, 292, 295, 299
Enlightenment/Renaissance/Eighteenth Century, 3, 61, 85, 210, 216, 219, 220, 229, 232–34, 252, 275
"Enuma Elish" (*see also* Babylon), 33
environment, environmental, 1, 2, 4, 5, 7, 9, 15, 28, 29, 31, 32, 34, 35, 36, 49, 55, 68, 79, 108, 165, 166, 168, 182, 186, 190, 192, 203, 204, 207, 226, 228, 229, 243, 256, 258, 261, 265, 272, 276, 293, 294, 296, 298, 299
environmentalists, -ism, -theology, 8, 9, 10, 11, 14, 35, 49, 55, 77, 94, 168, 223, 225, 256, 258, 261, 273, 274, 297
eschatology/eschatological
  and Eucharist/eucharistic, 145–46, 156, 238, 288
  (*see also* current realization, and modelling the Kingdom)
  and Jesus' resurrection, 268, 269, 271

and meatless cuisine, 142
and Sabbath, 40–41, 121–22, 130, 279, 281, 284
Christological aspects, 40, 60, 67, 230, 253, 279, 284
current realization (*see also* eucharist and the Kingdom), 127, 145, 184, 207, 214, 269, 271, 288, 300
implications for provisionality of knowledge, 60, 272
in Anabaptist communities, 214
in Augustine, 121–22, 124, 127, 130
in Basil of Caesarea, 156
in Benedict, 184
in Desert monasticism, 143, 145, 146
in Irenaeus, 48, 60, 67
modelling the Kingdom (*see also* current realization, and eucharist), 39
neglected interest, 10
potential dangers, 209, 273

feminist/feminism, 23–24
forests
and Apollo, grove of, 166, 175
and climate change, 293
and conflicted attitudes, 8, 175, 176–77
and conservation, 9, 189, 276
in Biblical vision, 262
in European lands, 176, 177–78
utilitarian use, 7, 179, 189
Francis of Assisi, 3, 12, 13, 18, 133, 200, 205, 220, 221–23, 224–25, 227, 243
idealized by White, 16, 199, 220–21, 229

Gnostic/Gnosticism, 202, 272, 295
see Irenaeus, 49–52, 54, 60, 65
see Augustine/Manichaeism, 92
see Desert monasticism, 135–37
see Benedict, 170
Guardianship/*Kaitiakitanga*/*Rahui* (*see also* New Zealand; Human Dominion as "caretaking" / governance/stewardship), 35, 46, 107, 114, 115, 211, 244
guardian spirits, 203
contested by Christ, 265

Holy Spirit, 3, 70, 89, 109, 114, 164, 174, 194
active in Creation, 62, 65, 88, 97–98, 99, 101, 103, 104, 105, 231
as mother, 153, 154
in cosmic dance, 239
in human transformation, 89, 94, 104, 128, 234, 248, 274, 287, 297
in resurrection faith, 234–35, 241, 269–70
one of God's "two hands", 27, 48, 67, 231, 232
human dominion, 14, 19, 63, 112, 57, 208, 266, 298
and Sabbath, 277–97, 300
and science, 89, 188, 209, 257
as "caretaking"/governance/stewardship (*see also* Guardianship/*Kaitiakitanga*/*Rahui*), 21–22, 44, 45, 54–55, 115–16, 130, 139, 162, 180, 185, 187, 195, 197–98, 211, 212–13, 214, 217, 221–22, 225, 231, 242–43, 255–57, 275, 289, 296
as corrupted, 210, 215, 220, 232–33, 257, 273, 293
as "Overlordship", 18, 195, 209, 215
as priestly, 246–54, 270, 299
as relational/contemplative, 43–47, 56, 88, 109–10, 118, 130, 157, 172, 195, 197, 206, 211, 217, 222, 231, 255
as representational, 42, 217, 228, 246, 279, 299
as servanthood, 159, 236–45, 296, 298
critiqued, 1, 2, 4–5, 15, 23, 200, 208, 213, 243
discerned not promoted, 7, 10
expressed in Christ, 66–67, 159, 195–96, 204–5, 230–31, 236–46, 270, 279, 282–84

for healing and peace, 8, 12, 17, 20, 58, 86, 88, 112–13, 159–60, 195, 198, 211, 215
  under restraint, 61–62, 106–7, 112, 156, 159, 175, 181, 217, 226
human subservience, 35
humanity as wondering onlooker, 18, 23, 214
humanity interconnected with/inextricable from creation, 13, 17, 19, 42–43, 67, 86, 88, 111, 113, 118–19, 135, 157, 170–71, 175, 194, 238–39, 247–48, 262–63, 289

image of God/*imago*
  and dominion, 19, 43, 44, 47, 109, 112
  and the arts, 54, 257–58
  as dignifying/affirming, 17, 42–43, 129, 157, 195, 248
  as representational/priestly/personal, 42, 43–44, 47, 57, 76, 193–94, 205, 217, 231, 246–49, 252–53, 299
  as servanthood, 26, 47, 87, 159, 180, 195, 240, 247, 275
  critiqued, 1, 4, 23, 240
  developing / fluid, 59, 63, 109–10, 130, 180, 231, 248, 274
  historical interpretations, 12, 20, 24, 42, 56–57, 110, 212, 232
  in Genesis, 39, 42–47
  in Jesus Christ, 66–67, 78–79, 122, 126, 195–196, 204, 211, 245–246, 248, 253, 299
  In Mesopotamia, 33–34, 37
  on Easter Island/*Rapanui*, 29–30, 35
  related to the *logos* / Word, 75, 76, 109, 195, 254
interpretation, 11, 12, 18–19, 24, 26, 44, 45
  Documentary hypotheses, 36–37, 46
  history of, 2, 44, 110, 182, 193, 198, 211, 234, 272
  in Augustine, 95, 96, 120, 122
  in Basil of Caesarea, 149, 150 152, 155
  in Benedictine monasticisms, 193, 194, 198
  in Desert monasticism, 136, 144
  (*see also* Christological interpretation)

Kingdom of God, 3, 18–19, 22, 235, 276, 294–95, 301
  "is creation healed", 272
  and Jesus' miracles/signs, 14, 267–69, 277–78, 300
  and Sabbath/Jubilee, 278–79, 282–84, 287–88, 295
  anticipated, 44, 241
  in Anabaptists, 214–15
  in Athanasius, 75, 84–85
  in Augustine, 107, 124, 127
  in Irenaeus, 65
  In Monasticism, 133, 142, 146, 147–48, 150, 161, 168, 184
  in New Testament and early Church, 272

Logikos, 53, 261, 266, 275, 297, 298, 299
Logos, The, 79, 84, 245, 249, 255, 270

Mani/Manichaeism/Manichees, 92–93, 95, 96, 97, 98, 100, 102, 103, 114, 130, 136, 137, 257, 295
Marsh, George Perkins, 7, 11
  being quoted in 19th century New Zealand, 9
  critical of paganism and Roman Catholicism, 8
  reviewing human dominion, 7–8
Mesopotamia, 33, 34, 35, 228
mind, 99, 104, 109, 128, 151, 157–58, 207
monasticism, 2, 17, 27, 133, 138
  and contemplation, prayer, worship, 143–45, 158–59, 169–70, 197, 206
  and environmental sustainability, 168, 187

and millenarian hopes/present
    experience, 145–46, 155–56, 168,
    207–8
as new social order, 133, 146,
    149–50, 160–62, 166–68
Cistercians, 188–90
corrupted, 135, 188, 190, 197–99,
    208
creating sacred space, 175–76, 177,
    179
engaging nature/creation, 134–35,
    137, 150–52, 158–59, 181, 189
ignored by White, 16, 26, 200
in Athanasius on Anthony, 87–88,
    132, 134, 136
in Augustine, 117, 128–29, 131,
    132, 146
in Basil of Caesarea, 148–65
in Benedict and Benedictines,
    165–98
in the Desert Fathers and Mothers,
    133–48
missional, 141, 147, 150, 160–61, 168,
    187
"New Monasticism", 56, 300
on time and Sabbath, 157, 165,
    173–75, 197
Pachomius/Pachomian, 140–42,
    146
Protestant, 217, 300
"secular"/lay expressions, 147–148
valuing work and farming, 114–16,
    138–41, 160–63, 183–90, 193
water management / spirituality,
    190–92

New Zealand, 8, 9, 31–32, 188, 200,
    276, 286
    European settlers' use of Biblical
        ideas, 8–9
    Maori impacts, 31–32, 200
    Moa, 31, 32
    Southern fur seal, 31, 32
    tapu, 35
    Wairau Bar and Waitaki River
        Mouth, 32
Nineveh, 33

pagan/paganism (*see also* Animist/
    animism), 1, 8, 19, 25, 38, 52, 64,
    71, 76, 86, 87, 104, 107, 108, 134,
    136, 174, 175, 176, 177, 180, 191,
    200, 201, 202, 210
patristic theologians/theology, 12, 13,
    22, 25, 112, 298
    and asceticism, 141
    and creation/new creation, 150,
        153, 183, 202, 203, 231, 263, 272,
        295
    and Trinitarianism, 27, 144, 153,
        202, 205, 230–31, 254
    frequently ignored, 14, 16, 17, 26,
        200–201, 203, 208, 229
    (*see also* Irenaeus, Augustine, Bede,
        Basil, History of Interpretation,
        sabbath)
place as significant space, 37, 59, 138,
    175, 186, 255–56, 263–66
Platonic/Platonism/Neo, 17, 84, 95,
    97, 98, 100, 101, 114, 120, 122,
    123, 124, 130, 225
prayer
    critiqued, 184, 188
    defining characteristic of humanity,
        251
    in Genesis 1/Jewish liturgies/"Lord's
        Prayer", 37, 277, 281, 283, 288
    in Monastic "Hours"/Eucharistic
        prayer, 138, 143, 144, 146, 148,
        156, 163, 171, 172, 173, 179, 191,
        253, 288
    integrating life, 139, 144, 163, 172,
        184, 190, 208, 225, 271
    of repentance/lament, 158–59
    (*see also* Contemplative life)
priest/priesthood/priestly, 22, 23, 68,
    118, 246–47, 249–50, 254, 266,
    278
    in Genesis, 36, 38, 44–45
    of Christ, 161, 240, 245, 248, 249,
        251–53, 264, 299
progress
    critiqued, 11, 60–61, 207, 209
    towards God/maturity, 60, 126, 207

rationality, 77, 84, 86, 154, 181, 183, 197, 204, 221
　includes love/relationality, 77, 118, 158, 180
religion as factor in environmentalism, 1, 4, 11, 16, 20, 29, 60, 215, 227, 248
resurrection, 3, 61, 145
　affirming materiality/the flesh, 65, 66, 67, 80, 82, 125, 126, 137, 194, 207, 226, 234, 263, 270
　and divine titles for Jesus, 230, 234–36
　and Lordship/dominion as service, 236–42
　and present reality/life in the Holy Spirit/hopeful living, 65, 126, 130, 145, 174, 207, 235, 269, 271–72
　and "psychic revolution", 206–8
　and the arts, 258
　as basis for doctrine of incarnation/restoration of *imago*, 245–46
　as vindication of Jesus' claims, 230, 267–84, 300
　of Christ, 80, 81, 82, 101, 125, 130, 173, 193–94, 207

Sabbath, 26, 47, 197, 300–301
　and contemplative living, 127–28, 213
　and ecological sustainability, 289–97
　as Christ working salvation, 125–26, 174, 207
　as God's rest, 129
　as the fulfilment of all things, 124–25, 229
　built into creation, 126, 173–75
　central to Jesus' ministry, 277–84, 300
　divine provision and human restraint, 287–90
　for contemporary living, 284–87
　in Augustine, 123–30
　in Basil of Caesarea, 156
　in Benedictine monasticism, 172–75, 188
　in Desert monasticism, 144–45
　in Genesis 1–2, 39–43
　in Intertestamental literature, 277–78
　model for living in grace, 127
sacralization/de-sacralization/sacralized/desacralized, 1, 27, 50, 64, 73, 76, 89, 106, 107, 165, 219
sanctuary / temple, 2, 3, 184
　as model of creation, 38–39, 42–43, 216, 247, 257, 264, 281
　Christ as "temple of life", 81
　in Baconian vision, 215
　in the ministry of Jesus, 278–84, 299
science
　and the Word/*Logos* of God, 203
　history of, 21, 28, 34, 154, 164, 165, 203, 204, 211, 227, 292
　in aiding proper care, 203–4, 256–57, 272, 292
　in Athanasius, 83
　in Basil of Caesarea, 148, 154, 164, 165, 255
　in Francis Bacon, 215
　in Irenaeus, 54
　in the contemplative life, 256, 257, 272
　limits and critiques of, 4, 13, 107, 209–10, 215, 216, 219, 227, 253, 257, 271
simplicity of life, 22, 56, 139, 165, 261, 289
stewardship. *See* Human Dominion
sustainable/sustainability, 71, 161, 167–68, 256, 258, 285, 289–90, 294, 295, 296
sustainable manufacturing, 296–97

Trinity/Trinitarian/Trinitarianism, 3, 25, 26, 27, 60, 70, 88, 97–100, 103, 110, 153, 154, 176, 195, 196, 204, 230–34, 238, 246, 249, 251, 258, 269

urban
　agriculture, 22
　design, 296

utilitarian attitudes to creation/nature, 7, 18, 41, 179, 216, 252, 266, 285, 299

water
  and chaos, 190–91
  conservation, 276, 294
  in interpreting Genesis, 1, 39, 97, 98, 99, 152, 153, 155, 196
  in spirituality, 144, 192
  into wine, 238, 241
  management/irrigation, 33–34, 167, 190, 192, 294
  salination and siltation, 34
wilderness, 5, 6, 9, 11–12, 152, 177
  as place of encounter, 6, 137–38, 213–14, 226
  as place of menace, 7, 16, 177
  conflicting impulses in American religion, 17–18
  Exodus wandering and Jesus' sacramental ministry, 238, 290
Word, The (see also *Logos*)
  active in creation, 38, 51–53, 55, 60, 62–63, 65, 72–76, 78, 83–86
  as one of God's "two hands", 48, 52, 67, 231–232
  eternally with the Father, 71, 80, 99, 100, 102, 106
  in human life, 54, 87, 89
  incarnate in Jesus, 3, 27, 50–55, 57, 60, 64–66, 71, 76–79, 80, 82, 85–86, 88, 97
work/labor
  as prayer, 163, 171–72, 183, 208, 252–53, 297
  as stewardship/partnership, 45, 63, 85, 114–15, 128, 138–39, 147, 161, 172, 184, 206, 211–12, 218, 245, 255–56, 274, 283, 289, 297, 301
  critiqued, 233, 284–85
  dignified, 184–86, 189–90, 211, 218, 290
  free or servile, 116–17, 127, 128, 140, 281–82, 290–91
  God's work (*see also* Sabbath; in Christ), 39, 41, 52, 62, 65, 88, 98, 129
  in Christ, 78, 79, 82, 126, 127, 241, 250, 262–63, 270, 287, 289

Scripture Index

OLD TESTAMENT

Genesis

1	10, 13, 14, 19, 21, 23, 26, 38, 39, 42, 59, 96, 112, 119, 150, 154, 193, 196, 207, 217, 228, 237, 246, 248, 253, 262, 289, 291
1:1—2:3	36, 123
1:24–31	262
1:6–10	191
1:11–13	105, 178, 194
1:6–7	155
1:26–27	12, 23, 53, 112, 157, 181, 193, 195, 244, 246
1:29–30	142, 181
1:14	37, 292
1:21	181
1:22	39, 276
1:25	194
1:28	15, 39, 59
1:31	39
2	21, 42, 178, 217, 218, 225, 228, 236, 262, 289
2:1–3	47
2:4–5	289
2:23–24	46
2:2	39
2:3	39
2:7	12, 114, 262, 262, 270
2:9	285
2:15	46, 244
3:1–5	119
3:19	63
6–9	46, 293
6:17	262
7:9–16	46
7:15	262
7:22	262
9	142, 262
13:4	236

Exodus

16:32–35	289
19:6	247
20:7	236
22	290
23:9–12	283, 291
23:10	291
23:19	213
24:16	38
29:4	240
34	283
40:29	240

Leviticus

8:6	240
16:4	240
19:9–10	283
23:22	283
25	290
25:8–17	291
25:3–7	291
25:23	291
25:38	291
26:34–35	291

Deuteronomy
6:4	236
10:17–21	236
15:12–15	290
23–24	290
24:19–21	283

Ruth
2	283

1 Kings
17:1	278

2 Kings
5:1–14	278

2 Chronicles
36:21	291

Psalms
3	172
8	10, 119, 246
36:6–10	119
48	257
65	262
67	172
68:18	242
68:27	44
72	262
84	257
85	262
87	257
96	262
98	262
104	262
122	257
147	262
148–150	172

Isaiah
9:6	67
11	58
11:1–9	44, 262
11:17	281
25:6	237
42:1–10	262
55:1	237
56:5	46
56:7	281
58:14	237
65:17–25	237, 262

Ezekiel
18:13	290
22:12	290

Jeremiah
7:11	281

Hosea
2:18	262

Joel
2:18–27	262
2:22	290

Amos
8:4–6	41
9:11–15	262

Micah
4:1–5	262, 290

Zechariah
3:10	290
14:20–21	184

NEW TESTAMENT

Matthew
3:11	278
4:4	261, 288
4:13–17	279
5:5	64
5:42	290
6:9–15	283
6:26–28	288
12	280
14:19	288

15:35	288	5:4	288
16:21	28, 268	6:1–11	280
20:24–28	237	8	14
20:17–19	268	9:16	288
21:23–27	281	9:21	268
21:31–32	147	11:2–4	283
21:12	281	12:16–21	283
21:14	281	12:35–38	238, 241
23:11	237	13:10–17	280
25:6	143	14:1–6	280
25:35	161	17:8	238
26:61–65	281	18:31–34	268
26:26–29	237, 288	18:19	151
27:39–44	281	19	288
		19:45	281
Mark		20:1–8	281
1:1	236	22	242
1:8	279	22:66–71	281
1:14	279	22:19–20	237, 288
2	288	22:27	159, 237
2:23–3:6	279	23:35–39	281
2:1–12	279	24:30	288
2:23–28	279, 281		
2:13–17	279	**John**	
2:22	241	1	99, 254
3:1–5	280, 281	1:1–6	99
6:41	288	1:10–11	244
8:31	268, 279	1:13–14	100, 126
9:10	268	1:1	255
9:12	279	1:3	51
9:35	237	1:14	50
10:42–45	237, 240	1:18	245, 246
11:27–33	281	2:1–11	237, 241, 270
11:15	281	2:13–22	278
11:17	281	3:3–8	234
13:35	143	3:2	126
14:58–64	281	3:5	240
14:22–25	237, 288	5:17–22	278
14:21	279	6	238, 288
14:41	279	6:30–51	237
15:29–32	281	6:11	237
		6:12	290
Luke		13	87
3:16	279	13:1–17	237, 240, 241
4	278, 292	13:20–30	244
4:16–21	278	14:1–5	237
4:25–27	278	19:32–34	241
5	288	20:21–23	270, 271

John (continued)
20:28	236
21:9–14	237

Acts
1:6–8	272
1:3	272
2:42–47	141
2:36	235, 236
4:32–35	141
14:15–17	73
14:22	272
20:25	272
28:23	272
28:31	272

Romans
1:8–11	269
1:3–4	236
1:20	73
5	246
5:14	50
6:3–4	234
8	58
8:17–24	262, 269, 275
8:10–11	234
8:23	270
8:29	269
11:17	65
14:9	236
14:17	272
15:1–3	240

1 Corinthians
1:20–25	263
3:7	114
6:9	272
6:14	234
8:1–12	240
8:5–6	236
10:31	163
11:23–26	237, 288
13:12	126
15	65, 246, 263, 274
15:12–58	275
15:24–28	65, 272
15:20	269
15:50	65

2 Corinthians
3:17–18	274
3:18	126
4:4–6	236, 246
5:17–18	235

Ephesians
1:14	269
1:20–23	275
1:20–22	235, 236
5:5	272

Philippians
2:5–11	244
2:6–11	236, 242, 246

Colossians
1	65
1:15–22	236, 244, 246
1:13	272
1:17	287
1:18	269, 275
1:27	145
2:12	234
2:15	240
3:10–11	158

1 Thessalonians
2:12	272
4:14–18	275
4:13	276

Hebrews
1	254
1:1–3	236
1:1–4	246
1:1–5	246
2:5–9	246
2:14–15	275
2:17–18	246
2:9	246
4	286

1 Peter
1:3–5	275
3:21–22	234

2 Peter

1:3	234	1:17–18	275
3:10	273	1:5	269, 275
		1:6	254
Revelation		4:11	254
1:5–9	269, 272, 275	5:13	254
1:5–6	236	21:4	275

www.ingramcontent.com/pod-product-compliance
Lightning Source LLC
Chambersburg PA
CBHW061425300426
44114CB00014B/1540